2ND EDITION

Metal Matters

Englisch für Metallberufe

von
Georg Aigner
in Zusammenarbeit mit der Verlagsredaktion

Cornelsen

Verfasser:	Dr. Georg Aigner, Landshut
Berater/innen:	Heike Hoppe, Arnstadt
	Jan Richter, Freiberg
	Sibylle Weiß, Mönchengladbach
Projektleitung:	Jim Austin
Verlagsredaktion:	Andreas Goebel
Außenredaktion:	Pete Oldham
Redaktionelle Mitarbeit:	Kieran Breen,
	Oliver Busch (Wörterverzeichnisse),
	Oliver Kenny
Bildredaktion:	Kieran Breen, Gertha Maly
Umschlaggestaltung:	vitaledesign, Berlin
Titelfoto:	Shutterstock (Zbynek Jirousek)
Layout und technische Umsetzung:	Klein & Halm Grafikdesign, Berlin
Illustrationen:	Oxford Designers & Illustrators, Carlos Borrell (Karten)

Erhältlich sind auch:
Handreichungen für den Unterricht mit CD-ROM und Audio-CD (ISBN: 978-3-06-520513-9)

www.cornelsen.de

Die Links zu externen Webseiten Dritter, die in diesem Lehrwerk angegeben sind, wurden vor Drucklegung sorgfältig auf ihre Aktualität geprüft. Der Verlag übernimmt keine Gewähr für die Aktualität und den Inhalt dieser Seiten oder solcher, die mit ihnen verlinkt sind.

1. Auflage, 4. Druck 2016

Alle Drucke dieser Auflage sind inhaltlich unverändert und können im Unterricht nebeneinander verwendet werden.

© 2011 Cornelsen Verlag, Berlin
© 2016 Cornelsen Verlag GmbH, Berlin

Das Werk und seine Teile sind urheberrechtlich geschützt. Jede Nutzung in anderen als den gesetzlich zugelassenen Fällen bedarf der vorherigen schriftlichen Einwilligung des Verlages.
Hinweis zu den §§ 46, 52a UrhG: Weder das Werk noch seine Teile dürfen ohne eine solche Einwilligung eingescannt und in ein Netzwerk eingestellt oder sonst öffentlich zugänglich gemacht werden. Dies gilt auch für Intranets von Schulen und sonstigen Bildungseinrichtungen.

Druck: M.P. Media Print Informationstechnologie GmbH, Paderborn

ISBN 978-3-06-520511-5

Metal Matters 2nd edition deckt die Lehrpläne für Englisch in Metallberufen ab und orientiert sich an den Lernfeldern, die der Ausbildung in Metallberufen zugrunde liegen. Das Lehrwerk bereitet außerdem auf die **KMK-Zertifikatsprüfung** (Stufe 2 und 3) vor. Ziel der Arbeit mit **Metal Matters** ist ein erfolgreiches Bestehen in beruflicher Kommunikation auf Englisch.

Die neue Ausgabe ist in 15 lernfeldbasierte Units untergliedert, denen eine *Introduction* vorgeschaltet ist. Diese soll erste kommunikative Handlungen üben lassen und den situativen Rahmen für die ersten Units vorgeben. Unit 1 bis 4 orientieren sich an den für alle Metallberufe identischen Lernfeldern 1 bis 4. Aus den anschließenden Units kann die Lehrkraft auswählen, welche Inhalte am besten zum Ausbildungsberuf passen. Den Abschluss jeder Unit bildet die Rubrik *Extra material*, die weitergehendes Übungsmaterial bereitstellt, häufig in Form von KMK-Prüfungsaufgaben.

Nach jeweils 3–4 Units gibt ein Kompetenz-Check (*I can …*) in Anlehnung an den **Europäischen Referenzrahmen** den Lernenden die Möglichkeit, die erworbenen Kompetenzen zu überprüfen.

Das Buch ist in erster Linie für die berufliche Ausbildung gedacht, eignet sich aber auch für innerbetriebliche Weiterbildungsmaßnahmen. Der Einsatz an Fachschulen für Maschinenbautechnik (**Technikerschulen**) und **Meisterschulen** wird ebenfalls empfohlen.

Zur Schulung des Hörverständnisses enthält jede Unit Hörübungen, zu der es in den Lehrerhandreichungen eine **Audio-CD** sowie Transkripte gibt. Zahlreiche *Role-plays*, Mediationsaufgaben und *Language Boxes* trainieren die **kommunikative Kompetenz**.

Der Grammatik kommt eine dienende Funktion zu, trotzdem ist es unerlässlich, ausgewählte Kapitel im Unterricht zu behandeln. Hierzu stehen in vielen Units *Grammar Boxes* mit Übungen zur Verfügung.

Durch die Tipps zu Lernstrategien in den *Learning Boxes* entspricht **Metal Matters** der Forderung nach lebenslangem Lernen und trägt zur Entwicklung von Methodenkompetenz bei. Ebenso fördert das Lehrwerk die Stärkung interkultureller Kompetenz, indem die Rahmenhandlungen der einzelnen Units nicht ausschließlich in englischsprachigen Ländern bzw. Firmen angesiedelt sind.

Im Anhang stehen umfangreiche Wörterverzeichnisse zur Verfügung, darunter eine deutsch-englische Liste mit *Basic technical vocabulary*, die die Schüler/innen spätestens am Ende der Ausbildung beherrschen sollten.

Dem Buch liegen authentische Materialien zugrunde, die Auszubildenden und Facharbeitern auch so in der englischsprachigen Berufswelt begegnen können. Durch Illustrationen, schrittweise aufgebaute Übungen und den technischen Sachverstand der Schüler/innen wird das Verständnis jedoch systematisch vorbereitet.

Wir hoffen, mit **Metal Matters** zu einem interessanten und motivierenden Englischunterricht beizutragen und wünschen viel Erfolg bei der Arbeit mit dem Buch.

Der Autor und der Verlag

CONTENTS

	UNIT	TITLE	CONTENTS	LANGUAGE AND SKILLS
LERNFELDER 1 BIS 4	Intro-duction	My job and workplace	• A metalworking firm • Welcoming a visitor • Describing metalworking jobs	• Greetings and introductions • Saying goodbye • Talking about yourself and your company
	1	Working with hand-held tools	• Tools and their functions • A technical drawing • Screws and screwdrivers	• Identifying tools and describing their function • Identifying and correcting mistakes • Writing an order
	2	Working with machine tools	• Lathe tools and turning operations • A milling machine • Measuring instruments	• Saying and writing numbers in English • Clarifying and solving problems with an order • Writing a summary
	3	Producing an assembly group	• A production schedule • A parts list • Fixing devices	• Describing production processes • A telephone conversation • Coping with difficult technical texts
	4	Maintenance of a lathe	• Lubrication • Environmental regulations • Circuit diagrams	• Writing a report • Telephoning • Finding information in a technical text
		I CAN ... (1)		
TECHNICAL OPTIONS	5	Producing a Stirling engine	• Basic principles of a Stirling engine • An organizational chart • Producing an estimate	• Showing someone around a building/firm • Querying an estimate
	6	Assembling components	• Radial bearings • Tolerances and fits • Assembly plan of a gripper • Warranty terms	• Understanding technical symbols and diagrams • Comparing technical data • Placing an order by telephone • Making a complaint
	7	Installing controlling systems	• Installation of a pneumatic system • Pneumatics and hydraulics • Safety signs and safety rules	• Understanding installation instructions • Comparing hydraulic and pneumatic systems • Problem-solving
	8	High-speed cutting	• conventional machining • CNC machining • Troubleshooting problems	• Talking to a customer • Working with an operating manual
		I CAN ... (2)		
	9	Connecting the Robobox	• A problem in Bangkok • Travelling around Bangkok • Troubleshooting	• Modernizing a packaging system • Filling out a form • Giving and understanding directions
	10	A ballpoint pen assembly system	• A new assembly system • A report • The spring disentangler	• Materials • Describing an automatic process • Calling a hotline service
	11	Quality control and safety at work	• A quality control problem • Industrial safety • An accident	• Talking about quality • Describing injuries • Mediation: Talking to a doctor
	12	Applying for a job	• Testing materials • Letters of application • A curriculum vitae	• Describing graphs • Applying for a job • Preparing for an interview
		I CAN ... (3)		
	13	Automation systems	• Planning a system • Choosing the right controller	• Finding information in technical texts • Giving a presentation • Translating technical terms
	14	Planning and realizing a project	• A construction team • A Work Breakdown Structure • Constructing an oat crusher	• Describing geometric shapes • Describing a technical system • Assessing a presentation
	15	Optimizing a technical system	• Improving the design • The Final Time Schedule • An Internet auction	• Assessing alternative technical solutions • Evaluating a planning phase • Using a specialist chat room
		I CAN ... (4)		

CONTENTS

LEARNING STRATEGIES AND GRAMMAR	EXTRA MATERIAL	PAGE
		6
• Wie Sie beim Hören mehr verstehen • Plural nouns • Simple present and present progressive	Maintenance and cleaning	11
• Wie Sie mit Mediation umgehen • Simple past and present perfect	Oral mediation: Helping a customer	20
• Wie Sie schwierige Fachtexte lesen • Future forms: *going to* and *will*	Mediation: A report	30
• Forming questions	Safety rules for working with electricity	39
		48
• The passive • Numbers and mathematical operations	Mediation: A summary	50
• How to write formal and informal e-mails	A letter of complaint	60
• Wie man Fachvokabeln mit Hilfe des Internets übersetzt • Modal verbs	Comparing hydaulic and pneumatic tools	68
• Gruppengespräche auf Englisch führen	Spoken mediation: At a trade fair	77
		86
• *If*-sentences types 1 and 2 • How to say e-mail addresses • How to say telephone numbers	Understanding a technical text: Stretch wrapper	88
	Language for marketing and advertising	98
• Adjectives and adverbs	Filling in an accident report	106
• The *–ing* form and the infinitive	Evaluating an interview	113
		126
• Wie kann ich mein Hörverständnis verbessern? • Wie kann ich mein Englisch verbessern?	Ordering food in a restaurant	128
• Comparative and superlative forms of adjectives and adverbs	Understanding a user's guide and warranty conditions	137
• Question tags with the verb *be* • Wie lese ich eine schwierigen Text?	A riding holiday in Scotland	145
		153

ANHANG							
Pairwork files	154	A–Z word list	190	Talking about measurements	206
Basic word list	162	Basic technical vocabulary German – English	204	Common irregular verbs	207
Unit word list	167	Talking about numbers	205	Acknowledgements	208

Introduction: My job and workplace

1 Meet Mandlmaier

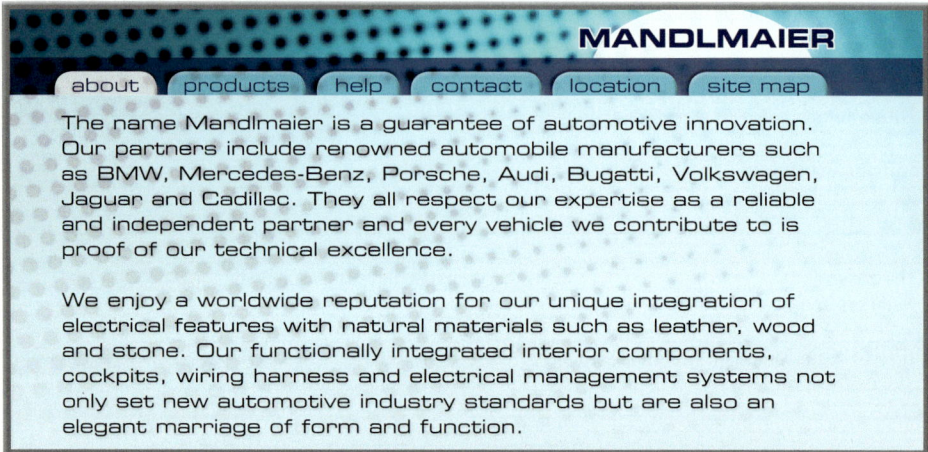

MANDLMAIER

about | products | help | contact | location | site map

The name Mandlmaier is a guarantee of automotive innovation. Our partners include renowned automobile manufacturers such as BMW, Mercedes-Benz, Porsche, Audi, Bugatti, Volkswagen, Jaguar and Cadillac. They all respect our expertise as a reliable and independent partner and every vehicle we contribute to is proof of our technical excellence.

We enjoy a worldwide reputation for our unique integration of electrical features with natural materials such as leather, wood and stone. Our functionally integrated interior components, cockpits, wiring harness and electrical management systems not only set new automotive industry standards but are also an elegant marriage of form and function.

1 What does the expression 'automotive innovation' mean?
2 Which car manufacturers do Mandlmaier work for? Which aren't German?
3 What do Mandlmaier produce?

2 All over the world

The Mandlmaier Group have their main headquarters in Rottenburg, Germany. They have subsidiaries in Shiyen (China), Detroit (USA), Sibiu (Romania) Warsaw (Poland), and York (United Kingdom). Match the letters A to F with the corresponding city.

3 Meet Mandlmaier staff

Young apprentices and skilled workers from Mandlmaier's subsidiaries are given the opportunity of working at the group's headquarters in Rottenburg. At the moment there are six young people working together in a group with Peter Vollmer, the training supervisor in Germany.

Look at their profiles, listen to the CD and write down the missing information in your exercise book.

NAME: Peter Vollmer
COUNTRY: Germany
JOB: training supervisor in ❶
AGE: 47 years
HOBBIES: travelling, family

NAME: Lisa Fellinger
COUNTRY: Germany
JOB: ❷
AGE: 17 years
HOBBIES: ❸, socializing

NAME: Ye Zhou
COUNTRY: China
JOB: ❹
AGE: 19 years
HOBBIES: ❺, reading

NAME: Ana Farcas
COUNTRY: ❻
JOB: energy engineer
AGE: ❼
HOBBIES: swimming, clubbing

NAME: Alan Pearson
COUNTRY: ❽
JOB: CAD engineer
AGE: 18 years
HOBBIES: playing drums, ❾

NAME: Michał Klimala
COUNTRY: Poland
JOB: ❿
AGE: 18 years
HOBBIES: ⓫, listening to music

NAME: Anthony Coleman
COUNTRY: ⓬
JOB: computer systems technician
AGE: 19 years
HOBBIES: ⓭, tennis

Introducing yourself

Hello, my name's Lisa Fellinger. / Hi, I'm Lisa.
I'm 17 (years old). I work for Mandlmaier in Germany.
I'm training to become an electrical engineer.
I work as a maintenance engineer.
I'm a computer systems technician.

I'm an apprentice at Mandlmaier in York.
I'm a trainee at Mandlmaier in the USA.
I live in Shiyen.
I like/enjoy/love playing tennis.
My hobbies are computing and football.

INTRODUCTION

4 Introducing yourself

Work with your partner. Using the language box on page 7, introduce yourself and give the following information:

- your name
- how old you are
- where you are from
- which job you are training for
  (see the box below for help)
- which company you are working for
- which school you go to
- what your hobbies are

5 Describing metalworking jobs

Match the job title with the correct description.

> CAD engineer • computer systems technician • electrical engineer •
> energy engineer • maintenance engineer • mechanic

a Their job is to reduce the costs of electricity, heating, air conditioning, etc.
b They check machinery that is often broken and think about alternatives.
c They are craftsmen who repair machinery.
d They are responsible for communications and computer systems within a company.
e They use computer technology to design real and virtual objects.
f Without these workers, there would be no lights, no computers and no TVs plugged into our walls.

Information

What's my job in English?

- Hier finden Sie eine Liste von Berufen in kleineren und größeren Unternehmen.

Elektriker *electrician, electrical engineer*	**Dreher** *turner*
Feinwerkmechaniker *precision mechanic*	**Maschinenbauer** *machine builder*
Schneidwerkzeugmechaniker *cutting tool mechanic*	**Werkzeugmacher** *toolmaker*
Mechatroniker *mechatronic systems engineer*	**Meister** *foreman*
Technischer Zeichner *CAD engineer*	**Auszubildender** *apprentice*
Energieingenieur *energy engineer*	**Facharbeiter** *skilled worker*
Konstruktionsmechaniker *construction mechanic*	**Techniker** *state-certified engineer*
Zerspanungsmechaniker *machining mechanic*	**Werkstattleiter** *workshop manager*
Ausbilder *training supervisor*	**Teilezurichter** *metal dresser*

- Viele Berufe können nicht 1:1 übersetzt werden. Deshalb müssen sie umschrieben werden, z. B. „Industriemechaniker": *I'm a mechanic who works in industry and in my training I have to produce workpieces out of steel and plastics, assemble them and automatize machine tool systems.*

- Häufig wird man auch nach seiner Schule gefragt:
  Berufsschule *vocational college*, **Berufsfachschule** *vocational technical college*, **Technikerschule/Meisterschule** *technical college of further education*, **Fachoberschule/Berufsoberschule/technisches Gymnasium** *technical college of higher education*

6 Meeting Anthony Coleman

Anthony Coleman from Mandlmaier Detroit has come to the headquarters in Rottenburg to meet Lisa Fellinger and Ye Zhou.

Put the conversation into the correct order and then listen to the dialogue to check your answer.

a	ANTHONY	Thank you.
b	ANTHONY	It was pretty early, but it was OK.
c	ANTHONY	I'm fine, and you?
d	ANTHONY	Yes, that's right. And I also wanted to see what the headquarters is like here in Rottenburg.
e	ANTHONY	I certainly would, because I just came from the airport and I didn't have time to get a drink there.
f	YE	Nice to meet you. How are you?
g	YE	Thank you, not too bad.
h	LISA	Hello, I'm Lisa. Pleased to meet you. Welcome to Rottenburg.
i	LISA	How was your flight?
j	LISA	Anthony Coleman, may I introduce you to my colleague Zhou Ye?
k	LISA	So, you are here to work with us on a common project, are you?
l	LISA	That's a good idea. But would you like a cup of coffee before we take a look around?
m	ANTHONY	Good morning, my name is Anthony Coleman, I come from Detroit.

Introductions

Hello, my name's Robert Brenner.

Hi, I'm Robert Brenner.

How do you do?* I'm Alan Symms.

I'm Sun Hai Jing. Pleased to meet you.

Nice to meet you. I'm Jiang Hua.

How do you do?* I'm Jiang Hua.

*„How do you do?" ist keine Frage, die eine Antwort verlangt. Es ist lediglich eine etwas förmliche Begrüßung, auf die normalerweise ebenfalls erwidert wird: „How do you do?".

Greetings

Hello, Robert. How are you?/
How are you doing?

I'm fine, too, thanks. Good morning/
afternoon/evening, Robert.

Fine thanks. And yourself?
Oh, not too bad.

OK, thanks. And how are you?
Good morning/afternoon/evening.

Saying goodbye

Goodbye, David. See you later.

See you. Bye.

INTRODUCTION

7 Role-play: Welcoming a visitor

A customer arrives at your company for a visit. In groups of three, act out a dialogue. Then swap roles. Before you start, read the language box on page 9.

Partner 1: Customer

- Grüßen Sie und stellen Sie sich vor.
- Danken Sie. Sagen Sie, es freut Sie ihn/sie kennenzulernen.
- Danken Sie. Sagen Sie, es freut Sie auch, ihn/sie kennenzulernen.
- Sagen Sie, dass die Fahrt ruhig war, Sie aber bereits seit 5 Uhr morgens unterwegs sind.
- Bejahen Sie die Frage nach der Besichtigung.
- Sagen Sie, dass wäre höchst willkommen.
- Sie trinken lieber Tee, und nach der Besichtigung würden Sie gerne den Chef kennenlernen.

Partner 2: Colleague A

- Grüßen Sie, stellen Sie sich und Ihren Kollegen vor und heißen Sie den Besucher in Ihrer Stadt willkommen.
- Erkundigen Sie sich nach der Anreise.
- Fragen Sie den Besucher, ob er/sie zuerst den Betrieb besichtigen möchte.
- Antworten Sie, das sei kein Problem und Sie werden ihn nachher dem Chef vorstellen.

Partner 3: Colleague B

- Grüßen Sie ebenfalls. Sagen Sie, es freut Sie, den Gast kennenzulernen und fragen Sie, wie es ihr/ihm geht.
- Fragen Sie den Gast, ob er vielleicht vorher etwas trinken möchte.
- Fragen Sie, ob der Gast Tee oder Kaffee möchte.

Working with hand-held tools

1 Identifying the sounds of tools

Listen to the five sounds of hand-held tools and match them to the pictures.

Sound A is a ...

- electric drill
- hacksaw
- handfile
- hammer
- jigsaw

2 Hand-held tools

Match the tool names in the box with the pictures below.

angle grinder • centre punch • chisel • counterbore • countersink • drill • height gauge • hex key • open-ended spanner • Phillips screwdriver • slotted screwdriver • tap

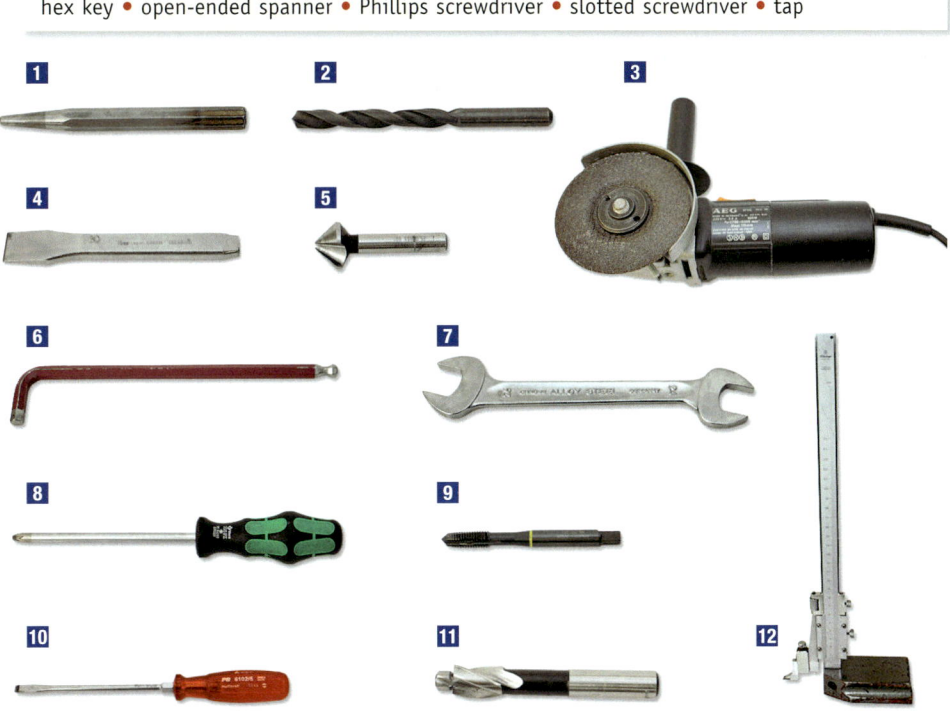

11

UNIT 1

3 The right tool for the job

a Form sentences to say what the tools are used for.

| We use a/an ... | angle grinder
centre punch
chisel
counterbore
countersink
drill
electric drill
file
hacksaw
hammer
height gauge
hex key
jigsaw
open-ended spanner
pozidriv screwdriver
slotted screwdriver
tap | to | bore holes through steel.
cut a thread.
cut away thick steel chips.
cut metal.
cut out shapes.
drive nails into walls.
grind metal.
hide conical screw heads.
hide cylindrical screw heads.
mark off.
punch mark.
shape metal surfaces.
turn a drill.
turn Allen-head screws.
turn cross-headed screws.
turn hexagonal-head bolts.
turn slot-headed screws. |

b Sort the tools in the table into two lists: manual tools and electric tools.

4 Producing the frame plate of a model lorry

Lisa, Ye and Anthony are in their first year of an apprenticeship at Mandlmaier. They are given the task of producing a model lorry in the apprentices' workshop.

a Read the beginning of Herr Vollmer's conversation with Lisa.

VOLLMER Lisa, Ye and Anthony, could you please take a look at this drawing of a frame plate. It's the first part of our lorry project and I want you to produce it with hand-held tools. I've prepared a piece of steel, 125 millimetres long, 40 millimetres wide and 8 millimetres thick. I want you to think about what kind of manual tools you'll need to produce the frame plate.

LISA Well, first, we'll need a hacksaw to cut the recesses. Then we'll ...

b Now look at the drawing on the opposite page and continue Lisa's description. The phrases in the box will help you to make sentences similar to Lisa's.

UNIT **1**

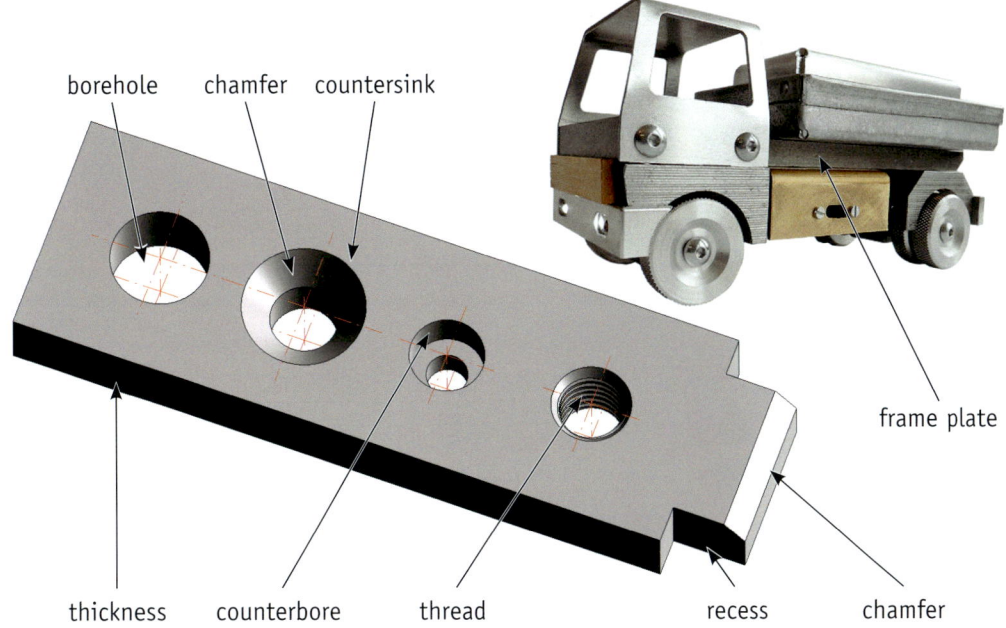

	a height gauge		cut the recesses.
Then we'll need …	an electric drill		cut threads.
Next we'll need …	a file		chamfer the holes.
In addition to	a hammer		produce the counterbores.
that, …	a centre punch	to	bore the holes.
After that, …	a hacksaw		make 90° angles.
Finally, …	a countersink		chamfer the edge.
	a tap		finish the side surfaces along the length.
	a counterbore		mark off the holes.

5 A technical drawing of the frame plate

Look at the technical drawing on the next page and answer the following questions.

1. Normally a technical drawing has a front view, a side view and a top view. Which of these can you find?
2. Which is the 3D view?
3. What are the dimensions of the recesses?
4. What are the diameters of the boreholes?
5. What are the dimensions of the chamfers?
6. What is the diameter of the counterbore?
7. What is the symbol for 'diameter'?
8. What is the symbol for 'radius'?
9. What is the 'centre line'?

13

UNIT 1

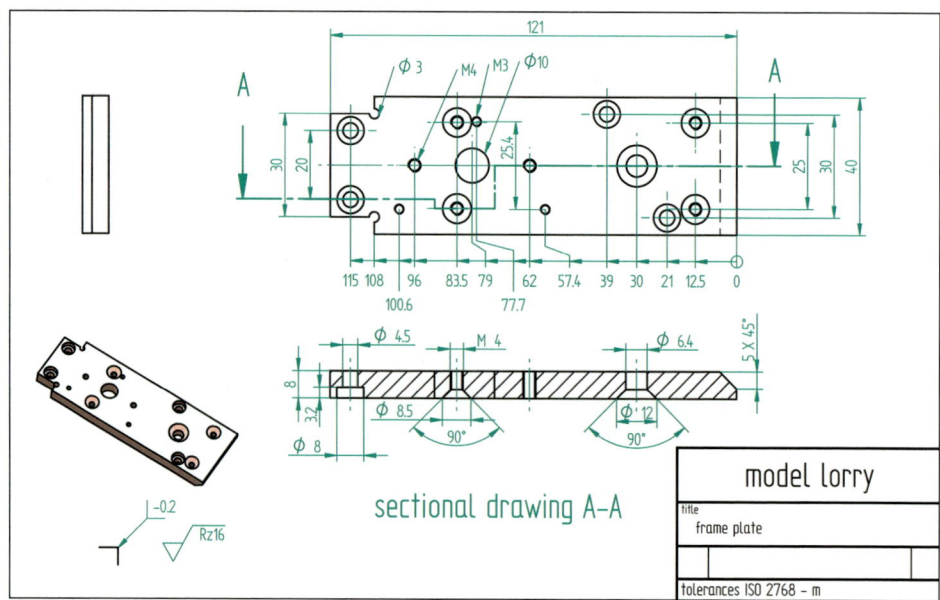

6 Examining the workpiece

 Ye and Anthony start producing the frame plate. Look at the dimensions in the drawing above carefully. Before you do the listening task, read the Learning box below.

a Herr Vollmer, their instructor, examined Alan's workpiece. Listen to the CD and check the technical drawing above to find out which mistakes there are in his workpiece.

b Which mistakes can be corrected and which will have to be taken care of later when manufacturing the counterparts?

> ### Wie Sie beim Hören mehr verstehen
>
> Richtig zu hören, so dass man das Gehörte auch versteht, kann man nur üben, indem man viel Englisch hört. Nutzen Sie daher jede Gelegenheit, Englisch zu hören. Beim Hören eines Textes sollten Sie folgende Punkte beachten:
>
> - Sehen Sie sich die Aufgabenstellung im Buch und eventuell vorhandene Bilder, die das Verständnis erleichtern können, vorher genau an.
> - Versuchen Sie bereits auf Grund der Aufgabenstellung herauszufinden, wovon der Text handelt.
> - Finden Sie bereits beim ersten Hören so viele Informationen wie möglich heraus und hören Sie sich den Text – wenn möglich – ein zweites Mal an. Machen Sie sich bei jedem Hören Notizen.
> - Das zweite Hören dient dazu, fehlende Informationen zu ergänzen und eventuelle Fehler zu verbessern. Wichtig ist, dass Sie versuchen, Ihnen nicht bekannte Ausdrücke einfach zu erraten. Dies nennt man *intelligent guessing*.
> - Geben Sie nicht auf und lassen Sie sich von zu schnellem Sprechen nicht entmutigen.

7 Screws and screwdrivers

In the workshop Ye finds a screw with a star-shaped head she has never seen before. Help her match the pictures and symbols with the correct terms from the box.

hexagon • pozidriv • security T • cross slot/Phillips • slotted • torx

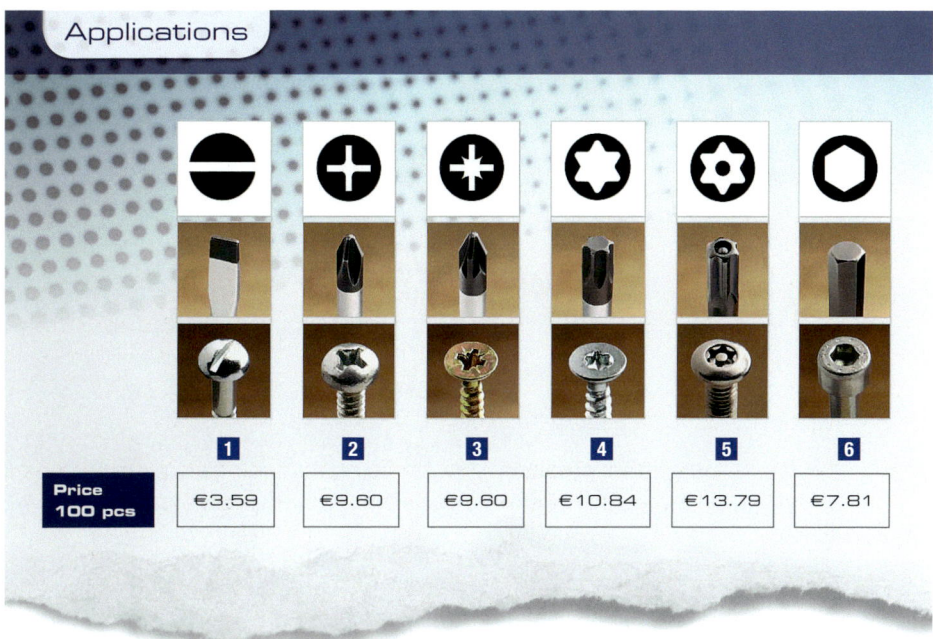

8 Ordering screws

Your boss asks you to order screws for €150. How many screws would you order of which kind? Write an e-mail to info@nutsandbolts.com and order them.

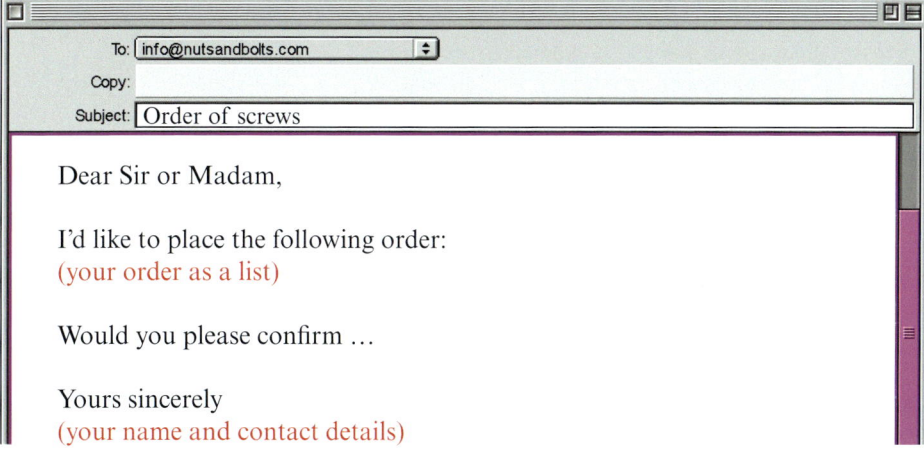

UNIT 1

9 A basic toolbox

Look at the catalogue description below and identify the tools in the photo.

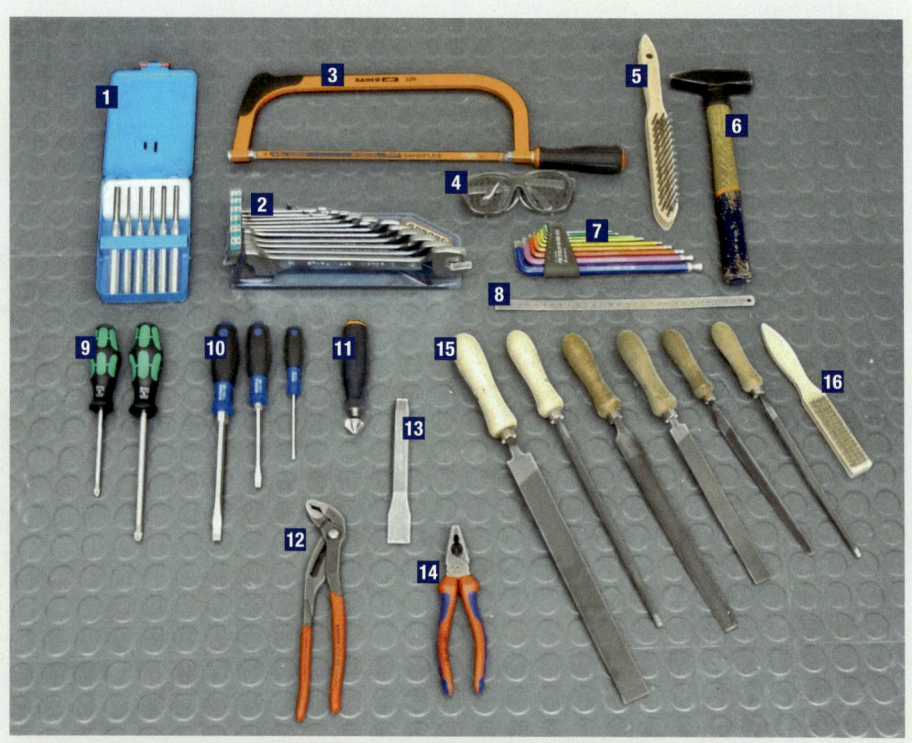

| 68 0302 | Assembly tool kit, 59 pieces with case No. 690200 | 306,- |

1	set of Allen keys 1.5 – 10
1	wire brush
1	file brush
1	hacksaw 300 mm
1	hammer 400 g
1	chisel 20 mm
1	countersink
1	set of 6 files 300 & 250 mm (2 flat, 2 round, 1 semicircular, 1 triangular)
1	pair of combination pliers
1	pair of waterpump pliers
1	box of pin punches 3-4-5-6-7-8
1	steel rule 300 mm
1	safety goggles
2	Phillips screwdrivers size 1 & 2
3	slotted screwdrivers 3 mm, 5.5 mm, 8 mm
1	set of open-ended spanners 6 – 32

UNIT **1**

Information

Talking about tools

In English, tools that have two distinct parts have only a plural form:
shears, pliers, pincers, scissors
These are special pliers for cutting, stripping and twisting wire.

These plural nouns can be used as a singular form by making them part of a group:
*Please pass me **a pair** of snipe nose pliers.*
*This **set of** pincers is made of chrome-vanadium steel.*
*Our toolbox contains **a** broad **range of** specialist pliers.*

10 Choosing the right tools

a Work with a partner. Choose two of the tasks below and say which tools you need to do them.

Example: *To repair a pump you need spanners or waterpump pliers. Then you need …*

repair a pump

produce the driver's cab of the lorry

mount an assembly line

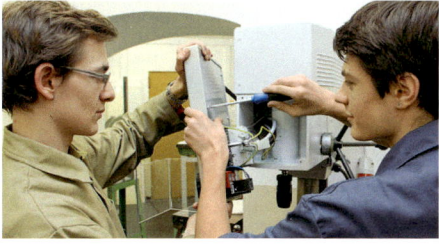

service a machine you know from your company

produce the frame plate of the lorry

b Name three tasks from your own job and say what kind of tools you need to do them.

17

UNIT 1

Grammar

Talking about the present

1 This is where we **keep** all the hand held tools.
2 And that's where Lisa normally **works**.
3 We **don't** just work in Germany, but also in China.
4 He**'s repairing** a pump at the moment.

- Das *Simple present* wird für **Gewohnheiten** und **regelmäßige oder häufig wiederkehrende Handlungen** und Vorgänge verwendet (1).
- Bei *he/she/it* wird *-(e)s* an das Verb angehängt (2).
  (Merke: He/she/it – das 's' muss mit!)
- **Fragen und Verneinungen** mit Vollverben werden mit dem Hilfsverb *do* bzw. in der 3. Person Singular mit der Form *does* gebildet (3).
- Das *Present progressive* wird dann verwendet, wenn ein konkreter, zeitlich begrenzter Vorgang beschrieben werden soll, der **zum Zeitpunkt des Sprechens im Gange** ist. Es wird gebildet mit einer Form von *to be*.
- An das Vollverb wird die Form *-ing* angehängt (4).

11 Practice

Complete the text with the simple present or present progressive of the verbs in brackets.

It's 11 o'clock on Monday morning at Mandlmaier. In the training department Ye …¹ (*make*) tea. Lisa is in a meeting with Herr Vollmer, the training supervisor. She …² (*have*) a meeting with him every Monday morning to discuss the week ahead. Across the corridor, in the meeting room, Ana and Michał …³ (*plan*) this week's production schedule for the lorry.

The training department of Mandlmaier has a lot of work at the moment but the company …⁴ (*not have*) many training supervisors, so it is important that work schedules are planned carefully.

Some of the trainees are out on a job this month. They …⁵ (*install*) wiring harnesses at Dongfeng Motor, a car factory in Shiyen in China. The factory is a good customer of Mandlmaier's and the engineers often …⁶ (*go*) there to install equipment.

Alan and Anthony are the only two apprentices in their second year in the training workshop. Ye …⁷ (*repair*) one of the company's oldest drilling machines. Michał is not in at the moment, he …⁸ (*get*) spare parts for the drilling machine. And finally, in construction, there is Simon Holmes. He …⁹ (*draw*) most of the plans for Mandlmaier's products. At the moment he and Alan …¹⁰ (*install*) some new CAD software onto the computer.

Extra material

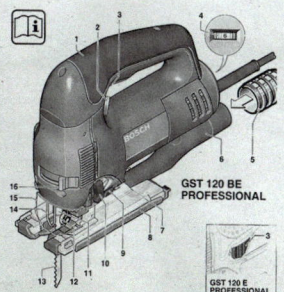

Maintenance and Cleaning

- Before any work on the machine itself, pull the mains plug.
- For safe and proper working, always keep the machine and the ventilation slots clean.
- In order to avoid operational malfunctions, do not saw gypsum board from below or overhead.

 In extreme working conditions, conductive dust can accumulate in the interior of the machine when working with metal. The protective insulation of the machine can be degraded. The use of a stationary extraction system is recommended in such cases as well as frequently blowing out the ventilation slots and installing a residual current device (RCD).

The guide roller 12 should occasionally be checked for wear and lubricated with a drop of oil. If it is worn, it must be replaced.
If the machine should fail despite the care taken in manufacturing and testing procedures, repair should be carried out by an after-sales service centre for Bosch power tools.
In all correspondence and spare parts orders, please always include the 10-digit order number given on the nameplate of the machine.

1 True or false?

Sind die folgenden Aussagen richtig oder falsch? In welchen Zeilen finden Sie die entsprechenden Aussagen? Wie lauten die richtigen Aussagen?

1 Vor der eigentlichen Arbeit an der Maschine soll der Netzstecker gezogen werden.
2 Lüftungsschlitze müssen stets sauber gehalten werden.
3 Gipskarton darf mit der Stichsäge nicht bearbeitet werden.
4 Die Schutzisolierung verliert ihre Wirkung, wenn sich bei der Bearbeitung von Metallen leitfähiger Staub im Inneren des Geräts absetzt.
5 Zum Schutz des Benutzers wird die Vorschaltung eines FI-Schutzschalters empfohlen.
6 Wenn sie abgenutzt sind, müssen die 12 Rollen ersetzt werden.
7 Um Ersatzteile zu bestellen, sind die digitalen Nummern auf dem Typenschild erforderlich.

2 Working with words

Find words in the text with the same meaning as these German words.

1 Abnutzungserscheinungen
2 Absauganlage
3 Führungsrolle
4 Kundendienststelle
5 leitfähig
6 Lüftungsschlitz
7 Netzstecker
8 Schutzisolierung
9 über Kopf
10 Wartung

2 Working with machine tools

1 Machine tools in a workshop

Match the machine tools 1–7 with their correct names.

bandsaw • centre lathe • drilling machine • grinding machine • milling machine • off-hand grinder • power hacksaw

2 Identifying sounds

Listen to the CD. You will hear five different machine tools. Which ones can you see in the photos above?

3 Turning a shaft

In a centre lathe a lot of lathe tools can be used for the different turning operations. Say what the ten lathe tools in the illustration are used for.

boring • chamfering • facing • in-copying • knurling • longitudinal turning • out-copying • parting-off • reaming • threading

Tool 1 is used for parting off.

UNIT 2

4 Producing parts for the model lorry

After producing the frame plate for the model lorry with hand-held tools (see Unit 1), Ana, Michał and Anthony are given the task of producing the two lorry parts shown in the photo with a lathe.

a Find the names of the two parts in the photo from the box below.

bumper • driver's cab • loading platform • rear axle • wheel

b Look at the drawing below and describe what you can see.

Examples: *The drawing shows ...*
In the front view ...   In the side view ...
On the left/right ...   At the top/bottom ...

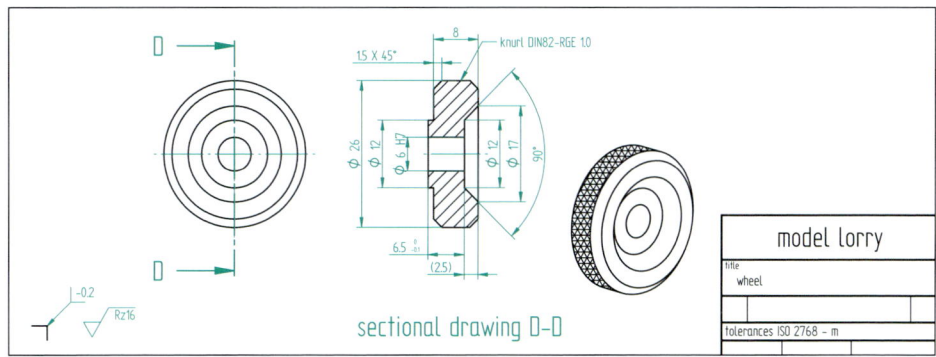

c Ana and Michał already know the next steps. Help them explain them to Anthony by putting these actions into the correct order using the words in the box.

first • now • then • afterwards • before • at last • finally

First we have to ...

- use a 6.0 reamer
- use a 5.8 mm drill
- turn the 45° rim recess
- turn a 45° chamfer left and right
- reduce to 26 mm
- part off at 9 mm

- knurl the outer surface
- face the rod
- cut in at 8 mm to a diametre of 12 mm
- clamp in an aluminium rod with a diametre of 28 mm
- centre

21

UNIT 2

Language

Saying and writing numbers in English

For a list of cardinal and ordinal numbers, see page 205 in the appendix.

45°	forty-five degrees
26 mm	twenty-six millimetres

Fractions

¾ hour	three quarters of an hour
⁷⁄₁₀ mile	seven tenths of a mile
³¹⁷⁄₅₀₉	three hundred and seventeen over five hundred and nine

Decimals

4.7	four point seven
0.375	nought/zero/oh point three seven five

Watch out!

Points are used for decimals:	26.79 = twenty-six **point** seven nine
Commas separate thousands, millions etc:	1,894,000 = one million eight hundred and ninety-four thousand
In English, units are used in the plural:	26 mm = twenty-six millimetre**s**

5 Partner files: Comparing two catalogues

Ana and Michał have to order new turning tools and check two catalogues from different suppliers. With a partner, compare the catalogues.

Student A: Go to File 1 on page 154.
Student B: Go to File 8 on page 158.

6 Clarifying problems with an order

a Michał Klimala has ordered some turning tools from Hoffman Tools by fax. Susanne Weinstock from Hoffmann Tools calls Michał to clarify some problems with the order.

7 Listen to the phone conversation and make a note of the problems.

Order quantity	Product Code	Size	Tool description	Unit price €	Quantity discount
3	24 0076	B01	Roughing bar	36	08
8	24 0086	B04	Thread-boring bar 60° metric	106	00
2	24 0086	B04L	Thread-boring bar 60° metric	116	00
3	24 0088	B04	Thread-boring bar 55° Whitworth	46	40
5	24 0078	B05	Recessing bar	74	24
3	24 0076	B06L	Roughing bar	121	00

b Use your notes to write the corrected order.

UNIT 2

Grammar

Talking about the past

1 How long **have** you worked for Mandlmaier?
2 Has Michał ever **told** you how to place an order?
3 Anyway, you **ordered** more than five pieces.
4 You **left** the roughing bar in the workshop.
5 **Did** you **check** the catalogue?

- Das *Present perfect* (1, 2) wird gebildet mit *have* und dem *past participle* (3. Form des Verbs). Man drückt damit aus, dass etwas in der Vergangenheit begonnen hat und bis in die Gegenwart – oder auch Zukunft – hineinwirkt (1). Der Zeitpunkt ist dabei entweder unbekannt oder unwichtig. Im Deutschen wird dafür manchmal die einfache Gegenwart verwendet (*Wie lange arbeiten Sie schon für …?*). Das *Present perfect* leitet oft ein Gesprächsthema ein: *Have you ever had/seen/been …?* (2)
- Das *Simple past* (3, 4, 5) drückt aus, dass etwas in der Vergangenheit begonnen und auch geendet hat. Im Gegensatz zum *Present perfect* geht es dabei um ein konkretes Ereignis bzw. einen Vorgang, das bzw. der zu einer bestimmten Zeit stattgefunden hat. Die Frageform wird mit *did* (+ Grundform) (5), die Verneinung mit *didn't* (+ Grundform) gebildet. Unregelmäßige Verben haben für die Vergangenheit eine eigene Form (4).

7 Practice

Complete the dialogue by using the simple past or present perfect of the verbs in brackets.

VOLLMER Anthony, how …¹ (*the turning/go*)? …² (*you/finish*) your work on the wheel yet?
ANTHONY No, not yet, Mr Vollmer.
VOLLMER What …³ (*you/do*) first?
ANTHONY Well, first I …⁴ (*clamp*) an aluminium rod into the three-jaw-chuck and …⁵ (*reduce*) it to 26 mm. …⁶ (*I/take off*) enough?
VOLLMER Yes, that's fine. What …⁷ (*be*) your next step?
ANTHONY I …⁸ (*face*) the rod, …⁹ (*centre*) it and then …¹⁰ (*drill*) a 5.8 mm hole into it.
VOLLMER Why …¹¹ (*you/use*) a 5.8 drill bit and not a 6.0 one?
ANTHONY Because there is this H7 fit and for that I …¹² (*use*) a reamer later on.
VOLLMER Very good. …¹³ (*you/have*) a lot of practice on the lathe?
ANTHONY Yes, quite a lot. …¹⁴ (*I/produce*) everything correctly?
VOLLMER Yes, you have. …¹⁵ (*you/do*) very well so far, Anthony. Please carry on.
ANTHONY Thank you, Mr Vollmer.

UNIT 2

8 Measuring instruments

a Match the names with the pictures. Which feature tells us the difference between the "go" and the "no go" side?

digital depth gauge • digital vernier calliper • micrometre • plug gauge • snap gauge • thread plug gauge • vernier caliper

b Look back at the drawing of the wheel on page 21 and decide which measuring instruments you will need.

9 Filling in an inspection sheet

Look at this inspection sheet for the rear axle then use the technical drawing below to write down the missing items 1–18.

MANDLMAIER		Inspection sheet				
Order number	15101	Drawing number	Lorry-13			
Name	rear axle					
Pos.	nominal dimension	tolerance ISO 2768-m	actual dimension	deviation	testing device	go/no go
1	67	±0.3	67.2	+0.2	vernier caliper	go
2	13 left	±0.2	12.8	1	2	3
3	13 right	±0.2	13.3	4	5	6
4	Ø 10	±0.2	10.05	7	8	9
5	Ø 6	−0.01/−0.05	5.94	10	11	12
6	M4	—	—	—	—	—
7	11		12	13	14	15
8	90°	—	—	—	—	—
9	2	±0.1	1.95	16	17	18

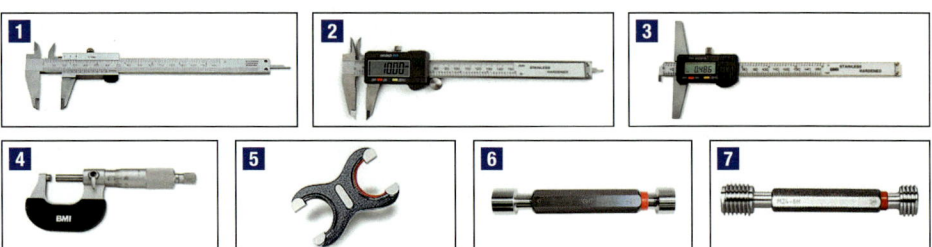

sectional drawing C–C

10 Describing a technical drawing

Describe the drawing in Exercise 9.

Example:
In the front view there is a shaft with a length of 67 mm and a diameter of 10 mm. ...

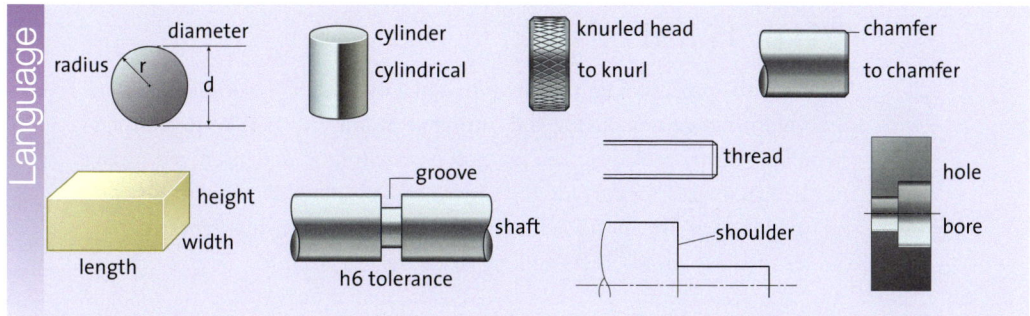

11 A new milling machine

Mandlmaier get a new milling machine for their training department. Ana, Michał and Anthony will work with it. They must be able to identify the different parts in English. Match the items in the box with the numbers in the drawing.

control panel • coolant hose • machine lamp • machine vice • milling cutter • spray protection cabin • vertical milling head

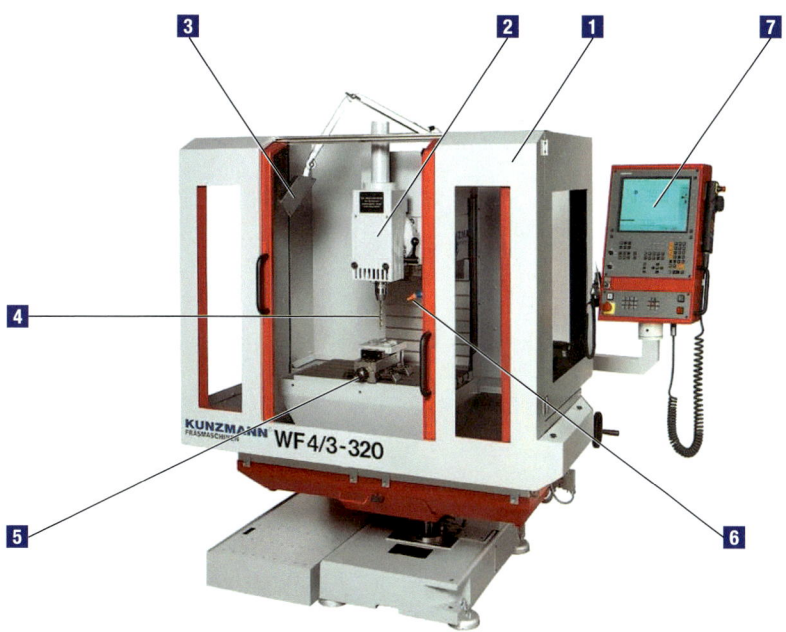

UNIT 2

12 Mediation

a Read the text about milling and give a summary in German. First, read the Learning box on page 28.

WHAT IS MILLING?

Milling is the process of cutting away material by feeding a workpiece past a rotating multiple tooth cutter. The cutting action of the many teeth around the milling cutter provides a fast method of machining. The machined surface may be flat, angular or curved. The surface may also be milled to any combination of shapes. The machine for holding the workpiece, rotating the cutter, and feeding it is known as the milling machine.

CLASSIFICATION OF MILLING

· *Face Milling*
In face milling, the cutter is mounted on a spindle having an axis of rotation perpendicular to the workpiece surface. The milled surface results from the action of cutting edges located on the periphery and face of the cutter.

· *End Milling*
The cutter in end milling generally rotates on an axis vertical to the workpiece. It can be tilted to machine tapered surfaces. Cutting teeth are located on both the end face of the cutter and the periphery of the cutter body.

· *Peripheral Milling*
In peripheral (or slab) milling, the milled surface is generated by teeth located on the periphery of the cutter body. The axis of cutter rotation is generally in a plane parallel to the workpiece surface to be machined.

b Types of milling

Which of the following sketches describes face, end and peripheral milling?

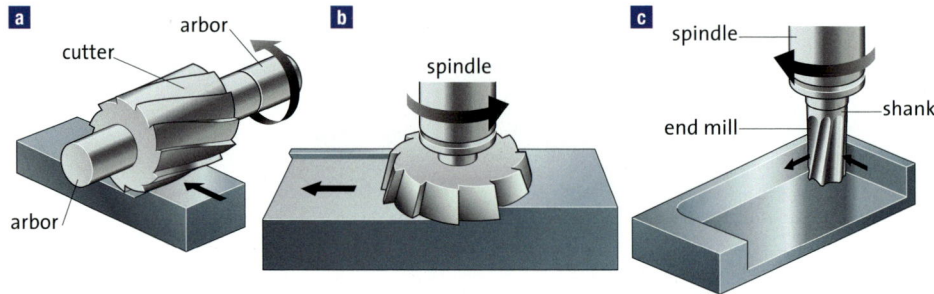

13 Comparing machinery

Listen to a sales representative of Kunzmann Milling Machines talking to a potential customer about the differences between the two machines and fill in the missing information in the table below.

Working range		WF 4/3-TNC 320	WF 7/3-TNC 320
X-axis (longitudinal)	mm	400	600
Y-axis (cross)	mm	350	❶
Z-axis (vertical)	mm	❷	400
Main spindle drive		❸	5,5
Spindle speed range	rpm	4.500	4.500
Tool taper		ISO 40	❹
Feed rate	mm/min	❺	2000
Rapid traverse	mm/min	5000	5000
Contouring control		TNC 320	❻
Weight	kg	approx. ❼	approx. 2.000
Clamping surface	mm	650 x 350	800 x ❽
Loading ability	kg	max. ❾	max. ❿

14 Talking about similarities and differences

Work with a partner. Compare two machines you are both familiar with.

Expressing similarity

The rapid traverse in the ... is (just) as fast as it is in the ...
Like the ..., the angular table of the ... is rigid.
Both models have the same ...
The ... is/are identical in both models.

Note:
axis (singular)
axes (plural)

Expressing difference

The ... is slightly lighter than the ...
The ... is more powerful/expensive/complicated/reliable/... than the ...
The ... weighs less/more than the ...
The ... has a different ...
The ... in the ... model is much bigger/smaller/heavier.
The new model has more features than the old one.
The new ... isn't as loud as the old one.

15 Translation: a technical leaflet

Your boss wants you to translate the characteristics of the WF 4/7 TNC 320 into German. Form groups and work together to produce a German version of the leaflet on the next page.

Universal Milling Machine
KUNZMANN WF 4/3-TNC 320

Major characteristics of KUNZMANN are:
- Stable cast iron construction with horizontal-/vertical spindle
- Hardened and ground flat guideways in all axes for the highest accuracy
- Automatic axis clamping for operational safety
- Stepless feed rate and spindle speed rate
- High-torque main spindle drive with 5,5 kW
- Hydraulic tool clamping
- Mechanical hand wheels in all axes
- Coolant fluid tank free-standing, capacity 70 litres
- Anti-splash protection with wide door openings
- Simple-to-use contouring control Heidenhain

TNC 320 with processing cycles and 3-axis digital readout

Options
- Rigid angular table
- Universal table 650 x 395 mm
- Electronic hand wheel
- Minimum-quantity lubrication system

Wie Sie mit Mediation umgehen

Mediation bedeutet Vermittlung. Der Sprachmittler drückt dabei nicht seine eigenen Gedanken aus, sondern vermittelt zwischen zwei Personen, die der Sprache des Anderen nicht mächtig sind. Das kann auf zwei Arten geschehen.

Schriftliche Mediation

Sie werden aufgefordert, den Inhalt eines englischsprachigen Dokumentes im Deutschen wiederzugeben. Hier kommt es weder darauf an, wörtlich zu übersetzen, noch einen geschliffenen neuen Text zu verfassen. Schriftliche Mediation dient der Informationsvermittlung, daher soll der Text für den Fachmann gut verständlich sein. Genauso selbstverständlich wie in der Technischen Mathematik eine Formelsammlung verwendet wird, benutzt man dabei ein zweisprachiges Wörterbuch.

Mündliche Mediation

Der Vorteil bei der mündlichen Mediation ist, dass man nicht wortwörtlich übersetzen muss, sondern Begriffe und Strukturen umschreiben und immer wieder nachfragen kann. Sie kommt zur Anwendung, wenn man z. B. Besucher durch den Betrieb führt, auf einer Baustelle Informationen weitergibt oder jemandem die fremdsprachige Aufschrift auf einem Schild in Deutsch erläutert.

Extra material

Oral mediation: Helping a customer

You are at a trade fair for machine tools. Ms Coleman, an English-speaking customer, wants some technical information about the Kunzmann WF 4 CNC Universal Milling Machine.

Mediate between her and Peter Reif, the Kunzmann sales representative. Use the excerpt from the data sheet to help you. Read the Learning box on page 28 first.

Universal Milling Machine KUNZMANN WF 4 CNC

Working range		
X-axis (longitudinal)	mm	400
Y-axis (cross)	mm	350
Z-axis (vertical)	mm	400
Main spindle drive	kW	5,5
Spindle speed range	rpm	5,000
Tool taper		ISO 40
Feed rate	m/min	up to 10
Rapid traverse	m/min	10
Weight	kg	approx. 2,000
Clamping surface	mm	650 x 350
Loading ability	kg	max. 250

English Customer	You	Peter Reif
Could you ask Herr Reif about the maximum workspace of the milling machine, please?	?	Auf der Längs- und auf der vertikalen Achse sind es 400 mm und auf der Querachse 350 mm.
All right. What is the power of the main spindle drive?	?	Bei voller Drehzahl liegt sie bei 5.500 Watt.
What is the top speed of the milling machine?	?	Sie liegt bei 5000 Umdrehungen pro Minute.
Well, that's not too fast, but what's the feed rate?	?	Sie kann bis 10 Meter pro Minute eingestellt werden. Aber es gibt auch einen Eilgang mit 10 m/min.
Right. And what's the maximum weight a workpiece can have?	?	Das Maximalgewicht liegt bei 250 kg.
Thank you for all the information.	?	Gerne.

3 Producing an assembly group

1 Work on the model lorry: an overview

a The frame plate, the wheels and the axles for the model lorry (see Units 1 and 2), are parts of an assembly group. Briefly explain what an assembly group is.

b Before the apprentices can assemble the group, they have to produce two more parts. Scan the dialogue below to find out what they are.

VOLLMER Welcome to this week's meeting. Before we talk about the next steps in the production schedule, I'd like to start with a quick review of what you've done so far on the lorry project. Lisa, can you start us off, please?
LISA Sure, well, first of all I worked with Ye and Anthony on the frame plate.
VOLLMER What exactly did you do?
YE We produced the frame plate to the right size and drilled all the holes.
VOLLMER And after that?
ANTHONY We cut the threads and filed all the chamfers.
VOLLMER Well Anthony, you had some problems, could you tell the others about them?
ANTHONY I'm afraid that some of my boreholes were not in the correct positions.
VOLLMER Ye, what do you think he could do about that?
YE Erm... I'm not sure, maybe take it into account when producing the counterparts?
VOLLMER Yes. So you'll have to be be careful when you get that far, Anthony.
ANTHONY I will, Mr Vollmer.
VOLLMER Anthony, this was the first time that you have produced such a complex workpiece as the wheel on a lathe. How did it go?
ANTHONY All the turning operations worked pretty well, but Michał and I had a problem with knurling.
VOLLMER What kind of problem was that?
ANTHONY The knurling tool was pretty old and blunt.
VOLLMER What did you do?
ANTHONY Michał got a new one from the storeroom.
VOLLMER Ah, all right. How was the fit?
ANTHONY I drilled holes of 5.8 mm in the wheels and then used a 6.0 mm reamer.
VOLLMER Did you check the holes with the axles?
ANTHONY Yes, everything fitted perfectly.
VOLLMER Fine, now, what's next?
YE Next, Lisa, Anthony and I will mill the wheelhousing and the axleguide. And then I think we can put the whole assembly group together.
VOLLMER Good. And when are you going to start work on the wheelhousing?
YE Tomorrow, but we have a few questions about the production schedule.
VOLLMER No problem, but perhaps later today? I've got some calls to make.
YE Perhaps after the lunch break, Mr Vollmer?
VOLLMER That's fine with me.

UNIT 3

c Now read or listen to the dialogue and put these actions into the correct order.

a check the holes in the wheels for the axles
b cut the material for the frame plate to the right size
c cut the threads and file the chamfers
d drill holes into the frame plate
e drill holes for the wheels and use a reamer
f get a new turning tool for turning the wheel
g mill the wheelhouse and the axleguide
h put the whole assembly group together
i turn the wheel

d Answer these questions.

1 How will Lisa, Ye and Anthony take into account that some of the dimensions of the frame plate in Unit 1 were wrong?
2 Why did they check the 6 mm fit with the axle?

2 Discussing the production schedule

The next job is the production of the wheelhousing.
Listen to the discussion and find out what 1–10 in the production schedule are.

Production Schedule		Name:	
Project	lorry		
Part	wheelhousing		
material	S235 [1] -2	size: 40 x 21 x 63	
Pos.	Operating Cycles	Tools	
1	clamp material [2]		
2	mill out cavity	90° indexable end mill 25/2 mm	
3	swivel [3] milling head 5°		
4	mill [4]	ball-nosed slot drill [5] mm	
5	clamp workpiece vertically		
6	mill left side	Roughing end mill stub 30 mm	
7	turn workpiece [6]		
8	mill right side	Roughing end mill stub 30 mm	
9	clamp workpiece [7]		
10	mill chamfer	45° indexable chamfer mill 16 mm	
11	drill at 4 corners of [8]	drill Ø 3mm	
12	drill in middle of square	Ø 12mm	
13	mill square [9]	MTC trapezoidal profile end mills stub TiAlN 4 mm	
14	mill square (finishing)	Universal end mill [10] -PM TiAlN 4 mm	
15	fit wheelhousing together with axleguide		

UNIT 3

Grammar

Talking about the future: *will* and *going to*

1. Alan **is going to order** new drill bits and reamers.
2. Alan **will order** new drill bits and reamers.
3. They **are going to adjust** the dimensions of some counterparts.
4. They **will adjust** the dimensions of some counterparts.
5. If the bore hole isn't deep enough, the bolt **won't fit** correctly.
6. I'm very busy at the moment, so **I'll deal with** that problem later.

- Bei einfachen Aussagen über die Zukunft können meist beide Futurformen verwendet werden, d.h. *going* to und *will*. (1–4)
- Das *will future* dient in *If*-Sätzen vom Typ I (siehe auch S. 96) dazu, die Folge einer Handlung zu beschreiben. (5)
- Das *will future* wird auch verwendet für spontane Absichtserklärungen oder Versprechen. (6)

3 Practice

Act out the dialogue with a partner. Look at the verbs in brackets and decide whether you could use either future form *(will/going to)* or just the will-future.

YE	When ...¹ (we/meet) again?
LISA	Can we meet after lunch at about 1.15?
VOLLMER	That's too early for me. I've got a meeting and ...² (I/not be) available until about 2.30. And I'm afraid ...³ (it/be) a short meeting because I have another meeting at 3.45.
ALAN	...⁴ (we/have) a lot to talk about, Mr Vollmer?
VOLLMER	Well, I'd like to discuss the next steps in the production of the model lorry. So study the prodution schedule over lunch, please.
YE	Mr Vollmer, none of us have a copy of the production schedule.
VOLLMER	I'm sorry, I thought I'd given it to you all. ...⁵ (I/make) photocopies straightaway.
YE	...⁶ (I/do) that for you, Mr Vollmer. Can you give me your copy, please?
VOLLMER	Thanks, Ye. Here. Is there anything else?
LISA	...⁷ (you/examine) us on how we did the previous processes?
VOLLMER	No, I'm afraid that ...⁸ (we/not have) enough time to do that.

UNIT 3

4 A telephone conversation

What does Mr Vollmer say? Complete the conversation with his sentences below.

a So you'd better do it either today or tomorrow.
b When will you be able to do that?
c What do you and the others plan to do this afternoon?
d Can I speak to Lisa, please?
e Let's have a meeting first thing on Monday and discuss the next steps.
f So when are you going to produce the wheelhousing?

VOLLMER	Hello Ana. ...¹
ANA	Just a moment, I'll get her for you. Lisa! It's Mr Vollmer for you!
LISA	Hello, Mr Vollmer.
VOLLMER	Hello, Lisa. ...²
LISA	We aren't sure yet. We'd like to produce the bumper.
VOLLMER	...³
LISA	We're going to do the wheelhousing the day after tomorrow on Thursday.
VOLLMER	Well, on Thursday the water jet cutting machine will be serviced. ...⁴
LISA	OK. But when can we work on the loading bed of the lorry?
VOLLMER	Well, that depends on you. But first you'll need to produce the angle pieces. ...⁵
LISA	We wanted to mill them on Friday.
VOLLMER	OK, that's fine. ...⁶

5 Assembling the lorry

a **Describe the drawing below. The parts list on the following page will help you.**

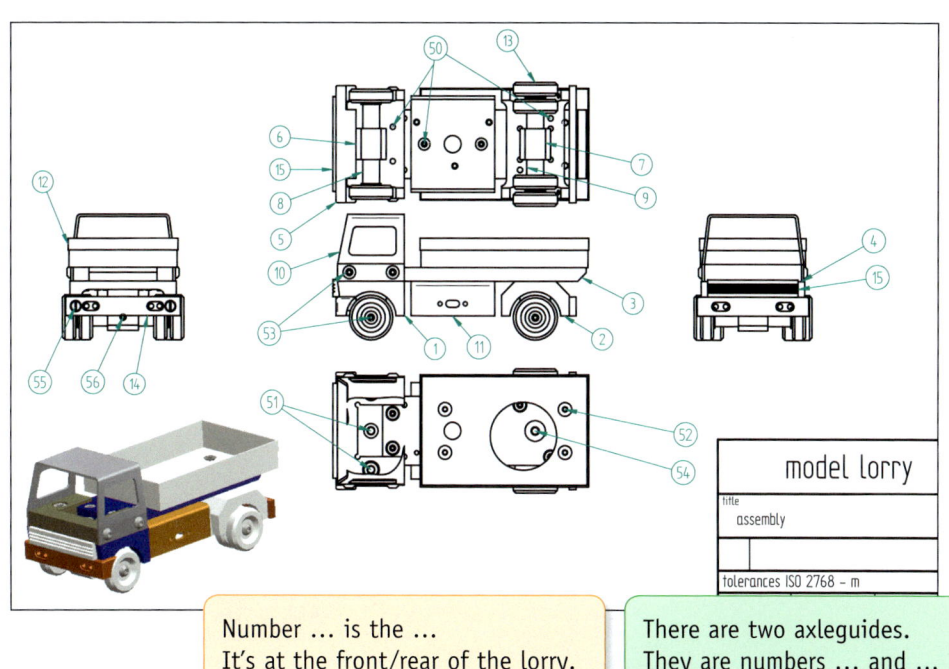

Number ... is the ...
It's at the front/rear of the lorry.

There are two axleguides.
They are numbers ... and ...

33

UNIT 3

b Match the German terms with the items in English in the parts list.

Abstandshalter • Achshalter hinten • Achshalter vorne • Fahrerhaus • Fahrerhausunterteil • Gewindestift mit Spitze • Hinterachse • Kühler • Ladefläche • Rad • Radkasten hinten • Radkasten vorne • Rahmen • Senkschraube • Stahlblech • Stoßstange • Unterfahrschutz • Vorderachse • Zylinderschraube

56	Allen set bolt	DIN 914 M4×6	2
55	cylinder head bolt	DIN EN ISO 4768 M4×16	2
54	countersunk bolt	DIN 7991 M6×20	1
53	cylinder head bolt	DIN EN ISO 4768 M4×6	8
52	countersunk bolt	DIN 7991 M4×8	4
51	cylinder head bolt	DIN EN ISO 4768 M 5×10	3
50	cylinder head bolt	DIN 6912 M4×12	6
15	cooling unit	CuZn	1
14	distance-piece	S235JR-K – 10×5×32	1
13	wheel	aluminium D28×10	6
12	loading bed	sheet steel galvanized 0.6 mm	1
11	underride guard	CuZn 2×90×40	2
10	driver's cab	aluminium sheet steel 1.5 mm	1
9	rear axle	10S20 DIN 671 D10×70	1
8	front axle	10S20 DIN 671 D10×60	1
7	rear axleguide	S235JR-K – 20×20×30	1
6	front axleguide	S235JR-K – 20×20×25	1
5	bumper	aluminium 12×80/14	1
4	base part driver's cab	S235JR-K – 40×10×62	1
3	frame	S235JR-K – 40×10×125	1
2	rear wheelhousing	U DIN 1026 – S235JR-2 – 65×42	1
1	front wheelhousing	U DIN 1026 – S235JR-2 – 65×42	1
Pos	Title	Material	No
	partslist	**Model Lorry**	
drawn by Vollmer 05.12.2010			

UNIT 3

Language

Fixing devices

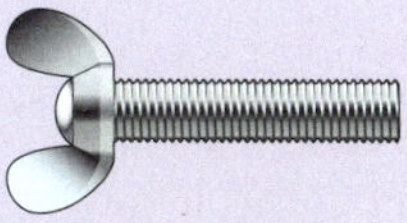

- wing screw
- hexagon head bolt 
- slotted cheesehead bolt 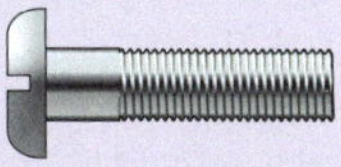
- slotted panhead bolt 
- slotted countersunk bolt 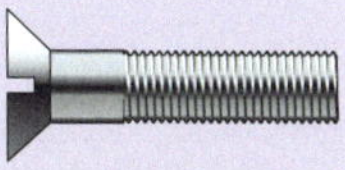
- hexagon socket cap bolt 
- round head screw 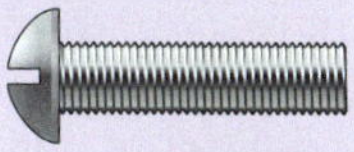
- Allen set screw 

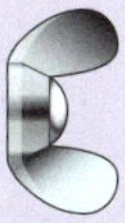

- wing nut
- nut 
- plain flat washer 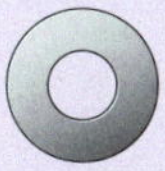
- spring washer 
- shakeproof washer 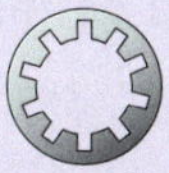
- panhead rivet 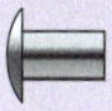
- roundhead rivet 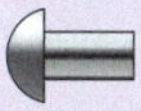
- countersunk rivet 

6 What fixing devices would you use?

Which items from the box above would you use to do the following tasks? Give examples and reasons for your choices.

build a steel bridge

fix a wheel to a lorry

fix a wheel to a bicycle

prevent a nut on a lawnmower from loosening

fix a movable hood on a lathe

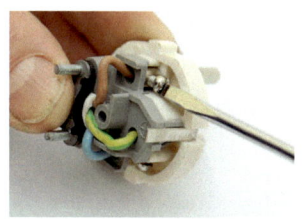

fasten a wire in a plug

35

UNIT 3

7 How to join materials

Listen to the dialogue on the CD and find out what is missing from the following chart.

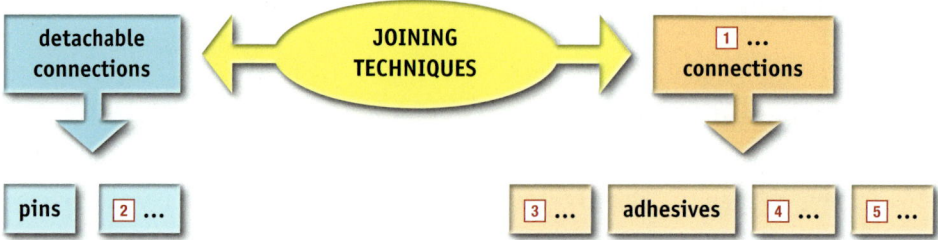

8 Welding

Read this text and do the exercises on the opposite page.

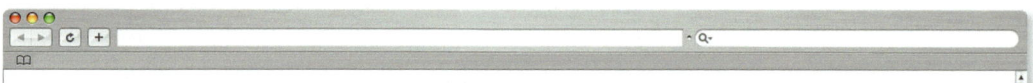

Welding is a process usually used to join metals but also thermoplastics. In contrast to brazing or soldering where a separate material is melted in order to join two objects, welding actually melts the work pieces themselves creating a very strong joint. A filler material is sometimes added whilst the pieces are melted and the process often takes place in the presence of an inert or semi-inert gas, known as a shielding gas or flux, which prevents the weakening of the joint through oxidation or other reactions.

Electric arc welding denotes the passing of an electrical current between an electrode and a base material. There are three main variants:
- Gas tungsten arc welding (GTAW) which uses a non-consumable tungsten electrode in the presence of a semi-inert gas; it is particularly useful for use with thin and light materials, especially stainless steel;
- Shielded metal arc welding (SMAW), one of the most common types of arc welding, uses a consumable steel electrode core which itself acts as the filler material and an inert gas to prevent oxidation taking place;
- Gas metal arc welding (GMAW) uses a continuous wire feed as an electrode and, a shielding gas against any contamination.

Gas welding, and most commonly oxyacetylene welding, is regularly used to join pipes and tubes and when undertaking repair work. Resistance welding involves passing a high current (between 1000 and 100 000 A) between two or more metal surfaces. Molten pools of metal then form around the weld area where resistance is at its highest. Spot welding uses this principle to join overlapping sheets of metal of up to 3 millimetres in thickness. Two electrodes simultaneously clamp the sheets together and pass a current between them securing the sheets. It is an easily automated process often undertaken by industrial robots; modern day cars are likely to have several thousand spot welds holding the chassis together.

The latest technological developments involve energy-beam welding which is very fast, easily automated and therefore highly useful in the production industry. While laser-beam welding focuses a high-powered laser onto a small area of material, electron beam welding follows the same principle but with electrons and inside a vacuum. Energy-beam welding has also been

UNIT 3

a What type of welding do these three photos show?

b Copy the word spider into your exercise book and complete it with the welding techniques described in the text.

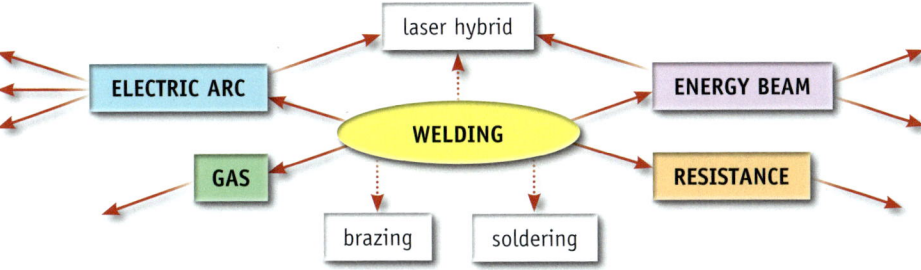

c Write a short step-by-step report (60–80 words) on a job you have done where you used any technique for joining materials. Use words like *first, then, after that, finally*.

Wie Sie schwierige Fachtexte lesen

- Technische Texte auf Englisch zu lesen ist gerade für Techniker gar nicht so schwierig, wie man oft glaubt. Viele Wörter sehen ähnlich wie ihre deutschen Entsprechungen aus und klingen auch so. Vergleichen Sie nur *press* und „Presse", *screw* und „Schraube" oder *electrical* und „elektrisch". Manchmal müssen Wörter auch nur vertauscht werden, wie bei *machine tool* = „Werkzeugmaschine". Wörter wie *elongation* klingen recht kompliziert; wenn man sich aber den Kern des Wortes – *long* – ansieht, kann man sich leicht erschließen, dass das Wort „Verlängerung" bedeutet.

- Bei den meisten Texten ist es nicht notwendig, dass man jedes einzelne Wort genau versteht. Oft können Sie von Ihrem technischen Sachverstand her einen Text besser verstehen als ein technischer Laie, der im Englischen sehr gut ist.

- Sie müssen auch nicht jedes unbekannte Wort im Wörterbuch nachschlagen oder in einer Datenbank suchen. Etwa dann nicht, wenn die Aufgabenstellung verlangt, einem Text lediglich spezifische Informationen zu entnehmen wie Maße, Eigenschaften von Stählen oder Herstellungsverfahren.

- Daher sollten Sie sich fragen, bevor Sie mit einem Text zu arbeiten beginnen: Welche Informationen suche ich im Text? Das wird Ihnen beim Lesen helfen, Unwichtiges zu ignorieren.

- Der wichtigste Aspekt für das Textverständnis ist die Tatsache, dass Sie ein Spezialist in Sachen Technik sind. Sie haben einen immensen Vorteil dadurch, dass Sie täglich mit technischen Dingen konfrontiert werden. Aus diesem Grunde können Sie sehr oft aus dem Zusammenhang erschließen, was bestimmte technische Ausdrücke auf Deutsch bedeuten.

UNIT 3

Extra material

Mediation: A report

Your firm is considering the introduction of a hybrid welding system. They ask you to write a short report in German on its main advantages. They also want to know if there are any disadvantages to the system.

KEIKO SYSTEMS INC.

- Conpany
- Innovations
- Industries and technologies
- Products and services
- Service
- Careers
- Press/Events
- Downloads
- Contact

In hybrid welding, any laser source (such as CO_2, Nd:YAG, diode, Yb fibre or Yb:YAG disc lasers) can, in theory, be combined with any arc source, such as MIG/MAG, TIG or plasma. In true hybrid welding, the two energy sources are usually combined so that the laser and arc operate in a single weld pool. This hybrid welding technology is gaining increasing acceptance as a viable production process in manufacturing sectors such as shipbuilding and the production of cars and rail rolling stock. KEIKO SYSTEMS has gained an international reputation for developing and implementing innovative and customer-oriented concepts for these types of application.

Hybrid welding with laser and arc brings many benefits for welding applications involving thick-walled materials such as construction steel, aluminium, or stainless steel. It combines the advantages of laser and arc welding, producing deep penetration welds comparable with laser welds, yet at the same time having an improved tolerance to joint fit-up when compared with laser welding. The combination of the gas metal-arc and laser beam welding processes also significantly increases the process stability.

The compact design of the KS HybridTec allows unhindered access to all workpieces, including three-dimensional subassemblies. The use of a filler material makes the process noticeably less dependent on workpiece tolerances and the ability to bridge gaps has been significantly improved.

Higher process speeds, along with excellent seam quality, ensure increased productivity. The risk of deformation is low due to greatly reduced heat input. This greatly reduces the need for reworking. Because of the higher weld penetration of the laser beam, time-consuming seam preparation is no longer necessary.

◀ back

Maintenance of a lathe

1 The Colchester Bantam 1600 lathe

Mandlmaier have several CNC machines for batch production. For single-part production Ana, Michał and Anthony use one of their Colchester Bantam 1600 lathes.

Match the following items with numbers 1–14 in the picture.

apron • bed • electrical controls • feedshaft • footbrake • gearbox • head-end plinth • headstock • leadscrew • main spindle • saddle and slides • tail-end plinth • tailstock • tool drawer

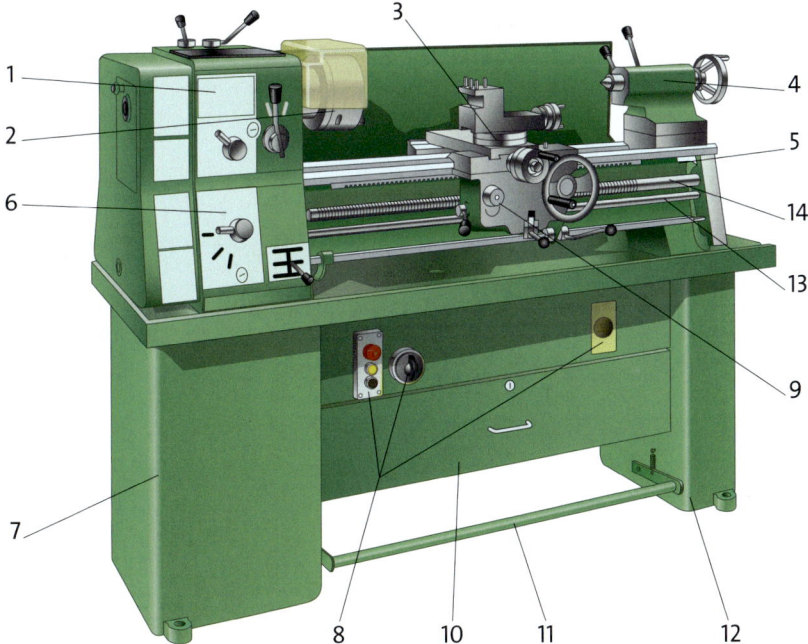

2 Changing the oil

a Before the apprentices can work with the lathe, they have to change the oil in the gearbox. The photos on the following page show this process step by step. Match the German instructions with pictures 1–11.

a Altöl vorschriftsmäßig entsorgen
b Öl ablassen
c Öl aus dem Gefahrstoffraum besorgen
d Öl mit Trichter einfüllen
e Ölablassschraube lösen
f Öleinfüllschraube lösen
g Ölsorte und Ölmenge aus der Betriebsanleitung übernehmen
h Spindelstockabdeckung abnehmen
i Spindelstockabdeckung wieder anbringen
j Stromunterbrechung sicherstellen
k Stromversorgung wieder herstellen

UNIT 4

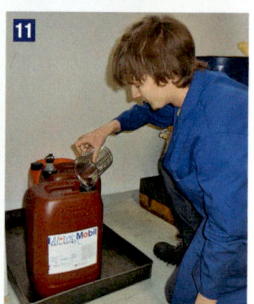

b Complete these English instructions with words from the box below.

drain screw • electrical • filler screw • funnel • headstock cover (2x) • operating manual • power source • store • waste oil

1 Make sure that the machine is disconnected from the electrical ....
2 Remove the ....
3 Loosen the oil ....
4 Drain off the ....
5 Check the ... for the grade and quantity of oil.
6 Get oil from the hazardous materials ....
7 Open the oil ....
8 Pour in the clean oil with a ....
9 Replace the ....
10 Reconnect the machine to the ... power source.

3 Writing a report

Write a working report on the oil change. Use the past tense and full sentences. Start like this:

First we pulled the plug of the cable out of the socket to make sure that the power supply was interrupted. Then we removed the ...

UNIT 4

4 The lubrication chart

 Listen to the telephone conversation between Anthony and the representative from Colchester Lathes and match the four icons to their meaning in the box.

- oil once a day/daily
- oil once a week/weekly
- grease once a week/weekly
- check level and top up once a week/weekly

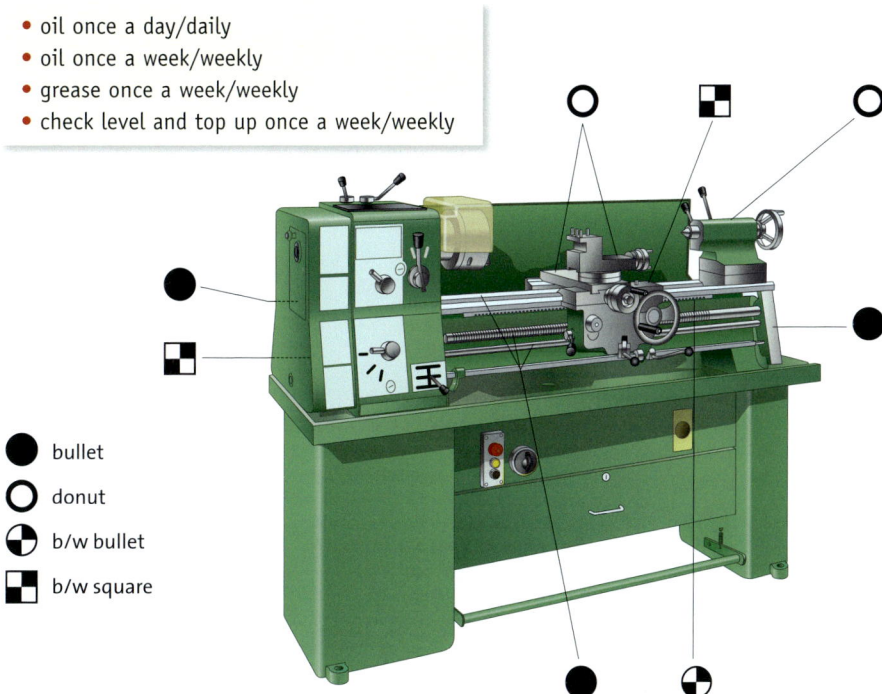

● bullet
○ donut
◐ b/w bullet
◼ b/w square

Language

Telephoning

Person called

- *Answering the phone*
  Good morning/afternoon. Colchester Lathes, how can I help you?

- *Asking who is calling*
  Who's calling, please?
  Could I have your name, please?
  Could you spell that?

- *Connecting the caller*
  One moment, please. I'll connect you.
  Could you hold the line, please?
  I'll put you through.

- *Answering a request*
  One moment, I'll have to check that.
  I'll have to ask Ms Fisher. I'll be right back.

- *Finishing the call*
  I'm glad I could help you.
  Thanks for calling. Bye.

Person calling

- *Saying who you want to speak to*
  Hello, could I speak to Anthony, please?
  Could you put me through to Anna, please?
  Could I have extension 487, please?

- *Saying your name*
  Hello, this is Anthony Coleman speaking.
  It's Anthony Coleman from Mandlmaier.
  This is Eric Mawdsley. That's M-A-W-…

- *Giving a reason for your call*
  I'm calling about the lubrication chart.
  Could you tell me how much the lathe costs?
  I'd like some information on prices, please.

- *Finishing the call*
  Thanks very much for your help.
  I'll call back later.

  Bye.

UNIT 4

5 Role-play: Ordering by telephone

You want to order gear oil. Work with a partner and act out the dialogue below. Then swap roles.

A	B
Melden Sie sich und grüßen Sie.	
	Grüßen Sie, geben Sie Ihren Namen und sagen Sie, dass Sie ein Getriebeöl für eine Drehmaschine benötigen.
Fragen Sie, für welche Drehmaschine es verwendet werden soll.	
	Sagen Sie, eine Colchester Bantam 1600.
Fragen Sie, welches Öl der Kunde braucht.	
	Antworten Sie, ein Shell Tellus 27.
Antworten Sie, dass Sie dies nicht mehr auf Lager haben und ob der Kunde die ISO Nummer kennt.	
	Antworten Sie, ISO 32.
Empfehlen Sie das IDEA Astron HLP 32, das den Vorteil hat, bei alten Maschinen nicht zu lecken.	
	Bestellen Sie 10 Liter an: Mandlmaier Automotive UK Ltd 11 Main Street Escrick York YO19 6JP
Sagen Sie, dass die Bestellung heute noch losgeschickt wird.	
	Bedanken Sie sich für die schnelle Erledigung.
Bedanken Sie sich für den Auftrag und verabschieden sie sich.	
	Verabschieden Sie sich ebenfalls.

Grammar

Forming questions

1. What **do** you do in York?
2. When **did** you get here?
3. Who **does** Markus work for?
4. Who **works** in Munich?
5. How **is** your hotel?

- Fragen mit Vollverben werden mit einer Form von *do* gebildet, d. h., *do/does* im *Simple present* (1, 3) und *did* im *Simple past* (2).
- Bei Fragen mit einer Form von *to be* rückt das Verb vor das Subjekt (5).
- Fragen nach dem Subjekt (mit *who* oder *what*) werden ohne eine Form von *do* gebildet (4).

who	fragt nach Personen	where	fragt nach dem Ort
what	fragt nach Handlungen und Sachen	why	fragt nach dem Grund oder Zweck
which	fragt nach Personen oder Sachen	when	fragt nach der Zeit
how	fragt nach der Art und Weise		

6 Practice

Ana meets Janet Steward, a CAD engineer, in the canteen of Mandlmaier in York. Complete the dialogue with questions.

JANET Hi, I'm Janet Steward. You must be Ana, the new trainee from Romania.
ANA Yes, I am. Pleased to meet you.
JANET …¹?
ANA I normally work at the subsidiary in Sibiu.
JANET …²?
ANA I'm training to be an energy engineer.
JANET I see. …³?
ANA I started working here this week, on Monday.
JANET Oh right, so you've only been here a few days then. …⁴?
ANA I'm working in one of the engineering groups.
JANET …⁵?
ANA Charlie Morrison is in charge of our group. He seems really nice.
JANET Yes, he is. So, …⁶?
ANA Well, I had to do three months' training somewhere abroad and I just thought it would be a good idea to do it here at the company's headquarters and in Manchester.
JANET You mean, to make good contacts?
ANA Not really. Just to see what the other subsidiaries are like, that's all.

7 Oil disposal: environmental regulations

a **Waste oil cannot simply be poured down the drain. That is why there are special stations for getting rid of oil. Read the text on the following page and find the English meanings of the following German words.**

entsorgen • Ölentsorgungsstelle • Verschmutzung • Schaden • Maschinenöl • Umweltbehörde • annehmen • Lösungsmittel • Anleitung • Lagerung

UNIT **4**

about the **oil care** campaign:
dispose of your **waste engine oil** for recycling at an **oilbank**

- Oil is a common and highly visible form of pollution where even a small quantity can cause a lot of harm to the environment.

- The Oil Care Campaign was set up by the Environment Agency, in association with SEPA in Scotland and Northern Ireland Environment Agency (NIEA), to reduce oil pollution by providing guidance on and facilities for the safe disposal and management of oil. Visit the Oil Care pages on their websites from the useful links section. From here you can also download some useful guidance notes on the safe use, storage and disposal of oil.

- The Environment Agency, SEPA and NIEA has installed a network of oil banks that accept used engine oil for recycling.

- Oil banks do not accept petrol, thinners, solvents, cooking oil, etc, or engine oil that has been mixed with white spirit, paint or solvents.

- If you live in the England, Wales, Scotland or Northern Ireland, you can find out where your nearest oil bank is by using our website or by telephoning the Oil Bank Line on 08708 506 506 or sending an email to enquiries@environment-agency.gov.uk.

find your nearest oil bank

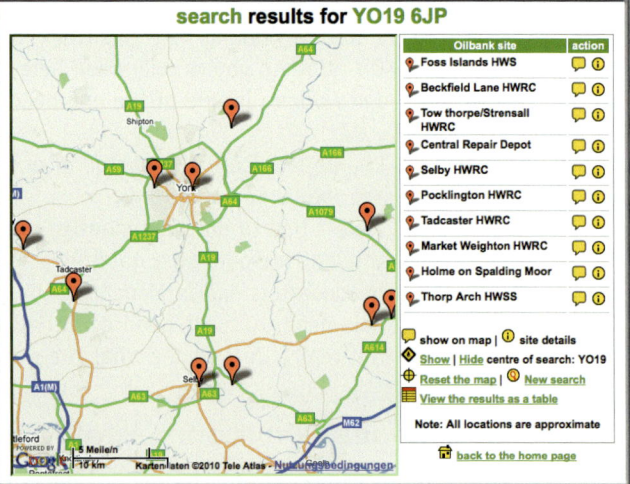

b What are the regulations for the disposal of waste oil in Germany? Find information on the Internet and write a short report (approx. 100–150 words) in English.

c Where are the oil banks in your local area?

UNIT 4

8 Describing a circuit diagram

a Match the definitions below with six of these symbols.

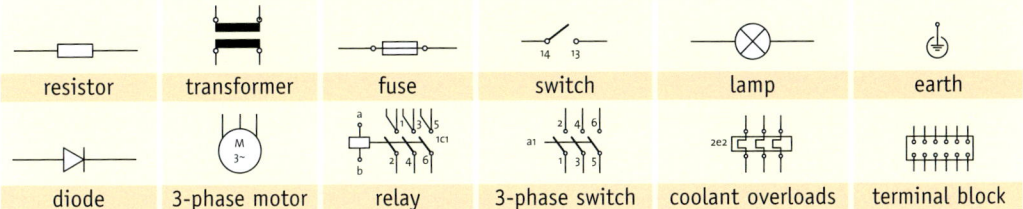

1. An electrical component that limits or regulates the flow of electrical current.
2. A device used in electrical systems to protect against excessive current.
3. An electronic component that conducts electric current in only one direction.
4. A device for reducing or increasing the voltage.
5. An electrically-operated switch. Many of them use an electromagnet to operate a switching mechanism mechanically.
6. An electrically-operated switch which is used to protect electrical circuits from overheating.

b Look at the circuit and complete the description.

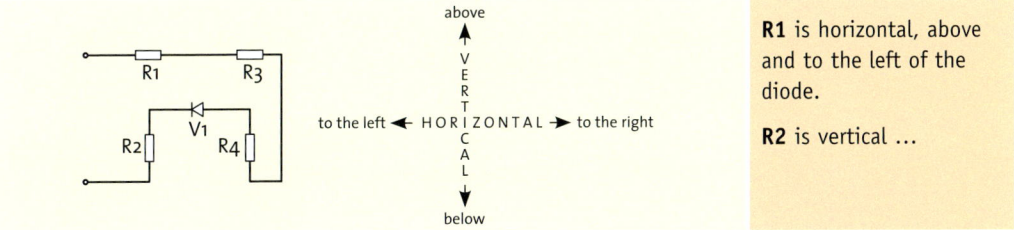

R1 is horizontal, above and to the left of the diode.

R2 is vertical ...

9 Describing the circuit diagram of an electric motor

Look at this circuit diagram and describe the position of the components.

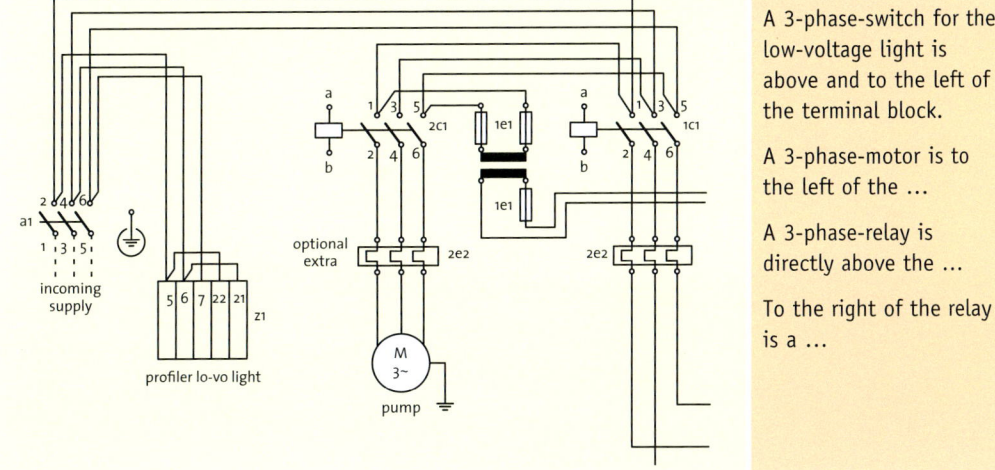

A 3-phase-switch for the low-voltage light is above and to the left of the terminal block.

A 3-phase-motor is to the left of the ...

A 3-phase-relay is directly above the ...

To the right of the relay is a ...

45

UNIT 4

10 Partner files: An electric motor control

Student A turn to file 2 on page 155.
Student B turn to file 9 on page 159.

11 How to connect the lathe to the mains

Lesen Sie den folgenden Text aus der Bedienungsanleitung der Bantam 1600 und beantworten Sie die folgenden Fragen in Deutsch.

1 Wo soll die Drehmaschine angeschlossen werden?
2 Wo soll die Anschlussleitung in die Maschine eingeführt werden?
3 An welchen Klemmen muss das Kabel am Lasttrennschalter angeschlossen werden?
4 In welche Richtung soll sich die Hauptspindel drehen?
5 Wie kann die Drehrichtung der Hauptspindel geändert werden?

ELECTRIC SUPPLY CONNECTION

Power supply must be through a separately-fused disconnect box, power input wires are connected to the lathe as follows:

1. Set the isolator switch on the electrical panel to the OFF position. Remove the panel cover.

2. Feed the power input wires through the entry hole located at the back of the panel under the tray, access to which is from the back of the machine (Fig. 4). The wires should be sheathed in armoured cable to the entry point.

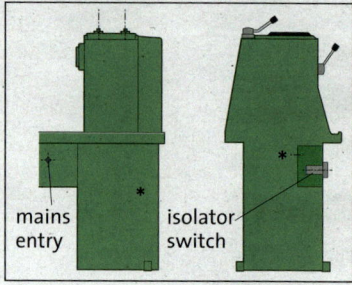

Fig. 4

3. Connect the power-input wires to terminals 1, 3 and 5 on the isolator switch.

4. Replace the panel cover. Check that the change-gear guard is secure and the spindle nose is clear of any obstruction.

5. Set the lathe-isolator switch to the ON Position, the two-speed switch to low and the headstock-speed levers to the lowest speed.

6. Raise the operating lever located on the RIGHT HAND side of the apron. The main spindle should rotate anticlockwise. If rotation is clockwise interchange any two of the power-input wires on terminals 1, 3 and 5 of the isolator switch after isolating the power supply at the source.

Refer to circuit diagrams on Pages 21–22.

Extra material

WORK SAFELY

Make sure that people who are working with electricity are competent enough to complete the job. Even simple tasks such as wiring a plug can be dangerous – ensure that people know what they are doing before they start.

Check that:
- suspect or faulty equipment is taken out of use, labelled 'DO NOT USE' and kept secure until examined by a competent person;
- where possible, tools and power socket-outlets are switched off before plugging in or unplugging;
- equipment is switched off and/or unplugged before cleaning or making adjustments.

More complicated tasks, such as equipment repairs or alterations to an electrical installation, should only be tackled by people with a knowledge of the risks involved and the precautions needed.

You must not allow work on or near exposed live parts of equipment unless it is absolutely unavoidable and suitable precautions have been taken to prevent injury, both to the workers and to anyone else who may be in the area.

You can find more information in our free download: www.hse.gov.uk/PUBNS/indg231.pdf

1 Working with electricity

Ihr Chef möchte, dass Sie bei Ihrem bevorstehenden Auslandseinsatz in Großbritannien keinen elektrischen Unfall erleiden und bittet Sie daher, die oben aufgeführten Grundsätze ins Deutsche zu übersetzen.

2 Internet task

Find more information about safety precautions and produce an audio-visual computer presentation.

I can ...

A Rezeption

Ich kann technische Texte verstehen und bearbeiten.

1 Lesen Sie den folgenden Text und setzen Sie die folgenden Ausdrücke ein.

after-sales service centre • fail • insulation • interior • mains plug • malfunctions • nameplate • residual current device • ventilation slots • wear

 Maintenance and Cleaning

- Before any work on the machine itself, pull the ...[(1)].
- For safe and proper working, always keep the machine and the ...[(2)] clean.
- In order to avoid operational ...[(3)], do not saw gypsum board from below or overhead.

In extreme working conditions, conductive dust can accumulate in the ...[(4)] of the machine when working with metal. The protective ...[(5)] of the machine can be degraded. The use of a stationary extraction system is recommended in such cases as well as frequently blowing out the ventilation slots and installing a ...[(6)]. The guide roller 12 should occasionally be checked for ...[(7)] and lubricated with a drop of oil. If it is worn, it must be replaced.
If the machine should ...[(8)] despite the care taken in manufacturing and testing procedures, repair should be carried out by an ...[(9)] for Bosch power tools. In all correspondence and spare parts orders, please always include the 10-digit order number given on the ...[(10)] of the machine.

2 Finden Sie die folgenden deutschen Ausdrücke im untenstehenden Text.

am höchsten • ausführen • bis zu • Fahrgestell • leiten • Punktschweißen • Strom • verbinden • Widerstand

Gas welding, and most commonly oxyacetylene welding, is regularly used to join pipes and tubes and when undertaking repair work. Resistance welding involves passing a high current (between 1000 and 100 000 A) between two or more metal surfaces. Molten pools of metal then form around the weld area where resistance is at its highest. Spot welding uses this principle to join overlapping sheets of metal of up to 3 millimetres in thickness. Two electrodes simultaneously clamp the sheets together and pass a current between them securing the sheets. It is an easily automated process often undertaken by industrial robots; modern day cars are likely to have several thousand spot welds holding the chassis together.

B Produktion

Ich kann den eigenen Beruf beschreiben.

3 Wählen Sie drei Berufe aus der untenstehenden Liste aus und beschreiben Sie sie Ihrem Partner in Englisch.

- Anlagenmechaniker/in für Sanitär-, Heizungs- und Klimatechnik
- Behälter- und Apparatebauer/in
- Feinwerkmechaniker/in
- Konstruktionsmechaniker/in
- Metallbauer/in
- Schneidwerkzeugmechaniker/in
- Technische/r Zeichner/in
- Zerspanungsmechaniker/in

Ich kann sozialen Kontakt herstellen durch Begrüßung und Sich-Vorstellen.

4 Führen Sie die folgenden sprachlichen Handlungen auf Englisch aus:

- Grüßen Sie.

I CAN ... 1

- Sagen Sie, dass es Sie freut Ihren Gesprächspartner kennenzulernen.
- Fragen Sie Ihren Gesprächspartner, wie es ihm geht.
- Sagen Sie, dass Sie ihm nun Ihren Chef vorstellen werden.

Ich kann Sachen bestellen.

5 Bestellen Sie in einer höflichen E-Mail bei order@megatools.co.uk folgende Werkzeuge. Bitten Sie um schnelle Lieferung.

- 1 x Schlitzschraubendreher
- 3 x Pozidriv-Schraubendreher
- 2 x Gewindebohrer M6 und M12
- 1 x Satz Gabelschlüssel 8 bis 19 mm

C Mediation

Ich kann Sachverhalte systematisch darstellen und wichtige Punkte hervorheben.

6 Lesen Sie den folgenden Text und vervollständigen Sie das Anweisungsschild, das an einer Fräsmaschine angebracht werden soll.

> **Sicherheitsanweisungen**
> - Sicherheitskleidung tragen
> - ...

Safety instructions
- Always wear appropriate clothes. These should include overalls, safety glasses, and safety boots with steel toecaps. Do not wear any loose clothing which could get caught by a moving part.
- Long hair should to be kept away from the face and safely restrained by a hairnet.
- Remove all jewelry, piercings or other body ornaments which could catch in moving parts.
- Before operating the machine, make a visual check and make sure there are no loose cables or loose components. If a loose cable or component is detected, turn the main power off and disconnect the 400V cable from the machine before handling the loose item.
- Do not turn switches on or off with wet hands.
- When operating the machine, keep your hands and any other part of your body away from moving parts while the machine is working.
- Do not attempt to do jobs that go beyond the capabilities of the machine. The operator should be knowledgeable about the material characteristics of the workpiece before attempting to work with it.
- The operator must know the location of the emergency button on the control panel so that it can be pushed immediately in an emergency.

D Interaktion

Ich kann mich in Situationen verständigen, in denen es um einen Austausch von Informationen in Zusammenhang mit der Arbeit geht.

7 Führen Sie das folgende Telefongespräch mit Ihrem Partner durch:

- **A** Melden Sie sich und grüßen Sie.
- **B** Sagen Sie Ihren Namen und dass Sie ein Getriebeöl für eine Fräsmaschine benötigen.
- **A** Fragen Sie nach dem speziellen Typ.
- **B** Antworten Sie, Sie hätten keine Herstellerangaben.
- **A** Empfehlen Sie das CLP 46 von Megol.
- **B** Fragen Sie nach dem Preis.
- **A** 20 Liter kosten € 86,00 plus Versandkosten.
- **B** Bestellen Sie das Öl mit Lieferung an Ihre Firma.
- **A** Nehmen sie die Bestellung auf und sagen Sie, dass Sie heute noch ausliefern werden.
- **A/B** Beenden Sie das Telefonat.

5 Producing a Stirling engine

1 The Stirling engine

The Stirling engine has been around since 1816 and is now making a comeback in many different fields, from micro engines which function with a temperature difference as little as one degree Celsius to powerful engines for industrial use. The primary energy can be the sun, oil, wood, gas or other energy sources.

Work with a partner: How do you think that Stirling engines could be used with the following things? The Language box below may help you with this.

1 a submarine

3 a satellite

2 a solar reflector

4 a refrigerator

5 a pellet furnace

6 a hybrid motor

Language

Antonyms: more – less, high – low, maximum – minimum, major – minor, main – auxiliary, primary – secondary, advantage – disadvantage

Synonyms: main – primary, secondary – additional, auxiliary, loud – noisy

Useful words and phrases

A Stirling engine can be used …

- in reverse to remove heat and lower the temperature.
- in conjunction with a conventional engine.
- together with a pellet furnace/fuel cell/…

Can a Stirling engine be used to …

- power an electric generator?
- produce electrical/motive power?
- lower the temperature of materials?

A Stirling engine …

- utilizes differences in temperature.
- operates at a high level of efficiency/is efficient.
- operates at a low noise level/runs quietly.
- is cost effective/cheap to operate.
- needs little maintenance.

UNIT **5**

2   How a Stirling engine works

Liu Xinzi and Hong Xaofeng teach engineering at Manchester Polytechnic College. Today they have to explain the basic principles of the Stirling Engine to a group of first-year students and they've printed out a text they found on the Internet.

The basic principles of a Stirling engine

Every Stirling engine has a sealed cylinder with one part hot and the other cold. The working gas inside the engine (which is often air, helium, or hydrogen) is moved by a mechanism from the hot side to the cold side. When the gas is on the hot side it expands and pushes up a piston. When it moves back to the cold side it contracts and pulls the piston back to the bottom of the cylinder. These two power pulses per revolution enable the engine to run very smoothly. There are two main types of Stirling engine: the displacer type and the two-piston type.

The displacer type Stirling engine has one power piston and a displacer piston. The space below the displacer piston is continuously heated by a heat source. The space above the displacer piston is continuously cooled. The displacer piston moves ('displaces') the air from the hot side to the cold side.

The two-piston type of Stirling engine has two power pistons. There is a heat source above the hot piston and a cooling mechanism above the cold piston.

a   Which type of Stirling Engine do the following illustrations show?

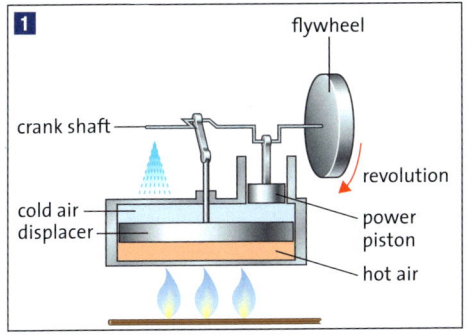

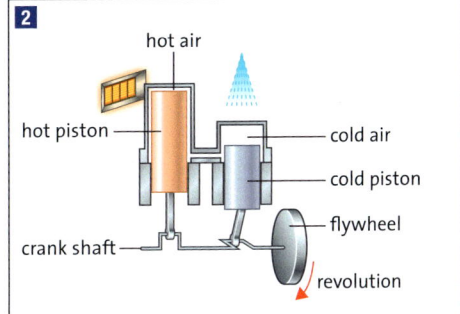

b   Are these statements correct? If not, correct them.

1. The Stirling Engine has a hot and a cold cylinder.
2. The piston is pushed upwards by cold gas.
3. The displacer type engine has only one piston.
4. In the two-piston type engine, hot and cold air cannot be exchanged.

UNIT 5

Grammar

The passive

1 The turning machines **are used** to produce the working cylinders.
2 **Have** all these products **been designed** here?
3 The factory **was built** by Gerald Faber about fifteen years ago.
4 All safety regulations **must be adhered to** exactly.

- Das Passiv wird mit einer Form von *to be* und dem *Past participle* (3. Form des Verbs) gebildet. (1–4)
- In technischen Texten wird im Englischen häufig das Passiv verwendet, um Handlungen zu beschreiben, ohne deren Urheber zu nennen, z. B., wenn der Urheber keine Rolle für die Aussage des Satzes spielt. (2)
- Wenn man hervorheben will, **von wem** etwas getan wird oder **wodurch** etwas geschieht, fügt man diese Information mit der Präposition *by* an. (3).

3 Practice

a Read the text in Exercise 2 on page 51 again and write down the passive constructions. There are three of them.

b Complete the answers by using the passive forms of the verbs. Use the same tense as in the question. The first one has been done for you.

FAQ

search

1 Who **invented** this type of Stirling Engine?
The Stirling Engine **was invented** by Robert Stirling in 1816.

2 Does the Stirling engine convert work into heat?
No! It's the other way round: in a Stirling engine, heat … (convert) into work.

3 Can I use a Stirling engine for my car?
No, Stirling engines … (can not / use) in cars because they start too slowly.

4 Is it true that the Stirling Engine is a clean and efficient engine?
Yes, because the heat driving the pistons … (supply) from outside the engine.

5 Does it produce any nitrogen oxides (NOx)?
No, because the fuel … (burn) constantly and slowly outside.

6 Is it true that Stirling Engines can also power refrigerators?
Yes, the reverse process … (can / use) for refrigeration without producing CFCs (chlorofluorocarbons).

7 What is this booklet for?
It's so that the world of Stirling Engines … (can / understand) much more fully.

52

2 How a Stirling engine works

Liu Xinzi and Hong Xaofeng teach engineering at Manchester Polytechnic College. Today they have to explain the basic principles of the Stirling Engine to a group of first-year students and they've printed out a text they found on the Internet.

The basic principles of a Stirling engine

Every Stirling engine has a sealed cylinder with one part hot and the other cold. The working gas inside the engine (which is often air, helium, or hydrogen) is moved by a mechanism from the hot side to the cold side. When the gas is on the hot side it expands and pushes up a piston. When it moves back to the cold side it contracts and pulls the piston back to the bottom of the cylinder. These two power pulses per revolution enable the engine to run very smoothly. There are two main types of Stirling engine: the displacer type and the two-piston type.

The displacer type Stirling engine has one power piston and a displacer piston. The space below the displacer piston is continuously heated by a heat source. The space above the displacer piston is continuously cooled. The displacer piston moves ('displaces') the air from the hot side to the cold side.

The two-piston type of Stirling engine has two power pistons. There is a heat source above the hot piston and a cooling mechanism above the cold piston.

a Which type of Stirling Engine do the following illustrations show?

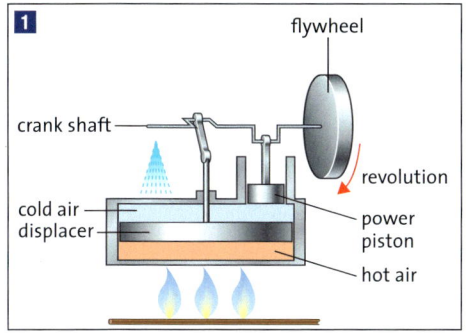

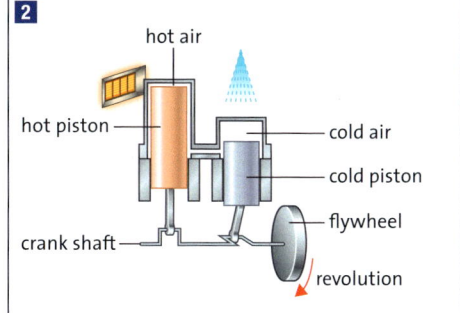

b Are these statements correct? If not, correct them.

1 The Stirling Engine has a hot and a cold cylinder.
2 The piston is pushed upwards by cold gas.
3 The displacer type engine has only one piston.
4 In the two-piston type engine, hot and cold air cannot be exchanged.

51

UNIT 5

Grammar

The passive

1 The turning machines **are used** to produce the working cylinders.
2 **Have** all these products **been designed** here?
3 The factory **was built** by Gerald Faber about fifteen years ago.
4 All safety regulations **must be adhered to** exactly.

- Das Passiv wird mit einer Form von *to be* und dem *Past participle* (3. Form des Verbs) gebildet. (1–4)

- In technischen Texten wird im Englischen häufig das Passiv verwendet, um Handlungen zu beschreiben, ohne deren Urheber zu nennen, z. B., wenn der Urheber keine Rolle für die Aussage des Satzes spielt. (2)

- Wenn man hervorheben will, **von wem** etwas getan wird oder **wodurch** etwas geschieht, fügt man diese Information mit der Präposition *by* an. (3).

3 Practice

a Read the text in Exercise 2 on page 51 again and write down the passive constructions. There are three of them.

b Complete the answers by using the passive forms of the verbs. Use the same tense as in the question. The first one has been done for you.

FAQ

search

1 Who **invented** this type of Stirling Engine?
The Stirling Engine **was invented** by Robert Stirling in 1816.

2 Does the Stirling engine convert work into heat?
No! It's the other way round: in a Stirling engine, heat ... (convert) into work.

3 Can I use a Stirling engine for my car?
No, Stirling engines ... (can not / use) in cars because they start too slowly.

4 Is it true that the Stirling Engine is a clean and efficient engine?
Yes, because the heat driving the pistons ... (supply) from outside the engine.

5 Does it produce any nitrogen oxides (NOx)?
No, because the fuel ... (burn) constantly and slowly outside.

6 Is it true that Stirling Engines can also power refrigerators?
Yes, the reverse process ... (can / use) for refrigeration without producing CFCs (chlorofluorocarbons).

7 What is this booklet for?
It's so that the world of Stirling Engines ... (can / understand) much more fully.

4 Welcome to Adler Heizsysteme GmbH

Adler have developed an innovative home heating system.

a Read this excerpt from their brochure and answer the questions below.

MR-703 Heizsystem

- Revolutionär ist das Zusammenspiel des völlig neu entwickelten Pelletbrenners mit einem technisch hochmodernem Stirlingmotor. Pellets sind sauber, umweltfreundlich, immer verfügbar und preiswert.
- Eine der Besonderheiten des neuen Pelletbrenners: Er wandelt die zugeführten Pellets rückstandsfrei in Gas um. Dabei entsteht praktisch keine Asche. Sie heizen nicht mit Festbrennstoff, sondern CO_2-neutral mit ökologisch sauberem, schadstofffreiem Gas aus eigener Herstellung.
- Die Erfindung des Upside-down-Brenners, bei dem die Flamme von oben nach unten auf einen Wärmetauscher düst, ist besonders effizient. Die extrem hohe Temperatur bringt den Stirlingmotor mit dem angeschlossenen Stromgenerator richtig zum Laufen.
- Sie bekommen absolut sauberen Strom ohne den üblichen Energieverlust. Denn mit der Abwärme der Stromproduktion heizen Sie Ihr ganzes Haus. 3 kW Strom speist der Motor unermüdlich ins Netz. Damit er das jahrzehntelang durchhält, haben wir ihn in kompromissloser Qualität gebaut. Allein das Kurbelwellenhauptlager aus Werkzeugstahl hat einen Durchmesser von 11 cm.
- Was von der Verbrennung übrigbleibt, ist tatsächlich nur die durch den Brennwerteffekt kondensierte Restfeuchtigkeit des Holzes mit wertvollen Mineralien und natürlichen Spurenelementen. Sie können es gefahrlos in die Kanalisation leiten oder für Ihre Pflanzen verwenden.

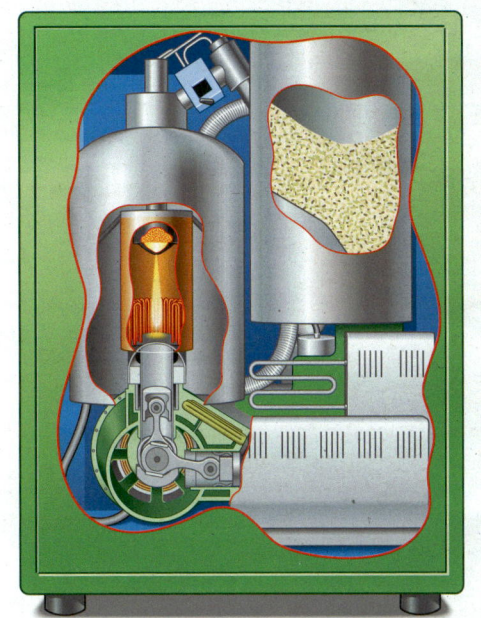

1. How is the MR-703 different from a conventional pellet heating system?
2. What makes the Stirling engine so efficient?
3. What is the function of the Stirling engine in this heating system?

b Describe the components of the MR-703 and their functions. The following Language box may help you with this.

- pellet hopper *Pellettrichter*
- worm screw *Schnecke*
- combustion chamber *Brennkammer*
- heat exchanger *Wärmetauscher*
- power generator *Stromgenerator*
- electric grid *Stromnetz*
- crankshaft *Kurbelwelle*
- main bearing *Hauptlager*

> The ... transports the pellets to the ...

> When the pellets are heated, they produce ...

UNIT 5

5 A visit to Castle Engineering

Adler GmbH want to market the MR-703 heating system at trade fairs around the world. They think that working models of Stirling engines would be a good way to impress potential customers. For this they'll need about 50 models. Klaus Schiller, the CEO (Chief Executive Officer) of Adler visits Castle Engineering in Huddersfield, England. Nigel Robinson, the CEO of Castle Engineering shows him around the factory and introduces him to some of the people who work there.

 a Listen to the recording and find out what 1–12 on the floor plan of the factory are.

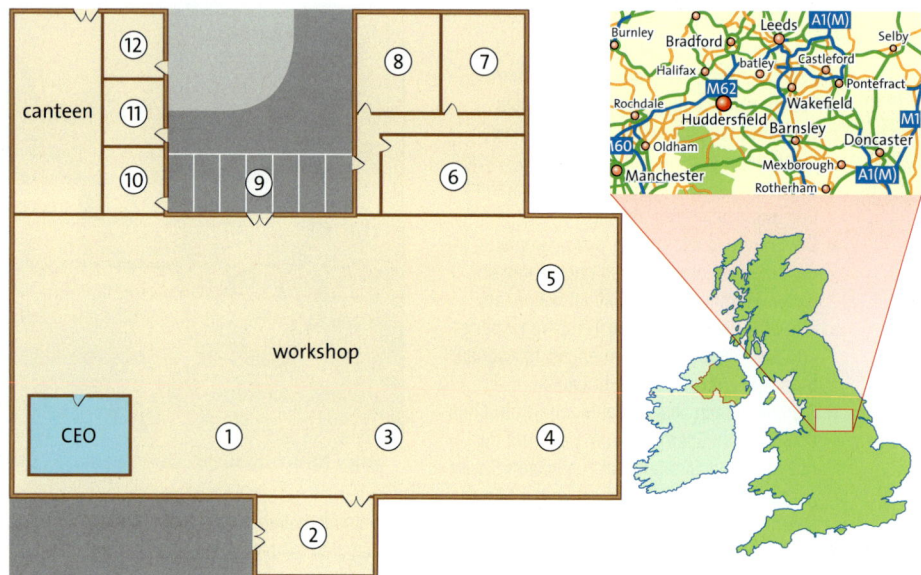

b Over lunch, Klaus Schiller meets some of the office workers at Castle Engineering. Read how they described their jobs on the next page. Then look at the organizational chart below and identify their names and the departments they are responsible for.

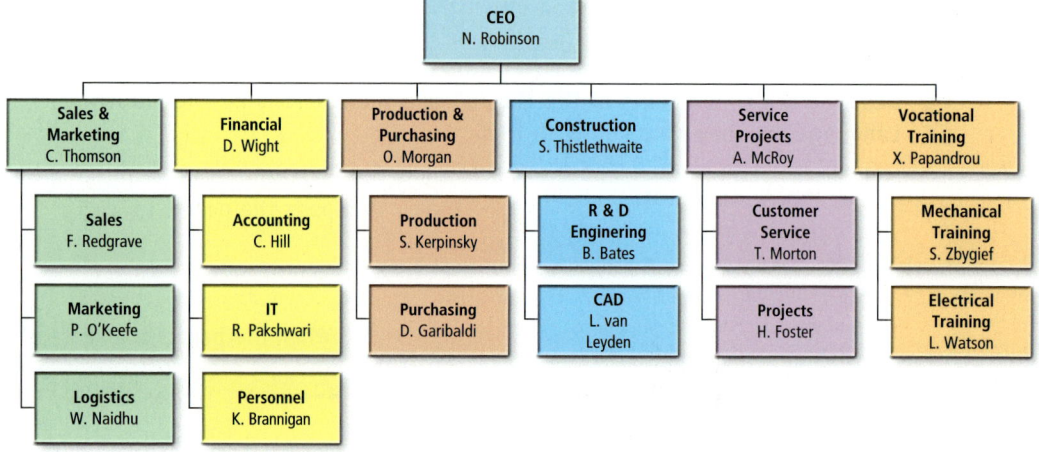

54

1

Well, I buy the materials we use, and all the machines and tools as well. I don't always buy the cheapest product. I look for a good quality product at a reasonable price. That can't always be found in a catalogue. I need to contact the producer and try to get a special price.
Name: Daniel ...
Dept.: Purchasing Department

2

I'm responsible for the training of seven young people who are learning how to do the electrical servicing and maintenance for all the machines and installations in the workshop and the offices. My department is a sub-division of Vocational Training.
Name: Laura ...
Dept.: ...

3

I work at the financial heart of the firm. It's my job to keep records of all the bills we send out and the bills we pay. I make profit and loss spreadsheets for all our projects so that we can check that everything is going well and we'll make a profit and not a loss.
Name: Christine ...
Dept.: ...

4

In my department all the technical drawings are produced with the help of special computer software. But before that stage my staff does a lot of research on how to combine the best materials with the best ways of production.
Name: Steve ...
Dept.: ...

5

I do the hiring and firing! Thankfully, firing is only a small part of my job and it doesn't happen often. Our company is expanding, so at the moment I'm doing a lot of interviewing. I have a BA in Applied Psychology, but I think I've learnt more working here than I ever did at university!
Name: Katy ...
Dept.: ...

UNIT 5

6 Working with measuring instruments

The Stirling Engine has a flywheel that has to be produced very precisely. To take all the necessary measurements the engineers use both a vernier caliper and a micrometre.

Give the following readings in numbers.

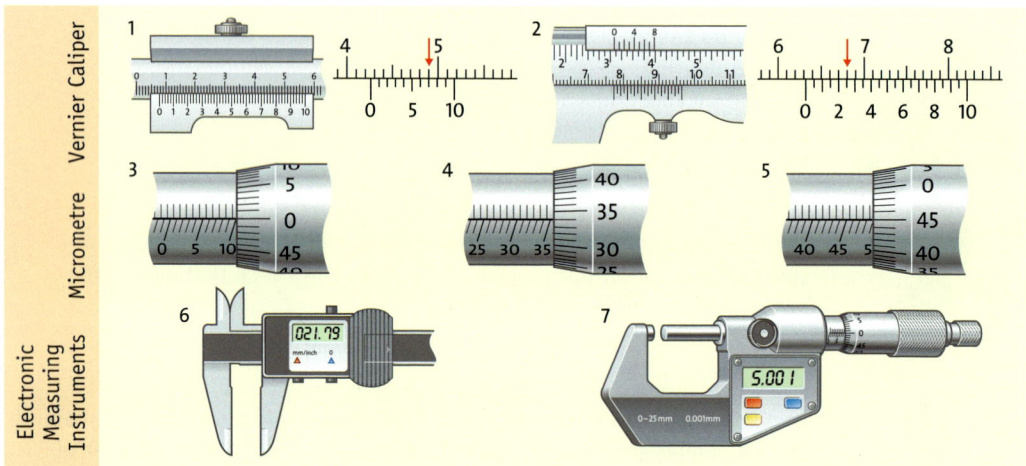

Information

Numbers
To repeat the numbers as well as decimal fractions look into the appendix.

Be careful:
four – fourteen – but: forty
five – but: fifteen – fifty
dt. 1Milliarde = 1 billion
1,894,876,273   commas separate thousands, millions etc.
   6.79 points are used for decimals

Mathematical Operations

a > b	a is greater (larger) than b
1.1	one point one
a < b	a is smaller than b
2 + 6 = 8	Two plus six is (equals) eight.
9 - 3 = 6	Nine minus three is (equals) six.
a ± b	a plus or minus b
3 x 3 = 9	Three times (multiplied by) three is (equals) nine.
16 ÷ 4 = 4	Sixteen divided by four is (equals) four.
$2^2 = 4$	Two squared is (equals) four.
$2^3 = 8$	Two cubed is (equals) eight.
$3^4 = 81$	Three to the power of four is (equals) eighty-one.
$\sqrt{9} = 3$	The square root of nine is (equals) three.

- Note that in English commas and dots are used differently:
  German   4.000,00 kg   0,7V
  English   4,000.00 kg   0.7V

- 0 is pronounced nought, oh or zero.

UNIT 5

7 An estimate

Klaus Schiller asks Nigel Robinson to produce a prototype before he places an order for the 50 model Stirling engines. Nigel Robinson wants to make an estimate of the costs for this prototype before he agrees to produce it.

Customer:	Adler Heizsysteme GmbH
Project:	Model-Stirling-Engine
Date:	19. April 2012

Estimate

		time required in hours	hourly rate in €	overhead rate in %	Costs total in €
Costs of materials					27
Work					
Sawing	labour costs	1	30		30
				35	11
Turning	labour costs	12	36		[1]
				80	[2]
Milling	labour costs	8	36		[3]
				90	[4]
Drilling	labour costs	5	36		[5]
				25	[6]
Assembly	labour costs	9	36		[7]
				15	[8]
Production Costs					[9]
Administrative overheads				5	100
Distribution overheads				5	[10]
Total Production Costs					[11]
Profit				10	[12]
sale price					[13]
VAT				17.5	[14]
retail price					[15]

a Work with a partner and calculate the numbers missing from the spreadsheet. One partner has a calculator. The other partner dictates the mathematical operation and writes down the results. Swap roles after every five numbers.

UNIT 5

b Klaus Schiller is surprised at some of the costs in the estimate. Look at his questions and find Nigel Robinson's answers (a–e).

KLAUS Oh, I didn't expect the prototype to be so expensive. I could buy a working model of a Stirling engine over the Internet for under 200 Euros. So why does your prototype cost 2,832 Euros? That's a big difference!

NIGEL …¹

KLAUS Let's go through the estimate step by step. We'll start with the materials.

NIGEL …²

KLAUS Yes I agree, the materials cost is reasonable. But why are the hourly rates different for the different production processes?

NIGEL …³

KLAUS OK, I understand that. But what are all these overheads that push the prices up so drastically?

NIGEL …⁴

KLAUS Well, I still think your administrative costs are on the high side, but perhaps we can discuss that detail later. Your profit margin bothers me. Is it really necessary for you to make this much profit with a single prototype? If we order 50 models, you could afford to reduce your unit profit.

NIGEL …⁵

a That's easy to explain. Sawing is a process that requires fewer skills than when working on a lathe or a milling machine. Therefore we can give that job to somebody who is less qualified and not as highly paid.

b Well, that's true, Klaus. But we haven't got that order for 50 models yet, have we? I'll make you an offer, if we get your contract for 50 model engines, I'll cancel the profit of 219 Euros for the prototype entirely and reduce our profit margin by 3%.

c Quality has its price, Klaus. You need a model which is robust and reliable and looks really good. You won't get that from something you buy over the Internet for a couple of hundred Euros.

d Well, the lowest costs are for the materials. That item is just 27 Euros. You can't complain about that.

e Overhead expenses are all costs not chargeable to specific projects. Our overheads include rent, utilities and insurance. These are fixed costs which are distributed equally over all ongoing projects. I can't imagine that your own overheads in Germany can be significantly lower than ours here in England. For lower overheads you'd have to use a firm in China or Vietnam or Cambodia.

c Do you accept Nigel Robinson's answers? If you don't, say why not.

d Work with a partner and act out a dialogue between the two CEOs.
Partner A: Write a list of questions that you are going to ask.
Partner B: Prepare convincing explanations to the questions.

Extra material

1 Mediation

Read this except from a brochure about a solar-powered Stirling engine and summarise it in German.

The Solar-powered Stirling engine

Selected Design

We chose a displacer design which incorporates the use of a regenerator that will improve the overall engine efficiency. This is a unique design as displacer engines do not normally incorporate regenerators. The displacer design uses one cylinder to expose the contained gas to either a hot or a cold source and a second cylinder to convert the hot gas expansion to power. The cylinders are connected by a conduit to allow the gas to be transferred.

Dominant factors that were considered when selecting the design were:
- simplicity and function as a demonstration tool,
- better efficiency by using a regenerator,
- ease of construction,
- a closed system which allows the use of gases other than air, i.e. helium,
- durability,
- a parabolic solar collector which reaches high temperatures quickly, can be positioned easily and is inexpensive to manufacture.

2 Working with language

Here is another excerpt from the brochure. Complete the text with the correct passive forms of the verbs in brackets.

To transmit the energy collected by the solar collector to the engine a rod assembly ...¹ (construct). The basic principle employed in the rod design was the conduction of heat through a highly conductive medium (copper). The heat energy ...² (focus) to a focal point near the top of the copper rod by the collector. This rod ...³ (attach) to the solar collector, passing through the hole in its base. The bottom of the rod ...⁴ (thread) into the copper top of the displacer chamber. Heat ...⁵ (conduct) down the rod and into the copper top, which heats the enclosed air by radiation.

3 Working with words

Look at the illustration and say where the following components are and what they do.

conducting rod • displacer • framework • power piston • solar collector

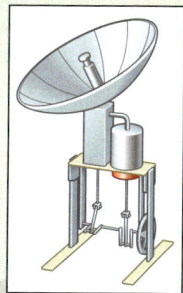

The ... is a parabolic mirror at the top of the ... and it collects sunlight and focuses the heat on to ...

4 Discussion

Work in groups and discuss where the solar-powered Stirling engine could be implemented. Write a list.

6 Assembling components

1 Fits in everyday objects

Work with a partner and decide how exact the fit of each item should be on a scale of 1 (fairly loose) to 6 (very tight). Can you think of other examples?

bike pedal • car door • car shock absorber • cogwheels in a watch • door hinge • DVD tray • lid of a bowl • lid of a pressure cooker

cogwheels   shock absorber   plastic lid   pressure cooker lid

2 Types of radial bearings

a Which types of radial bearings do the three illustrations show: ball, roller or plain?

b Look at the illustration of bearings and roller bearings. Match the following terms in the box below with the numbers.

cage (2x) • inner race • outer race • roller • rolling ball

c Look at the four illustrations on the right and answer the following questions.

1 Which are ball bearings and which are roller bearings?
2 Which arrows show radial forces and which show axial forces?
3 Some bearings have more than one pair of rolling elements. Can you give a reason for this?

 d Listen to an instructor at Castle Engineering describing different types of bearings to a group of trainees. Complete the table below.

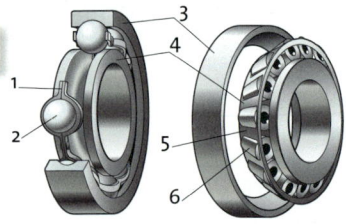

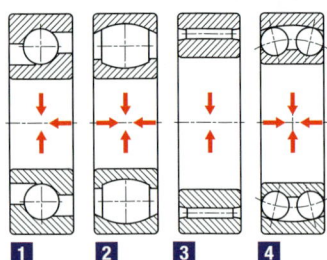

German name	English name	Number of illustration
Schrägkugellager	...	...
Pendelkugellager	...	...
Nadellager	...	...
Tonnenlager	...	...

3 Tolerances and fits

The team at Castle Engineering is still working on the prototype model of a Stirling engine (see Unit 5). Their next task involves the production of the supporting plate which you can see in the drawing on the right. Here a ball bearing has to be pressed into a borehole.

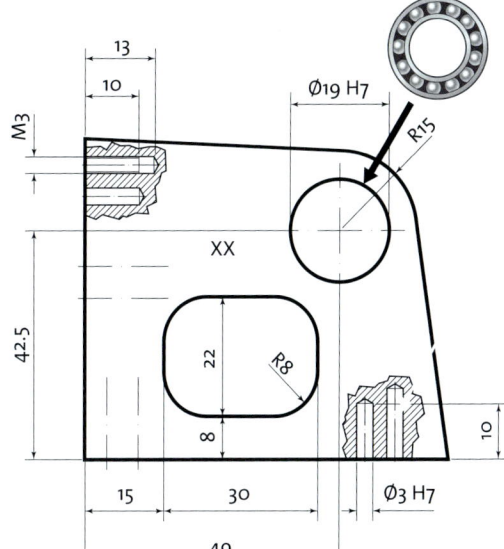

a Answer the following questions.

1 What are the diameters (ø) and tolerances of the ball bearing and the borehole?
2 Why are there two different symbols for tolerance?

b Look at the table of clearance fits below and check which of the following statements is correct.

1 H7 means that the diameter of the borehole can be no more than 21 millimeters.
2 H7 means that the diameter of the borehole can be no more than 21 hundredths of a millimeter.
3 H7 means that the diameter of the borehole can be no more than 21 thousandths of a millimeter.

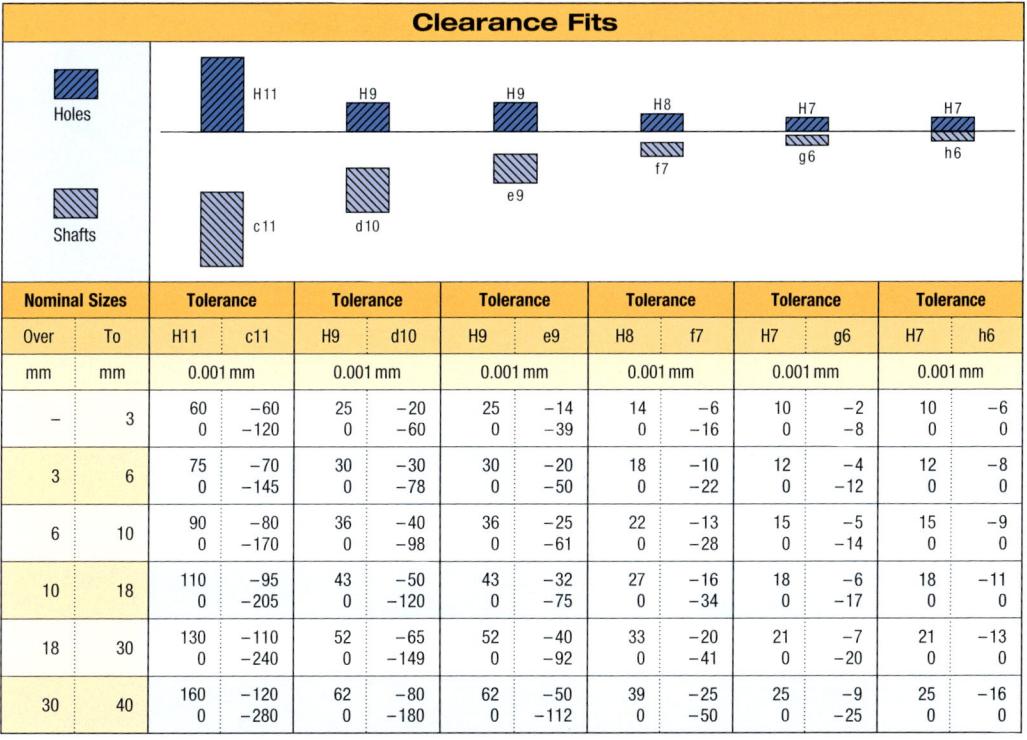

4 What happens if...

a Now think about the following three situations and say what you think will happen in each one. The box below can help you.

The borehole is (1) 18.89 mm, (2) 19.03 mm, (3) 19.31 mm.

The bearing	will won't	fit fall	into the borehole at all. the borehole perfectly. fall through the borehole.

b Find out whether the following dimensions are within tolerance (go) or outside tolerance (no go)?

H7 4.008 • g6 4,000 • H7 12.17 • g6 11.085 • H8 33.022 • f7 31.97

5 Partnerwork files: comparing technical data

Student A: Turn to file 3 on page 155.
Student B: Turn to file 10 on page 159.

6 The gripper

Castle Engineering also mounts grippers onto industrial robots. Look at the gripper and the chart below and then decide which of the shapes (A, B, C) show the following special movements.

1 From 'swiveling open' to 'swiveling close'.
2 From 'parallel open' to 'parallel close'.
3 From 'parallel open' to 'swiveling close'.

SPECIAL MOVEMENTS

Shape A	Shape B	Shape C

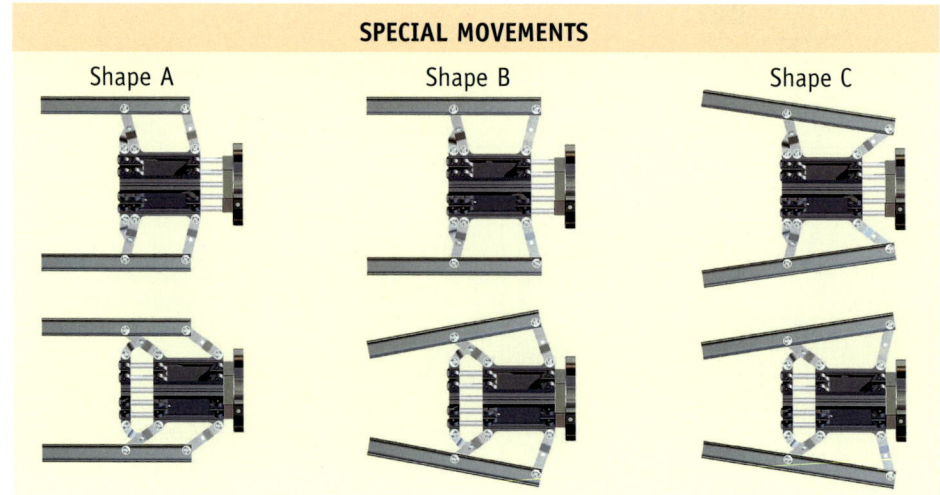

UNIT 6

7 The assembly plan of a gripper

a Castle Engineering need to order the following four components for the gripper mounting. Look at the table on the right and find out the names of these parts.

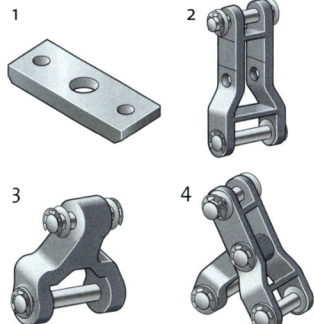

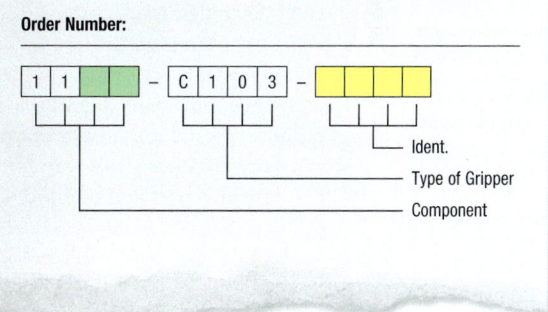

Pos. 4+5	Link, Crank, Crank Mechanism, Counter Plate		
Article	Component	Ident.	Scope of Delivery
Link	02	LE04	Link (3), Slide Bearing (22), Bearing Pins (15), Washer and Circlips.
Crank	03	KU04	Link (4), Slide Bearing (22), Bearing Pins (14+15), Washer and Circlips.
Crank Mechanism	51	KT04	Link (3), Crank (4), Slide Bearing (22), Bearing Pins (14+15), Washer and Circlips.
Counter Plate	05	GP03	Counter Plate for shoe attachment. Only for fingers with finger length F=0 and standard bore template.

Order Number: _____

1 1 ☐ ☐ — C 1 0 3 — ☐ ☐ ☐ ☐

— Ident.
— Type of Gripper
— Component

b Now use the information in the table and in the order number key to find the order numbers of the four parts above.

link: 1102-C103-...
crank: 1103-C103-...
crank mechanism: ...
counter plate: ...

c Role-play a telephone conversation.

Partner A: You work for Castle Engineering and you have to order spare parts for grippers. Call GMG-Systems and order the following parts.
Partner B: You work for GMG-Systems. A customer orders different spare parts. Find out the prices for them.

A: Mitarbeiter von Castle Engineering	B: Mitarbeiter von GMG-Systems
Rufen Sie bei GMG-Systems an und bestellen Sie: 5 Stück Gegenplatten 10 Stück Kurbeln 10 Stück Kurbelgetriebe 5 Stück Lenker Fragen Sie nach dem Preis und bitten Sie um schnellstmögliche Lieferung.	Ein Mitarbeiter von Castle Engineering ruft bei Ihnen an und bestellt verschiedene Ersatzteile. Fragen Sie nach den Bestellnummern und errechnen Sie den Gesamtpreis. Sagen Sie, dass die Teile noch heute von GMG ausgeliefert werden. Hier ist die dazugehörige Preisliste: 1102-C103-LE04 £24 1103-C103-KU04 £52 1151-C103-KT04 £89 1105-C103-GP03 £18

UNIT 6

8 A case of warranty

a Strohmeier are specialists in the repair of 4-wheel drives. About six months ago they repaired a bearing on an H2 Hummer. Now it has failed again.

Partner A: Call Ajax Wheel Bearings in the United States and ask for a new wheel bearing and the warranty terms.
Partner B: Use the website below to answer the call.

AJAX WHEEL BEARINGS

search

- HOME
- PRODUCTS
- SERVICE
- CONTACT
- IMPRESSUM
- HELP

The following is Wheel Bearings Inc., limited warranties as wholesaler of aftermarket front wheel and rear wheel hub units:
The wholesaler guarantees to the first user and/or purchaser that the product will be free from defects in material and workmanship for a period of 1 year, or 12,000 miles. Malfunctions resulting from abuse, accidents, misapplications, improper installation, improper removal, or normal wear and tear are not covered by this warranty.
In the event a Wheel Bearings Inc., part fails or is not fit for its intended purpose for any reason attributable to Wheel Bearings Inc., as defined by this warranty disclosure, this warranty is limited to the cost of the replacement of the defective part and does not include labor nor any consequential damages.

PARTS DETAIL

Make **Hummer**
Model **H2**
Year **2003**
Part Number **515058**
Description
wheel bearing module

back

---

b Read the text below and decide whether the following statements are true or false. Correct the false statements.

1 Wheel bearings are only produced for the second-hand market.
2 The warranty includes damage to the axles or differential caused by a defective bearing.
3 Buying the car second hand with a milage of 10,000 is included in the warranty.
4 Improper installation is covered by the warranty.
5 A broken bearing on a vehicle with a mileage of 13,000 will not be covered by the conditions of the warranty.
6 The hourly wages for the car mechanics to replace the bearing will not be covered by the warranty conditions.

9 Calling the bearing manufacturer

Operator	Mechaniker bei Strohmeier
Melden Sie sich und grüßen Sie.	Grüßen Sie, geben Sie Ihren Namen und sagen Sie, dass das Kugellager für einen Hummer H2 bereits nach 6 Monaten kaputt war.
Fragen Sie nach Kundennummer und Rechnungsdatum.	Antworten Sie, die Kundennummer ist 1325558 und das Rechnungsdatum ist der 15. Februar.
Fragen Sie, wie viele Meilen das Fahrzeug seitdem gefahren ist.	Antworten Sie, 15 000 km. Geben Sie auch die gefahrenen Meilen an. (1 Meile = 1,6 km)
Fragen Sie, ob das Fahrzeug in einen Unfall verwickelt war.	Verneinen Sie. Sagen Sie, dass das Lager von Facharbeitern ein- und ausgebaut wurde.
Bitten Sie um eine kurze E-Mail, das die Bedingungen für einen Garantiefall nochmals auflistet.	Fragen Sie, wer die Kosten für die Arbeitszeit trägt.
Sagen Sie, dass die Garantiebedingungen dies nicht abdecken.	Bedanken Sie sich und bestätigen Sie, dass Sie die E-Mail schicken werden.
Danken Sie und sagen Sie, dass nach Erhalt der E-Mail das Lager per Express versandt wird.	Bedanken und verabschieden Sie sich.

UNIT 6

> **Language**
>
> **How to write an e-mail**
> Write the topic of the e-mail onto the subject line.
> Start with: *Dear Sirs,*
>   *Dear Ms* Abercrombie,
>
> Keep your problems short and simple.
> Mention all the necessary numbers and codes.
> Finish with: *Yours faithfully* (wenn Sie mit *Dear Sirs* begonnen haben)
>   *Yours sincerely* (wenn Sie mit *Dear* + Name begonnen haben)

10 An e-mail confirmation

To confirm the order, the mechanic writes an e-mail to WBI. Complete the text of the e-mail with the words from the box below.

> accident • bearing • confirm • delivered • miles • qualified • replace • warranty

Subject: Our customer number: 1235558.

Dear Sirs,

I would like to ⎡1⎤ ... the contents of our earlier telephone conversation.

Please ⎡2⎤ ... according to your ⎡3⎤ ... conditions the wheel ⎡4⎤ ... module no. 505158 for a Hummer H2 which was ⎡5⎤ ... with an invoice dated February 14 this year. The car was not involved in any ⎡6⎤ ... and the mileage on the bearing is about 15,000 ⎡7⎤ .... The bearing was assembled and disassembled by ⎡8⎤ ... personnel.

Please deliver the bearing a.s.a.p.

Yours faithfully,
Karl Landendinger

11 A complaint

Schreiben Sie eine E-Mail an die Firma Inmat (info@inmat.in).
Beklagen Sie sich, dass Sie bereits vor drei Wochen ein Dreibackenfutter für eine Bantam-Drehmaschine bestellt hätten, die Firma aber bis heute noch nicht darauf reagiert hat. Sollte die Bestellung nicht unverzüglich geliefert werden, soll der Auftrag storniert werden.

Extra material

1 Writing a complaint

Benutzen Sie die sprachlichen Hilfen, um einen Beschwerdebrief zu schreiben.

Sie haben bei Wholesale Tool einen konkaven Fräser (*milling cutter*) für $438,00 bestellt. Bereits nach kurzer Zeit sind zwei Fräserzähne (*miller teeth*) abgebrochen. Benutzen Sie die sprachlichen Hilfen oben, um einen Beschwerdebrief zu schreiben. Stellen Sie die folgenden Dinge klar:

- Im Katalog wurde eine besonders lange Standzeit (*tool life*) versprochen.
- Tatsächlich brachen bereits nach 12 Betriebsstunden zwei Zähne heraus.
- Zeigen Sie Ihre Unzufriedenheit mit dem Produkt.
- Außerdem zeigte der Fräser bei Lieferung bereits leichte Gebrauchsspuren.
- Fordern Sie, dass Wholesale Tool Ihnen entweder einen komplett neuen Fräser schickt oder
- Ihnen der Betrag von $467,00 (einschließlich der Liefergebühren) auf Ihr Konto zurücküberwiesen wird.

Language

Phrases in a formal letter or e-mail of complaint

Formal letters of complaint often follow the simple structure set out below.

The greeting
Dear Sir,/Dear Sirs,   Dear Sir or Madam,   Dear Mr …,/Dear Ms …,

The reason for the complaint
I am writing to you to complain about …
- the product sent to me/your product number …/the delay in delivery of …

I am writing to you to express my strong dissatisfaction …
- with the product I was sold/with the condition of the delivery

Further details
According to (the brochure, your website), … but in reality it was …
When I ordered I was expecting a high-quality product and not a …
The product was not up to standard/did not work correctly/was defective/was damaged

Demands, expectations and threats
Under the circumstances, I feel that a refund/replacement is in order.
I will expect some form of compensation for the inconvenience/lost orders/…
Please pay the refund into the following bank account: …
If this matter is not dealt with to our satisfaction, we will cancel the order/look for a new supplier.

Polite ending
Yours sincerely/Yours faithfully

Vocabulary

refund	*Rückerstattung*	compensation	*Vergütung, Entschädigung*
dissatisfaction	*Unzufriedenheit*	to expect	*erwarten*
replacement	*Ersatz, Austausch*	to cancel	*kündigen, stornieren*

7 Installing Controlling Systems

1 Pneumatics in modern industry

Pneumatic devices and tools such as the air pistols used in modern industry need a certain amount of compressed air to work. It is generated centrally by a compressor and distributed by a pipe system. Castle Engineering is currently planning to equip their production area with an interlinked pipe system which will consist of a loop with additional cross connections. This will make it possible to work with compressed air anywhere in the production area. All sections of the pipe system can be closed for repair or inspection by shut-off valves.

a Find the English equivalents of the German terms in the text opposite.

1. pneumatische Einrichtung, 2. Druckluftwerkzeug, 3. Rohrsystem,
4. Produktionsfläche, 5. Querverbindung, 6. Absperrventil

b Work with a partner and compare the pneumatic systems at your companies.

2 Installing the new system

Sauter Klimatec from Wuppertal in Germany will install the peneumatic system at Castle Engineering. Two German engineers, Petra Berger and Orhan Tosun, are on-site to discuss the installation with the British factory manager and three plumbers from a local firm.

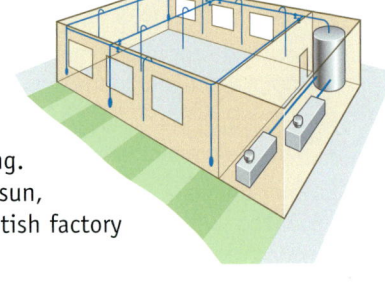

🎧 15 Listen to the CD and find out which role each of the following people will play in the installation of the pneumatic system. Take notes as you listen.

Petra Berger + Orhan Tosun
engineer
works for ...
plans the ...
sets up ...
commissions ...

John Watford
factory ...

Garry Ward
foreman at ...

Eric Johnson + Paul Weller
worker at ...

3 Compressed-air distribution

The statements below are incorrect. Read the following installation instructions and then correct them.

Sauter Components — Installation instructions for pneumatic plants

1 High-pressure line, approx. 6 bar
The high-pressure lines are usually laid with copper or plastic pipes. The pipes must be laid at a slope and drained periodically at the lowest points. With treated air, the operating temperature must not fall below 3 °C; otherwise water may condense.

2 Supply and signal-pressure lines
Polyethylene, polyamide or soft copper pipes will mostly be used for piping installed with screwed connections. In most cases, the softer and less expensive polyethylene tubing can be used if no special requirements (fire hazard, damage caused by rodents etc.) need to be observed. Copper pipes are to be laid in such a manner that no strong forces are acting on the connected equipment (particularly in case of plastic housings). To ensure this, the last 30 cm before any connection with equipment should consist of plastic tubing.
A flexible tube made of special polyurethane has been developed for lines which need only to be pushed onto a nipple.
In order to prevent condensation, the temperature within the system must never fall below the lower limit of −2 °C. The normal pipe section dimensions are 6 x 1 (external diameter 6 mm, wall thickness 1 mm). For long lines and high air throughput, the additional pressure drop in the supply line must be taken into consideration.

3 Equipment connection
Sauter equipment is usually provided with an internal thread Rp 1/8 (ISO 7/1). It therefore fits the widely used conical screw-in nipples R 1/8 (ISO 7/1). Teflon tape or a special sealing stick (Accessory No. 297169) are recommended as sealing materials (do not use Loctite on plastics). Limited torque must be applied when metal nipples are screwed into plastic housings (use plastic nipples if possible).
Push the tube off the nipple instead of pulling. Use the tube remover (Service Set 297508). Cut off excessively widened tube ends.

1 It doesn't matter whether the pipes are laid straight or sloped.
2 Soft copper pipes can be used for the high-pressure lines.
3 The signal pipes must be welded together.
4 Rodents such as mice or martens aren't a problem for polyethylene fittings.
5 Condensation can be a problem at temperatures below 2 °C.
6 A pressure drop in the supply lines is not a problem.
7 The screw-in nipples should be fixed with Loctite.

UNIT 7

4 Discussing installations

Today, Kilian Linz, a representative of Sauter Klimatec, is over in Great Britain to monitor the ongoing installation. As his English isn't so good, he asks Petra to mediate between him and John.

Work with two partners and act out the following dialogue.

Kilian	Petra	John
Wo bekommt ihr das notwendige Werkzeug?	?	You can get everything you need from the engineers' workshop.
Müssen die Hochdruckleitungen bestellt werden, oder sind sie schon in der Firma?	?	All necessary high pressure lines have been ordered and are already outside in the staff car park.
Wie werden die Rohrleitungen an der Wand befestigt?	?	The ones on the walls are fixed with wallplugs and screws and the ones on the ceiling are fixed to the steel beams.
Dürfen wir Löcher in die Stahlträger bohren?	?	No, I'm afraid not. This is not allowed for security reasons. We have special clamps for the steel beams.
Gibt es dafür ein Montagegerüst?	?	Of course, there is a special scaffolding which we will set up for you.

The following illustrations may help you.

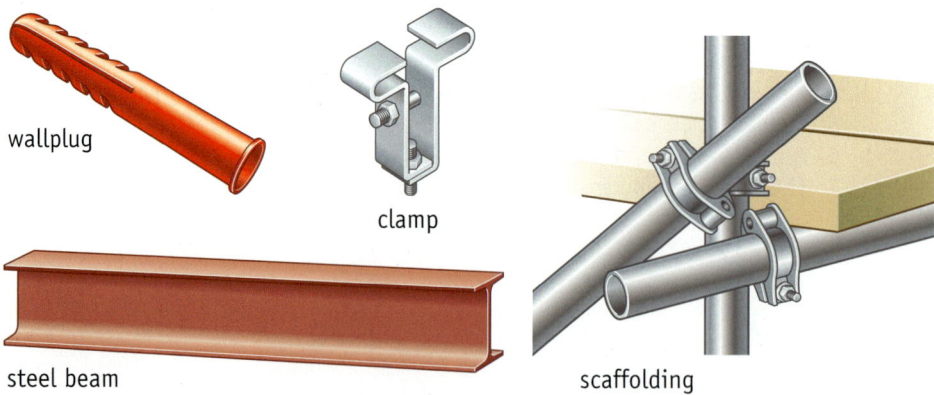

wallplug

clamp

steel beam

scaffolding

5 Installation of compressed-air hoses

Compressed-air hoses should always be slightly slack because the hose expands under pressure and therefore becomes shorter. If the hose is fitted too tightly, it could be torn apart.

Look at the following drawings of different hoses. Say which of them are correctly or incorrectly installed and why.

These words may help you:

> minimum radius • sharp bend • straight piping • large radius • tight hose • loose hose, • tight bending • straight fitting/connection piece • round fitting/connection piece

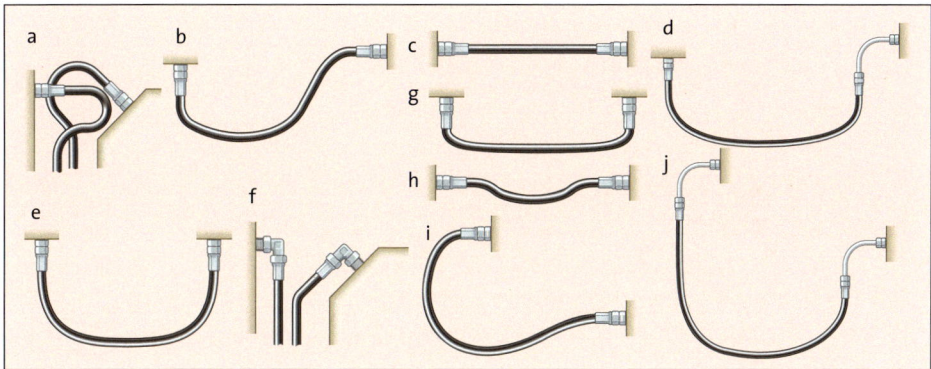

6 Pneumatics or hydraulics?

During their installation work Eric Johnson and Paul Weller start a discussion about whether it makes sense to install a pneumatic system or whether a hydraulic system would have been better. Eric thinks pneumatics would make more sense but Paul prefers hydraulics.

a Work in a group and from what you know so far make a list of the advantages and disadvantages of both systems.

pneumatics		hydraulics	
☺	☹	☺	☹

b Now work together with your partner

Student A: You prefer pneumatics. Go to file 4 on page 156.
Student B: You prefer hydraulics. Go to file 11 on page 160.

UNIT 7

7 Commissioning the system

a Work with a partner: Find the German equivalents of the following English verbs in the text below.

> check • adjust • set • close • open • raise • eliminate • ventilate • fix • document

Tätigkeiten bei der Inbetriebnahme

✓ Zunächst Schläuche noch einmal auf festen Sitz überprüfen.

✓ Zum Schutz für Mensch und Material Druck durch das Druckregelventil auf einen niedrigen Wert einstellen.

✓ Die Steuerung in die Grundstellung bringen.

✓ Vor dem Belüften alle Drosselventile schließen.

✓ Drosselventile langsam öffnen und Steuerung testen.

✓ Den Druck am Druckregelventil langsam auf den für die Anlage maximal zulässigen Betriebsdruck erhöhen.

✓ Leckstellen beseitigen.

✓ Endgültiges Justieren der Grenztaster und Einstellen der Drosseln.

✓ Bei auftretenden Fehlern in der Steuerung ist diese zunächst zu entlüften.

✓ Funktionsfehler beheben, indem der Weg der Druckluft von Bauteil zu Bauteil verfolgt wird.

✓ Die Inbetriebnahme ist zu dokumentieren, Einstellwerte werden festgehalten, Schaltpläne werden eingeheftet.

b Castle Engineering needs documentation of the commissioning, so Petra translates the steps into English. Use an online dictionary to translate the text.

Wie man Fachvokabeln mit Hilfe des Internets übersetzt

Wenn Sie eine Fachvokabel im zweisprachigen Wörterbuch nicht finden, können Sie natürlich in einem Online-Wörterbuch danach suchen. Werden Sie dort nicht fündig, sollten Sie nicht gleich aufgeben, sondern es mit ein paar Kniffen versuchen, z. B.:

- Einen deutschsprachigen Wikipedia-Artikel aufrufen und auf die englische Version umschalten.

- Bei Google das Wort durch Eingabe von Kontextwörtern (d. h. Wörtern, die normalerweise zusammen mit dem gesuchten Wort auftreten) suchen. Sie können auch versuchen, das englische Wort zusammen mit deutschen Kontextwörtern zu suchen.

- Technische Seiten wie www.howstuffworks.com aufrufen, den Artikel für das Oberthema suchen und die englisch bezeichneten Teile anhand der Abbildungen erkennen.

Sie möchten z. B. wissen, was „Entlötlitze" auf Englisch heißt. Rufen Sie den Artikel über Löten in Wikipedia auf und wechseln Sie zur englischprachigen Seite. Dort werden in dem Abschnitt über *desoldering* (Entlöten) auch *desoldering wicks* erwähnt. Die Google-Suche nach „desoldering wicks entlötlitze" bestätigt, dass es sich um das gesuchte Wort handelt.

UNIT 7

8 Safety signs

a During their installation work at Castle Engineering Petra and Orhan discover lots of safety signs. What do the different colours mean?

> The yellow signs warn people about …

> The blue signs tell people what they …

> The red signs …

b Match the signs (a–o) with the meanings below.

1 fork-lift trucks in operation
2 laser hazard
3 no entry
4 no naked lights
5 ear protectors must be worn
6 goggles must be worn
7 hard hat/safety helmet must be worn
8 highly flammable
9 high voltage
10 no fork lift trucks
11 protective footwear must be worn
12 gloves must be worn
13 visors must be worn

Grammar

Modal verbs

1 Compressed air **can** be used for power tools.
2 A hydraulic system **could** save maintenance costs.
3 This lathe **must** be lubricated weekly.
4 Tom **will be able to** use it after training.
5 We **won't be allowed** to use it without supervision.
6 We **should** compare the costs of both systems.
7 The old lathe wasn't up to modern standards and **had to** be replaced.
8 You **mustn't** operate this machine with loose clothing.

Modale Hilfsverben haben folgende Eigenschaften:
- Sie haben in allen Personen dieselbe Form.
- Bei der Verneinung gibt es zusammengezogene Kurzformen. (5, 8)
- Alle werden mit dem Infinitiv ohne *to* verwendet. (Beachte: *be able to* und *have to* sind Vollverben.)
- Wenn andere Zeitformen nötig sind, benutzt man die Ersatzverben *be able to* (für *can*), *be allowed to* (für *may*), und *have to* (für *must*). (4, 5, 7)

Achtung: *must not* = nicht dürfen, *don't/doesn't have to* = nicht müssen

UNIT 7

9 Practice

Replace the German modal verbs in brackets with the most suitable English modal.

1 You (*müssen*) ... be 100% accurate when you measure a workpiece.
2 You (*nicht dürfen*) ... leave equipment switched on without supervision.
3 The new electronic scales (*können*) ... weigh extremely small objects exactly.
4 The team (*müssen*) ... work faster if they want to complete everything by tomorrow.
5 Tomorrow Petra (*dürfen*) ... try out the system for the first time.
6 We (*nicht brauchen*) ... give the oscilloscope back until next Thursday.
7 (*Könnten*) ... I use your calculator, please?
8 What (*sollten*) ... we do this afternoon? (*Sollten*) ... we tidy up the workshop?

10 Problems and remedies

a Read the text and write a headline for each problem (1–7).

SAFETY WITH PNEUMATIC TOOLS

Air powered tools present many of the same hazards as their electrically powered counterparts, plus hazards you may not have considered. Here are things to remember when using air tools:

1 ...
Air may be delivered at varying pressures and flows. If the pressure/flow exceeds the manufacturer's rating, the tool itself could over-speed, delivering too much torque or other excessive force. This is hazardous due to the increased possibility of tool or work piece breakage. (Remedy: ...)

2 ...
Pneumatic tools discharge exhaust air at the tool itself or nearby. Frequently, this air is not muffled and therefore pneumatic tools can be much noisier than electric tools. As prolonged exposure to loud noise can damage your hearing, precautions should be taken. (Remedy: ...)

3 ...
The air feeding the tool may contain oil or antifreeze, discharging contaminated air into the environment around you. If oil-contaminated air discharges near where you grip the tool, your hands may become oily, resulting in a dangerous loss of grip. (Remedy: ...)

4 ...
If the air discharges on your hand, you can feel that it is cold. Under certain conditions, the temperature could be low enough to cause frostbite or stiffen your fingers. (Remedy: ...)

5 ...
Air powered tools are not grounded or double insulated so if you contact a live wire while working with a pneumatic tool, you can be shocked. (Remedy: ...)

6 ...
A severed air hose can whip around violently until the air is shut off. You may be injured by the whipping hose or while scrambling to get out of its way. (Remedy: ...)

7 ...
Compressed air or particles may fly from equipment such as chipping hammers, rock drills, rotary drills or sanders, and cause pain or injury. (Remedy: ...)

74

b Now match the correct remedies (a–g) from the box below to the problems (1–7).

a Protect the hose from physical damage. When using quick-disconnect type fittings, install the male end on the tool.
b Ensure that all electric power in the immediate work area is isolated.
c It helps to frequently wipe both your hands and the tool and to be sure you are not over-oiling the tool. To eliminate the hazard, find a replacement tool with a better design.
d Gloves may help if they can be worn without creating the additional hazard of becoming caught up in any rotating or reciprocating parts.
e Either effective mufflers can be installed on the exhaust, or hearing protection should be worn.
f Don't take chances with your eyesight!
g Adjust your air pressure to the manufacturer's rating. Make sure hoses are of the correct internal diameter and are not kinked or crushed.

11 Safety when using pneumatics

After the installation of the new pneumatic system, John asks whether Petra and Orhan have brought a sign with the safety rules in English. They haven't, so Orhan sends an SMS to the firm in Wuppertal and asks them to send the safety rules in German.

Work together with your partner and translate the following instructions into English.

Sicherheitsmaßnahmen an pneumatischen Anlagen

✓ Niemals mit Druckluft auf Personen blasen.
✓ Hauptluftleitung erst dann öffnen, wenn der Luftkreislauf geschlossen ist.
Nicht angeschlossene Schläuche können umherschlagen und Verletzungen verursachen.
✓ Luft abschalten bei Luftaustritt aus einem Verbindungsstück.
✓ Bei Änderungen am Luftkreislauf immer Luft abschalten.
✓ Pleuel nicht berühren.
✓ Bei Arbeiten mit und an pneumatischen Anlagen Schutzbrille tragen.

Übersetzungstipp

Wenn Sie Schwierigkeiten haben, versuchen Sie mit dem zweiten Teil des deutschen Satzes anzufangen, z. B.:

Always turn off the air supply before making …
Wear safety goggles when working with or on …

UNIT 7

Extra material

1 Hydraulic tools vs. pneumatic tools

Look at the following comparison between hydraulic and pneumatic tools. Give each advantage a score of +1 and each disadvantage a score of −1. Give each item (a–x) a score. Do your results correspond with the results at the bottom of the 'score' columns?

Issue	Hydraulic	score	Pneumatic	score
Life-Span	Hydraulic tools are known for their durability – It isn't uncommon for them to last 15+ years.	a	Pneumatic tools, if properly maintained, can be expected to last from 5–10 years.	m
Initial Cost	Initial cost of hydraulic tools is fairly significant; about twice the cost of pneumatic tools.	b	Initial cost of pneumatic tools is about half that of hydraulic tools.	n
Maintenance Required	Very little maintenance required, as internal parts are always bathed in oil. (General cleaning of tool after use, and keeping hydraulic couplers clean).	c	Significantly more maintenance required for pneumatic tools than hydraulic tools. Includes draining moisture from air tanks, and constantly keeping tools oiled.	o
Noise	Hydraulic tools are very quiet.	d	Pneumatic tools are very loud, by comparison, and can even damage hearing in some situations.	p
Confined Space Issues	None.	e	Exhaust air may contain oil or antifreeze, and the tool may be discharging contaminated air into the environment. Special precautions may be needed in confined or poorly ventilated spaces.	q
Temperature	Hydraulic tools will operate in sub-zero temperatures. They will not freeze up.	f	Due to moisture in the air, pneumatic tools can freeze up and become inoperable in freezing temperatures.	r
Wet Conditions	Many hydraulic tools can be operated underwater.	g	Water pumps aside (see below), pneumatic tools cannot be operated underwater.	s
Power	Hydraulic tools are more powerful, because they use pressurized liquid (oil) which does not compress like air does.	h	Pneumatic tools cannot deliver the same power (especially when torque is required) as they are using pressurized air, which will compress.	t
Broken Hose	Creates a mess, but not dangerous. As with pneumatic tools, a broken hose is never a good thing.	i	Can become a safety hazard if the hose whips around uncontrollably. As with hydraulic tools, a broken hose is never a good thing.	u
Tools Available	There are far more hydraulic tools available than pneumatic tools.	j	There are fewer pneumatic tools available, in comparison to hydraulic tools.	v
Water Pumps	The largest hydraulic water pump available requires 9 gpm, weighs 21 lbs, and can pump up to 500 gpm.	k	The largest pneumatic water pump available requires 110 cfm, weighs 58 lbs, and can pump up to 340 gpm.	w
	The largest hydraulic trash pump available requires 9 gpm, weighs 65 lbs, and can pump up to 800 gpm.	l	The largest pneumatic sludge/trash pump available requires 85 cfm, weighs 152 lbs, and can pump up to 250 gpm.	x
Total Score	Out of 12	10+/2−	Out of 12	1+/11−

High-speed cutting

1 Different tasks of a machining centre

CNC machining centres are used in a wide variety of industries, from medical to automotive or electronic. A modern machining centre can drive speeds up to 60,000 rpm. This is called high-speed cutting and is used to work economically, especially with smaller tools.

a Match the pictures of objects manufactured by using machining centres with the words in the box.

> artificial hip joint • base plate for a clock • dental inlay • die making for a mobile phone • electrode • impeller for a jet engine • impeller for artificial ventilation • stamping tool • wheel rim

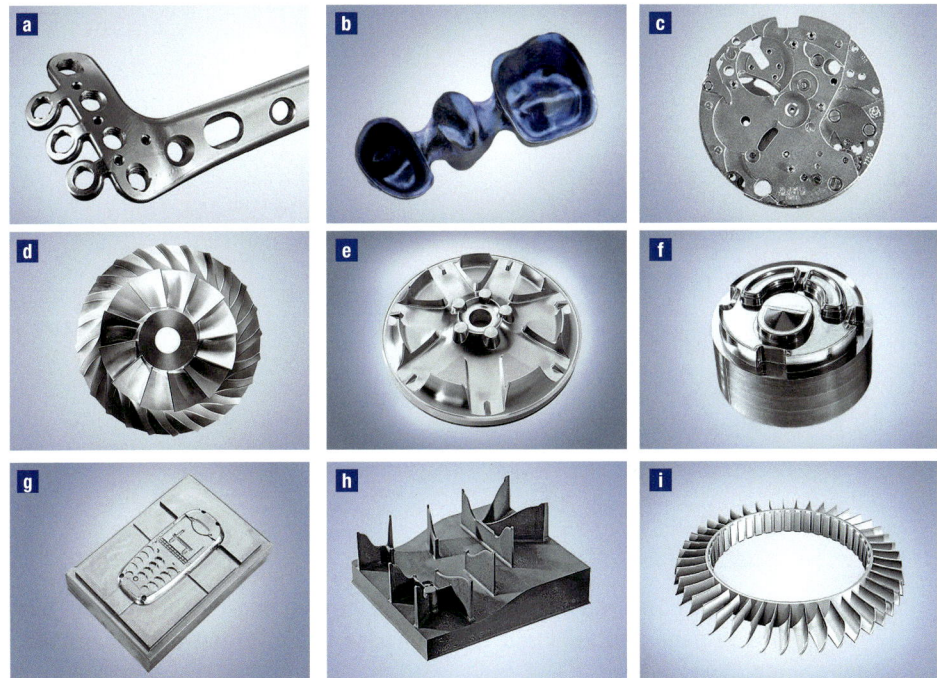

b Now make sentences about machining centres using the table below.

Machining centres	are used can be found	in for to produce	the automotive/ aerospace industry medical engineering dental equipment clockwork welding tasks	for example, for the production of artificial hip joints/ dental inlays/…	as shown in Photo C. as you can see in Photo E. like the one in Photo H.

77

UNIT 8

2 Conventional machining vs. CNC machining

With a partner, sort the following expressions into two lists: conventional machining and modern CNC machining. You can add your own ideas as well.

- always expensive
- comparatively cheap
- complex design of workpiece
- complex programming
- different machines for turning/milling/drilling/grinding
- easy to operate
- fast production
- faults are created by machine operator
- for batch production
- for smaller number of workpieces
- highly accurate production
- one machine for turning/milling/drilling/grinding
- operates in 2 or 3 axes
- operates in 5 axes
- simple designs of workpiece
- slow production

conventional machining	CNC machining
– comparatively cheap	

3 High-speed cutting

a Describe the photo and explain what you know about high-speed cutting.

> In the photo I can see a machine …

b Your boss shows you the brochure for a high-speed-cutting system on the opposite page and asks you to summarise the information in German.

MEMO		
von: GHS	**an:** SFH	**Datum:** 6.11.20
Ich brauche folgende Infos aus beiliegender Broschüre auf Deutsch: – Material des Maschinenbetts – max. Beschleunigung – Design – max. Drehzahl Motorspindel – Traversgeschwindigkeit		

HSC newly defined
The highest precision and dynamics

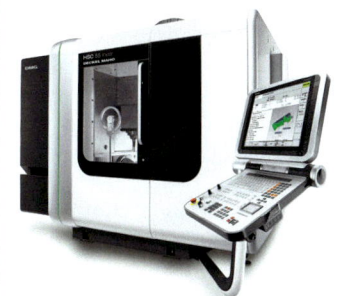

This is the next generation of high-speed cutting. The combination of a highly stable design, the latest drive technology and high-end spindle technology give the **HSC 55 *linear*** unparalleled performance during HSC machining. The foundation for the outstanding dynamics and precision of the **HSC 55 *linear*** is the mineral-composite machine bed in the closed gantry design. The thermo-symmetric design ensures long-lasting precision. Linear drives in all axes allow rapid traverses up to 80 m/min and 2.3 g acceleration. In the Standard version, the 28,000 HSC spindle, combined with the HSK-A 63 receiver guarantees not only better tool durability, but also improved surface qualities for simultaneous, high chipping-time volumes in this precision class.

4 Working with words

a Match the expressions 1–5 with the definitions. The expressions are all from the brochure above.

1 durability
2 machine bed
3 performance
4 precision
5 surface

a the ability to withstand wear, pressure, or damage
b the process of carrying out a task
c the outer part or layer of something
d the quality of being exact or accurate
e the transfer rack of the machining centre

b Now explain one of the words 6–11 to your partner. He/She has to guess which one matches your description. Swap roles after each word.

Example: *This word means that something ...*
The next word describes something that is ...

6 acceleration
7 design
8 high-end
9 rapid
10 simultaneous
11 stable

UNIT 8

5 At a trade fair: talking to a customer

With a partner, act out this conversation at a trade fair.

Student A: You work for DMG. Turn to file 5 on page 156.
Student B: You are a visitor at the Metavak fair in the Netherlands. At the DMG stand, a manufacturer of high-speed cutting systems, you are interested in the HSC 75/105 because of the automatic pallet exchange.

Turn to file 12 on page 160.

6 Operating the HSC 55

The HSC 55 is operated by a control pad. Match the words in the box with numbers 1–6 in the picture below.

agreement key • emergency stop • machine-specific softkeys • operating field • operating panel of the control system • screen

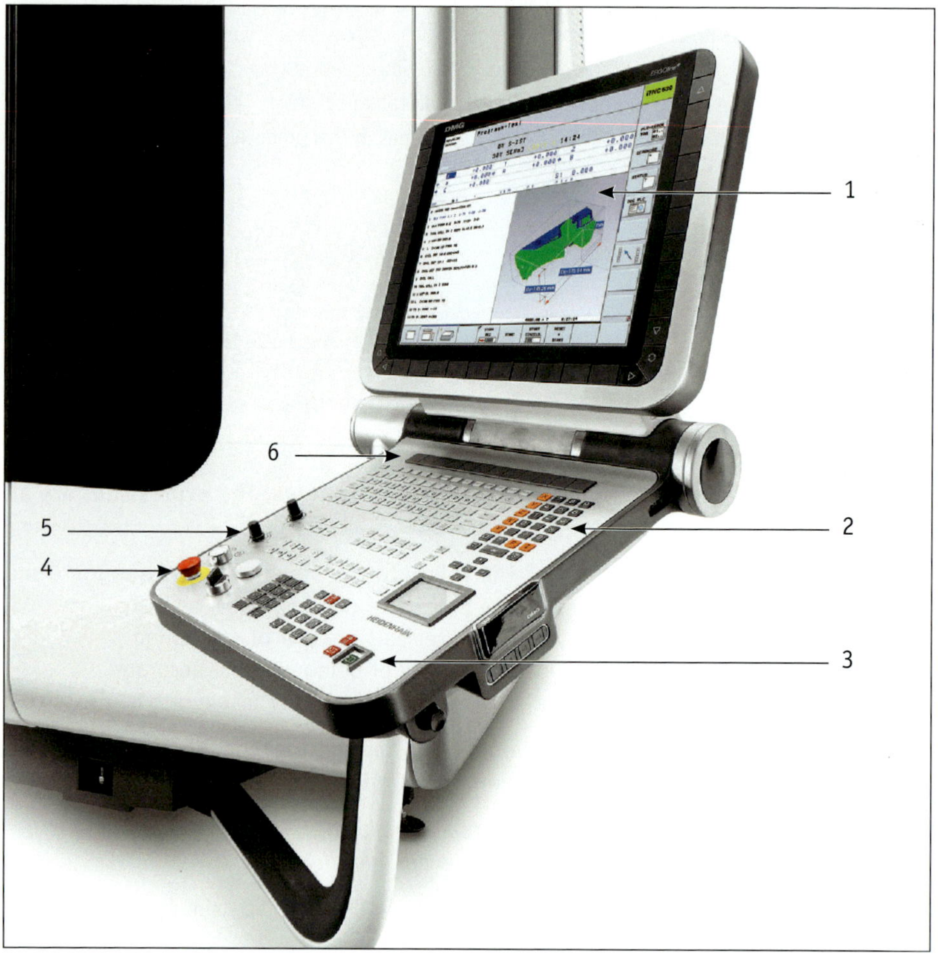

UNIT 8

7 Utilization of the machine

Look at the excerpt below from the operating manual of the HSC 55 and find the correct place for the following words and expressions.

- drilling
- glass-fibre reinforced plastic
- metal
- milling
- plastic
- the use of rotating tools/workpieces
- turning

Utilization of the machine

The metal-removing machining with rotating tools/workpiece with at least one geometrically-defined cutting edge.

The machine may only be used for the following machining techniques:
- ... 1
- ... 2
- ... 3

This machine is intended for:
- ... 4,
- the handling of workpieces, raw parts and tools from the peripheral units connected to the machine.

Material

The following materials may be machined in milling operations:
- ... 5
- wood
- ... 6

The following materials may be machined in milling-and-turning operations:
- metal
- plastic
- ... 7

Note

The "production package" option is strongly recommended for machining light metals and non-metallic materials.

8 Sound maze

Can you get from *rotating* to *removing*? Move one square at a time either vertically or horizontally. You can only move onto squares that have a word with the stress on the second syllable like *roTAting* or *reMOving*. Write this path down on a separate piece of paper and then listen to the CD to check your answers.

rotating	machine	utilization	drilling	milling
workpiece	defined	techniques	massive	plastic
limited	geometrically	intended	turning	recommended
interesting	connected	peripheral	metal	reinforced
raw parts	delivered	wood	surface	package
operations	production	machining	material	removing

81

UNIT 8

9 SMARTkey® operating mode selector switch

a Complete the following excerpt from the manual of the HSC 55 with the following verbs in their correct form.

> appear • indicate • insert (2x) • save • transmit

3.5 SMARTkey® operating mode selector switch

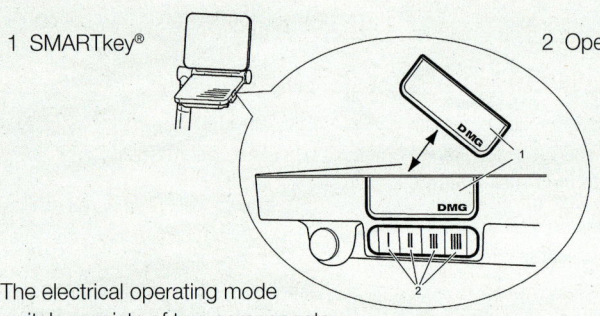

1 SMARTkey®   2 Operating mode selector switch

The electrical operating mode switch consists of two components:

Component	Function
SMARTkey®	Key and data memory for authorizations on the machine.
Operating mode selector keys	These keys are used to select the operating mode.

3.5.1 Description

When ... ¹ the SMARTkey® into the reading station, the data (operating modes) ... ² on the key is ... ³ to the control system.

Note!
If a SMARTkey® without authorization for the operating mode selected in the machine is ... ⁴, the "NO AUTHORIZATION" message ... ⁵.

The active operating mode is ... ⁶ via the illuminated operating mode selector key.

b Now answer these questions in German.

1 Was ist der Unterschied zwischen dem SMARTkey® und dem 'operating mode selector switch'?
2 Was passiert nach dem Einlegen des SMARTkey®?

10 Missing headlines

On the opposite page you can see another excerpt from the same manual. The following instructions are missing from the excerpt. Match them with letters A–E.

- Switch on the machine – apply the supply voltage
- Select the desired operating mode with the door open
- Important: Always remove the SMARTkey® after each operating mode change
- Insert the SMARTkey®
- After removing the SMARTkey®, the selected operating mode remains unchanged.

5.2 Operating mode selector switch SMARTkey®

5.2.1 Selection of an operating mode

▷ [a]

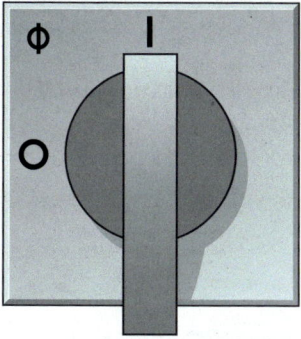

▶ Operating mode 1 is selected automatically. It is permanently defined as AUTOMATIC and is therefore the safest operating mode.

▷ [b]

▶ The status on the SMARTkey® is transferred to the control system.

▶ At the control display, a window with the current status information, authorizations operating mode, current operating mode selection (keys), and the currently active operating mode (machine) are displayed.

▷ [c]

▶ The active operating mode is displayed by the highlighted operating mode selector keys.

▶ [d]

Note! [e]

11 Discussion: troubleshooting

Work in small groups. Tell each other about a problem you have had with machinery at work. Discuss possible solutions and say what you did about it. The Learning box on the next page will help you.

UNIT 8

Gruppengespräche auf Englisch führen

Sich zu Wort melden
Can I just say that … ?
Well, if you ask me, …

Die eigene Meinung äußern
I think that …
In my opinion, …

Jemand anderen ins Gespräch einbringen
What do you think, Tim?
What's your opinion, Susan?

Höflich widersprechen
You may be right, but …
I don't think that's quite right.

Nachfragen, ob man verstanden wurde
Do you see what I mean?

Nachfragen, ob man etwas richtig verstanden hat
Do you mean that …?

Auf den Gesprächspartner reagieren
I see./Oh, right.   Ach so.
Really?   Echt?
Right.   Ah ja.

12 Listening and role-play

a Now look at the excerpt from the manual of the HSC 55 below. Unfortunately, some things have got mixed up in the table, so users call the DMG hotline to ask questions about the correct steps to deal with the problem. Listen to the two telephone calls on the CD and say which fault message goes with which cause and what the method of troubleshooting is.

Fault message	Cause	Troubleshooting
"OM SMARTkey® – No authorization"	E. g. two operating mode selection keys have been pressed simultaneously.	To be defined.
"OM SMARTkey® – Selection error"	No valid signal on the BCD interface.	Select operating mode for which there is authorization on the SMARTkey® (see information window). Use SMARTkey® with the appropriate authorization.
"Device malfunction"	Due to the selection of an operating mode using the OM selector keys, for which there is no authorization for the SMARTkey® inserted.	Select again the desired operating mode.

b Listen again to the two phone calls. Which of the following phrases do you hear?

Phone call 1
1 a What can I do for you?
   b How can I help you?
2 a What's the problem?
   b What seems to be the problem?
3 a Thank you very much for your assistance.
   b Thanks very much for your help.

Phone call 2
4 a DMG after-sales service, you're talking to Jane Galtress.
   b DMG after-sales service, Galtress speaking.
5 a But what can I do?
   b So what can I do about it?
6 a Thank you for using the DMG hotline.
   b Thanks for phoning us.

c Now act out the phone call about the remaining fault message with a partner. Use the phrases from above.

Extra material

Mediation

At a trade fair, your boss takes you to the stand of a British producer of CNC software. He has a few questions to ask the representative of the British company and asks you to mediate between them.

German engineer	You	British representative
Fragen Sie den Vertreter, was diese Software alles kann.	?	You can write your program on a PC and then simulate it on the screen.
Kann man die Daten auch auf die Maschine übertragen?	?	Of course, but it depends on what kind of controller you have.
All unsere Maschinen haben Heidenhain- oder Siemens-Steuerungen.	?	Heidenhain, Siemens, Fanuc, Allen-Bradley and many others are compatible.
Fragen Sie, ob es möglich ist, Maschinen-Crashs bei der Simulation zu erkennen.	?	Sure, the software detects crashes and near-misses between tools and workpieces.
Sagen Sie, sie hatten schon einmal einen Crash mit einem Werkzeugwechsler. Kann man das auch verhindern?	?	Of course, tool-changers are also integrated in the software and you can also define other objects you want to protect.
Das klingt gut. Gibt es noch weitere Vorteile?	?	The most important advantage is that you can train the CNC program without using production time on the machine.
Fragen Sie, ob ein Vertreter mit der Software in unserer Firma vorbei kommen könnte.	?	Sure, we could fix a date right now if you like.

I can ...

A Rezeption

Ich kann einem Hörtext wichtige Informationen entnehmen.

 1 Listen to the instructor and answer the following questions.

1. Which bearings can't be dismantled?
2. Which bearings have tapered rollers?
3. Which bearing has a double row of ball bearings?
4. Which bearings are the most suitable for high speeds and heavy loads?

Ich kann Fragen zu einem authentischen Fachtext beantworten.

2 Beantworten Sie die folgenden Fragen zu dem unten stehenden Fachtext auf Deutsch.

1. Welche Verletzungen können beim Arbeiten mit hydraulischen Systemen passieren?
2. Wo in der Landwirtschaft sind hydraulische Systeme besonders beliebt?
3. Warum wird hydraulische Energie gespeichert?
4. Warum sind nadellochgroße Lecks in den Schlauchleitungen so gefährlich?

Hydraulic Systems Safety

Quick Facts ...

Hydraulic systems must store fluid under high pressure. The fluid, under tremendous pressure, is also hot. Three kinds of hazards exist: burns from the hot, high pressure spray of fluid; bruises, cuts or abrasions from flailing hydraulic lines; and injection of fluid into the skin. Safe hydraulic system performance requires general maintenance. Proper coupling of high and low pressure hydraulic components and pressure relief valves are important safety measures. Hydraulic systems are popular on many types of agricultural equipment because they reduce the need for complex mechanical linkages and allow remote control of numerous operations. Hydraulic systems are used to lift implements, such as plows; to operate remote hydraulic motors; and to assist steering and braking.

Many systems store hydraulic energy in accumulators. These accumulators are designed to store oil under pressure when the hydraulic pump cannot keep up with demand, when the engine is shut down, or when the hydraulic pump malfunctions. Even though the pump may be stopped or an implement disconnected, the system is still under pressure. To work on the system safely, relieve the pressure first.

Pinhole Leak Injuries

Probably the most common injury associated with hydraulic systems is the result of pinhole leaks in hoses. These leaks are difficult to locate. A person may notice a damp, oily, dirty place near a hydraulic line. Not seeing the leak, the person runs a hand or finger along the line to find it. When the pinhole is reached, the fluid can be injected into the skin as if from a hypodermic syringe. Immediately after the injection, the person experiences only a slight stinging sensation and may not think much about it. Several hours later, however, the wound begins to throb and severe pain begins. By the time a doctor is seen, it is often too late, and the individual loses a finger or an entire arm. Unfortunately, this kind of accident is not uncommon. To reduce the chances of this type of injury, run a piece of wood or cardboard along the hose (rather than fingers) to detect the leak (see Figure 1).

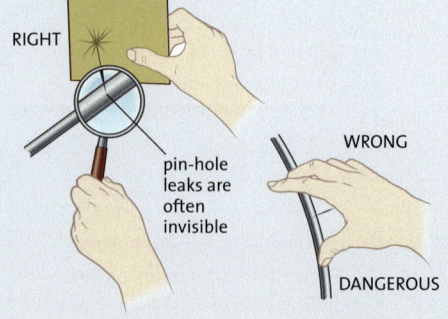

B Interaktion

Ich kann mich am Telefon über einen Sachverhalt beschweren.

3 Führen Sie das folgende Telefongespräch mit Ihrem Partner.

A Stellen Sie sich vor und sagen Sie, von wo Sie anrufen.
B Begrüßen Sie den Anrufer und fragen Sie, was Sie für ihn/sie tun können.
A Erklären Sie, dass es einen Unfall mit einer wild umherschlagenden Hydraulikleitung gab.
B Fragen Sie, was mit der Hydraulikleitung passiert ist.
A Anworten Sie, dass das Überdruckventil nicht funktioniert hat.
B Fragen Sie, wie die Leitung umherschlagen konnte.
A Antworten Sie, dass ein Schlauch geplatzt sei.
B Sagen Sie, dass Sie nur Sicherheitsschläuche verkaufen.
A Antworten Sie, dass genau ein solcher Schlauch geplatzt sei, obwohl im Prospekt absolute Sicherheit versprochen wurde.
B Fragen Sie, was der Anrufer zur Lösung des Problems vorschlägt.
A Antworten Sie, Hydraulicsworld soll einen Mechaniker schicken, um den Schaden sofort zu beheben.
B Antworten Sie, dass heute noch jemand vorbeikommen wird. Bitten Sie um eine kurze E-Mail über den Vorfall.
A Sagen, dass Sie gleich eine E-Mail schreiben werden und beenden Sie das Gespräch.
B Beenden Sie das Gespräch.

C Produktion

Ich kann über die Arbeit in meiner Firma sprechen.

4 Denken Sie an Ihre Firma und nennen Sie Beispiele, welche Aufträge in der Regel mit konventionellen Werkzeugmaschinen und welche mit CNC-Maschinen ausgeführt werden.

Ich kann mich schriftlich über einen Sachverhalt beschweren.

5 Schreiben Sie eine E-Mail mit einer Beschwerde an support@hydraulicsworld.co.uk, in der Sie die folgenden Punkte erwähnen.

- Unfall
- wild umherschlagende Hydraulikleitung
- Überdruckventil hat nicht funktioniert
- Schlauch geplatzt
- im Prospekt wurde absolute Sicherheit versprochen
- Hydraulicsworld soll einen Mechaniker schicken

9 Connecting the Robobox

1 The international drinks market

Work with a partner. In which countries are the products below produced?

> Where does ... come from?

> It's made/ produced in ...

2 Drinks from Thailand

The Boon Rawd Brewery in Thailand is already one of the biggest producers of beer and soft drinks in South-East Asia and they are expanding into other markets around the globe, including Europe.

Read the newspaper report on Boon Rawd below. What will they have to do in order to cope with the expected increase in sales?

Think of the following:
– build new production plant
– need for larger supplies of raw materials
– more efficient packaging system
– ...

Boon Rawd on the way up

A sponsorship deal with Manchester United will help Boon Rawd Trading International make its Singha brand one of England's top Asian beers. The tie-in deal with the English Premiership side will see Singha become the only lager sold at its Old Trafford stadium. The Bangkok-based

UNIT **9**

3 The Krones Robobox

Boon Rawd want to modernize their packaging system so that they can cope with the increase in production. The plant manager is considering buying several Robobox modules produced by the German manufacturer Krones. The system is highly adaptable and can be connected to other components on a conveyor system and the compact modules would only take up a small area of the shop floor.

a Here are some sentences from a Robobox brochure. Match the two sentence halves correctly.

1 Its precision and versatility make the Robobox an ideal
2 It can be adapted to fit all kinds of
3 Its precision gripper can cope with
4 Its compact modular structure means

a that it requires only a minimum of space.
b choice for the reliable palletising of bottles and cans.
c bottles of any shape, size and material.
d conveyor systems.

b Read the following text from a Krones brochure and match the highlighted terms with the numbers in the diagram below.

The practical modular system enables multiple **Robobox modules** to be combined in order to increase performance. This diagram shows two Robobox modules with a single **conveyor lane**. The Robobox modules can handle either single or double conveyor lanes. The filled bottles pass under the **portal** of the first module into the **assembly stage**. The **gripper** comes down, grasps the bottles and assembles them into whatever groups have been preselected. The gripper contains a guiding device which ensures that it can turn precisely in any direction. It can handle bottles with complicated shapes and pick up and rotate disposable bottles made of soft plastic without damaging them. It arranges the bottles in packs at preset locations around the assembly stage. The Robobox is the ideal supplement to the Modulpal series of robotic palletising devices. In this diagram there are two **palletising modules** and a **shrink-wrapper**. The shrink-wrapper wraps a foil around a set of bottles and shrinks it together so that they are bound together tightly. Together they form a fast and flexible team capable of high performance.

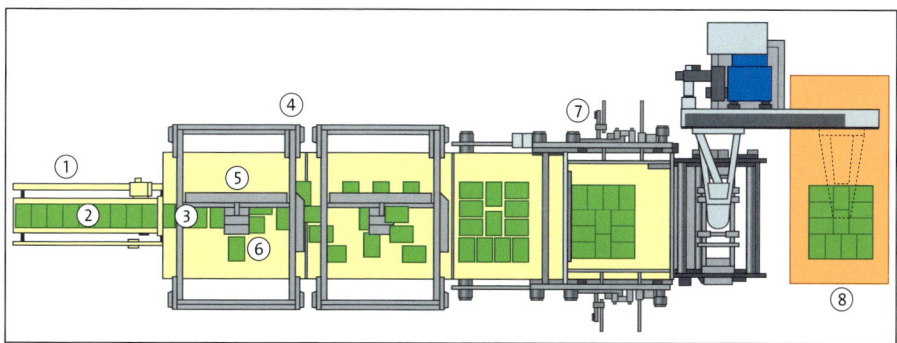

89

c Match the statements below with the following photos.

 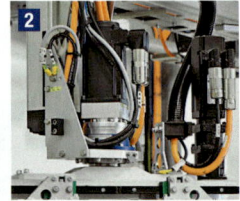  

a The turning unit above the gripper head is compact and easily accessible for mounting and repairs.
b The plastic fins on the gripper heads guarantee the gentle handling of packs.
c To control the Robobox the Krones iPanel can be operated simply by using the touch screen.
d The gripper places the packs being conveyed into the Robobox into the correct position and also into the desired format.

4 A problem in Bangkok

At their brewery in Bangkok Boon Rawd drinks are packed and palletised for global distribution. Boon Rawd has bought a Robobox from Krones in Germany to palletise their famous *B-ing* soft drinks. This was delivered completely disassembled and Sigi and Martina from Krones have to travel to Bangkok to install it. When they arrive at Bangkok Airport they discover that their suitcases have arrived, but not their toolbox with all the special tools they'll need for the assembly and installation of the conveying system.

a What should they do now and which airport sign can help them?

① baggage claim   ② baggage trolley   ③ banking & currency   ④ barber shop   ⑤ buses   ⑥ coffee shop

⑦ drinking water   ⑧ first aid   ⑨ hotel telephones   ⑩ left baggage   ⑪ lost property   ⑫ meeting point

⑬ post office & telegraph   ⑭ souvenir shop   ⑮ telephone rental   ⑯ tour service

Where can we report that our toolbox is missing?

b With a partner, take turns to ask and answer questions about the airport signs.

Which sign should you look for if …
– your luggage is too heavy to carry?
– you have severe stomach pains and you feel dizzy?
– your hair looks terrible and you have an interview later in the day?
– … ?

UNIT **9**

 c Sigi and Martina find the lost property office. Listen to the dialogue, then copy and complete the following report into your exercise book.

Lost Luggage Report

1 Passenger's full name
2 Mobile telephone number
4 Current address or name of hotel
7 E-mail address
8 Flight number [xxxxxxxxxxxx] from [xxxxxxxxxxxxxxxxxxxxx] to [xxxxxxxxxxxxxxxxxxxxxx]
9 Luggage tag number [xxxxxxxx]
10 Description of luggage

Language

How to say e-mail addresses
@ = at
- = hyphen
_ = underscore
. = dot

How to say telephone numbers
0049 – 179 3957809
= double oh four nine, one seven nine, three nine five, seven eight, oh nine

5 Checking into the Narai Hotel

a From the left luggage office at Bangkok Airport Martina and Sigi go to the Narai Hotel on Silom Road and check in. In groups of three, act out the roles of Martina, Sigi and a hotel receptionist. The phrases in the Learning box on the next page may help you.

Guests	Receptionist
Grüßen Sie und sagen Sie, dass für Sie zwei Einzelzimmer gebucht sind.	Fragen Sie nach den Namen und bitten Sie um die Pässe. Sagen Sie, dass für die beiden ein Zweibettzimmer gebucht wurde.
Antworten Sie, Sie möchten lieber zwei Einzelzimmer.	Sagen Sie, dass es heute nur ein einziges freies Zimmer mit Klimaanlage gibt, das andere ist nicht klimatisiert.
Fragen Sie, ob in den nächsten Tagen ein zweites Zimmer mit Klimaanlage frei wird.	Bejahen Sie, spätestens übermorgen kann das Zimmer gewechselt werden.
Fragen Sie, ob die Zimmer Nichtraucherzimmer sind.	Bejahen Sie, fast alle Zimmer mit Klimaanlage sind Nichtraucherzimmer, das andere Zimmer jedoch nicht.
Fragen Sie, ob es möglich wäre, ein Allergikerkissen zu bekommen.	Das ist kein Problem, das Zimmermädchen wird eines auf das Zimmer bringen.
Fragen Sie, ob Sie die Zimmer sehen können.	Zeigen Sie dem Gast die Zimmer.
Fragen Sie nach dem Zimmerpreis mit Frühstück.	Antworten Sie: 62 US-Dollar für das Zimmer mit Klimaanlage und 50 US-Dollar für das Zimmer ohne.
Sagen Sie, dass Sie die beiden Zimmer nehmen werden.	Sagen Sie, dass das zweite Zimmer dann spätestens übermorgen frei wird.
Erklären Sie, dass Ihr Werkzeugkoffer am Flughafen nicht angekommen ist.	Sagen Sie, dass vor einer Stunde vom Flughafen ein Koffer für Sie gebracht wurde.
Zeigen Sie sich erfreut und sagen Sie, dass Sie den Koffer gleich mitnehmen werden.	Sie übergeben den Koffer und bitten die beiden Gäste, die Anmeldeformulare auszufüllen.

UNIT 9

Language

What to say at a hotel

Checking in
Do you have a … available, please?
single room
double room (with twin beds/with a double bed)
I have a reservation under the name of …
Do I need to fill in a registration form?
I'll pay with cash/with a credit card/debit card.

Specific wishes
We'd prefer a room with an en suite bathroom, please.
I'd like a non-smoking room, please.
with air conditioning
on the second/third/…floor
overlooking the front/rear of the hotel/the pool
an extra blanket
a non-allergic pillow

Asking for information
Does the price include breakfast/an Internet connection/parking/…?
Is the room equipped with cable television/…?
Where is the breakfast room/fitness centre/bar/…, please?
When do you start/finish serving meals in the restaurant?

Checking out
I'm checking out tomorrow morning.
Would you have my bill ready by … a.m., please?
Would you mind preparing my bill, please?
Here's the key to my room/the minibar list.

b Pairwork: Filling in a registration form

Student A: Go to File 6 on page 157.
Student B: Go to File 6 on page 157.

6 Travelling around Bangkok

a Martina and Sigi take a 'tuk-tuk' from the hotel to the Boon Rawd Brewery. Listen to the driver's sat nav and follow their route with the map on the opposite page.

b **Work with two partners and write sat nav directions for the following situations. Then read your script to one of your partners – you are the sat nav voice and your partner is the tuk-tuk driver and must follow your directions on the map.**

- Roadworks on the Phaya Thai Road are causing a severe traffic jam. The sat nav suggests an alternative route from the Narai Hotel to the Boon Rawd Brewery.
- A guest at the Narai Hotel asks the tuk-tuk driver to take her to the zoo on Rama the Fifth (V) Road.
- Outside the zoo the tuk-tuk driver picks up an Australian couple who want to go for a meal at a Chinese restaurant in Worachak Road, Chinatown.

UNIT 9

> **Language**
>
> **Giving directions**
> Turn around and drive north/south/east/west.
> Turn left/right at the next crossroads/set of traffic lights/road junction.
> Turn left/right in 500 metres/at the next turn-off /crossroads/road junction.
> Turn left/right into …
> Stay on … for 2.7 kilometres.
> There is a roundabout/bridge/monument/tunnel 180 metres ahead.
> The National Gallery/main station/zoo /… is on your left/right.
> You're travelling/driving/going in the wrong direction. You must turn around.
> You've missed/driven past the turn-off for …
> Drive on and take the next turn-off on the left/right.

7 Troubleshooting

At the brewery Martina and Sigi meet the Boon Rawd team who will help them with the assembly of the Robobox. As often happens, there are unexpected problems during the assembly. Martina and Sigi discuss each problem with the Boon Rawd team and agree on a solution.

a Look at the table below. In small groups, discuss possible solutions to each problem in English and agree on a solution. You may also add your own ideas. Try to think of other problems that might occur during the assembly.

> The old conveying system is still in place. Should we try to integrate it with the new system?

> If we do that, it will take up too much valuable floor space and adapting it to fit the new system would be …

The old conveying system is still in place. Should we try to integrate it with the new system?	If we do that, it will … − take up too much valuable floor space. − be very difficult and cause even more problems. − …	We'll have to … − adapt the old system to fit the new one. − modernize the old system. − …
The height of the conveyor is too low. Should we adjust the rack?	If we do that, it will … − become unsteady. − …	We'll have to … − adjust the stand. − …
The sensors are not compatible. Should we replace the sensors?	If we do that, … − the system will be more expensive. − …	We'll have to … − replace the sensors. − …
The relay controllers are outdated and 48V. Should we replace the relays?	…	…
…	…	…

94

b Before they leave, Martina and Sigi have to write an error log in English for Boon Rawd. Copy and complete their error log into your exercise book using one of the problems you discussed above. The words in the box below can help you. You can also use a German-English dictionary.

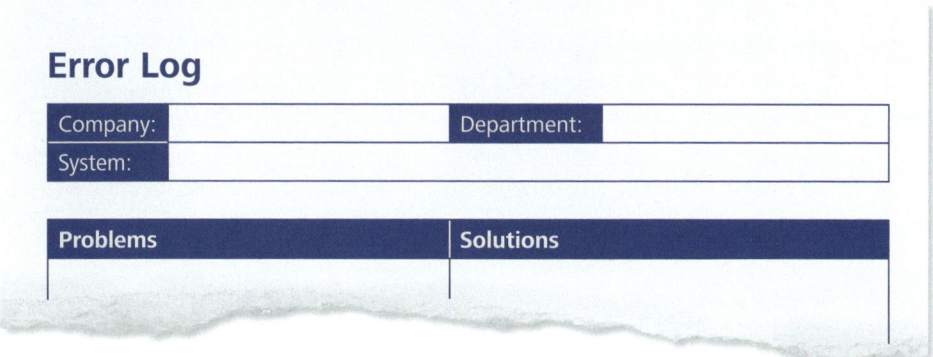

Error Log

Company:		Department:	
System:			

Problems	Solutions

Useful words

Gestell	rack
vor Ort	on-site
demontieren	dismantle
veraltet	outdated
uneben	uneven
ausgeglichen	level, well-balanced
Motorschutzschalter	motor-circuit-breaker
auslösen	trigger, set off

c On their return, Martina and Sigi also write an error log in German for their records. Copy their error log into your exercise book and complete it.

Fehlerprotokoll

Firma:		Abteilung:	
Anlage:			

festgestellte Fehler	Problemlösungen

UNIT 9

Grammar

If sentences types 1 and 2

1. If the old conveyor is still in place, it **will** cause even more problems.
2. We **will have** to **dismantle** the old conveyor if we **want** to fit the new one.
3. If we **had to use** the old controlling system, it **would fail** sooner or later.
4. If it **came** to that, the costs **would be** even more expensive.
5. It **could cause** a lot of problems if we **continued** using the old sensors.

- *If*-Sätze vom Typ 1 drücken eine erfüllbare Bedingung aus. Beachten Sie die Zeitenfolge: Der *if*-Nebensatz steht im *Simple present*, im Hauptsatz steht das *will future*. (1, 2).

  ⚠ Merke: *If plus will makes teachers ill!*

- *If*-Sätze vom Typ 2 drücken eine möglicherweise erfüllbare, meist unwahrscheinliche Bedingung aus. Beachten Sie die Zeitenfolge: Der *if*-Nebensatz steht im *Simple past*, im Hauptsatz wird *would* + Infinitiv verwendet (3, 4), wobei *would* durch *could*, *might* oder *should* ersetzt werden kann (5).

  ⚠ Merke: *If plus would is no good!*

- Steht der if-Nebensatz an erster Stelle, wird er vom Hauptsatz durch ein Komma getrennt. (1, 3, 4)

8 Practice 1: *If* sentences type 1

Complete the sentences using the correct form of the verbs in brackets.

1. If the height of the conveyor ... (to be) too low, the bottles ... (not be transported) evenly onto the Robobox.
2. If the old conveyor ... (to be) still on-site, it ... (take) a lot of time to dismantle it.
3. If the sensors ... (not to be) compatible with the new PLC system, we ... (have to) exchange them.
4. The new PLC ... (guarantee) a smooth operation, even if the old relay controllers ... (to be) outdated.
5. If the floor ... (to be) uneven, the mechanics ... (level) it.
6. If the old conveyor ... (deliver) the bottles too fast, they ... (not connect) it to the PLC.
7. ... (it/delay) the project if we ... (replace) the motor-circuit-breakers next week?

9 Practice 2: *If* sentences type 2

Describe the following chain reaction using if sentences.

Example:
If Martina and Sigi used the old conveyor, the sensors would fail.
If the sensors failed, ...

Martina & Sigi / use old conveyor / sensors fail

- PLC / get wrong signals
- delivery / stop
- bottles / jam
- bottles / fall off
- production / stop
- boss / be angry

UNIT 9

Extra material

The TopTier Stretch Wrapper

TopTier offers our compact and cost-effective palletisers with integrated concurrent stretch wrapping. Available in both high- and low-infeed models.

Concurrent Stretch Wrap Features

- Fully automated operations including film grip, cut, and wipe down
- 18" heavy duty turntable bearing
- Easy Load film head with 200% pre-stretch
- Fully enclosed Category 3 safety cage
- The palletising speeds are generally not impacted by stretch wrapping as layer build continues during the wrap cycle.
- The Integrated Allen Bradley controls with touchscreen interface allow for the adjustment of all palletiser and stretch wrapper parameters.
- Wrapping during load build is fully adjustable including number of start wraps, film overlap, number of top wraps and film tension.
- The layer head continues to receive product during the wrap cycle for continual palletising operations even when a full pallet is exiting the system.
- Easy access to the film carriage and palletiser through large safety relay-protected doors
- The Stretch Wrapper does not increase the footprint of palletiser other than the positioning of the film tower.

All TopTier palletisers focus on operator safety.

- The palletiser is enclosed by safety doors with automatic emergency stop.
- The safety cage creates a Category III enclosure.
- The door sensors are connected via fibre-optic cable to a redundant contact safety relay.
- On automatic models, pallet exit equipped with light curtain protection including automatic blanking when load exits.
- The infeed conveyor is protected by a safety tunnel to prevent access to row pushing area.
- The touchscreen controls allow all devices to be cycled and motors to operate at slow speeds for safe machine set-up or clearing jams.
- A light tree indicates the machine operation status.
- All systems are equipped with OSHA-compliant pneumatic and electrical lockouts.

1 Understanding the text

Briefly explain what the TopTier Stretch Wrapper is.

2 Working with words

Find expressions in the text that match the following definitions.

1 a rotating support placed between moving parts to allow them to move easily
2 closed in on all sides
3 an extremely thin plastic film in which something is wrapped
4 to leave
5 switch to shut off the system if there is an accident or a malfunction
6 multiple light beam safety device
7 a computer monitor with sensitive area which registers the touch of a finger

3 Role-play: At an industrial fair

Ask and answer questions about the TopTier Stretch Wrapper.

Partner A: You are a representative of the company that produces the TopTier Stretch Wrapper.
Partner B: You are a visitor at the fair.

10 A ballpoint pen assembly system

1 What ballpoint pens are made of

a What is your ballpoint pen made of?

b What do you think are the advantages and disadvantages of these materials?

chromium-plated plastic/steel
eloxated aluminium
gold-plated steel
plastic
stainless steel

Plastic is…

light/lighter than…
rustfree/luxurious/
cheap to produce/manufacture
durable/hard-wearing
soft/easy to work

2 A new series

Ballpoint Peak Ltd produce exclusive ballpoint pens in small batches. They want to manufacture a new line of ballpoint pen developed by the Research Division.

First look at the different parts of the new pen. Three parts are not correctly labelled. Work together with your partner and find out which ones they are.

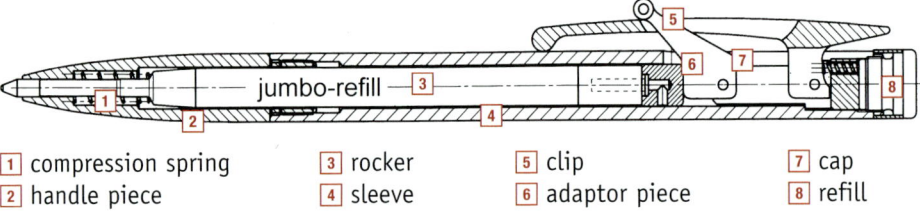

[1] compression spring   [3] rocker   [5] clip   [7] cap
[2] handle piece   [4] sleeve   [6] adaptor piece [8] refill

3 A new assembly system

Matthias Baumeister from the company's R & D department has been asked to construct an assembly system for the new series of ballpoint pens. Matthias is working with two British engineers, Eric Clancy and Felix Trees. As a first step, Matthias draws a rough sketch of the system to help him explain things to them.

a The box below is the answer key in German to the sketch on the opposite page. Produce an answer key in English with the terms in the box below.

1. Schaftzuführung	adaptor piece and refill
2. Baugruppenzuführung Kipphebel	cap insert
3. Montagestation für Kappe	compression spring separation and feed
4. Wendestation	removal station
5. Minenzuführung	rocker insert
6. Federvereinzelung und –zuführung	screw in handle piece
7. Griffstückmontage	sleeve feed
8. Auswurfstation	turn around unit

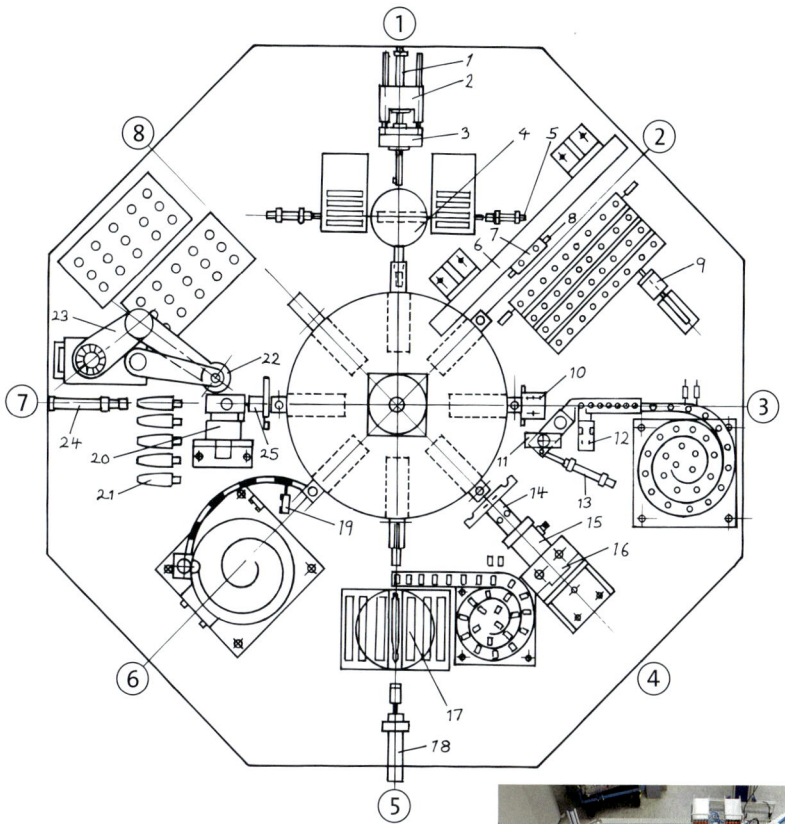

b Martin and the two British engineers then produced a working model of the new assembly system. Compare it with the sketch and identify the components by using the sentence structures given below.

The	mechanism apparatus construction	on the left in the middle at the bottom	is a … is the … corresponds to number … in the sketch.

c The model performs eight actions. Put them into the correct order:

a A robot picks up and removes the fully assembled ballpoint pens.
b The front piece of the ballpoint pen is turned.
c The small rod which presses downwards on the refill is fitted.
d The refill and the small part above it are inserted.
e The partly-assembled ballpoint pen is turned vertically.
f The shaft of the ballpoint pen is inserted.
g The spring components which depress the refill are disentangled and fed into the shaft.
h The button on the top of the ballpoint pen is fitted.

UNIT 10

4 The Functional Specification Document (FSD)

Matthias is currently working on the central station, i.e. the turntable in the middle of the assembly system. Before he starts work he writes a report in the FSD and then uses online translation software to translate it into English for the British engineers. The British engineers are confused and send it back with some words and phrases highlighted that they don't understand.

Compare both versions below and correct the English translation with the help of a good German-English dictionary.

Pflichtenheft "Zentralstation" (Drehstation)

Verfasser: *Matthias Baumeister*

Zweck:
Die Zentralstation dient
- *zur Aufnahme des zu montierenden Werkstückes*
- *zur lagerichtigen Bereitstellung des Werkstückes*
- *zum Weitertransport des Werkstückes zu allen Stationen*

Pflichten:
Die Zentralstation ist als pneumatisch betriebene Drehstation zu konzipieren und muss alle 45° exakt definiert anhalten können. Bei erreichter jeweiliger Endlage ist ein elektrisches Signal zu geben.

Die Drehstation umfasst insgesamt 8 Aufnahmeköcher

Der maximal zulässige Durchmesser beträgt 500 mm.

Die 8 Aufnahmeköcher müssen am Umfang der Drehstation eingebaut werden und über eine kinematische Zwangsschwenkung verfügen, die das Werkstück entweder in die Vertikal- oder Horizontalstellung bewegen.

Folgende Stellpositionen sind in dieser Reihenfolge 1 – 8 einzuhalten: horizontal – horizontal – vertikal – horizontal – horizontal – horizontal – vertikal – vertikal – vertikal.

Alle Aufnahmeköcher müssen in den Endlagen durch Stellschrauben feinjustierbar sein (gegenüber der Vertikal- und Horizontalstellung).

Durch geeigneten Mechanismus ist das Werkstück im Köcher sowohl radial als auch axial in Position zu halten.

Die Schwenkzeit über 45° sollte bei maximal 2 Sekunden liegen.

http://www.technical-translator.net/

FSD "Central Station" (Turning Station)
Author: Matthias Baumeister

Purpose:
The purpose of the central station is:
- to receive the ==to be assembled workpiece==
- to position the workpiece correctly
- to ==ship== the workpiece onto further stations

==Obligations:==
The central station has to be ==formulated== as a pneumatically-powered turning station and ==must precisely every 45° be able to stop.== An electrical signal must be given upon reaching the respective end position.

The turning station ==includes== 8 collecting arms.

The maximum ==allowable== diameter is 500 mm.

The 8 collecting arms must be built into the circumference of the turning station and have a kinematic ==Zwangsschwenkung== that ==either in the workpiece vertical or Horizontalstellung move.==

The following ==Stellpositionen are in this order must be kept:== horizontal – horizontal – vertical – horizontal – horizontal – vertical – vertical – vertical.

All collecting arms must ==in their Endlagen by set screws== be finely adjustable (as opposed to the vertical and ==Horizontalstellung).==

The workpiece in the ==quiver is== to be held in position by a suitable mechanism both ==radial== and ==axial.==

The ==Schwenkzeit== 45° should not exceed 2 seconds.

5 Talking to English-speaking workmates

Work with a partner and act out the following discussion in English.

Matthias Baumeister	British engineer
Fragen Sie, wie weit die Arbeit an der Anlage schon ist.	Antworten Sie, die Zentralstation ist gefertigt und die Aufnahmeköcher sind montiert. Nun muss die Station auf dem Tisch befestigt werden.
Fragen Sie, welche weiteren Stationen schon gefertigt sind.	Antworten Sie, die Schaftzuführung, die Wendestation und die Montagestation für die Kappe.
Erkundigen Sie sich nach dem Stand der Minenzuführung.	Antworten Sie, die Konstruktion und die 3D-Modellierung sei bereits abgeschlossen.
Fragen Sie, wann mit der Fertigung begonnen wird.	Antworten Sie, die Materialien sind bereits bestellt. Die Teile werden nächste Woche gefertigt.
Fragen Sie, wann die Montage erfolgt.	Antworten Sie, dass dies für übernächste Woche vorgesehen ist. Dann folgt auch die Inbetriebnahme.
Fragen Sie nach dem Zeitpunkt der Inbetriebnahme der Federvereinzelung.	Antworten Sie, etwa drei Tage nach dem Eintreffen des Geräts.

UNIT 10

6 Commissioning the refill feeder

Matthias has written the commissioning certificate in German and Felix is explaining it to David Swaby in English, but unfortunately he misses some important points.

a Listen to Felix and compare what he says in English with the original text in German below. Which points did he miss?

b Now try to explain the points he did not mention in English.

Inbetriebnahmeanweisung

 Durchführung nur von an dieser Anlage eingewiesenen Personen!

1. Kontrollen, die vor dem Einschalten der Anlage durchzuführen sind

1.1 Es muss überprüft werden, ob Bauteile im Minen- oder Kappenprisma sind, gegebenenfalls müssen diese entfernt werden.

1.2 Eine Sichtkontrolle der elektrischen und pneumatischen Bauteile ist durchzuführen.

1.3 Eine Überprüfung der Freigängigkeit aller beweglichen Teile muss vorgenommen werden.

2. Einschalten der Energieversorgung

2.1 Hauptschalter der Elektrik einschalten, SPS Start überwachen

2.2 Pneumatik Druckluft einschalten

2.3 Start-Taste 2 Sekunden drücken, um Grundstellung anzufahren. Wenn Grundstellung erreicht ist, gegebenenfalls Bauteile aus Minen- oder Kappenprisma entfernen.

3. Befüllen der Anlage

3.1 Trennwand in dafür vorgesehene Schlitze in den Minenbehälter einführen (gegebenenfalls Restminen beiseite schieben)

3.2 Minen in Minenbehälter einlegen, Position der Minen kontrollieren und wenn nötig ausrichten

3.3 Minenbehälter-Trennwand entfernen und an dafür vorgesehene Position ablegen

4. Automatik starten

4.1 Start-Taste 2-mal drücken, um Automatikablauf zu starten

4.2 Automatikablauf kurzzeitig überwachen, um Beschädigungen zu vermeiden

UNIT 10

7 The spring disentangler

Before compression springs can be fitted into the pens they must be disentangled. Ballpoint Peak uses a drum conveyor to do this.

a Match the springs (1–6) with the terms in the box.

coil springs • helical spring with closed ends • plate ring
saw ring • snap ring • tension springs with closed loops

 1  2  3  4  5  6

b Do you use any of these parts in your company? What are they used for?

c Read the following text and find out whether the four statements below are true or false. Correct the false statements.

Equipment and machines from **BADEX** guide hard-to-disentangle mass-produced parts into the proper position for processing. Snap rings, saw rings, helical springs with closed ends, tension springs with closed loops, plate springs and coil springs can be disentangled with these machines. **BADEX** solutions automate different operations, depending on the application. Most small parts are supplied as bulk goods, like the ones mentioned above. They are often heavily interlocked with one another and thus very difficult to separate. **BADEX** feeding technology automates and accelerates this process, even with parts that can usually only be separated by hand. Up to 99 % of parts can be gently disentangled and fed into an assembly system, depending on the design.

1 BADEX-Produkte führen schwer entwirrbare Masseteile lagerichtig der Verarbeitung zu.
2 Auch Federn mit geöffnetem Schenkel können entwirrt werden.
3 Schüttgut ist in der Regel leicht zu entwirren.
4 BADEX-Produkte sind nicht für Teile geeignet, die normalerweise von Hand entwirrt werden.
5 Viele Teile können nur von Hand separiert werden.

d The assembly station for the new ballpoint pens uses low-voltage electric motors. Which of these motors would you choose to drive the system? Give reasons.

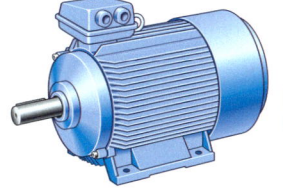 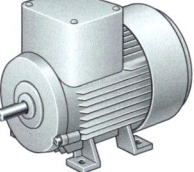 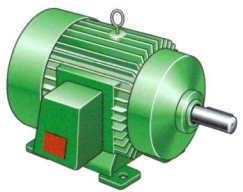 

squirrel cage motors   slip-ring motor   direct current motors   stepper motor

UNIT 10

8 Calling a hotline service

a Sometimes problems arise that you can't solve yourself. You need help from a specialist. In groups of three, read the following telephone conversation aloud.

A Power Engine Ltd, technical hotline, Chris speaking. How can I help you?

B Hello, this is Markus Schnelzer from Metago Metalltechnik in Leipzig speaking. We've got a problem with one of our three-phase motors.

A OK, can you give me the product number, please?

B Sure. It's 302160-2180-400V.

A Sorry, what was the last number again?

B 302160-2180-400V.

A Right. I'll put you through to the Technical Department. Hang on a second, please.

C Power Engine Ltd, Technical Department, Alan Bates speaking. What can I do for you?

B Hello, Mr Bates. We've got a problem with a squirrel cage motor. We can't get it to start. It's the 302160-2180-400V model.

C Well, let me check the machine fault chart. There might be a cable break or perhaps there's no power at all. There could also be a failure of the line protection devices, such as fuses for example. And the worst-case scenario is that the windings are defective.

B OK, I'll check the things you mentioned. Thank you for your help

C Not at all.

b Now act out similar dialogues with a hotline service.

Partner A: Turn to file 7 on page 158. Use phrases from the dialogue above.
Partner B: Choose one of the motor types from the table below and use phrases from the dialogue above to say what the problem is.
Partner C: Turn to file 13 on page 161. Use the chart and phrases from the dialogue above to advise the caller.

Squirrel cage motors	Motor doesn't start
Slip-ring motors	Motor doesn't start
Squirrel cage motors	Motor starts but makes loud noise
Slip-ring motors	Motor has not enough power under load
Squirrel cage motors	Motor gets too hot
Direct current motors	Motor speed too high under load
Slip-ring motors	Sparks at the brushes can be seen
Direct current motors	Motor starts jerkily
Squirrel cage motors	Motor makes strange sound
Direct current motors	Sparks at the brushes can be seen

Extra material

1 Language for marketing and advertising

Without using a dictionary, guess the German equivalents of the words and phrases below. Then compare your results with your classmates.

- your firm's logo engraved on the barrel
- a fitting gift for your most valuable customers
- a combination of elegant design and technical precision make the … a collector's item
- the impressive and luxurious appearance is due to the superb finish
- the … is manufactured to the highest standards using the finest materials
- the … is produced as a limited edition
- is only available for a limited time

2 Designing an advertising brochure

Before the new line of ballpoint pens go into production, a sales team must develop a marketing strategy for the pens. Form a group and design a flyer.

Consider the following questions:
- What are you going to call the new pens?
- Who are your potential customers?
- What technical information might customers find interesting?
- What other information about the new pens might be interesting?
- What information would customers need to order the new pens?

3 A customer enquiry

Write the following e-mails using the information in your flyer.

1 You work for the ordering department of an Australian firm in Melbourne. You want to order 500 pens, but you need some information first:
   - delivery time
   - technical format for the logo
   - method of payment
   - currency: Australian dollars or Euros

2 You work in the sales department of Ballpoint Peak Ltd. Answer the e-mail from the firm in Melbourne and quote a price for the pens they want to order.

4 Avoiding mistakes in e-mails

Find nine mistakes in the following e-mail.

> Dear Sir or Madam,
>
> We would like to order 150 idems, order number BZ 348. We would like our log-gia on the puns and we have encased this in a PFD-file at the rear of this mailing.
>
> Yours affectionately,
>
> Siley Dawkins

11 Quality control and safety at work

1 Quality control in developing countries

Look at the following photos from developing countries. What problems do they show?

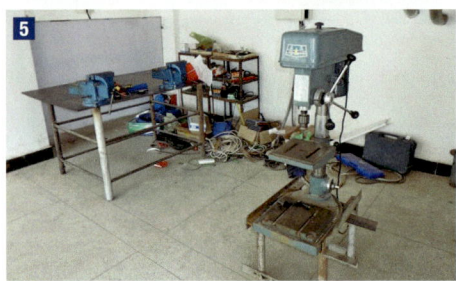

2 A quality control problem

The ballpoint pens that come out of the assembly station (see Unit 10) have scratches on the surface. Discuss possible reasons for this with a partner.

a The gripper surface has a burr.
b The arrangement of the mounting station was changed for some reason.
c … (your own ideas)

UNIT 11

3 Quality control

a Read this definition of quality. Does it match your own idea of quality or do you find other aspects more important?

> **Quality means staying in business**
> Noriaki Kano, the developer of a customer satisfaction model, presents a two-dimensional model of quality: "must-be quality" and "attractive quality". The former concerns "fitness for use" and the latter is what the customer would love but has not yet thought about. Supporters characterise this model more succinctly as "products and services that meet or exceed customers' expectations".

b Make a mind map based on the term *quality control* and complete it with everything that comes to mind. As a first step, check the meaning of the terms in the box and add them to the mind map.

customer satisfaction • measuring and testing equipment
• regular inspection • sample test • stress testing

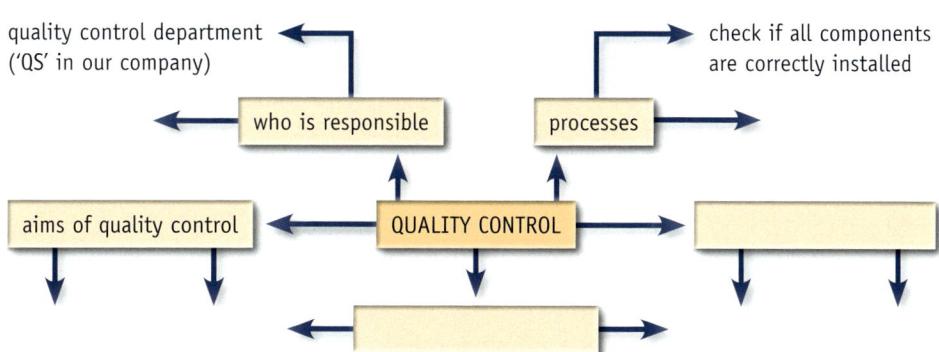

c Now present your ideas on quality control to the class using terms from your mind map. You may use the following questions to structure your presentation. You have five minutes to prepare.

- What role does quality control play in your company?
- How is quality checked in your company?
- Do you have a quality control department?
- What do the people in that department do?

4 Talking about quality

Peter Drabble, a foreman of Oxley's Metalworking Company, talks to his apprentice Dave Sandywell about quality control at their company.

a Listen to their conversation and take notes on the information given about quality management. Compare your notes with your neighbour.

b Briefly explain what an audit is.

UNIT 11

5 Industrial safety

The National Institute for Occupational Safety and Health (NIOSH) publishes materials which promote industrial safety.

Read the text and say whether statements 1–5 below are true or false. Correct the false statements.

> Young people under the age of 18 can be an asset to your workforce. They are enthusiastic and eager to learn. However, like other new and inexperienced workers, these young workers can be injured on the job when they do not receive adequate safety training and supervision. Some injuries have a lifelong impact, and some are even fatal. Furthermore, on-the-job injuries to young workers can be costly.
>
> Young workers get hurt when …
> - they take on jobs for which they are not trained – sometimes without being asked,
> - they do not have appropriate supervision,
> - they work with dangerous tools or equipment.
>
> Work on a construction site is especially hazardous. In fact, the construction industry, which employs less than 3 % of all young workers, ranks third in the number of work-related fatalities among young people – at 14 % of all occupational deaths for workers under 18.

1 Employing younger workers is a problem in your team.
2 Providing an apprenticeship is not enough. You also have to control what they do.
3 Younger workers can handle dangerous tools well.
4 Working on buildings is less dangerous because only 3% of all work-related accidents happen there.

6 Guidelines for working with young employees

a Sort the points below into two lists: DO and DO NOT tasks. Then compare your list with a partner and discuss any differences.

a Allow young workers to do tasks for which they are not trained or that break the law.
b Ask young workers to demonstrate that they understand what was said.
c Assume that young workers understand what they have been told.
d Do not correct mistakes.
e Give young workers a task if they have not been trained for that specific task.
f Give young workers tasks that require the use of power tools or the operation of heavy equipment.
g Let young workers work alone.
h Make sure young workers get clear instructions for each and every task.
i Provide adequate supervision.
j Set a firm rule that young workers may ONLY work on tasks for which they are trained.
k Stress safety to supervisors.
l Train young workers on what tasks they can and can't legally perform.

DO	DO NOT
b Ask young workers to …	Allow young workers …

Extra material

1 Language for marketing and advertising

Without using a dictionary, guess the German equivalents of the words and phrases below. Then compare your results with your classmates.

- your firm's logo engraved on the barrel
- a fitting gift for your most valuable customers
- a combination of elegant design and technical precision make the … a collector's item
- the impressive and luxurious appearance is due to the superb finish
- the … is manufactured to the highest standards using the finest materials
- the … is produced as a limited edition
- is only available for a limited time

2 Designing an advertising brochure

Before the new line of ballpoint pens go into production, a sales team must develop a marketing strategy for the pens. Form a group and design a flyer.

Consider the following questions:
- What are you going to call the new pens?
- Who are your potential customers?
- What technical information might customers find interesting?
- What other information about the new pens might be interesting?
- What information would customers need to order the new pens?

3 A customer enquiry

Write the following e-mails using the information in your flyer.

1 You work for the ordering department of an Australian firm in Melbourne. You want to order 500 pens, but you need some information first:
   - delivery time
   - method of payment
   - technical format for the logo
   - currency: Australian dollars or Euros

2 You work in the sales department of Ballpoint Peak Ltd. Answer the e-mail from the firm in Melbourne and quote a price for the pens they want to order.

4 Avoiding mistakes in e-mails

Find nine mistakes in the following e-mail.

> Dear Sir or Madam,
>
> We would like to order 150 idems, order number BZ 348. We would like our log-gia on the puns and we have encased this in a PFD-file at the rear of this mailing.
>
> Yours affectionately,
>
> Siley Dawkins

11 Quality control and safety at work

1 Quality control in developing countries

Look at the following photos from developing countries. What problems do they show?

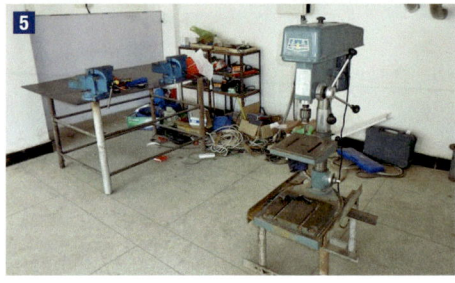

2 A quality control problem

The ballpoint pens that come out of the assembly station (see Unit 10) have scratches on the surface. Discuss possible reasons for this with a partner.

a The gripper surface has a burr.
b The arrangement of the mounting station was changed for some reason.
c ... (your own ideas)

UNIT 11

3 Quality control

a Read this definition of quality. Does it match your own idea of quality or do you find other aspects more important?

Quality means staying in business
Noriaki Kano, the developer of a customer satisfaction model, presents a two-dimensional model of quality: "must-be quality" and "attractive quality". The former concerns "fitness for use" and the latter is what the customer would love but has not yet thought about. Supporters characterise this model more succinctly as "products and services that meet or exceed customers' expectations".

b Make a mind map based on the term *quality control* and complete it with everything that comes to mind. As a first step, check the meaning of the terms in the box and add them to the mind map.

customer satisfaction • measuring and testing equipment
• regular inspection • sample test • stress testing

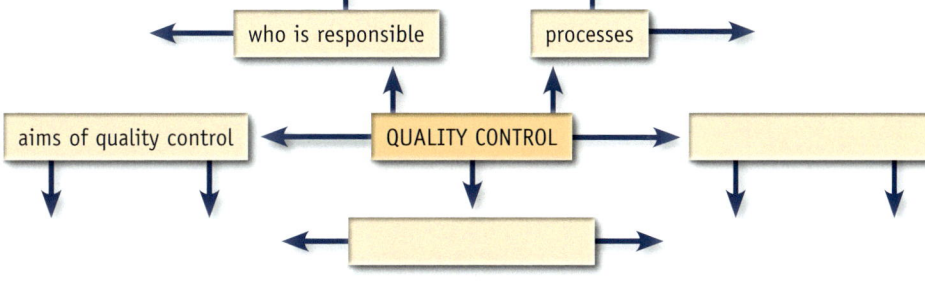

c Now present your ideas on quality control to the class using terms from your mind map. You may use the following questions to structure your presentation. You have five minutes to prepare.

- What role does quality control play in your company?
- How is quality checked in your company?
- Do you have a quality control department?
- What do the people in that department do?

4 Talking about quality

Peter Drabble, a foreman of Oxley's Metalworking Company, talks to his apprentice Dave Sandywell about quality control at their company.

a Listen to their conversation and take notes on the information given about quality management. Compare your notes with your neighbour.

b Briefly explain what an audit is.

107

5 Industrial safety

The National Institute for Occupational Safety and Health (NIOSH) publishes materials which promote industrial safety.

Read the text and say whether statements 1–5 below are true or false. Correct the false statements.

> Young people under the age of 18 can be an asset to your workforce. They are enthusiastic and eager to learn. However, like other new and inexperienced workers, these young workers can be injured on the job when they do not receive adequate safety training and supervision. Some injuries have a lifelong impact, and some are even fatal. Furthermore, on-the-job injuries to young workers can be costly.
>
> Young workers get hurt when …
> - they take on jobs for which they are not trained – sometimes without being asked,
> - they do not have appropriate supervision,
> - they work with dangerous tools or equipment.
>
> Work on a construction site is especially hazardous. In fact, the construction industry, which employs less than 3 % of all young workers, ranks third in the number of work-related fatalities among young people – at 14 % of all occupational deaths for workers under 18.

1 Employing younger workers is a problem in your team.
2 Providing an apprenticeship is not enough. You also have to control what they do.
3 Younger workers can handle dangerous tools well.
4 Working on buildings is less dangerous because only 3% of all work-related accidents happen there.

6 Guidelines for working with young employees

a Sort the points below into two lists: DO and DO NOT tasks. Then compare your list with a partner and discuss any differences.

a Allow young workers to do tasks for which they are not trained or that break the law.
b Ask young workers to demonstrate that they understand what was said.
c Assume that young workers understand what they have been told.
d Do not correct mistakes.
e Give young workers a task if they have not been trained for that specific task.
f Give young workers tasks that require the use of power tools or the operation of heavy equipment.
g Let young workers work alone.
h Make sure young workers get clear instructions for each and every task.
i Provide adequate supervision.
j Set a firm rule that young workers may ONLY work on tasks for which they are trained.
k Stress safety to supervisors.
l Train young workers on what tasks they can and can't legally perform.

Do	Do Not
b Ask young workers to …	Allow young workers …

UNIT **11**

b Now compare the rules above with the way young employees are treated in your own company.

Example:
Most young workers in my company are only given tasks that they have been trained to do. However, I once had to ...

7 An accident

There has been an accident at a factory and a trainee has been injured. Listen to the conversation between the patient and the company doctor and find out from the following list of illnesses and injuries what is wrong with him.

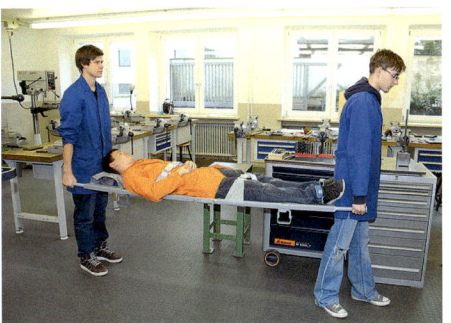

wounded forehead	cough
bleeding nose	cold
broken tooth	sore throat
injured back	flu
bruised chest	redness of the eyes
broken arm	pain in the bones
broken finger	itching
upset stomach	stomach and bowel
broken leg	problems
injured knee	nose bleeds
sprained ankle	nausea
crushed foot	diarrhoea
crushed toe	toothache

8 Describing injuries

Think of an accident you or one of your colleagues have had at work. Alternatively, recall an accident from your childhood. Describe what happened using the words and phrases above.

9 Medical objects

  a Name the medical objects in the photos below.

  b Which of these objects would you find in a first-aid kit?

antiseptic ointment • bandage • basin • blood pressure monitor • eye pads • ice pack • inhaler • pills • safety pins • scalpel • scissors • stretcher • syringe • thermometer

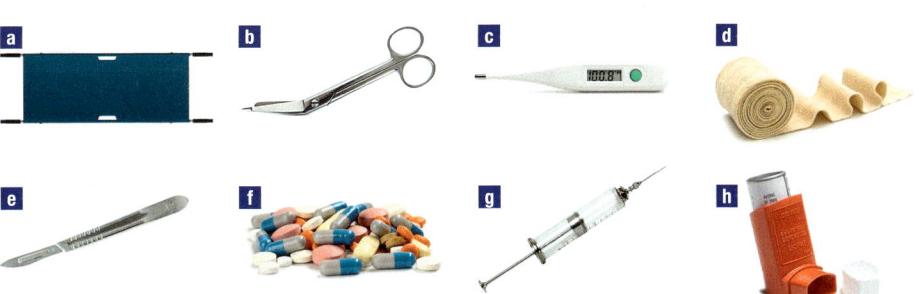

UNIT 11

10 Describing symptoms

Complete the table with the adjectives in the box. Add any other relevant words you can think of.

acute • bleary • burning • dislocated • dizzy • giddy • painful • stiff • sharp • shooting • stabbing • unclear • unfocussed

pain	head	vision	joints
sharp		unclear	

Adjectives and adverbs

1 I have a **sharp** pain in my back.
2 I thought it was **broken**.
3 You must learn how to lift heavy things **properly**.
4 How **fast** is your pulse after the exercise?
5 It was a **really** boring presentation

- Adjektive beschreiben, wie jemand oder etwas ist, und beziehen sich auf ein Nomen. (1, 2)
- Adverbien bezeichnen, wie etwas gemacht wird, und beziehen sich auf ein Verb. (3, 4)
- Im Englischen werden die meisten Adverbien von einem Adjektiv abgeleitet, indem man *-ly* anhängt. (3)
- Das zu *good* gehörende Adverb ist *well*.
- Die Adverbien *hard, fast, early* und *late* sind identisch mit dem Adjektiv. (4)

11 Practice

Choose the correct word in *italics*.

1 Dave Sandywell is a *young/youngly* apprentice.
2 He solved the problem with the gripper *easy/easily*.
3 The Romanian trainee was *severe/severely* injured.
4 The trainees don't have *appropriate/appropriately* supervision.
5 The boy was standing on an 8-inch *wide/widely* steel beam.
6 Make sure young workers get *clear/clearly* instructions.
7 Make sure young workers are *clear/clearly* instructed.
8 Provide young workers with *proper/properly* sized personal protective equipment
9 The foreman was angry and spoke *sharp/sharply* to the trainee.
10 I told the doctor that I wasn't feeling *good/well*.
11 You must follow the installation instructions *exact/exactly*.
12 The model they produced was an *exact/exactly* replica of the original.
13 Fasten the nut *gentle/gently* until it fits *tight/tightly*.
14 Alice is a *high/highly* experienced metalworker.

UNIT **11**

12 At a doctor's surgery

Who might say the following: a) a doctor, b) a patient, or c) a receptionist at a surgery?

1 Can I have your health insurance card, please?
2 Excuse me. Could you tell me how to get to the X-ray department, please?
3 Let's have a look at your leg then. Please lie down on the stretcher.
4 Have you been to this surgery before?
5 I feel terrible. The wound keeps itching all the time. When I scratch it, it starts bleeding.
6 I'm not taking any medication at the moment.
7 We'll have to take your blood pressure first. Can you roll up your sleeve, please?
8 What seems to be the problem?
9 I slipped on an oil stain after lubricating the machine.
10 Would you like to make another appointment? How about Thursday at 9.30?

13 Mediation: talking to a doctor

A Czech trainee working in your company has had an accident at work. As he doesn't speak any German you have to mediate between him and the company doctor. When you have finished, swap roles.

Company doctor	You	Patient
Was ist passiert?	She wants to know...	I ran into a fork lift.
Wie ist denn das passiert?	?	I guess I wasn't paying attention. And I wasn't wearing my helmet.
Ich sehe, Sie haben versucht, die Blutung zu stoppen. Hat es stark geblutet?	?	Yes, it bled quite a bit. I also think the wound is very dirty.
Wir werden sie sofort reinigen. Sind Sie gegen Tetanus geimpft *(vaccinated against tetanus)*?	?	Yes, I had a vaccination before coming to Germany. That was only three months ago.
Na ja, die Wunde ist nicht so tief, aber wir werden sie nähen müssen. Sie sollten nächstes Mal Ihren Helm tragen. So, tut sonst noch etwas weh?	?	Well, I think I've sprained my ankle. And my knee hurts as well.
Aha, das werden wir gleich versorgen. Wir kühlen das Knie und den Knöchel mit einem Eisbeutel.	?	

UNIT 11

Extra material

Filling in an accident report

Read the following article and note down the information required in the report below. Make up details not mentioned in the article.

18-year-old trainee Ana Farcas was severely injured in an accident at one of the lathes at the Mandlmaier factory in York the day before yesterday. The trainee energy engineer was working on a turning project at about 3 p.m. when suddenly the right arm of her overall was caught in the chuck. Her arm was twisted badly before the foreman could press the emergency stop button. The young girl was brought to York Hospital where she had to undergo an operation on her arm which had been broken in several places. Three ligaments also had to be sewn.

Filling in this form
This form must be filled in by an employer or other responsible person.

Health and Safety at Work etc. Act 1974
The Reporting of Injuries, Diseases and Dangerous Occurrences Regulations 1995

Part A About you

1 What is your full name?

2 What is your job title?

3 What is your telephone number?

About your company
4 What is the name of your company?

5 What is the address and postcode?

6 What type of work does the company do?

Part B About the incident

1 On what date did the incident happen?

2 At what time did the incident happen?
(Please use the 24-hour clock, e.g. 0600)

Part C About the injured person

1 What is their full name?

2 What is their home address and postcode?

3 What is their home phone number?

4 How old are they?

5 Are they ☐ male ☐ female
6 What is their job title?

Part D About the injury

1 What was the injury? (e.g. fracture, laceration)

2 What part of the body was injured?

3 Was the injury (tick the box that applies)
☐ fatal? ☐ a major injury?
☐ an injury to an employee or self-employed person which prevented them from doing their normal work for more than 3 days?

Part E Describing what happened

Give as much detail as you can. For instance
- the name of any substance or substances involved
- the name and type of any machine involved
- the events that led to the incident
- the actions undertaken by the other workers

12 Applying for a job

1 Testing materials

Because the rear axle of this giant dumper has broken twice while doing routine transportation work in a quarry, the manufacturer has asked a laboratory to find out whether the steel used for the axles is up to the required standard.

a Testing steels can be done either by destructive testing (DT) or non-destructive testing (NDT). Use the following table to describe different testing methods.

| The | ultrasonic test magnetic-particle test tension test pressure test vibration test hardness test | is | destructive non-destructive | and is used to | find measure test | surfaces. toughness. imperfections in steel. discontinuities in ferroelectric materials. springs. the tension of steel. |

b Talk to your neighbour. Does your company test any materials? How do they do it? Report back to the class.

2 Testing methods

Match the pictures to the testing methods in the box below.

hardness test • pressure test • ultrasonic test • vibration test

3 The tension test

a Look at the photos of a steel rod that was torn apart in a tension test for a tension/extension diagram. Describe what happened and why.

b Copy the following diagram into your exercise book and label points 1–5 with the terms in the box.

> lower yield point • original length •
> stress at failure • ultimate stress •
> upper yield point

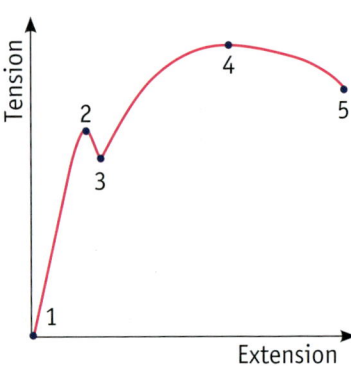

c Now match these photos to three of the five points shown in the diagram. Explain what happens at each stage.

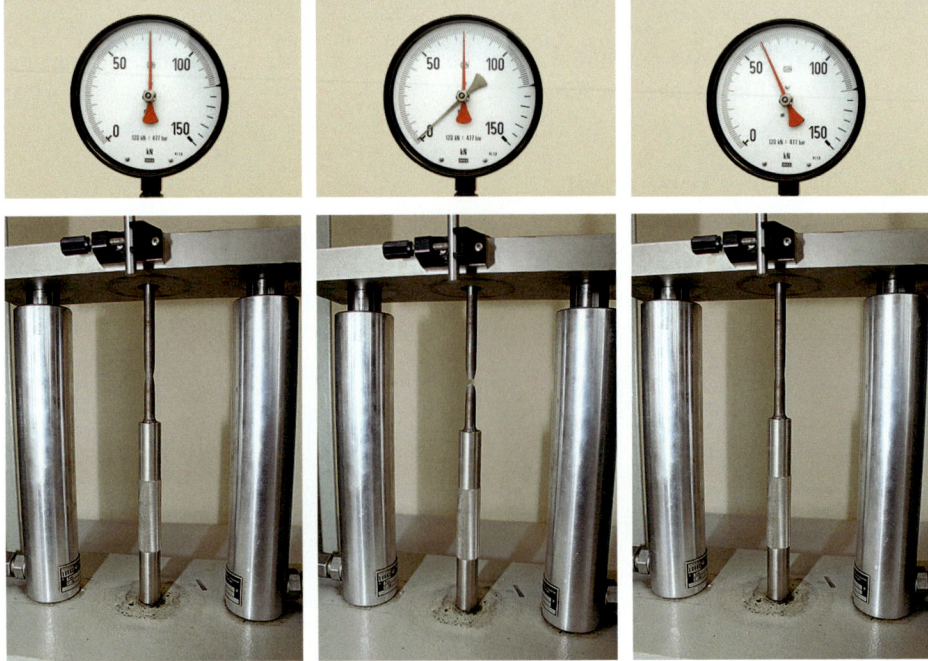

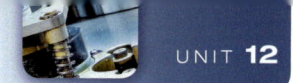

4 Describing graphs

a Use the table to describe the graphs on the opposite page. Sometimes you can use more than one expression.

The	line voltage velocity torque tension	drops flattens out fluctuates goes up/down hits a maximum levels off peaks plunges rises shoots up	drastically gradually sharply steadily suddenly	at ... between ... and ... from ... to ...	in ... after ... over a period of ... (percent/seconds)
		remains constant.			

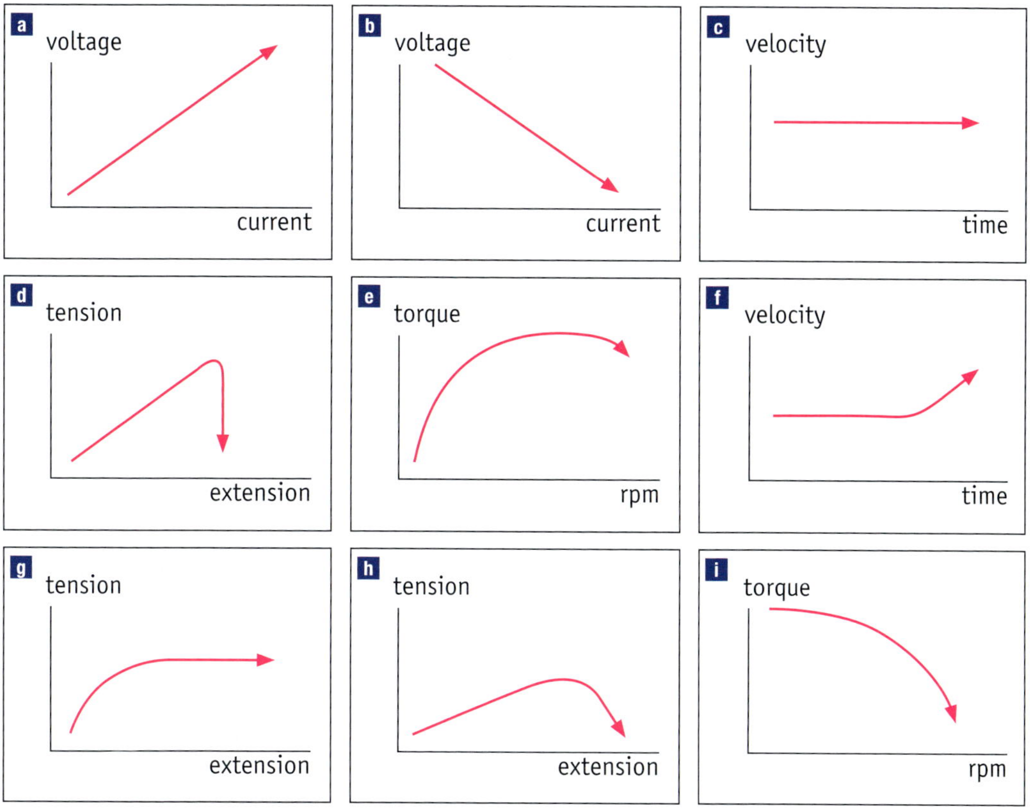

a voltage / current

b voltage / current

c velocity / time

d tension / extension

e torque / rpm

f velocity / time

g tension / extension

h tension / extension

i torque / rpm

b Draw three graphs and describe them to a partner who must draw them. Compare your partner's version with the original. Then swap roles.

5 The universal testing machine

A universal testing machine is used to test the tensile and compressive stress of materials either by tearing them apart or pressing them together.

a Which of the following drawings shows tensile stress and which compressive stress?

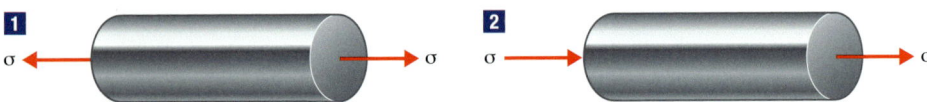

b Look at the following data sheet and say whether statements 1–4 below are true, false or not in the text.

Computerised Twin Screw Dual Channel Universal Testing Machine – Embedded touch screen version. The equipment can also be used to conduct peel, bond and friction tests by attaching different fixtures (optional).

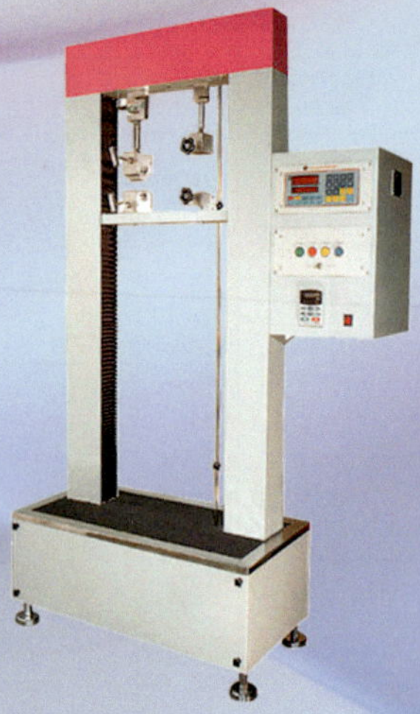

Specification:

Load capacity: up to 1000 kg.

No. of load cell: two.

Cross travel: up to 1000 mm.

Horizontal daylight: 450 mm.

Speed: from 2 mm/minute to 500 mm/minute.

Paint: powder coated.

Power: 230 volts, 50 Hz, single phase.

Direct display and printout through embedded controller

1 Two material samples can be tested at the same time.
2 The width of the machine is 1 metre.
3 You need an additional printer to print the stress-strain diagram.
4 A speed of 5 mm/s is possible.

The -ing form and infinitive

1 The specialists **suggested using** a different type of steel for the axles.
2 I **plan to test** the alloyed steel next.
3 I'll **start looking** at my first test results now.
4 You'll really **start to** understand the system.
5 Can we **begin by looking** at the diagrams of the other types of steel?
6 He's **good at giving** presentations.
7 It's **a waste of time trying** to test the hardness of copper.

- Die *-ing*-Form folgt auf Verben wie *enjoy, imagine, involve, suggest*. (1)
- Auf andere Verben wie *agree, choose, decide, expect, hope, learn, plan, prefer, want* folgt der Infinitiv. (2)
- Auf einige Verben wie *begin, continue, hate, like, love, stop* und *start* kann sowohl die *-ing*-Form als auch der Infinitiv folgen. (3, 4)
- Wenn auf eine Präposition ein Verb folgt, muss man die *-ing*-Form verwenden. (5)
- Nach bestimmten Wendungen wie *It's a waste of time …, to be good at, to be afraid of, How about …?* steht ebenfalls die *-ing*-Form. (6, 7)

6 Practice 1

Complete the sentences.

1 Could you imagine … (work) abroad?
2 She enjoys … (learn) about properties of materials.
3 Our company has decided … (buy) a new universal testing machine.
4 The next step in the testing procedure involves … (check) the results.
5 Could you go on with … (prepare) the presentation of the results, please?
6 It's a waste of time … (ask) questions before the end of the presentation.
7 Steel can be hardened by … (alloy) it with chrome and vanadium.
8 Press the bandage on the cut until it stops … (bleed).
9 Can you imagine … (work) under those conditions?
10 We must start … (test) the new assembly as soon as possible.

7 Practice 2

Talk about your hobbies and interests.

> I like playing darts in my free time. What do you like doing?

> I'm good at drawing and painting. What are you good at?

> I like visiting little pubs and collecting beer mats.

> My dog likes throwing a stick and I like running after it.

UNIT 12

8 Looking for employees

When a company is looking for new employees they usually place an advert in a regional or national newspaper. Many companies also advertise on the Internet. Companies that operate internationally often write their advert in English.

Compare the job advert in German with the job advert in English. Translate the underlined words and phrases into either English or German as appropriate.

Techniker/in – Application Support

Fourpoint ist <u>weltweit</u>[1] einer der <u>führenden Hersteller</u>[2] von Hard- und Software für Maschinen und Anlagen im <u>Materialtestgewerbe</u>[3]. <u>Zum nächstmöglichen Termin</u>[4] suchen wir eine(n) Techniker(in) für den Bereich Application Support.

<u>Zu Ihren Hauptaufgaben gehört</u>[5] die Installation und Wartung von Testsystemen, sowohl vor Ort als auch Remote. <u>Sie schulen die Anwender</u>[6] und sind für die Dokumentation mitverantwortlich. Sie betreuen außerdem unsere firmeneigenen IT-Systeme. Sie haben <u>gute Kenntnisse</u>[7] in den Bereichen Windows Client-Server Betriebssysteme/Netzwerktechnik. Fundierte SPS-Kenntnisse <u>sind von Vorteil</u>[8]. <u>Reisebereitschaft ist unbedingt erforderlich</u>[9], dabei ist die mündliche und schriftliche Verständigung auf Englisch für Sie kein Problem. Idealerweise haben Sie einen Abschluss als Techniker.

Wir bieten Ihnen neben einer <u>leistungsorientierten Bezahlung</u>[10] abwechslungsreiche und verantwortungsvolle Aufgaben mit viel Raum für Eigeninitiative in einem erfolgreichen Unternehmen.
Senden Sie Ihre Bewerbung in englischer Sprache an:
Fourpoint GmbH
Neuwies 1, D-35794 Mengerskirchen
Tel: + 49 6476 13-0, Fax: +49 6476 13-13
<u>human.resources@fourpoint-software.com</u>

Maintenance Engineer

Job Description: Siwamet S.A. in Warsaw wishes to recruit a multi-skilled maintenance engineer <u>as soon as possible</u>[11]. He or she should have either an electrical or a mechanical bias to ensure optimal levels of <u>plant performance and reliability</u>[12]. His or her main responsibility will be to <u>minimize plant downtime</u>[13] through effective and efficient planned preventive maintenance (PPM). Fault-finding through PLCs and <u>rectifying breakdowns and faults</u>[14] quickly and efficiently are vitally important skills. He or she must be a multi-skilled engineer with proven <u>hands-on experience of maintenance and repairs</u>[15] within a machine manufacturing environment.

Qualifications:
Ideally apprentice-trained with certificates in vocational training or a qualification in a <u>relevant engineering discipline</u>[16].

9 Letters of application

Ralf Schweiger is a trained precision mechanic who will soon finish a higher vocational course. He will then have a qualification as an engineer.

Norbert Hoffmann is a trained mechanical engineer who will soon finish his vocational training. He wants to work abroad.

a **Ralf decides to apply for the Fourpoint job (Exercise 8), so he writes a letter of application. Complete his letter with the words from the list below.**

> advert • apply • attention • challenge • currently • faithfully • grateful • hearing • maintenance • responsible • spoken • Vacancy

Dear Sirs,

… (1) **for an engineer in Application Support**

I saw your … (2) in the Internet and I would like to … (3) for the above post of engineer in the area of Application Support.

As you can see from my CV, I am … (4) working in the mechanical engineering department of Mandlmaier GmbH in Rottenburg. My most recent job was at a factory in Shenyang, China where I was part of a team … (5) for the installation and commissioning of conveying appliances and training operatives in its operation and … (6).

Your advert caught my … (7) because I am looking for a new … (8) and am interested in expanding my work experience abroad. My … (9) and written English is quite good and I am used to working in an international environment.

I would be … (10) if you would invite me for an interview.

I look forward to … (11) from you in the near future.

Yours … (12),

Ralf Schweiger

Enclosures:

UNIT 12

b **Norbert Hoffmann decides to apply for the job in Warsaw (Exercise 8). Write his letter of application. Ralf Schweiger's letter and the Language box below may help you.**

Applying for a job

Dear Ms/Mr/Mrs …,
Dear Sir or Madam,

Human resources manager/Personnel manager

I wish to apply for the above post, advertised in …
I read/saw your advert in … *(Zeitschrift mit Datum bzw. Online-Stellenbörse)*
I found your advert interesting because …
Your advert caught my attention because …

I am currently working in a small company called …
The company I now work for specializes in …
Since I have started here I have learned …
I have a very wide range of responsibilities which include …
My main task at present is the maintenance/installation/…

I am seeking a new position that …
– offers responsibility for the full range of …
– provides me with the opportunity to meet and work with a wide range of people.
I like to think that I bring enthusiasm and adaptability to my work.

I am interested in finding a position
– which offers me greater responsibility/an interesting challenge.
– where I can apply and expand my skills as a …

I would welcome the opportunity to discuss …
I am available for an interview at any time.
I look forward to hearing from you.

Yours sincerely/faithfully,

c **Discuss the types of job that would interest you.**

> I'm interested in …, so I'd be interested in a job that allowed me to …

> I don't want to work abroad or a long way from home, so I'll look for …

> For me, the most important things in a job are …

security? • adventure? • good pay? • working conditions? • career opportunities? • training? • …?

UNIT **12**

10   A curriculum vitae* (CV)

Lisa Fellinger has downloaded the Europass CV from the Internet. It can be used to apply for a job in any European country.

(*AE: résumé)

a Read Lisa's CV on the following two pages and complete the missing subheadings 1–9 from the list below.

- Driving licence
- Education and training
- First name(s) / Surname(s)
- Gender
- Main activities and responsibilities
- Mobile:
- Mother tongue(s)
- Name and type of organisation providing education and training
- Occupation or position held

b Find the English equivalents in the CV for the following German words and expressions.

1 Facharbeiter/in
2 freiwilliges soziales Jahr
3 Geschlecht
4 Handy
5 künstlerische Fähigkeiten
6 Lebenslauf
7 Muttersprache
8 Schul- und Berufsbildung
9 Selbstbeurteilung
10 soziale Fähigkeiten

c Read the information that Lisa provides in her CV and answer the following questions.

1 What is Lisa's middle name?
2 Where is she working now?
3 What does she do there?
4 What vocational qualifications does she have?
5 What exams did she take at school?
6 Where did she do her training?
7 What work experience does she have?
8 What skills does she have?
9 What are her free time interests and hobbies?

d Download the English template of the Europass CV from the Internet or ask your teacher for the file. Then write your own CV.

Europass Curriculum Vitae

Personal information

(1)	Lisa Maria Fellinger
Address(es)	Corneliusstrasse 3, D-84028 Landshut, Germany
Telephone(s)	+49 871 201 295 **(2)** +49 179 7662075
E-mail	lisa@fellingerfamily.de
Nationality	German
Date of birth	Nov. 8, 1989
(3)	female

Desired employment / Occupational field: Energy Engineer at Mandlmaier York

Work experience: Qualified Electrical Engineer at Mandlmaier Rottenburg

Dates	08/2010 – present
Occupation or position held	Qualified Electrical Engineer at Mandlmaier Rottenburg
(4)	Responsible for automation of conveying systems
Name and address of employer	Mandlmaier GmbH, Industriestrasse 4, D-84056 Rottenburg
Type of business or sector	Automotive components

Dates	08/2009 – 07/2010
(5)	voluntary social year
Main activities and responsibilities	Responsible for Children- and Youth work, organizing events
Name and address of employer	Turngemeinde Landshut
Type of business or sector	Sports Club

(6)

Dates	09/2006 – 07/2009 Training as an Electrical Engineer
Title of qualification awarded	Qualified Electrical Engineer
Principal subjects/occupational skills covered	Planning and carrying out electrical installations; installing and adapting PLCs; selecting and integrating electrical drive systems
(7)	Mandlmaier GmbH Rottenburg; Berufsschule 1 Landshut (Vocational College)
Level in national or international classification	ISCED 3
Dates	08/2005 2 weeks work placement at EST electronics in Dingolfing
Dates	09/2000 – 07/2006 Realschule Landshut (Secondary Modern School)
Title of qualification awarded	Mittlerer Schulabschluss (School Leaving Certificate)

UNIT **12**

Personal skills and competences (8)	German				
Other language(s)	**English, Italian**				
Self-assessment European level (*)	**Comprehension**		**Speaking**		**Writing**
	Listening	Reading	Spoken interaction	Spoken production	
English	B1	B1	B1	B1	B1
Italian	A1	A1	A1	A1	A1

(*) *Common European Framework of Reference for Languages*

Social skills and competences	Captain in a ladies' football team
Computer skills and competences	MS Office; CAD HiCAD
Artistic skills and competences	Playing the piano
(9)	for cars Type B; for motorcycles Type A
Additional information	I have been a member of the Landshut Disaster Relief Organisation since 2005
	Last summer I went to the U.K. with my football team and I decided to stay there and work for the rest of my holiday.

11 Mediation: do's and don'ts for job applications

Schreiben Sie eine kurze Liste in Deutsch mit Dingen, die für eine erfolgreiche Bewerbung zu beachten sind.

- DO **research the company, the career area and the actual job** for which you are applying. Make sure you can offer the qualifications, experience and personal skills that the employer is seeking.
- DO **make sure you are using the right form** – some employers have different forms for different job functions. DON'T use a Standard Application Form or CV where the employer specifies that you should use their own application form.
- DON'T **start to write on the form** itself until you are perfectly certain of what you are going to say. **Do your first draft on a photocopy of the form** to make sure that you can fit everything you want to include into the space available.
- DO **find a quiet place** to fill out the form – the library, your room or wherever suits you. Keep coffee cups, chocolate bars and small children at a safe distance.
- DO **read the form through and follow all instructions.** DO use black ink – your form will probably be photocopied and this makes it easier to read.
- DO **keep your own photocopy** of each application form. When it comes to the interview stage, it is immeasurably useful to remember what you have told the employer!

UNIT 12

12 Interview tips

Work with a partner and read the following ten sentences with advice on how to for an interview. Discuss how useful you think these tips are. In your exercise book, write the list in the order of their usefulness to you, i.e. from 1 (the most useful) to 10 (the least useful).

- Start preparing for the interview well in advance.
- Find out everything you can about the company on the Internet.
- Make friends with people who work for the company.
- Always drive to the interview.
- Change your CV to match the company's job advert.
- Practise the interview several times with a friend or a colleague.
- Buy new clothes for the interview.
- If you're a woman, look sexy; if you're a man, look cool and dynamic – it might help you get the job.
- Have a relaxing bath on the day of the interview.
- Drink lots of coffee to stay awake.

13 Interview questions

Work with a partner and practise an interview. The following Language box may help you.

Interviews

Interviewer

Where are you working now?
How long have you been working there?
What do your duties include?
What qualifications have you got?
Where did you study/train?
What are your hobbies and interests?

What do you enjoy most about your current job?
Why do you want to leave your present employer?
What are your strengths and weaknesses?
How would you describe yourself?
What relevant skills do you have?
Why are you interested in this job?

Interviewee

At the moment I'm working for a company that makes/produces/installs/…
I work for a company called …
I've been with them for … years/since 20…
My duties/responsibilities include …
I'm responsible for maintaining/the maintenance of …
I have a School Leaving Certificate from a German technical school/grammar school/…
After school I went to … for a two-year/… course in engineering /metalworking /…
I've worked abroad/in Australia/… and my English/Spanish/… is quite good.
I have the following vocational qualifications: …
The thing I enjoy most about my present job is …
I'm good at …, but I'm not so good at …
I see myself as someone who enjoys a challenge/can work independently und reliably/…
I'm interested in … and I'm an active member of a local …
In my free time I usually/often …

Extra material

1 Tips for an interview

Work together in a group and make a list of all the useful tips you can think of for someone going for a job interview.

2 The day of the interview

a Ralf Schweiger is invited to an interview. Before you listen to the interview, copy the following table into your exercise book.

Questions	Answers (+2 = very good, +1 = good, 0 = not so good, -1 = bad, -2 = very bad)
1	
2	

b Listen to the interview with a partner and evaluate Ralf's answers to the questions as shown in the table above.

c After the interview, compare how you evaluated Ralf's answers. Which of Ralf's answers were definitely bad? Discuss your evaluations and decide whether you would offer Ralf the job or not.

3 Teamwork vs. individuality

Discuss the advantages and disadvantages of each.

> In any group of people, one person usually becomes a leader who tells the others what to do.

> A team has more experience than any single person.

> When they work together, a team can achieve much more than one person alone.

> Some problems need radical solutions, but teams generally think conventionally. Only individuals can think "out of the box".

> A team is like a committee – it stifles initiative and innovative ideas.

I can ...

A Mediation

Ich kann einem deutschen Kollegen helfen, in ein Hotel im Ausland einzuchecken.

1 Sie übersetzen für einen deutschen Kollegen, der kein Englisch spricht, bei einem Gespräch an der Hotelrezeption.

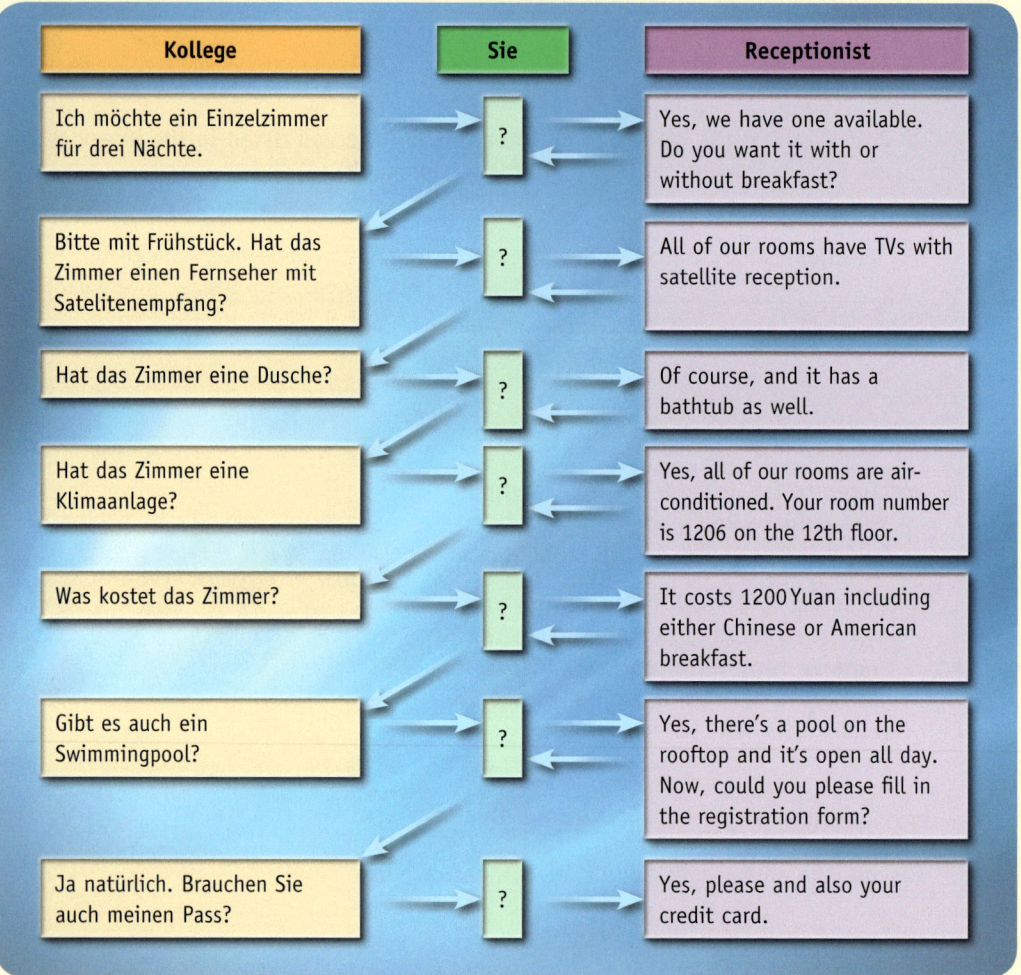

B Produktion

Ich kann Sicherheitsanweisungen auf Englisch geben

2 Formulieren Sie die folgenden Sätze in Englisch.

1. Stellen Sie den Arbeitern Sicherheitsschuhe und Schutzhelme zur Verfügung.
2. Verbessern Sie Fehler der Auszubildenden.
3. Geben Sie jungen Arbeitern keine Aufgaben, bei denen sie schwere Werkzeuge verwenden müssen.
4. Geben Sie jungen Arbeitern keine Aufträge, für die sie nicht ausgebildet sind.
5. Lassen Sie junge Arbeiter nicht alleine arbeiten.

C Rezeption

Ich kann eine Diskussion über das Qualitätsmanagement verstehen

3 Hören Sie sich den Dialog an und finden Sie jeweils die richtige Lösung.

1. Dave and Peter are talking about the Quality Management ...
   a) assurance manual.   b) insurance manual.   c) durance manual.
2. The company sells their products ...
   a) to the UK.   b) to the UK and Europe.   c) globally.
3. Each country has different product ...
   a) facilities.   b) liabilities.   c) sensibilities.
4. When products are tested to ensure they have no harmful effects, this is called environmental ...
   a) responsibility.   b) compatibility.   c) adaptability.
5. An audit test whether Oxley fulfills the requirements of the...
   a) ISO 9001 norm.   b) ISO 9009 norm.   c) ISS 9007 norm.

Ich kann einem authentischen Fachtext spezifische Informationen entnehmen.

4 Lesen Sie den folgenden Text und beantworten Sie die Fragen.

EM 2 Series Rockwell Hardness Testers

The EM-2 Series Rockwell hardness testers can be supplied in three models: advanced, basic and analog. Combination packages are also available that include both the regular and superficial tester model.

The EM-2RSD Series is our advanced digital tester featuring our advanced digital readout. The advanced digital test head is password protected and can be used to display your hardness result, plus a variety of advanced functions including tolerances, SPC, etc. Save over 2400 results to memory for recall and analysis. Print reports including averages of results and statistical analysis including standard deviations, etc. Use the digital readout's RS232 output with our optional ViewData® software for more comprehensive reporting and analysis. This series may also be equipped with optional motorized major load control.

The EM-2RBD Series are equipped with our basic digital test head that displays the hardness result. Prompts guide you through the setup process. Tolerances can be applied to your results to indicate OK, High or Low. An internal memory within the digital readout can stored results or use its RS232 serial data output to transmit information to a personal computer. This model can also be used with our optional ViewData® software for more comprehensive reporting and analysis using the tester's RS232 output and a personal computer.

The EM-2R Series measures and indicates the hardness result on the analog dial with direct-reading Rockwell hardness numbers. The dial resolution is 0.1 Rockwell points.

1. Welche drei Modelle des Härtetesters gibt es?
2. Welche Anzeige hat der EM 2RSD?
3. Wie viele Testergebnisse kann der Härtetester speichern?
4. Was wird am Testkopf des EM 2RBD angezeigt?
5. Wie wird das Setup durchgeführt?
6. An welchem Ausgang kann ein externer Rechner angeschlossen werden?
7. Was unterscheidet den EM-2R vom EM-2RSD und dem EM-2RBD?

13 Automation systems

1 Planning a new PLC system

Klaus Schicha, a young trainee from Hundt Automation systems in Graz, is in Detroit to work with his American colleagues Dave, a mechatronics technician, and Eric, a mechanic, on the automation system of a production line for welding cars. Their task is to replace an old and outdated control system which often causes downtime and unnecessary expenses. These control systems become more difficult to service as time goes by and modern systems become more commonly used.

a Describe what can you see in these four photos.

b Do you have PLCs in your company? Explain what they control.

c Listen to the text and write a list of the things Dave, Eric and Klaus need to install the new PLC system.

```
3x handling robots
3x magazines for sheet metal
10 welding robots
```

Wie kann ich mein Hörverständnis verbessern?

Je häufiger Sie Englisch hören, desto leichter wird es Ihnen fallen, Muttersprachler zu verstehen. Möglichkeiten zum Üben gibt es zuhauf:

- englischsprachige Radio- und Fernsehsender (z. B. BBC World, CNN)
- DVDs bzw. Videos im Originalton
- Audiofiles aus dem Internet (eine wahre Fundgrube ist z. B. www.bbc.co.uk, wo man sich BBC-Radiosendungen als Livestream anhören kann – der große Vorteil dabei ist natürlich die Möglichkeit, vor- und zurückzuspringen oder sich die Sendung noch mal anzuhören)

Tipps zum leichteren Verständnis beim Hören

- Machen Sie sich vor dem Zuhören klar, um was es beim Hörtext gehen wird. (Welche Thematik? Worauf lässt der Titel schließen? Gibt es Fotos oder Illustrationen?)
- Versuchen Sie beim ersten Zuhören, den Text sinngemäß zu erfassen, und verzichten Sie auf das Verstehen von Details.
- Wenn Sie sich einen Text zum zweiten Mal anhören, können Sie auf Einzelheiten achten. Notieren Sie sich vorher, wo beim ersten Mal Verständnislücken geblieben sind – und achten Sie beim Hören darauf, wo Sie etwas falsch verstanden haben.
- Bleiben Sie nicht an Einzelwörtern hängen, sondern versuchen Sie, die Gesamtaussage zu erfassen.

2 A SIMATIC S7-presentation

Klaus, Dave and Eric go to a presentation of the SIMATIC S7. Before the presentation they prepare a list of questions that they want to ask the representative.

a What questions would you ask the representative? Work with a partner and write a list of questions. Think about the following areas of interest:

The company:
- technical know-how?
- amount of experience in the automotive industry?

The system:
- future expansion?
- adaptability/flexibility?
- maintenance?

General problems:
- vibration?
- breakdowns/downtime?

b Now work with your partner and think of possible answers to your questions. Act mini-dialogues of questions and answers.

c Listen to the presentation. Which of the questions on your list were asked? Did you hear questions about aspects you hadn't thought of? Make notes about the answers the representative gave and compare them with the answers you thought of in your mini-dialogues.

UNIT 13

3 Choosing the right controller

a Der amerikanische Chef bittet Sie, für acht verschiedene Aufgabenarten in der Firma (siehe unten) die richtige Steuerung auszuwählen. Verwenden Sie hierzu die Informationen des Informationsblatts auf die gegenüberliegenden Seite.

1   Wartungsfreie Steuerung
2   Steuerung, die in STEP 7 programmiert werden kann
3   Steuerung, die die Stückzahl pro Palette abzählen kann
4   Steuerung, bei der die Module während des Betriebs ausgetauscht werden können
5   Steuerung, bei der die Konfiguration während des Betriebs geändert werden kann
6   Steuerung mit Verbindungsmöglichkeit zu PROFIBUS und PROFINET
7   Steuerung für eine kleinere Montageeinheit, die einfach zu programmieren ist
8   Ausfallsichere Steuerung

b Now present the results to your the American boss in English and explain why each one is the right controller for the required task. The following example may help you.

For task number 1 either the Simatic ET 200 or Simatic S7-300 would be suitable as both claim to be maintenance-free.

UNIT **13**

SIMATIC Modular Controllers

LOGO!
Logic module for switching and controlling

- Simple automation in industry, trade and utility building as a replacement for mechanical switchgear
- Simplest possible programming with LOGO! Soft Comfort

More information about LOGO! at:
www.siemens.com/logo

SIMATIC S7-1200
Modular, compact controller for discrete and stand-alone automation solutions

- Scalable and flexible design for compact solutions
- Integrated Industrial Ethernet/PROFINET interface for programming, I/O and HMI connection and CPU-to-CPU communication
- Integrated technology functions for counting, measuring, closed-loop control, and motion control
- Simple and efficient programming with STEP 7 Basic

SIMATIC ET 200
Bit-modular, distributed I/O system with local intelligence

- Design with degree of protection IP20 (in the control cabinet) and IP65/67 (without control cabinet)
- Module replacement during operation
- Fail-safe version
- Maintenance-free thanks to data retentivity on Micro Memory Card*)

SIMATIC S7-300
The modular controller for system solutions in the manufacturing industry

- Compact design, mounting on DIN rail
- Many functions are integrated into the CPU (I/O, technology functions, PROFIBUS/PROFINET connection)
- Maintenance-free thanks to data retentivity on Micro Memory Card*)
- Isochronous mode on PROFIBUS and PROFINET
- Fail-safe versions
- Fail-safe technology controller

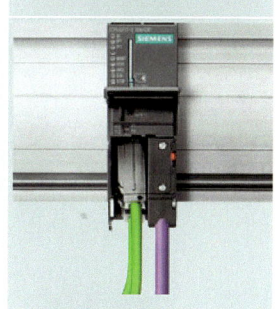

SIMATIC S7-400
The powerful controller for system solutions in the manufacturing and process industries

- Rack system with various rack types
- Extremely high-speed processing and communications performance
- Changes to the configuration during operation
- Isochronous mode on PROFIBUS and PROFINET
- Fail-safe and fault-tolerant versions
- Hot swapping

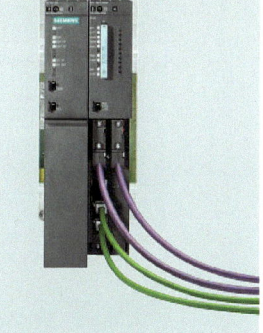

*) without battery

UNIT 13

4 Application of the SIMATIC S7-400

a Match eight of the industrial sectors mentioned in the following leaflet with the photos below.

SIMATIC S7-400: The Power Controller for system solutions in the following sectors of industrial manufacturing and process automation.

- Automotive industry
- Standard mechanical equipment manufacture, including custom mechanical equipment manufacture
- Warehousing systems
- Building engineering
- Steel industry
- Power generation and distribution
- Paper and printing industries
- Woodworking
- Textile manufacture
- Pharmaceuticals
- Food, beverages and tobacco industries
- Process engineering, e.g. water and wastewater utilities (sewage)
- Chemical industry and petrochemicals

UNIT **13**

b Work with a partner. Look at the list of industrial sectors in the leaflet on page 132 where the Simatic S7-400 can be applied. What exactly do you think it might control in each sector? And if the Power Controller failed, what could happen in each case?

c Ihr Chef möchte von Ihnen die Anwendungsbereiche der SIMATIC S7-400 wissen. Übertragen Sie diese ins Deutsche.

Wie kann ich mein Englisch verbessern?

Englisch kann man auf viele unterschiedliche Weisen lernen. Hier sind ein paar Tipps – aber bestimmt fallen Ihnen noch mehr Möglichkeiten ein!

- Haben Sie Zugang zu englischsprachigem Radio oder Fernsehen (BBC World Service, CNN)? Nachrichten ändern sich bekanntlich von Stunde zu Stunde kaum, daher versteht man beim zweiten oder dritten Mal oft viel mehr. Und man kann zwischendurch nachschlagen, was man nicht verstanden hat.
- Filme auf DVD in Originalfassung sind mit englischen Untertiteln leichter zu verstehen – und vielleicht klappt es beim zweiten Mal schon ohne Untertitel!
- Auch in Großbritannien oder den USA gibt es Arbeitsplätze – haben Sie schon mal im Internet gesucht?
- Ein Magazin für Ihr Hobby gibt es ganz bestimmt auch in englischer Sprache.
- Noch einfacher geht's im Internet. Hier schon mal ein Tipp: Auf der Seite www.howstuffworks.com werden unzählige Dinge aus Alltag, Umwelt und Technik auf Englisch erklärt.
- Warum nicht mal eine SMS oder E-Mail auf Englisch schreiben?
- CDs haben meist Booklets mit Texten – wer mitliest, versteht mehr.

5 Using modal verbs

Complete the following sentences with the correct form of the verbs from the list below.

be allowed to • can • have to • may • mustn't • needn't • should

1 Car bodies ... be welded with 100 % accuracy.
2 You ... leave equipment switched on overnight because it wastes energy.
3 This new user interface ... show almost any step of the welding process.
4 Please find and repair the defect quickly because this unit ... be back on line within an hour.
5 Although Klaus was still a trainee, he ... to program some of the PLC routines.
6 We've got plenty of time. We ... start to fix the new light barriers till next Friday.
7 ... I use your programming unit, please? Mine's not working.
8 What do we do next? ... we fix the new sensors?

6 The PLC for extreme conditions

Read the text below and answer the questions below.

Robustness

Maximum industrial suitability – through increased robustness

With any standard product from the SIMATIC range, you rely on maximum quality and robustness – perfect for use in industrial environments. Specific system tests ensure the planned and required quality of each individual component. For example, SIMATIC IPCs undergo more than 50 tests to ensure industrial compatibility.

Of course, SIMATIC components meet all relevant international standards and are certified accordingly. Components remain functional within a temperature range between +5 to +45 °C. The degree of resistance to shock and vibration are defined in the SIMATIC Quality Guidelines as well as their electromagnetic compatibility (EMC) resistance. This robustness make our products suitable for use in hazardous areas. The SIMATIC ET 200 range also includes standard products with an IP67 degree of protection, i.e. they are dustproof and can tolerate temporary submersion.

SIPLUS extreme modules from the SIMATIC spectrum, e.g. SIMATIC ET 200 in special design, are available for industrial applications with difficult to extreme operating conditions. SIPLUS extreme components are suitable for use in an expanded range of ambient temperature as well as in corrosive environmental conditions, salty ambient air, condensation and deposits of conductive dust.

This enables their use in harsh industrial environments or outdoors, without the need for additional precautions such as enclosures or air conditioning.

Suitable for industry – even under difficult operating conditions

- An integrated range of products for all industrial application areas and extremely rough conditions
- Maximum robustness at all levels of automation and for all applications: from field devices to control units to operator panels
- Can be used direct on the machine or close to the process – even without a control cabinet, i.e. without requiring installation and wiring

1 Could the SIMATIC range operate at a temperature of – 20°C?
2 What characteristics of the SIMATIC range are defined in the Quality Guidelines?
3 What extra characteristics does the IP67 degree of protection offer?
4 Which range of components is suitable for outdoor operation?
5 What makes the SIPLUS range the most suitable modules for operation in coastal areas?

7 Technical translation

Translate the following terms into English.

1. stoßfest, 2. vibrationsgeschützt, 3. eine lackierte Baugruppe, 4. EMV-Schirmung, 5. Temperaturbereich, 6. Klemmbox, 7. Anschlussklemmen, 8. Kontaktstifte

8 Working with definitions and synonyms

Read the following text and find words in the text that match the synonyms and definitions below.

> The automation of many different processes, such as controlling machines or factory assembly lines, is is acheived by using small computers called programmable logic controllers. A PLC is actually a control device that consists of a programmable microprocessor, and is programmed using a specialized computer language. Typically, the program is written in a development environment on a computer, and then is downloaded onto the programmable logic controller directly through a cable connection. The program is stored in the programmable logic controller in non-volatile memory. Programmable logic controllers are designed for real-time use, and often must withstand harsh environments on the shop floor. The programmable logic controller circuitry monitors the status of multiple sensor inputs, which control output actuators, which may be things like starter motors, solenoids, lights and displays, or valves.
>
> Today, programmable logic controllers deliver a wide range of functionality, including basic relay control, motion control, process control, and complex networking, as well as being used in distributed control systems (DCS).
>
> Digital signals yield an on or off signal, of which the programmable logic controller sees only two states: true or false. Analog signals may also be used, such as those from devices like volume controls, and these analog signals can be seen by the programmable logic controller as floating point values.
>
> There are several different types of interfaces that are used when people need to interact with the programmable logic controller to configure it or work with it. It might be configured with simple lights or switches, or a text display. More complex systems might use a web interface on a computer running a supervisory control and data acquisition (SCADA) system.
>
> Programmable logic controllers were first created to serve the automobile industry. The first programmable logic controller project was developed in 1968 for General Motors to replace hard-wired relay systems with an electronic controller.

1. production line
2. a digital computer used for the automation of electromechanical processes
3. unstable (adj.)
4. a mechanism that performs an automatic action
5. a coil of wire around an iron core
6. produce (verb)
7. numbers that would be too large or too small to be represented as integers
8. an electrical circuit which links one machine, especially a computer, with another
9. substitute (verb)

UNIT 13

Extra material

Wining and dining

a In the evening Klaus goes out with Dave and Eric to a typical American restaurant. Take a look at the menu and decide what you want to eat. Ask your classmates for help if you don't know what something is.

> Does anybody know what "pulled pork" is?

> Has anyone ever eaten "…"?

APPETIZERS

Slider Trio: Slices of Turkey, Beef, and Pulled Pork	$11.00
Corn Dogs: Served with Mustard Cream	$10.00
Mini Shrimp Rolls: Spiced Poached Shrimp, Tarragon Mayonnaise	$12.00
Buffalo Chicken Wings: served with Blue Cheese Crumbles, Carrots, and Celery	$11.00
Classic American Chilli: Turkey and Chicken with Bell Peppers, Onions, and Tomato	$8.00
Tomato Soup with Grilled Cheese Toasts	$9.00

SALADS

Wedge Salad: Iceberg lettuce, Cucumber, Tomato, Bacon Bits, Pickled Shallots, Blue Cheese	$10.00
Caesar Salad: House Made Caesar Dressing, Parmesan Croutons, Kalamata Olive Tapenade	$10.00
Wedge Salad: Iceberg lettuce, Cucumber, Tomato, Bacon Bits, Pickled Shallots, Blue Cheese	$10.00
Caesar Salad: House Made Caesar Dressing, Parmesan Croutons, Kalamata Olive Tapenade	$10.00
Caesar Salad with chicken	$14.00
Caesar Salad with shrimps	$15.00
Classic American Salad: Iceberg lettuce, Radish, Beans, Avocado, Cucumber, Tomatoes, Champagne Vinaigrette	$9.00

BURGERS & SANDWICHES

The Classic American Burger: With melted cheddar, lettuce, onions and secret sauce with French Fries	$14.00
Turkey Burger: With Muenster Cheese, Cranberry Mustard and Arugula with Sweet Potato Fries	$15.00
Pulled Pork Sandwich: Classic Slaw, Smokey BBQ Sauce and Classic Baked Beans	$15.00
Turkey Swiss Club: With Avocado, Bacon and Lettuce served with Classic Slaw	$13.00
Cubano: Ham, pulled pork, Dijon mustard, dill pickle on a French baguette	$14.00

ENTREES

Smoked Half Chicken: Served with Roasted Root Vegetables	$16.00
10 oz. Skirt Steak: Served with House Made Steak Sauce with French Fries	$19.00
Classic Meatloaf: Served with Mashed Potatoes and Green Beans	$15.00
Beer Battered Fish: With French Fries and Malt Vinegar Tartar Sauce	$13.00
Pot Roast: Served with Roasted Root Vegetables	$17.00
Pasta Primavera: With Chicken, Vegetables sautéd in a Roasted Garlic Sauce	$18.00

DESSERTS

Ice Cream Sandwiches: Chocolate Chip Pecan Walnut Cookie with Vanilla Bean Ice Cream	$7.00
Oatmeal Cookie Sandwich: With Dulce de Leche Ice Cream	$7.00
Smores: Graham crackers, Marshmallow Fluff, Chocolate Sauce	$7.00
Banana Split: Caramelized Bananas, Vanilla and Strawberry Ice Cream, Nuts, Whipped Cream	$9.00

b Then ask your classmates what they would like to eat. Act out the situation in the restaurant. The words an phrases in the box below may help you.

Language

In a restaurant

Waiter/Watress
Would you like to order now, Sir/Madam?
Can I bring you anything to drink?
Under what name was the reservation made?

Guest
I'd like to look at the wine list, please.
We'd like a table for three, please.
Do you accept Matercard/Visa/…?

Planning and realizing a project

1 At the farm

Listen to the sounds made by the following machines. Then listen again and say which machine made each sound.

a milking machine

an oat crusher

a tractor

a lawnmower

a chainsaw

a forestry harvester

2 A construction team

Oats must be ground and crushed before they can be used for feeding animals. Grange Farm Livery Stables in Arthington need new oat crushers to prepare the cereals for their horses and they ask Chodiltech Ltd. in Worcester if they can produce them. Chodiltech put together the following design and construction team.

> First we should produce a WBS. That will give us a rough overview of all the steps necessary for the planning phase.

> A Work Breakdown Structure? OK, I'll draw it.

> Thanks, Emily. What will the first heading be?

Daniel

Emily

Archie

Use the completed WBS on the next page to complete the team discussion which produced it. Write the missing words in your exercise book and then act out the dialogue with two classmates.

137

UNIT 14

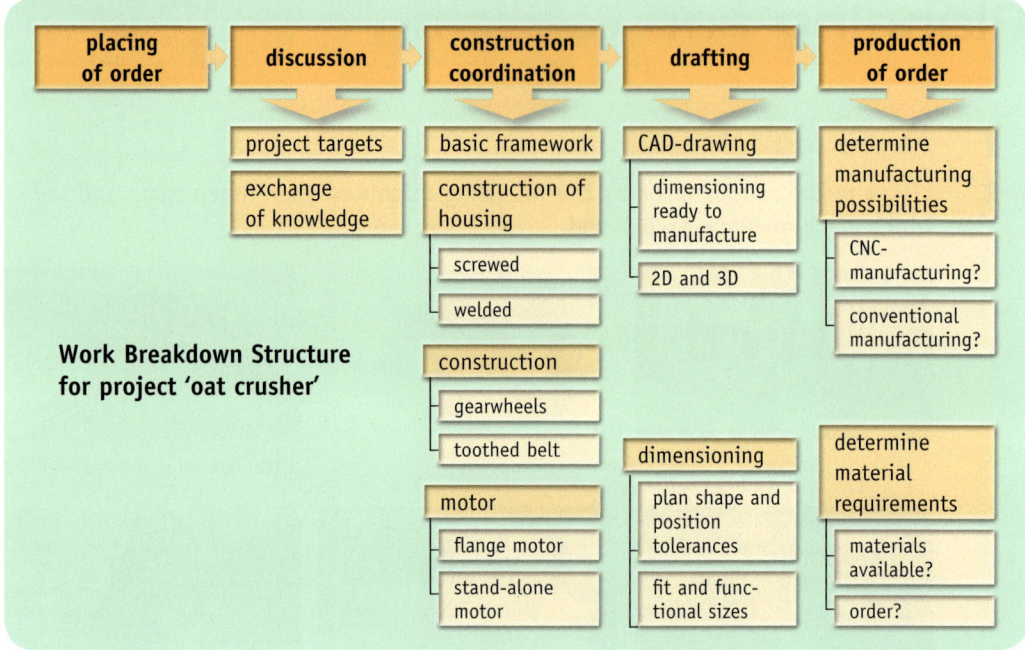

Emily The first heading is the placing of the order, isnt it? Then we'll need a couple of meetings to discuss the project. I'll give that the heading '...¹'.
Archie In these discussions we must define our ...².
Emily I'll put that as the step under the heading 'Discussion'. Does anything else come under this heading?
Archie Yes, we make suggestions and exchange ideas and knowledge.
Emily OK. I'll write 'Exchange of knowledge'.
Daniel The next step in the first level is 'Construction and coordination', isn't it?
Archie That's right. Here we have to draft a ...³ for the production process.
Emily That would start with the construction of the housing.
Daniel Yes, we must decide whether the housing is ...⁴ or welded together.
Archie We also need to discuss the other components in the construction. How should they be driven: by ...⁵ or a toothed belt?
Daniel And what about the motor? Do we need a flange motor or a ...⁶?
Emily OK, I've got that. The next step is the drafting, isn't it? We'll have to produce a ...⁷ with dimensioning ready to manufacture.
Daniel Yes, and it will have to be in both ...⁸.
Archie When we do the dimensioning we have to plan both shape and position tolerances and we also have to specify the fits and functional sizes.
Emily OK. I've written all that down. The final step is ...⁹, isn't it? And the first thing we have to do is determine the manufacturing possibilities.
Daniel Yes, we must decide what can be done by ...¹⁰ and what by can be produced by conventional manufacturing.
Archie Then we have to determine ...¹¹. We must find out which materials are available and which materials we need to ...¹².
Emily OK. I'll draft the Work Breakdown Structure on the computer and print it out.
Daniel Great, thank you. And I suggest meeting at four for our first discussion.

UNIT 14

3 Who does what?

Work with two partners, take over the roles of the team members and discuss in English who will do what in the process of constructing the new oat crushers.

Daniel	Emily	Archie
Fragen Sie, was die Haferquetsche eigentlich können soll.	Antworten Sie, sie soll Hafer zu Flocken verarbeiten.	Sagen Sie, dass die Haferquetsche besonders robust für den Einsatz am Bauernhof sein muss.
Fragen Sie, ob nur eine Flockengröße hergestellt werden oder ob die Quetsche verstellbar sein soll.	Antworten Sie, die Quetsche soll für verschiedene Flockengrößen verstellbar sein.	Fragen Sie, ob es Sicherheitsmaßnahmen gibt, die zu beachten sind.
Antworten Sie, ja, die Finger dürfen nicht in die Maschine gelangen.	Fragen Sie, wieviel Hafer in die Quetsche geschüttet werden soll.	Antworten Sie, mindestens 2 Liter. Fragen Sie, welche Motorleistung dafür benötigt wird.
Antworten Sie, dass ein Motor mit 1,1 Kilowatt ausreichen sollte.	Fragen Sie, wer die Motorleistung berechnen kann.	Sagen Sie, Sie werden das berechnen, wenn Sie die Quetsche konstruieren.
Sagen Sie, dass Sie drei nun die Arbeit für die Entwicklung der Haferquetsche unter sich aufteilen müssen.	Sagen Sie, dass Sie gerne die CAD-Zeichnungen machen würden.	Sagen Sie, dass Sie gerne die Konstruktion planen und die Berechnungen durchführen würden.

4 The oat crusher project

a At the first meeting of the team, Daniel draws a sketch of the oat crusher. Use the following sentence pattern and the Language box on the next page to describe his sketch.

The ... must be the

- motor housing.
- hopper.
- oat bin.
- power cable.
- oat crusher.
- ...

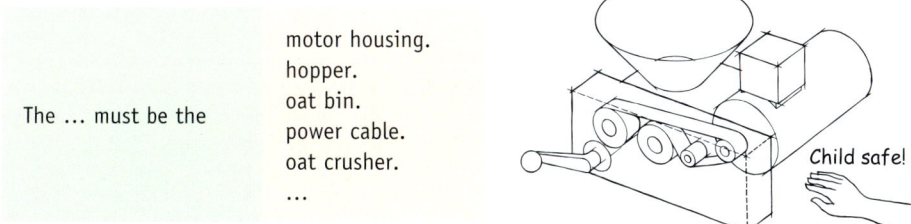

Child safe!

139

UNIT 14

Language

Forms and shapes

2-D shapes

shape	noun	adjective
	square	square
	rectangle	rectangular
	triangle	triangular
	circle	circular
	semi-circle	semi-circular
	–	convex
	–	concave

3-D shapes

shape	noun	adjective
	cube	cubic
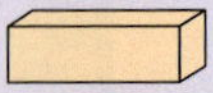	rectangular solid	rectangular
	cylinder	cylindrical
	sphere	spherical
	hemisphere	hemispherical
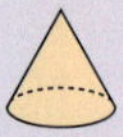	cone	conical

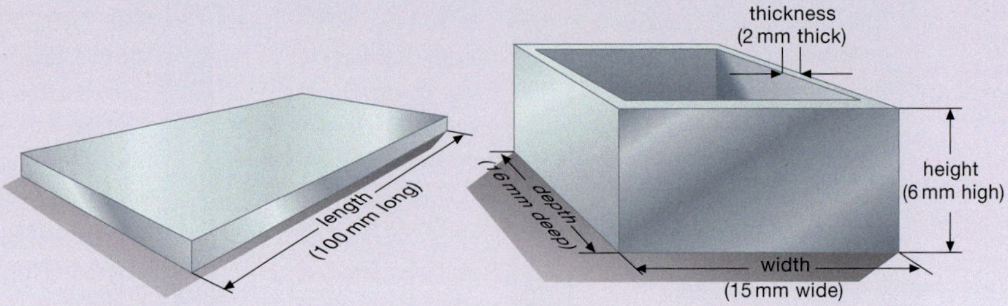

length (100 mm long)

thickness (2 mm thick)
depth (6 mm deep)
height (6 mm high)
width (15 mm wide)

b Describe the requirements of the system by completing the following sentences.

1 The hopper   should be able to be wall mounted.
2 The power supply   must be child safe.
3 The oat crusher   should be portable.
4 The machine   has to be 230 v AC.
5 The oat crusher   has to hold a minimum of 2 litres of oats.

c Discuss other characteristics you think the new oat crusher should have. Use the following sentence patterns.

| I think the new machine should be
I don't think the new machine needs to be | maintenance free
easy to operate
very cheap
robust
rustproof
quiet
… | because … |

UNIT **14**

5 Construction of the oat crusher

a Match the following technical terms with the definitions (A–I) below.

> rollers • torque • hopper • casing • belt drive • handwheel • switch • brackets • slip

- a a covering that protects components in a machine; a synonym for 'housing'
- b a device which is fixed to a wall and can support a piece of machinery
- c metal tubes placed close together which turn towards each other and crush grains of cereal by forcing them into the space between them
- d a wheel that can be turned by hand and which adjusts or moves some component
- e a V-shaped container open at both ends which feeds grain into a machine
- f a band of rubber or leather which is used to rotate components in machine
- g a device for turning electrical power to a machine on or off
- h a twisting force that causes things to rotate
- i to fail to grip something tightly

b Archie from Chodiltech presents the first version of the oat crusher to Rob Sefton, the manager of Grange Farm Livery Stables. Listen to their conversation and then identify the components 1–6 in the following illustration.

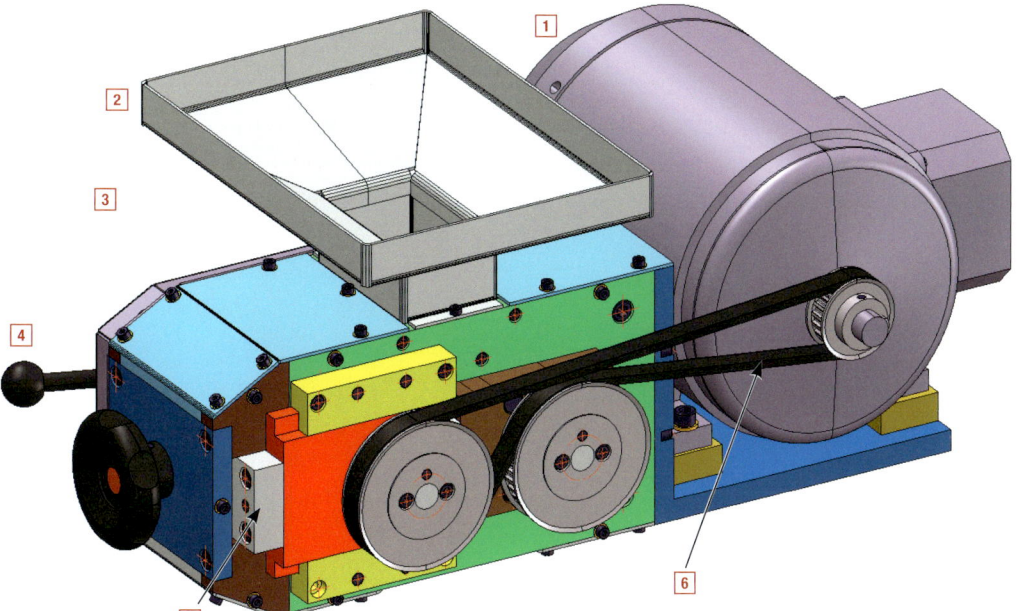

c Listen to Archie's presentation again and answer the following questions.

1. What is the power in kilowatts of the electric motor in Archie's design?
2. What is the voltage of the electric motor in the design?
3. How much torque in Newtonmetre does the 1.1 kW electric motor produce?
4. What is the volume in litres of the grain hopper in Archie's design?
5. What changes to the design does Rob Sefton suggest?

6 An ideal presentation?

Read the following presentation rules and then assess Archie's presentation. Which of the points did he get right? What did he do either badly or not at all?

THE RULES OF PRESENTATION

Organization
- Introduction
- Title slide
- Background information
- Statement of problem

Results/Discussion
- What was done
- What it means

Conclusion
- What was achieved
- What it means
- Have a clear ending for your talk so your colleagues will know it's time to clap.

Slides
- Have a title for each slide.
- Don't use too many different colours!
- Not too much information on a slide.
- Use bullets and very little text – tell the story with pictures.

Presentation
- Test your equipment before you start.
- Memorize the important points of your presentation – don't read it out word for word!
- Look at audience while you are talking.
- Point to the screen.
- Don't wave things about nervously or gesture too much.
- Don't stand in front of the overhead projector or beamer.
- Don't walk around too much.

Voice
- Practice speaking loudly, but not shouting.
- Don't speak too quickly.
- Speak clearly and confidently. Avoid saying "um" or "er".

Answering questions
- Don't give too many details or be overly specific.
- Answer the question asked. Don't try to show how much you know by answering questions that weren't asked!
- If the question is difficult, say: "That's a good question" and take time to think about it carefully before giving an answer.

(abridged: http://www.chemistry.mcmaster.ca/~chem4d3/4d3pres.htm)

UNIT **14**

7 Making a good presentation

Form groups of four and make your own multimedia presentation of the new oat crusher using the information from this unit. One student from each group gives the presentation and the members of the other groups listen and ask (critical) questions.

> **Grammar**
>
> ### The comparative and superlative forms of adjectives and adverbs
>
> 1 When the gap between the rollers is **smaller**, the oats are crushed **more thinly**.
> 2 The motor in the revised design is **more powerful** than in the first version.
> 3 The smooth belt drive worked **well** enough, but the toothed belt drive worked **better**; it was the **best** way of preventing slip.
>
> ⚠ bad – worse – worst ⚠ little – less – least
>
> - Einsilbige Adjektive sowie zweisilbige Adjektive, die auf *y* enden, werden gesteigert, indem man *er* oder *est* an das Wort anhängt. (1)
> - Adverbien, die auf *ly* enden, werden mit *more* oder (*the*) *most* bzw. *less* oder (*the*) *least* gesteigert. (1)
> - Adjektive mit zwei oder mehr Silben werden mit *more* oder (*the*) *most* bzw. *less* oder (*the*) *least* gesteigert. (2)
> - Das Adjektiv *good* und das Adverb *well* haben die gleichen unregelmäßigen Steigerungsformen. (3)
>
> Achten Sie auf die Rechtschreibung: *thin – thi**nn**er, big – bi**gg**er, heavy – heav**i**er*

8 Practice

Fill in the correct form of the adjectives in brackets.

1 The construction team for the new oat crusher tried to find the … (good) solution for each task.
2 They decided that a stand-alone motor would work … (good) than a flange motor.
3 They decided that construction steel was the … (suitable) material for the casing.
4 The new oat crusher had to be not only … (robust) than the old machine, but also … (easy) to operate.
5 It also had to work … (efficiently) than the old one.
6 Some grains are … (thick) than others and this makes them … (difficult) to crush.
7 When the gap between the rollers is … (wide), the oats can be crushed … (quick).
8 When the gap between the rollers is … (narrow), the oats can be crushed … (quick).
9 When the gap between the rollers is at its … (wide), the oats can be crushed … (quick).
10 The electric motor in the first design version was … (powerful) than the one used in the final construction.
11 In the revised design the team made the hopper … (big).
12 The team decided that a … (powerful) motor and a toothed belt drive was the … (good) way of preventing slip.

Extra material

The Chodiltech oat crusher user's guide

The Chodiltech Oat crusher is designed and built to give many years of service. Before the first use, clean the crusher with a dry cloth. THE ROLLERS MUST REMAIN DRY – DO NOT WASH. Use only grain which has been cleaned of all impurities. **The guarantee does not cover damage caused by foreign bodies (i. e. pieces of metal or plastic, sand, grit, etc.).**

Always close the lid of the hopper while grinding, as large grains can fly out of the hopper. Always disconnect the machine from the power outlet when not in use, before removing or replacing components and before cleaning. Never use harsh abrasive cleansers or aggressive chemicals cleaners. Clean components carefully with a soft cloth or a nylon brushes. Never use a wire brush. Avoid all contact with moving parts. Never put your hand into either the discharge opening or the hopper. Never put a hard object in the hopper while the machine is operating. **Inappropriate handling will invalidate the guarantee.**

Specially designed mounting brackets are available for wall mounting.

1 Operational and maintenance advice

Beantworten Sie die folgenden Fragen zu der Gebrauchsanleitung auf Deutsch.

1. Was ist vor dem ersten Gebrauch zu tun?
2. Was ist von der Garantie ausgeschlossen?
3. Warum darf während des Quetschvorgangs nicht in den Fülltrichter geblickt werden?
4. Was ist bei der Reinigung zu beachten?
5. Wie soll die Haferquetsche an der Wand befestigt werden?

2 Warranty conditions

Fill in the gaps 1–10 in the warranty conditions below with the following words.

crate • defect • expires • foreign bodies • misuse • order number • padding • prepaid • replace • within

Choldiltech oat crusher: LIMITED WARRANTY

Chodiltec, Ltd. agrees to repair or …¹ any defective product or part at their expense, provided the oat crusher is returned with …² freight costs. This warranty is non-transferable. This warranty does not apply to damage incurred through negligence, …³, faulty packing or mishandling in transit by the carrier or damage caused by …⁴ in the grain. Missing or damaged components must be reported …⁵ two weeks of receipt of the oat crusher. The warranty covers only the original components and …⁶ in total if these are replaced with non-original parts.

SHOULD SERVICE BE REQUIRED:
1. Carefully pack the oat crusher in the original …⁷ or any other suitable container with sufficient protective …⁸ to avoid damage to the product during transport.
2. Please quote the …⁹ and the date of purchase together with a note describing the …¹⁰.

15

Optimizing a technical system

1 Improving the design

a In Unit 14 the Chodiltech team produced an initial design for an oat crusher and showed it to Rob Sefton, the manager of Grange Farm Livery Stables. What changes did he want and why?

| He wanted | a more powerful motor
a bigger hopper
a toothed belt
wall brackets | so that it would
so that it wouldn't
because
so that it could | slip.
be fixed to a wall.
start more reliably.
tired horses need more food. |

b Look at the following revised design for the oat crusher and the 3D-drawings and descriptions on the opposite page. Which construction option do you think that the Chodiltech team chose. Explain why. The words and phrases in the box below may help you.

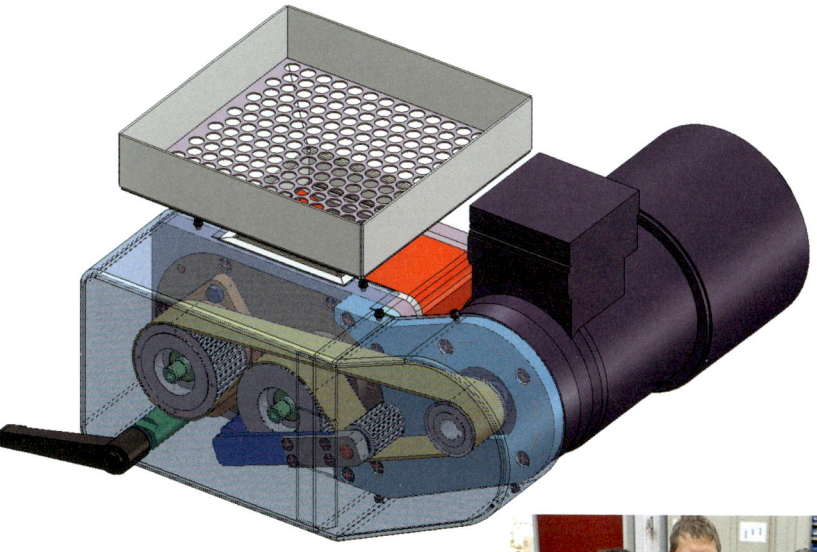

They decided to use the ... because it was ...
After discussing the advantages and disdvantages, the team chose the ...
They agreed that ... was more important than ... and chose ...

145

UNIT 15

guiding slide: advantages: – high precision – no slackness, i.e. too much play – can be adjusted precisely disadvantages: – sensitive to dirt and dust	**excentric adjustment:** advantages: – simple parts to manufacture – insensitive to dirt disadvantages: – less adjustment precision
gear drive: advantages: – prefabricated parts can be used disadvantages: – axis-centre distance for different grain sizes can't be changed easily	**toothed belt drive:** advantages: – smooth operation – simple reversion of rotation disadvatages: – belt tightener necessary
stand alone motor: advantages: – cost-effective disadvantages: – complex motor mounting bracket necessary	**flange motor:** advantages: – can be fixed on a simple motor bracket disadvantages: – expensive
Sheet metal belt guard: advantages: – sturdy disadvantages: – not every shape is possible – heavy – lots of screws or rivets for fixing necessary	**3D-printer plastic belt guard:** advantages: – different colours possible – lightweight disadvantages: – less sturdy – expensive

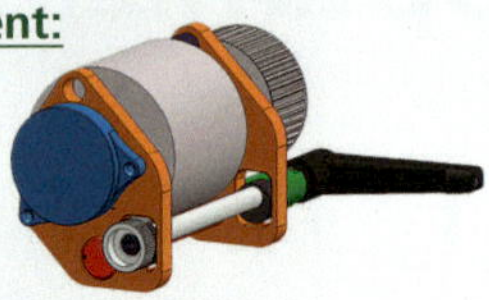

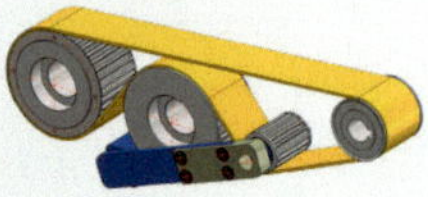

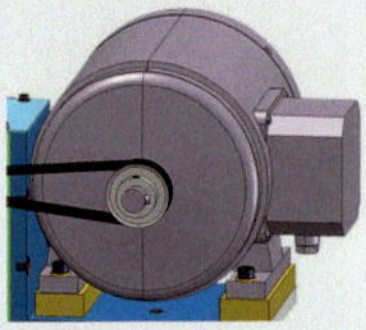

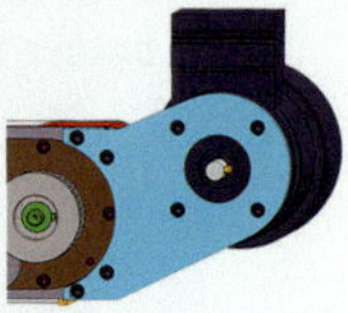

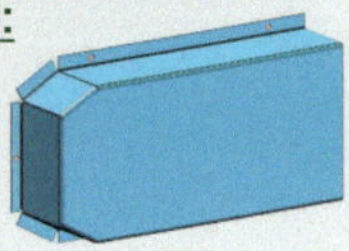

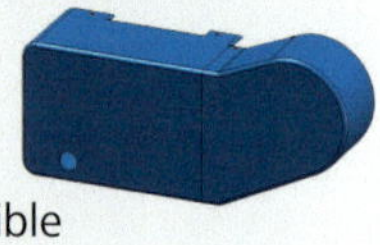

c There is no such thing as a perfect machine. Every machine is a compromise – a 'trade off' between competing factors such as price, weight, stability, reliability, etc. Form groups of four and decide which factors you think are important for an oat crusher on a U.S. ranch. Decide how to construct it and produce a design. Present your design to the other groups.

COMPETING FACTORS

reliability
durability
power
portability
low maintenance
safety, childproof
ease of operation

material costs
manufacturing costs
operational costs
weight
dimensions
simplicity
…

> We think … is / are more important for a ranch than …

> … is probably less important on a ranch than …

2 Safety stickers and technical data

a These four safety signs had to be applied to the Chodiltech machine before shipping. Explain what they mean in English.

b A plate containing important technical information is also screwed onto the casing of the oat crusher. Use a dictionary to translate the information into English.

Motordaten:
Antriebsleistung: 1,1 kW

Motordrehzahl: 1350 1/min
Nennspannung: 230 V; 50 Hz
Nennstrom: 5,2 A

Haferquetsche:
Außenmaße:
375 mm x 400 mm x 220 mm
Trichtervolumen: 2 l
Masse bei 2 l Hafer: 1,2 kg
Durchsatz: 36 kg/h

3 The Final Time Schedule

After completing the construction of the oat crusher, a Final Time Schedule was produced. This evaluates the planning by comparing the time planned for each phase with the time it actually took. Discuss the evaluation of the planning using the FTS on the opposite page.

- The exchange of ideas took exactly as long as was planned.
- The ... took ... days longer than was planned.
- The ... took ... fewer days than was planned.
- How long did the ... take?
- Did the ... go according to plan?
- The time estimated for the ... was accurate / reasonably accurate / inaccurate.

UNIT 15

oat crusher — Date

Task	May 3–6	May 7–11	May 12–18	May 19–25	May 26–31	June 1–9	June 10–16	June 17–25
1. Exchange of ideas	planned: 3–6; actual: 4–7							
2. Construction		planned: 7–11 (blue); actual: 5–12 (orange)						
3. Constr. changes			planned: 14–16; actual: 17–21					
4. Component drawing				planned: 21–24 (blue); actual: 19–28 (orange)				
5. Operating Manual				planned: 23–24; actual: 24–31				
6. Ordering				planned: 18–19				
7. Production					planned: 28–June 3; actual: June 9–11			
8. Assembly & Commissioning						planned: 7–11 (blue); actual: 14–18 (orange)		
9. Presentation							planned: 14–18; actual: 21–25	

planned: ▇ (blue)   actual: ▇ (orange)

4 Another oat crusher

a Read the following text from an Internet website and find the English equivalents of these German words:

1. Mischfutter, 2. Getreide, 3. verschleißfest, 4. Quetschgut, 5. Halter,
6. Zahnräder, 7. Schnellversteller, 8. Metallseparator, 9. Zugriff,
10. Strommessgerät, 11. wartungsfrei

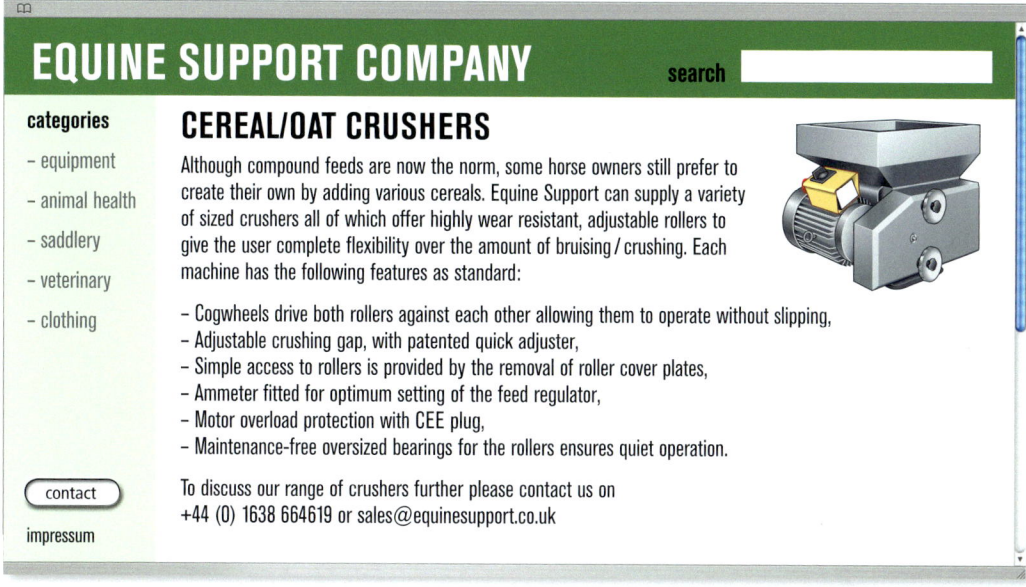

b Schreiben Sie eine E-Mail an Equine Support und fragen Sie nach …

- einer Wandhalterung oder einem Ständer für die Haferquetsche,
- einem automatischen Metallteile-Entferner,
- der Spannung mit der der Motor betrieben wird,
- die Stromstärke mit der der Motor abgesichert werden muss.

5 An Internet auction

a A second-hand oat crusher is being offered on an Internet auction site. The questions (1–6) on the opposite page are from potential buyers. They are all written in a very informal language. The answers to the questions (a–f) are mixed up. Rewrite them in the correct order.

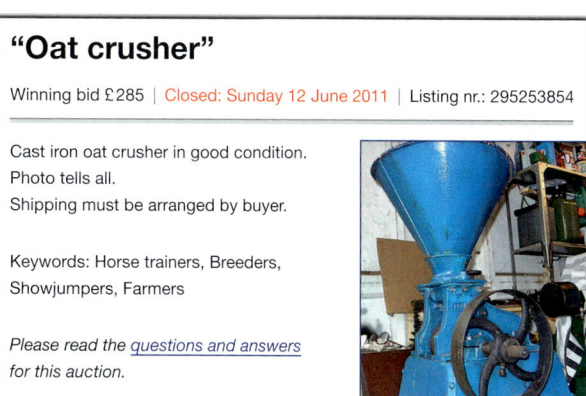

"Oat crusher"

Winning bid £285 | Closed: Sunday 12 June 2011 | Listing nr.: 295253854

Cast iron oat crusher in good condition.
Photo tells all.
Shipping must be arranged by buyer.

Keywords: Horse trainers, Breeders, Showjumpers, Farmers

Please read the questions and answers for this auction.

UNIT 15

Q 1 Hi there! Is the motor single phase? cheers **norm13** (652 ⭐) 8:16 am, Mon 7 Jun	A (a) Hi. I have no idea as I don't use it – that's why it's for sale. Thanks. 9:43 pm, Thu 10 Jun
Q 2 Would it crush barley **ginny222** (6 ⭐) 8:44 am, Mon 7 Jun	A (b) Hi. The rollers can be adjusted by the lever on the front, it was mainly used to crush oats but dad also put barley through it. Thanks. 8:10 pm, Sun 13 Jun
Q 3 Hello, I am very interested in the crusher. Could I please come and have a look at it and put some barley through it. My ph. no. is 021 215-2265. Thanks **savvyup** (14 ⭐⭐) 6:41 pm, Mon 7 Jun	A (c) Hi Yes. No problem. 1:51 pm, Mon 7 Jun
Q 4 Hi there. If the hopper was full of barley or wheat, how long would it take to crush? Cheers **dogbond** (62 ⭐⭐⭐) 8:54 pm, Thu 10 Jun	A (d) Sure. I'll call on you back this evening. 8:20 pm, Wed 9 Jun
Q 5 Hi there! Can you tell me the part of town for pick up please **norm13** (652 ⭐) 2:00 pm, Sat 12 Jun	A (e) Hi. Pick up is Leeston. Thanks. 11:24 am, Sun 13 Jun
Q 6 I am interested but you say you have not used it, yet you say it will crush barley?? How do you know ?? Cheers **stacker59** (18 ⭐⭐) 7:34 pm, Sun 13 Jun	A (f) Hi! Yes the motor is single phase. Thanks. 1:50 pm, Mon 7 Jun

b Now join in the chat room and ask questions in English about the following.

- ob der Anschluss an 400V möglich ist?
- die Füllmenge des Trichters?
- ob es eine Abdeckung für die Riemenscheibe gibt?
- …?

Question tags with the verb *be*

1 Emily **is** a useful member of the team, **isn't she?**
2 This **isn't** the best solution to the problem, **is it?**
3 I'**m not** making a mistake, **am I?**
4 I'**m** giving the presentation, **aren't I?**
5 Tom **was** in a hurry, **wasn't he?**

„Frageanhängsel" werden verwendet, wenn man auf eine Frage eine Bestätigung erwartet. Sie entsprechen der Wendung *nicht wahr?* bzw. *oder?* im Deutschen.

- Ein bejahter Satz wird im Frageanhängsel verneint (1), ein verneinter Satz bejaht. (2, 3)
- Bei *I'm* ist das verneinte Frageanhängsel unregelmäßig. (4)
- Das Verb im Frageanhängsel bekommt die gleiche Zeitform wie das Verb im Hauptsatz. (5)

6   Practice

Complete the sentences with the correct question tag.

1 We aren't going to give another presentation, ...?
2 You're going to choose the belt drive, ...?
3 I think I'm the oldest trainee on the team, ...?
4 Fred was a very competent engineer, ...?
5 Anna isn't very happy with the result, ...?
6 Daniel and Emily were going to write the report, ...?
7 This isn't the best time for a meeting, ...?
8 That's my notebook, ...?

Wie lese ich einen schwierigen Text?

Wenn Sie längere, schwierige Texte lesen, ist es wichtig zu wissen, worauf Sie Wert legen: auf ein allgemeines Textverständnis oder auf ein detailliertes Verständnis bestimmter Textabschnitte oder des ganzen Textes.

Wählen Sie die Lesetechnik, die Sie am besten ans Ziel bringt.

1 Vorwissen abklären als Vorbereitung auf das Lesen

Bevor Sie einen schwierigen Text lesen, sollten Sie sich vergegenwärtigen, was Sie bereits zur Thematik wissen.

2 Schnelles Lesen zum Erfassen des allgemeinen Textverständnisses

Verschaffen Sie sich einen ersten Eindruck vom Text, indem Sie sich zunächst die Überschrift, evtl. auch Zeichnungen und Bilder ansehen und dann den Text rasch überfliegen.

3 Selektives Lesen zum Erfassen wichtiger Textabschnitte

Nach dem ersten Lesen merkt man oft, dass nur ein Teil des Textes wichtig ist. Suchen Sie den Text nur auf die Gesichtspunkte oder Fakten ab, die Sie interessieren.

4 Genaues Lesen zum Erfassen des Detailverständnisses

Wollen Sie bei einem schwierigen Fachtext den Zusammenhang, Fakten oder einzelne Wörter genau verstehen, müssen Sie den Text oder die entsprechenden Textabschnitte langsam, Satz für Satz lesen. Ein Wörter- oder Fachwörterbuch sollte auch hier nur dann zu Rate gezogen werden, wenn Sie alle sprachlichen Differenzierungen verstehen wollen.

5 Den Text strukturieren und grafisch veranschaulichen

Wenn Sie sich den Textinhalt effektiv einprägen wollen, sollten Sie ihn strukturieren (z. B. indem Sie wesentliche Textstellen durch Markierung hervorheben) und grafisch veranschaulichen (z. B. indem Sie die wichtigsten Aussagen ineiner Mind Map festhalten).

6 Umgang mit unbekannten Wörtern

Schlagen Sie nur dann unbekannte Wörter im Wörterbuch nach, wenn das Wort aus dem Satzzusammenhang nicht erschlossen werden kann und für das Textverständnis unabdingbar ist.

UNIT 15

Extra material

A riding holiday in Scotland

Lisa and Anthony are planning a riding holiday in the Scottish Highlands in the summer. Look at the website text below and write a list in German of the information it provides about food, accomodation and outdoor activities, particularly riding.

Essen	Übernachtung	Aktivitäten	Reiten
– exzellentes Essen aus der Region	– Buchung mit und ohne Übernachtung möglich	– Golf	– pro Tag mit Ü/F £210

Riding Holidays UK ~ Horse Riding Holidays Scotland

Your exclusive horse riding holiday

At Auchencairn House you will enjoy the finest hospitality throughout your stay and excellent local food served in style. All our riding holidays are designed for small parties of 2–6 people. Non-riders are welcome and can explore our undiscovered corner of Scotland with golf, fishing and mountain biking as alternative entertainment. Non-riders can also meet their partners each day for their gourmet picnic lunch.

Other horse riding options

If you are touring Scotland or visiting relatives you can stop off here for a day's riding with or without accommodation. The route will follow the spectacular coast going east or west with cliff tops and beach rides, breaking for a picnic lunch after approximately 10 miles. Lunch will be outdoors if possible. If the weather is poor we will have lunch round the kitchen table.

The terrain throughout varies from beach to quiet roads, hills, fields and tracks. The breathtaking views speak for themselves and we will take time to enjoy the wealth of flora and fauna along the route. There will be opportunities to alter the pace of the ride, you can walk, trot, canter and gallop at various stages. There are plenty of cross-country jumps en-route for those seeking more excitement!

At the end of the day, riders and non-riders will get a welcome cream tea before departure.

In the evening the horses are turned out in a field for the night and you will again enjoy a fine dinner and comfortable night back at Auchencairn House.

Your Accommodation

Your horse riding holiday includes bed and breakfast, luxury picnic or barbecue lunch and three course dinner. You will be staying at Auchencairn House, the family home of your hosts Piet and Sue Gilroy. Throughout your stay you will dine on the finest local produce (all included). Our attention to detail helps to ensure that your holiday is second to none. The spacious accommodation comprises:

- 2 double rooms
- 2 twin rooms
- 1 single room

All rooms have adjacent bathroom facilities.

You will stay at our base at Auchencairn House. Here you can enjoy the genuine experience of a working Estate in an untouched area of beaches, woodland, hills, fields and dramatic coastal views. Set in its own impressive grounds near the idyllic coastal village of Auchencairn, and with spectacular views across Auchencairn Bay, this is a quiet oasis you will want to return to again and again.

Contact us for availability and to book your horse riding holiday.

I can ...

A Rezeption

Ich kann Produktbeschreibungen verstehen.

1 Lesen Sie den Text auf Seite 134 (Unit 13, Exercise 6) nochmals durch und sagen Sie, ob die folgenden Aussagen richtig oder falsch sind.

1. The SIMATIC IPCs have to pass more than fifty tests.
2. SIMATIC components can be used outside, even in the European winter.
3. The SIMATIC ET 200 can be submerged in water for a short time.
4. The SIMATIC ET 200 can function even if it is covered in metallic, conductive dust.
5. The control units aren't designed for heavy industrial use and must be treated with care.

B Interaktion

Ich kann auf einer Messe Gespräche führen.

2 Sie befinden sich auf einer Messe und führen ein Gespräch zu einer großen Haferquetsche. Dabei werden Fragen zu technischen Details gestellt und beantwortet.

Kunde Fragen Sie nach ...	Vertreter Antworten Sie in ganzen Sätzen.
– der notwendigen Spannung,	– 400 V
– der Leistung,	– 3 kW
– der Drehzahl,	– 1500 rpm
– dem Volumen des Fülltrichters,	– 4 litres
– dem Gewicht der Haferquetsche.	– 24 kg

C Produktion

Ich kann technische Details per E-Mail erfragen.

3 Schreiben Sie eine E-Mail an support@horsegadgets.co.uk und fragen Sie nach den folgenden Dingen.

- Gibt es einen Ständer, um die Haferquetsche auf den Boden zu stellen?
- Sind die Rollen gehärtet?
- Ist die Riemenabdeckung aus Kunststoff oder Blech?
- Gibt es die Haferquetsche auch in anderen Farben außer Blau?
- Wieviel kostet der Transport an Ihren Heimatort?
- Kann man das Gerät auch selber abholen?

D Mediation

Ich kann technische Details auf Deutsch zusammenfassen.

4 Fassen Sie die sechs Merkmale der Haferquetsche auf Seite 145 (Unit 15, Exercise 4a) auf Deutsch zusammen.

Pairwork files

File 1   Unit 2, Exercise 5

Partner A:

Describe the specifications of the different boring bars to your partner and find the differences between the two catalogues.

Start like this:
Let's start with size B00. In my catalogue the price for form G and form F is the same: 36 Euros and 8 cents. The boring depth is 10 mil. What is it in yours?

Hoffmann Catalogue

Boring bars for bores from 2.5 mm ø

HSS
Co10 P20
Version: Microscopically tested, precise cutting profile.
Cost-efficient due to multiple regrinding of the cutting face.
Tool material:
24 0074/0078/0084 – HSS/Co10 – for difficult to machine materials

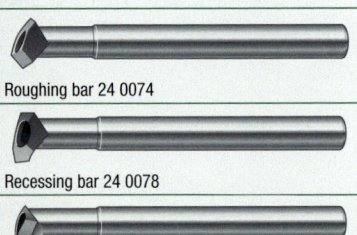

Roughing bar 24 0074

Recessing bar 24 0078

Internal thread boring bar 24 0084

Size = (L = long)	24 0074 Roughing bar Form g HSS/Co10	24 0078 Recessing bar Form f HSS/Co10	24 0084 Internal thread boring bar HSS/Co10	Boring depth 24 0074 24 0078	For bores from ø	Overall length	Shank ø
	€	€	€	mm	mm	mm	mm
B00	36.08	36.08	–	10	2.5	50	8
B01	36.08	36.08	37.12	20	3	60	8
B02	37.82	37.82	39.90	24	5	60	8
B02L	–	57.65	–	24	5	125	8
B03	39.09	39.09	40.72	26	7	65	8
B03L	–	59.16	–	26	7	125	8
B04	44.31	44.31	46.40	45	9	75	8
B04L	62.64	62.64	–	80	9	125	8
B05	53.71	53.71	57.19	50	12	80	8
B05L	74.24	74.24	78.88	80	12	125	8
B06	73.08	73.08	76.56	60	14	95	10
B06L	93.96	93.96	98.60	90	14	125	10

File 2 Unit 4, Exercise 10

Partner A:
Listen to your partner describe an electric circuit for controlling the direction of rotation in an electric motor and draw a diagram of the circuit and its components on the blackboard. You can refer to this rough sketch, but be careful: it isn't accurate!

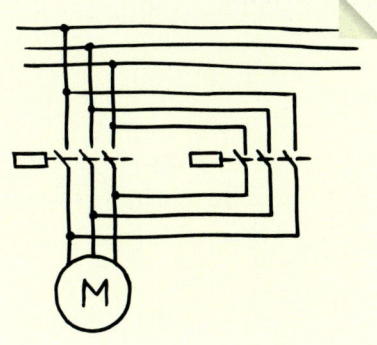

File 3 Unit 6, Exercise 5

Partner A:
Complete your list by asking your partner questions.

For example:
What is the width of the SL 18 2220?

Use your table to answer your partner's questions.

SL18 22 Series Semi Locating Full Complement Cylindrical Roller Bearings

Bearing Reference	Dimensions			Load Rating		Mass
	Bore	OD	Width	Dynamic	Static	Kg
SL18 2220	100	180		395000	550000	5.20
SL18 2222	110		53	455000	625000	7.30
SL18 2224		215	58	535000	765000	9.10
SL18 2226	130		64	625000	910000	11.30
SL18 2228	140	250	68	715000	1060000	
SL18 2230	150	270	73	820000	1225000	
SL18 2232	160	290		1010000	1535000	23.00
SL18 2234	170	310	86		1735000	28.70
SL18 2236	180	320	86		1835000	29.80
SL18 2238	190		92	1380000	2165000	35.70
SL18 2240	200		98	1510000	2335000	43.20
SL18 2244	230		108	1820000	2990000	57.00

PAIRWORK

File 4   Unit 7, Exercise 6b

Partner A:

You prefer pneumatics. Think about the advantages of pneumatics and the disadvantages of hydraulics and start a discussion.

Start like this:
One advantage of a pneumatic system is that air is easily available.

Advantages of Pneumatic Systems

- Air is easily available
- Fast response
- Air is non-flammable

Disadvantages of Hydraulic Systems

- Fluid might leak out
- Fluid flow speed is limited
- Pipes are complicated
- Working fluid is often flammable.

File 5   Unit 8, Exercise 5

Partner A:

You work for DMG and you are at their stand at the Metavak Trade Fair in the Netherlands.

Use the following excerpt from a brochure in German to answer questions from potential customers in English.

HSC 75/105 linear – Vollautomatischer Palettenwechsel durch das Portal.

Die HSC 75 linear und HSC 105 linear sind beide optional mit einem 20-fach-Palettenspeicher erhältlich. Auf standardisierten Palettenträgern können Bauteile bis zu 100 kg Handlingsgewicht vollautomatisch ein- und ausgewechselt werden. Zum Erreichen kürzester Bereitstellungszeiten lässt sich das System durch das innovative 180-fach Werkzeugmagazin ergänzen.

HSC75/105 linear mit Palettenspeicher
- Palettenspeicher für 20 Werkstücke für HSC 75/105 linear:
  – Vollautomatische Wechsel der Paletten durch das Portal,
  – Palettengröße 320 x 320 mm, Transfergewicht bis 100 kg.
- Geringer Platzbedarf und uneingeschränkte Zugänglichkeit zur einfachen Bestückung.
- Modulares Palettenmagazin mit Transfergewicht bis 500 kg.
- Werkzeugmagazin mit bis zu 180 Plätzen.

PAIRWORK

File 6 Unit 9, Exercise 5b

Partner A:

You are a receptionist at the Narai Hotel and you are filling in the the following registration form for a guest who is checking in. Ask your partner for the information you need to fill in the form.

Then swap roles with your partner. Now you are the guest and you must give the receptionist the necessary information.

NARAI HOTEL — Registration Form

Guest Name: surname _____ First name _____

Arrival Date: day / month / year _____ Departure Date: day / month / year _____

No. of Rooms: Room Type: ☐ single ☐ double (one bed) ☐ twin (2 beds)

Address _____

City _____ Country _____

Tel _____ Fax _____

E-mail _____

Name of Credit Card Holder _____

Credit card number _____ Exp. date: month / year _____

Card type: ☐ Visa ☐ Mastercard ☐ Diners Club ☐ American Express

Signature _____ Date: day / month / year _____

Partner B:

You are checking into the Narai Hotel. Give the receptionist the information he or she needs to fill in the registration form. Then swap roles with your partner.

PAIRWORK

File 7 Unit 10, Exercise 8b

Partner A:

You work for a technical hotline service. Answer the call from Partner B and then transfer the call to partner C.

File 8 Unit 2, Exercise 5

Partner B:

Describe the specifications of the different boring bars to your partner and find the differences between the two catalogues.

Start like this:
Size B00. Well, in mine the prices for the F and G forms are the same, but the boring depth is 12 mil. Let's have a look at Size B01 ...

Toolhouse Catalogue

Boring bars for bores from 2.5 mm ø

HSS
Co10 P20
Version: Microscopically tested, precise cutting profile.
Cost-efficient due to multiple regrinding of the cutting face.
Tool material:
24 0074/0078/0084 – HSS/Co10 – for difficult to machine materials

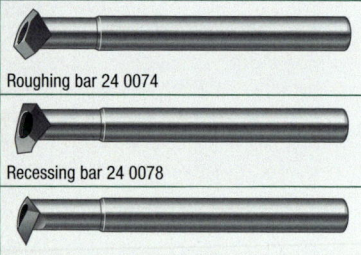

Roughing bar 24 0074

Recessing bar 24 0078

Internal thread boring bar 24 0084

Size = (L = long)	24 0074 Roughing bar Form g HSS/Co10	24 0078 Recessing bar Form f HSS/Co10	24 0084 Internal thread boring bar HSS/Co10	Boring depth 24 0074 24 0078	For bores from ø	Overall length	Shank ø
	€	€	€	mm	mm	mm	mm
B00	36.08	36.08	–	12	2.5	50	8
B01	36.08	36.08	37.12	20	4	60	8
B02	37.82	38.72	39.90	24	5	60	8
B02L	–	–	57.65	24	5	125	8
B03	39.09	39.09	40.72	24	7	65	8
B03L	–	59.16	–	26	7	135	8
B04	44.31	44.31	46.40	46	9	75	8
B04L	62.64	62.64	–	80	10	125	8
B05	53.71	57.19	53.71	50	12	80	8
B05L	74.24	74.24	78.88	80	12	125	10
B06	73.08	73.08	76.56	80	14	95	10
B06L	93.96	93.96	98.60	90	14	125	12

File 9 Unit 4, Ex. 10

Partner B:

Listen to your partner describe an electric circuit for controlling the direction of rotation in an electric motor and draw a diagram of the circuit and its components on the blackboard. You can refer to this rough sketch, but be careful: it isn't accurate!

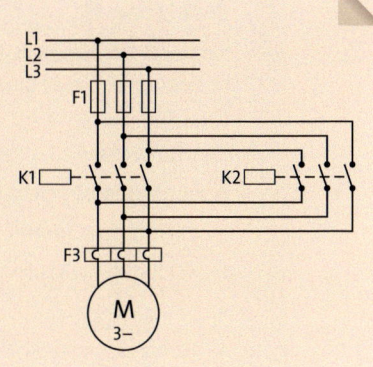

File 10 Unit 6, Exercise 5

Partner B:

Complete your list by asking your partner questions.

For example:
What is the loading mass of the SL 18 2220?

Use your table to answer your partner's questions.

	Bore	OD	Width	Dynamic	Static	Kg
SL18 2220	100	180	46	395000	550000	
SL18 2222	110	200	53	455000		7.30
SL18 2224	120	215	58		765000	9.10
SL18 2226	130	230	64			11.30
SL18 2228	140	250	68	715000	1060000	14.50
SL18 2230		270	73	820000	1225000	18.50
SL18 2232		290	80	1010000	1535000	23.00
SL18 2234	170	310	86	1125000	1735000	
SL18 2236	180	320	86	1165000	1835000	
SL18 2238	190	340		1380000	2165000	35.70
SL18 2240	200	360	98			43.20
SL18 2244	230	400	108	1820000	2990000	

PAIRWORK

File 11   Unit 7, Exercise 6b

Partner B:

You prefer hydraulics. Look at the advantages of hydraulics and the disadvantages of pneumatics and start a discussion.

Start like this:
One advantage of a hydraulic system is that it has a high output force.

Advantages of Hydraulic Systems
- High output force
- Accurate hydraulic pressure
- No corrosion
- Continuous variable transmission

Disadvantages of Pneumatic Systems
- Output force is limited
- Compressibility of air
- Corrosion may occur
- Pipe length is limited

File 12   Unit 8, Exercise 5

Partner B:

You are a visitor at the Metavak fair in the Netherlands. At the DMG stand, a manufacturer of high-speed cutting systems, you are interested in the HSC 75/105 because of the automatic pallet exchange. Ask your partner:

- if the pallet storage comes automatically with the HSC 75/105
- what the maximum weight of the workpieces in the pallet storage is
- what size the pallets are
- how many tools the magazine can hold

File 13 Unit 10, Exercise 8b

Partner C:

You are a specialist in the Technical Department of a hotline service. Use the following troubleshooting chart and phrases from the dialogue on page 104 to advise callers.

Types of machine fault

Fault	Possible causes		
	Squirrel cage motors	Slip-ring motors	Direct current motors
Motor fails to start, no noise	Cable break. No power. Failure of line protection devices, windings defective.		
		Starter defective or damaged.	
			Field rheostat defective.
Motor fails to start, loud buzzing noise	Bearing damaged. One phase interuppted e. g. one fuse blown.		
Motor fails to start under load	Countertorque too high. Line voltage too low.		
Motor starts jerkily			Interruption in starter. Armature winding short. Core short.
Motor does not pull properly under load	Feed cable break, overloading.		
	Rotor bars broken. Short-circuit rings loose.	Break in rotor circuit.	Brushes wrongly adjusted. Voltage drops.
Motor races and hunts under load			Brushes wrongly adjusted. Field current circuit interrupted or drop resistor too large. Wrong wiring.
Motor heats up too much during operation	Motor on overload. Voltage too high or too low. Motor only on one phase. Rotor rubs stator.		Overload. Short-circuited windings. Cooling faulty.
Motor heats up even in no-load operation	Stator windings wrongly connected. Line voltage too high. Inadequate cooling. Incorrect direction of rotation (if motor is designed to run in one direction only).		
Localized heating	Short circuit between turns. Winding breaks.		
Brushes spark (observe air humidity)		Brushes not making proper contact. Brush pressure too low. Dirt accumulation. Wrong type of brushes.	
		Slip-rings out of true.	Commutator out of true. Commutator grooved. Brushes damaged. Core short. Overloading. Excessive speed.
Motor sounds abnormal	Electrical causes (disappear when motor is switched off). Bearing damage. Damaged gears. Damaged transmission. Out of balance. Changes in baseplate. Defect in gear drive.		

Basic word list

Diese Liste enthält ca 860 Grundwörter, die in *Metal Matters* als bekannt vorausgesetzt werden. Nicht aufgeführt, jedoch vorausgesetzt, sind einige elementare Wörter, wie Präpositionen, Pronomen, Zahlen und Wörter, die im Englischen und Deutschen die gleiche Bedeutung haben, wie z. B. *hotel, restaurant, hobby*.

A

able, to be ~ können, in der Lage sein
abroad im/ins Ausland
absolutely absolut, völlig
accept annehmen, akzeptieren
accident Zufall, Unfall
action Handlung
active aktiv(iert)
activity Tätigkeit, Aktivität
ad(vertisement) Werbung, Anzeige
add zusammenzählen, hinzufügen
addition, in ~ to zusätzlich zu
address Adresse; adressieren
advantage Vorteil
advice Ratschlag, (guter) Rat
afraid, I'm ~ leider
after (all) schließlich (doch)
afternoon Nachmittag
again wieder
age Alter
agree zustimmen, vereinbaren, sich einigen
aim Ziel, Absicht
air Luft
airport Flughafen
all alle(s)
allow erlauben, gestatten, (zu)lassen
almost fast, beinahe
alone allein(e)
along entlang
already schon, bereits
also auch, außerdem
alternatively alternativ
although obwohl
altogether insgesamt
always immer
among zwischen, unter
amount Menge, Betrag
angry wütend, verärgert
animal Tier
another noch eine/r/s
answer Antwort; (be)antworten
any irgendetwas, -welche, jede
anybody/anyone jemand, jede/r
anything etwas, alles
anyway jedenfalls, sowieso
anywhere irgendwo(hin)
apart from abgesehen von, außer
appendix Anhang
apprentice Auszubildende/r
area Gebiet, Bereich
arrange arrangieren, vereinbaren
arrival Ankunft
arrive ankommen, eintreffen
art Kunst

as well ebenso, auch
ask fragen, bitten
assistant Assistent/in
attend teilnehmen (an)
attractive attraktiv, reizvoll
average Durchschnitt
away weg, entfernt

B

back Rückseite, Rücken; zurück
bad schlecht, schlimm
bag Tasche, Tüte, Beutel
ball Kugel
basic einfach, grundlegend
basically grundsätzlich, im Grunde
because weil
become werden
before vor(her)
begin anfangen, beginnen
beginning Anfang
behind hinter, hinten
believe glauben
belong gehören
below unter, unten(stehend)
beneath unter(halb), unten
best beste, am besten
better besser
between zwischen
big groß
bike Fahrrad
birth Geburt
blue blau
body Körper
bone Knochen
book Buch; buchen, bestellen
bored gelangweilt
born geboren
boss Chef/in
both beide
bottle Flasche
bottom Unterseite, Unterteil, Boden
box Kasten, Kiste, Kästchen
boy Junge
bracket Klammer
break Pause
breakfast Frühstück
bring bringen, holen
broad breit
broken kaputt
brother Bruder
build bauen, errichten, aufbauen
building Gebäude
business Geschäft
busy beschäftigt, besetzt
button Taste, Knopf

buy kaufen
buyer Käufer/in

C

call Anruf; (an)rufen
caller Anrufer/in
can dürfen, können
cannot nicht können
canteen Kantine
car Auto
car park Parkplatz, Parkhaus
care, take ~ of sich kümmern um
careful(ly) vorsichtig, sorgfältig, genau
case Fall, Kiste
cash Bargeld
cause Ursache, Grund; verursachen
centre Zentrum, Mittelpunkt
certain(ly) sicher, gewiss, bestimmt
chain Kette
chair Stuhl
change (Ver-)Änderung; (aus)wechseln, (sich) ändern
cheap billig, günstig
check überprüfen, kontrollieren
cheque Scheck
child Kind
choice Wahl, Auswahl
choose (aus)wählen
city (Groß-)Stadt
class Klasse
classmate Klassenkamerad/in
clean sauber; reinigen, säubern
clear klar, deutlich
clever klug, intelligent
clock Uhr
close schließen, zumachen
close (to) nahe
clothes Kleidung, Kleider
coffee Kaffee
colleague Kollege, Kollegin
collect sammeln
collection Sammlung
college Fachhochschule
colour Farbe
combine verbinden, kombinieren
come kommen, geliefert werden
common üblich, gemeinsam
commonly häufig, gewöhnlich, üblicherweise
company Unternehmen, Gesellschaft
compare vergleichen
comparison Vergleich
complain sich beklagen, sich beschweren, reklamieren
complete vollständig; vervollständigen

completely völlig
complicated kompliziert
confirm bestätigen
connect (miteinander) verbinden, anschließen
construct bauen, konstruieren
contact Kontakt, Verbindung
contain enthalten
contents Inhalt
control Kontrolle; kontrollieren, regeln, steuern, überwachen
conversation Gespräch, Unterhaltung
copy Exemplar, Kopie; abschreiben, kopieren
corner Ecke
correct richtig, genau; korrigieren
cost Kosten; kosten
could konnte/n, könnte/n
count zählen
country Land, Staat
couple Paar
course Kurs, Lehrgang
create (er)schaffen, erstellen, herstellen
cross (an)kreuzen
culture Kultur
cup Tasse
current gegenwärtig, aktuell
customer Kunde, Kundin
cut Schnitt; schneiden

D
damage Schaden; beschädigen
danger Gefahr
dangerous gefährlich
dark Dunkelheit, dunkel
date Datum, Termin
date of birth Geburtsdatum
day Tag
dear liebe/r
decide entscheiden, beschließen
decision Entscheidung
definite(ly) (ganz) sicher, bestimmt
delay Verzögerung; verzögern
delete löschen
deliver (aus)liefern
delivery Zustellung, Lieferung
depend abhängen (von)
describe beschreiben
description Beschreibung, Schilderung
design Entwurf, Konstruktion, Gestaltung; entwerfen, konstruieren, gestalten
desk (Schreib-)Tisch, Arbeitsplatz
details Daten, Angaben
dialogue Gespräch, Dialog
diary (Termin-)Kalender
dictionary Wörterbuch
die sterben
difference Unterschied
different unterschiedlich, verschieden
difficult schwer, schwierig
dinner (Abend-)Essen
direct direkt, gerade
direction Richtung
dirt Schmutz

dirty schmutzig
disadvantage Nachteil, Schaden
disappear verschwinden
discover entdecken, feststellen
dislike nicht mögen
do tun, machen
door Tür
draw zeichnen
drawing Zeichnung
drink Getränk; trinken
driver Fahrer/in
during während

E
each jede/r/s
early früh
east Osten
easy, easily leicht, einfach
education Erziehung, (Aus-, Schul-) Bildung
effective effektiv
either entweder
electrical elektrisch, Strom-
electronic elektronisch
else andere/r/s
employ beschäftigen, einstellen
employee Arbeitnehmer/in, Beschäftigte/r
employer Arbeitgeber/in
empty leer
end Ende, Schluss; (be)enden
ending Ende
energy Energie
engineer Ingenieur/in, Techniker/in
enjoy genießen, gefallen, gern tun
enough ausreichend, genug
enquiry (An-)Frage, Untersuchung
environment Umwelt, Umfeld
environmental Umwelt-
equal gleich
especially besonders
essential (absolut) notwendig
even sogar (noch)
evening Abend
ever je(mals)
every jede/r/s
everybody jede/r
everyone jede/r/s, alle
everything alles
exactly exakt, genau
examine untersuchen
example Beispiel
excellent hervorragend, ausgezeichnet
excited aufgeregt, begeistert
exciting aufregend, spannend
exercise Übung
exercise book (Schul-)Heft
expect erwarten, annehmen
expensive teuer
experience Erfahrung
expert Fachmann/frau
extra zusätzlich
extreme äußerst, extrem
eye Auge

F
fact Tatsache
factory Fabrik
fairly ziemlich
false falsch
familiar vertraut, bekannt
family Familie
famous berühmt
far weit (entfernt)
fast schnell
feel (sich) fühlen, meinen, glauben
feeling Gefühl
female weiblich, Frauen-
(a) few ein paar, wenig/e
fight Kampf; (be)kämpfen
file Ordner, Datei
final letzte/r/s
finally schließlich, endlich
financial finanziell
find finden, suchen
find out herausfinden
fine gut, schön
finish (be)enden, abschließen, fertig werden
firm Firma
first(ly) erst; zuerst
fish Fisch
fishing Angeln
fix festlegen, reparieren
flat flach, eben
flight Flug
floor Etage, (Fuß-)Boden
fly fliegen
follow (be)folgen
(the) following der/die/das Folgende
food Essen, Nahrung
football Fußball
foreign ausländisch, Auslands-, fremd
forget vergessen
form Form, Formular; bilden, formen
formal(ly) förmlich, formell
forward nach vorne
free frei; gratis, kostenlos
friend Freund/in
friendly freund(schaft)lich
friendship Freundschaft
front Vorderseite
full voll
fully völlig
funny komisch, merkwürdig
further weitere
future Zukunft; (zu)künftig

G
gap Lücke, Spalt
gas Gas
general allgemein, generell, normal
generally im Allgemeinen, normalerweise
get holen, bekommen, werden
girl Mädchen
give geben
glad froh
go gehen, fahren
go on weitermachen, fortfahren
go out ausgehen

BASIC WORD LIST

good gut
goodbye auf Wiedersehen
grandparents Großeltern
great groß(artig)
greatly in großem Maße
green grün
greet (be)grüßen
greeting Gruß(formel), Begrüßung
ground Boden, Grund
group Gruppe; gruppieren
grow wachsen, werden
guarantee Garantie
guess Annahme; raten, schätzen
guest Gast

H

half Hälfte; halb
handle umgehen mit, bearbeiten, fertigwerden mit
happen passieren, geschehen
happy glücklich, zufrieden
health Gesundheit
hear hören
heart Herz
heavy schwer
height Höhe, Größe
help Hilfe; helfen
helpful hilfreich, nützlich
here hier
hide verbergen, verstecken
high; highly hoch; äußerst
hire mieten, leihen, anstellen
history Geschichte
hole Loch
holiday Ferien, Urlaub, Feiertag
home Zuhause, Heim; nach Hause
honest ehrlich, anständig
hope Hoffnung; hoffen
horse Pferd
hot heiß
hour Stunde
house Haus
how wie
however doch, jedoch
huge riesig
human menschlich

I

idea Vorstellung, Idee, Gedanke
ideally möglichst, im Idealfall
if wenn, falls, ob
immediately sofort, unverzüglich
important wichtig
impossible unmöglich
impressive beeindruckend
improve verbessern, sich bessern
include enthalten, umfassen
individual einzeln, individuell
industry Branche, Industrie
informal ungezwungen, inoffiziell, informell
information Auskunft, Information(en), Angaben
instead stattdessen
interest Interesse; interessieren
interested interessiert
interesting interessant
introduce (sich) vorstellen, (miteinander) bekannt machen, einführen
introduction Einleitung, Einführung, Vorstellung
invitation Einladung
invite einladen
invoice Rechnung
ironic ironisch

J

job Arbeit(sstelle), Aufgabe
just einfach, nur, genau

K

keep (be)halten
key Schlüssel, Taste
kind freundlich; Art, Sorte
knee Knie
knife Messer
know kennen, wissen
knowledge Wissen, Kenntnis(se)

L

lamp Lampe
language Sprache
large groß
last dauern; letzte/r/s
late spät
later später
latest neueste/r/s
law Gesetz
lead führen
learn lernen, erfahren
least, at ~ wenigstens
leave lassen, verlassen, ab-/wegfahren
left links; übrig
length Länge
less weniger, abzüglich
let erlauben, (zu)lassen
letter Buchstabe, Brief
level Ebene, Niveau
lie Lüge; (be)lügen
life Leben
lift Fahrstuhl, Aufzug
light Licht, Lampe; hell, leicht
like mögen; (ähnlich) wie
likely wahrscheinlich
limited beschränkt
line Linie, Leitung, Zeile
list Liste; auflisten, notieren
listen hören, zuhören
little klein, wenig
live wohnen, leben
load laden
local örtlich, lokal
located gelegen
location (Stand-)Ort, Lage
long lang
look Blick, Aussehen; (aus)sehen, blicken
look after sich kümmern um
look for suchen nach
look forward to sth sich auf etw freuen
lose verlieren
lots of/a lot of viel, viele
love Liebe; lieben, sehr gern mögen
low niedrig
lunch Mittagessen

M

machine Gerät, Maschine
main Haupt-, wichtigste/r/s
make machen
make sure sicherstellen, gewährleisten
male männlich
manage leiten, verwalten, regeln, (es) schaffen
many viele
map Karte, Plan
match zuordnen, (zusammen) passen
matter Angelegenheit, Sache
maximum Maximum; maximal
may dürfen, können, mögen
maybe vielleicht
meal Essen, Mahlzeit
mean bedeuten, meinen, heißen
meaning Bedeutung
mediation Vermittlung
medium mittlere; Medium, Mittel
meet (sich mit jdm) treffen, begegnen
meeting Sitzung, Besprechung, Treffen
memory Gedächtnis, Speicher
message Meldung, Nachricht
metal Metall
method Methode, Verfahren
middle Mitte, mittlere/r/s
might könnte(n) (vielleicht)
mile Meile
minimum Minimum; minimal
miss verpassen, vermissen
missing fehlende/r/s
mistake Fehler, Irrtum
mobile mobil
mobile (phone) Mobiltelefon, Handy
moment Augenblick, Moment
money Geld
month Monat
monthly monatlich
more mehr
morning Morgen
most der/die/das meiste, die meisten
mountain Berg
mouse Maus
move (sich) bewegen, umziehen
movement Bewegung
much viel
must müssen

N

name Name; nennen, benennen
national national, staatlich
nationality Staatsangehörigkeit
nearly beinahe, fast
necessary nötig, notwendig, erforderlich
need Bedarf, Bedürfnis; brauchen, benötigen
neighbour Nachbar/in

BASIC WORD LIST

neither ... nor weder ... noch
never nie(mals)
new neu
news Neuigkeit(en), Nachricht(en)
next nächste/r/s; danach
night Nacht
normal(ly) normal(erweise)
north Norden
note Notiz; beachten, notieren
nothing nichts
now nun, jetzt
nowadays heutzutage
number Nummer, Zahl

O

object Gegenstand
of course natürlich, selbstverständlich
offer Angebot; anbieten, bieten
office Büro
often oft, häufig
oil Öl
old alt
once einmal, einst; sobald
only nur, einzig
open öffnen; offen, geöffnet
opinion Meinung, Ansicht
opposite Gegenteil; gegensätzlich, gegenüber(liegend)
option Möglichkeit, Option
or oder
order bestellen
otherwise sonst
own eigene/r/s; besitzen

P

page Seite
pain Schmerz
paint Farbe
pair Paar
paper Papier, Zeitung
parents Eltern
part Teil, Bauteil
passport Pass
path Weg, Pfad
pay Lohn, Bezahlung; zahlen, bezahlen
per cent Prozent
perfect vollkommen, perfekt
perfectly völlig
perhaps vielleicht, eventuell
period Zeit(raum)
personal persönlich
phone Telefon; anrufen
photo Foto
phrase Redewendung, Satz(teil)
pick up aufheben, abholen
picture Bild
piece Stück, Teil
place Stelle, Platz; setzen, stellen
plain einfach
plane Flugzeug
plastic Plastik, Kunststoff
plenty viel, reichlich
point Punkt; Komma
poor arm, schlecht, mangelhaft
popular beliebt, populär

possibility Möglichkeit
possible möglich
power Kraft, Strom; antreiben
powerful mächtig, stark
practical praktisch
practice Praxis, Training
practise (ein)üben
prefer vorziehen, besser finden, mögen
preparation Vorbereitung
prepare (sich) vorbereiten, zubereiten, erstellen
present Gegenwart; Geschenk; gegenwärtig; vorstellen, präsentieren
press drücken
previous vorherige/r/s, frühere/r/s
price Preis
print Druck; drucken, ausdrucken
printer Drucker/in
printout (Computer-)Ausdruck
priority Vorrang
private privat, persönlich
probably wahrscheinlich
produce Produkt(e); produzieren, herstellen
product Produkt, Erzeugnis
production Produktion, Herstellung
promise versprechen
properly richtig
protect (be)schützen
protection Schutz
provide liefern, bieten
pub Kneipe, Gaststätte
pull ziehen
push schieben, drücken
put setzen, stellen, legen

Q

quality Qualität
quarter past/to Viertel nach/vor
question Frage
quick(ly) schnell
quite ziemlich, ganz

R

rapid schnell, rasch
rather than lieber/eher als
reach erreichen
read lesen
reader Leser/in
ready bereit, fertig
real echt, wirklich
really wirklich, eigentlich, tatsächlich
reason Vernunft, Grund
receive erhalten, empfangen, bekommen
recent aktuell, neu
recently neulich, kürzlich
recommend empfehlen
regular(ly) regelmäßig
relation Verwandte/r, Verhältnis
relative Verwandte/r, relativ
relatively relativ, verhältnismäßig
remain (ver)bleiben
remember sich erinnern, daran denken
remove entfernen
repair reparieren

repeat wiederholen
replace ersetzen, austauschen
report Bericht; melden, berichten
require benötigen, erfordern
reservation Reservierung, Buchung
response Reaktion, Antwort
responsible verantwortlich, zuständig
result Resultat, Ergebnis; folgen, resultieren
return zurückkehren, zurückgeben
right rechts, richtig
risk Risiko; riskieren
road (Land-)Straße
role Rolle
role play Rollenspiel
room Zimmer, Raum
round Runde; rund
rule Regel, Vorschrift
run laufen (lassen), betreiben

S

safe(ly) sicher
sales Verkauf, Vertrieb, Umsatz
same gleiche/r/s, der-, die-, dasselbe
sauce Soße
save retten, sichern, (ein)sparen
say sagen
school Schule
score Ergebnis, Punkt(estand)
screen Bildschirm
search Suche; (durch)suchen
second zweite(r,s), Sekunde
secondary school weiterführende Schule
see sehen, besuchen, verstehen
seem (er)scheinen
sell (sich) verkaufen
send senden, schicken
sentence Satz
serious ernst, ernsthaft
service Dienst, Dienstleistung, Service
set setzen, stellen
several etliche, einige, mehrere
shall sollen, werden
shape Form, Gestalt
share teilen, gemeinsam (be)nutzen
sharp scharf
shelf Regal
shop Laden, Geschäft; einkaufen
short kurz, klein, knapp
shorten kürzen
should solle/n, sollte/n
show zeigen
shut schließen
side Seite
sign Zeichen, Anzeichen, Schild
similar ähnlich
simple einfach
since da, weil, seit
single einzig, einzeln
sit sitzen, sich hinsetzen
size Größe
slow langsam
small klein
so also, damit, deshalb, so
solution Lösung

BASIC WORD LIST

some einige, etwas
someone / somebody jemand
something etwas
sometimes manchmal
somewhere irgendwo(hin)
soon bald
sorry traurig; Verzeihung
sound Klang, Geräusch; klingen, sich anhören
south Süden
space Raum, Platz, Abstand
speak sprechen, reden
special besondere/r/s
specially speziell, extra, besonders
speed Geschwindigkeit, Gang
spell buchstabieren, schreiben
spend (Geld) ausgeben, (Zeit) verbringen
square Viereck, Quadrat
staff Angestellte, Mitarbeiter/innen
stand stehen, aushalten
standard Standard; normal, üblich
start Beginn; anfangen, starten
statement Aussage, Feststellung, Behauptung
stay Aufenthalt; bleiben
step Schritt, Stufe
still still, trotzdem, (immer) noch
stop (an)halten, aufhören (mit)
street Straße
strong stark, heftig
study studieren
stuff Material, Stoff
subject (Schul-)Fach, Thema
success Erfolg
successful erfolgreich
such as wie zum Beispiel
suggest vorschlagen, andeuten
suggestion Vorschlag
summarise zusammenfassen
sun Sonne
sure sicher
surname Nachname, Familienname
surprise Überraschung; überraschen
swim schwimmen

T
table Tisch, Tabelle
take nehmen, bringen, dauern
take off ausziehen, abnehmen, abheben
take part teilnehmen, mitmachen
talk Gespräch, Vortrag; sprechen, reden
task Aufgabe
tax Steuer
teach unterrichten, lehren
teacher Lehrer/in
team Mannschaft
technical technisch
technology Technik, Technologie
telephone (call) Telefon(anruf)
television Fernsehen, Fernseher
tell sagen, erzählen
test untersuchen, prüfen
than als
thank you danke

thanks Dank; danke
then dann
there da, dort(hin)
these diese
thick dick
thin dünn
thing Sache, Ding, Gegenstand
think denken, meinen, finden, glauben
thorough(ly) gründlich
those jene
though obwohl
through durch
throw werfen
ticket Karte, Fahrschein
time Zeit, Mal
timetable Fahr-, Stundenplan
tiny winzig, klein
tip Hinweis, Tipp
today heute
together zusammen
tomorrow morgen
tonight heute Abend/Nacht
too zu, auch
tool Werkzeug
tooth Zahn
top Spitze, Gipfel; Spitzen-
topic Thema
total (Gesamt-)Summe; gesamte/r/s, Gesamt-
touch anfassen, berühren
tower Turm
town Stadt
traffic Verkehr
train Zug; ausbilden
trainee Auszubildende/r, Praktikant/in
training Ausbildung
translate übersetzen
translation Übersetzung
travel Reisen; reisen, fahren
trip Ausflug, Reise
trouble Mühe, Umstände, Problem(e)
true wahr, richtig
try versuchen, probieren
turn (sich) drehen, wenden, werden
twice zweimal
type Art, Sorte, Typ; tippen
typical typisch

U
unable unfähig
understand verstehen, begreifen
unfortunately leider
unit Einheit, Lektion
university Universität
unless es sei denn, außer wenn
unlike anders als, im Gegensatz zu
until bis
use Gebrauch; gebrauchen, benutzen, verwenden
useful nützlich
useless nutzlos, unbrauchbar
user Anwender/in, Benutzer/in
usual gewöhnlich, normal, üblich
usually gewöhnlich, normalerweise, meistens

V
vary variieren, schwanken
visit Besuch; besuchen, besichtigen
visitor Besucher/in, Gast
voice Stimme

W
wait warten
wall Wand, Mauer
want wollen
watch Armbanduhr
water Wasser
way Weg, Methode, Art (und Weise)
weather Wetter
week Woche
weekend Wochenende
weekly wöchentlich
welcome Willkommen; begrüßen, willkommen heißen
well gesund, gut; also
west Westen
wet feucht, nass
whatever was auch immer
wheel Rad
when wenn, als, wann
whenever immer wenn
where wo(hin)
whether ob
which welche
while während
white weiß
who(m) wen, wem
whole ganz
why warum
wide breit, weit
width Breite
will Wille; werde(n), wollen
window Fenster
wine Wein
wish Wunsch; wünschen
woman Frau
wonderful wunderbar
wood Holz
word Wort
work Arbeit; funktionieren, arbeiten
worker Arbeiter/in
workplace Arbeitsplatz
world Welt
worldwide weltweit
worried besorgt, beunruhigt
would würde/n
write schreiben
wrong falsch

Y
year Jahr
yesterday gestern
young jung
Yours sincerely Mit freundlichen Grüßen

Unit word list

Die neuen Wörter sind in der Reihenfolge ihres Vorkommens im Text verzeichnet. Nicht aufgeführt sind die Wörter aus der Liste des Grundwortschatzes (Basic word list).
T = das Wort befindet sich in den *Transcripts* (Hörverständnistexte).
P = Das Wort befinder sich in den *Pairwork files*.

6 workplace ['wɜːkpleɪs] — Arbeitsplatz
automotive [ˌɔːtəˈməʊtɪv] — Automobil-
to include [ɪnˈkluːd] — einschließen, umfassen, einbeziehen
renowned [rɪˈnaʊnd] — bekannt, renommiert
automobile [ˈɔːtəməbiːl] — Auto, Automobil-
manufacturer [ˌmænjuˈfæktʃərə] — Hersteller
to respect [rɪˈspekt] — schätzen, respektieren
expertise [ˌekspɜːˈtiːz] — Fachwissen, Know-how
reliable [rɪˈlaɪəbl] — zuverlässig
independent [ˌɪndɪˈpendənt] — unabhängig
vehicle [ˈviːəkl] — Fahrzeug
to contribute to sth [kənˈtrɪbjuːt tə] — zu etw einen Beitrag leisten
proof [pruːf] — Nachweis, Beweis
excellence [ˈeksələns] — ausgezeichnete Qualität, hohes Niveau
to enjoy [ɪnˈdʒɔɪ] — sich erfreuen, genießen
reputation [ˌrepjuˈteɪʃn] — Ruf
unique [juːˈniːk] — einzigartig, einmalig
electrical [ɪˈlektrɪkl] — elektrisch
feature [ˈfiːtʃə] — Merkmal, besondere Eigenschaft
leather [ˈleðə] — Leder
wood [wʊd] — Holz
stone [stəʊn] — Stein
functional(ly) [ˈfʌŋkʃənli] — funktional
integrated [ˈɪntɪgreɪtɪd] — integriert
component [kəmˈpəʊnənt] — Bauteil, Element
interior [ɪnˈtɪərɪə] — Innen-, Inneneinrichtungs-
wiring harness [ˈwaɪərɪŋ hɑːnɪs] — Kabelbaum, Kabelstrang
management system [ˈmænɪdʒmənt sɪstəm] — Steuerungs- und Regelungssystem
marriage [ˈmærɪdʒ] — Verbindung
expression [ɪkˈspreʃn] — Ausdruck
headquarters [ˌhedˈkwɔːtəz] — Zentrale
subsidiary [səbˈsɪdɪəri] — Niederlassung
corresponding [ˌkɒrɪˈspɒndɪŋ] — entsprechend

7 staff [stɑːf] — Personal, Belegschaft
skilled worker [ˌskɪld ˈwɜːkə] — Facharbeiter/in
opportunity [ˌɒpəˈtjuːnəti] — Gelegenheit
training supervisor [ˌtreɪnɪŋ ˈsuːpəvaɪzə] — Ausbilder/in
profile [ˈprəʊfaɪl] — Profil, Beschreibung, Porträt
travelling [ˈtrævlɪŋ] — Reisen
socializing [ˈsəʊʃəlaɪzɪŋ] — Ausgehen, unter Leute gehen

engineer [ˌendʒɪˈnɪə] — Ingenieur/in, Techniker/in
CAD engineer [siː eɪ ˌdiː endʒɪˈnɪə] — Technische/r Zeichner/in
drums [drʌmz] — Schlagzeug
technician [tekˈnɪʃn] — Techniker/in
to train to be [ˈtreɪn tə bi] — eine Ausbildung zum/r ... machen
maintenance [ˈmeɪntənəns] — Wartung, Instandhaltung
to enjoy doing sth [ɪnˈdʒɔɪ] — etw gern tun
computing [kəmˈpjuːtɪŋ] — Computer(wesen)
mechanical engineering [mɪˌkænɪkl endʒɪˈnɪərɪŋ] — Maschinenbau *T*
to introduce [ˌɪntrəˈdjuːs] — vorstellen, bekannt machen *T*
to socialize with sb [ˈsəʊʃəlaɪz wɪð] — sich mit jdm treffen *T*
equipment [ɪˈkwɪpmənt] — Geräte *T*
to break down [ˌbreɪk ˈdaʊn] — kaputtgehen *T*
to repair [rɪˈpeə] — reparieren *T*
to replace [rɪˈpleɪs] — ersetzen, austauschen *T*
to be one's turn [bi ˌwʌnz ˈtɜːn] — an der Reihe sein, dran sein *T*
spare time [ˌspeə ˈtaɪm] — Freizeit *T*
motorcycling [ˈməʊtəsaɪklɪŋ] — Motorradfahren *T*
usually [ˈjuːʒuəli] — normalerweise *T*
to discuss [dɪˈskʌs] — besprechen *T*

8 following [ˈfɒləʊɪŋ] — folgende/r/s
metalworking [ˈmetlwɜːkɪŋ] — metallverarbeitend, in der Metallverarbeitung
mechanic [mɪˈkænɪk] — Mechaniker/in
to reduce [rɪˈdjuːs] — senken, reduzieren, verringern
electricity [ɪˌlekˈtrɪsəti] — Strom, Elektrizität
heating [ˈhiːtɪŋ] — Heizung
air conditioning [ˈeə kəndɪʃnɪŋ] — Klimatisierung, Klimaanlage(n)
machinery [məˈʃiːnəri] — Maschinen
broken [ˈbrəʊkən] — kaputt
to think about sth [ˈθɪŋk əbaʊt] — über etw nachdenken
craftsman [ˈkrɑːftsmən] — Handwerker
responsible for [rɪˈspɒnsəbl] — verantwortlich für, zuständig für
communications [kəˌmjuːnɪˈkeɪʃnz] — Kommunikation
technology [tekˈnɒlədʒi] — Technik, Technologie
virtual [ˈvɜːtʃuəl] — virtuell
object [ˈɒbdʒɪkt] — Gegenstand, Ding, Objekt
to plug sth in [ˌplʌg ˈɪn] — etw einstecken, anschließen

167

UNIT WORD LIST

workpiece ['wɜːkpiːs]	Werkstück	surface ['sɜːfɪs]	Oberfläche
steel [stiːl]	Stahl	slot-headed screw	Schlitzschraube
plastics ['plæstɪks]	Plastik	[ˌslɒthedɪd 'skruː]	
to assemble [əˈsembl]	zusammenbauen, montieren	cross-headed screw	Kreuzschlitzschraube
to automatize ['ɔːtəmaɪz]	automatisieren	[ˌkrɒshedɪd 'skruː]	
machine tool [məˈʃiːn tuːl]	Werkzeugmaschine	Allen-head screw	Innensechskantschraube
9 order ['ɔːdə]	Reihenfolge	[ˌælən hed 'skruː]	
solution [səˈluːʃn]	Lösung	bolt [bəʊlt]	Schraube
pretty ['prɪti]	ziemlich	hexagonal [heksˈægənl]	sechseckig
I'm fine. [aɪm 'faɪn]	Mir geht es gut.	hexagonal-head bolt	Sechskantschraube
Pleased to meet you.	Schön, Sie kennen zu lernen.	[heksˌægənl 'hed bəʊlt]	
[ˌpliːzd tə 'miːt ju]		to sort [sɔːt]	sortieren
colleague ['kɒliːg]	Kollege/-in	manual ['mænjuəl]	Hand-
to take a look around	sich umsehen	frame plate ['freɪm pleɪt]	Rahmenplatte
[ˌteɪk ə ˌlʊk əˈraʊnd]		lorry ['lɒri]	Lastwagen
10 visitor ['vɪzɪtə]	Besucher/in	apprenticeship [əˈprentɪʃɪp]	Lehre, Ausbildung
customer ['kʌstəmə]	Kunde/-in	task [tɑːsk]	Aufgabe, Auftrag
visit ['vɪzɪt]	Besuch	workshop ['wɜːkʃɒp]	Werkstatt
to swap [swɒp]	tauschen	to prepare [prɪˈpeə]	vorbereiten
11 tool [tuːl]	Werkzeug	wide [waɪd]	breit
hand-held tool	Handwerkzeug	recess [rɪˈses]	Aussparung
[ˌhændheld 'tuːl]		to continue [kənˈtɪnjuː]	fortführen, weiterführen
to identify [aɪˈdentɪfaɪ]	bestimmen, identifizieren	phrase [freɪz]	(Rede-)Wendung, Satz
sound [saʊnd]	Klang, Geräusch	13 borehole ['bɔːhəʊl]	Bohrloch
drill [drɪl]	Bohrmaschine	chamfer ['tʃæmfə]	Fase
electric drill [ɪˌlektrɪk 'drɪl]	Elektrobohrmaschine	countersink ['kaʊntəsɪŋk]	Spitzsenkung
handfile ['hændfaɪl]	Handfeile	counterbore ['kaʊntəbɔː]	Stirnsenkung
hammer ['hæmə]	Hammer	thickness ['θɪknəs]	Stärke, Dicke
hacksaw ['hæksɔː]	Bügelsäge	in addition to [ɪn əˈdɪʃn tə]	zusätzlich
jigsaw ['dʒɪgsɔː]	Stichsäge	to chamfer ['tʃæmfə]	(an)fasen
angle grinder	Winkelschleifer	angle ['æŋgl]	Winkel
['æŋgl graɪndə]		edge [edʒ]	Kante
centre punch ['sentə pʌntʃ]	Körner	to finish ['fɪnɪʃ]	polieren
chisel ['tʃɪzl]	Meißel	view [vjuː]	Ansicht
counterbore ['kaʊntəbɔː]	Zapfensenker	front view [ˌfrʌnt 'vjuː]	Ansicht von vorn
countersink ['kaʊntəsɪŋk]	Spitzsenker	side view ['saɪd vjuː]	Seitenansicht
height gauge ['haɪt geɪdʒ]	Höhenanreißgerät	top view ['tɒp vjuː]	Ansicht von oben
hex key ['heks kiː]	Innensechskantschlüssel	dimensions [dɪˈmenʃnz]	Abmessungen, Dimensionen
open-ended spanner	Maulschlüssel,	diameter [daɪˈæmɪtə]	Durchmesser
[ˌəʊpən ˌendɪd 'spænə]	Gabelschlüssel	centre line [ˌsentə 'laɪn]	Symmetrieachse
Phillips screw(driver)	Kreuzschlitz-	14 instructor [ɪnˈstrʌktə]	Ausbilder/in
[ˌfɪlɪps 'skruːdraɪvə]	schraube(ndreher)	to take care of sth	sich um etw kümmern
pozidriv screw(driver)	Pozidriv-Schraube(ndreher)	[ˌteɪk 'keər əv]	
[ˌpɒzɪdrɪv 'skruːdraɪvə]		to manufacture	herstellen; fertigen
slotted screw(driver)	Schlitzschraube(ndreher)	[ˌmænjuˈfæktʃə]	
[ˌslɒtɪd 'skruːdraɪvə]		calliper ['kælɪpə]	Messschieber T
tap [tæp]	Gewindebohrer	micrometer [maɪˈkrɒmɪtə]	Messschraube T
12 thread [θred]	Gewinde	to fill in [ˌfɪl 'ɪn]	eintragen T
chip [tʃɪp]	Span	overall [ˌəʊvərˈɔːl]	Gesamt- T
to drive [draɪv]	treiben, schlagen	point [pɔɪnt]	Komma T
nail [neɪl]	Nagel	distance ['dɪstəns]	Abstand T
shape [ʃeɪp]	Form	apart [əˈpɑːt]	(voneinander) entfernt,
to grind [graɪnd]	schleifen, abschleifen		auseinander T
conical ['kɒnɪkl]	kegelförmig, konisch	to take care [ˌteɪk 'keə]	aufpassen T
screw head ['skruː hed]	Schraubenkopf	15 star-shaped ['stɑː ʃeɪpt]	sternförmig
cylindrical [səˈlɪndrɪkl]	zylindrisch	term [tɜːm]	Begriff
to bore [bɔː]	bohren	security [sɪˈkjʊərəti]	Sicherheit
to mark off [ˌmɑːk 'ɒf]	anzeichnen, anreißen	slotted ['slɒtɪd]	geschlitzt, Schlitz-
to punch mark	ankörnen	to order ['ɔːdə]	bestellen
['pʌntʃ mɑːk]		nut [nʌt]	Mutter
to shape [ʃeɪp]	formen	order ['ɔːdə]	Auftrag, Bestellung

UNIT WORD LIST

to place an order [ˌpleɪs ən 'ɔːdə]	einen Auftrag erteilen, eine Bestellung aufgeben	
to confirm [kən'fɜːm]	bestätigen	
16 toolbox ['tuːlbɒks]	Werkzeugkasten	
catalogue ['kætəlɒg]	Katalog	
assembly [ə'sembli]	Montage	
case [keɪs]	Kasten, Koffer	
Allen key ['ælən kiː]	Innensechskantschlüssel	
brush [brʌʃ]	Bürste	
wire brush ['waɪə brʌʃ]	Drahtbürste	
file [faɪl]	Feile	
file brush ['faɪl brʌʃ]	Feilenbürste	
flat [flæt]	flach, eben	
semicircular [ˌsemi'sɜːkjələ]	halbrund	
triangular [traɪ'æŋgjələ]	dreikantig	
pliers ['plaɪəz]	Zange	
combination pliers [ˌkɒmbɪ'neɪʃn plaɪəz]	Kombizange	
waterpump pliers [ˌwɔːtəpʌmp 'plaɪəz]	Wasserpumpenzange	
pin punch ['pɪn pʌntʃ]	Schlagdorn	
rule [ruːl]	Lineal	
safety goggles ['seɪfti gɒglz]	Schutzbrille	
17 distinct [dɪ'stɪŋkt]	unterschiedlich, verschieden	
shears [ʃɪəz]	Schere	
pincers ['pɪnsəz]	Pinzette, Zange	
scissors ['sɪzəz]	Schere	
to strip [strɪp]	abziehen	
to twist [twɪst]	drehen, verdrehen, verdrillen	
to pass [pɑːs]	reichen	
snipe nose pliers [ˌsnaɪp nəʊz 'plaɪəz]	Flachrundzange	
a broad range of [ə ˌbrɔːd 'reɪndʒ əv]	eine große Auswahl von	
specialist ['speʃəlɪst]	Spezial-	
pump [pʌmp]	Pumpe	
to mount [maʊnt]	montieren	
assembly line [ə'sembli laɪn]	Montagestraße, Fertigungslinie, Fließband	
to service sth ['sɜːvɪs]	etw warten	
driver's cab [ˌdraɪvəz 'kæb]	Fahrerhaus	
18 to keep [kiːp]	aufbewahren	
department [dɪ'pɑːtmənt]	Abteilung	
meeting ['miːtɪŋ]	Besprechung	
ahead [ə'hed]	nächste/r/s	
corridor ['kɒrɪdɔː]	Flur, Gang	
schedule ['ʃedjuːl]	(Termin-)Plan	
to install [ɪn'stɔːl]	installieren	
factory ['fæktəri]	Fabrik, Werk	
drilling machine ['drɪlɪŋ məʃiːn]	Bohrmaschine	
construction (department) [kən'strʌkʃn]	Konstruktionsabteilung	
to load [ləʊd]	laden	
19 cleaning ['kliːnɪŋ]	Reinigung	
mains plug ['meɪnz plʌg]	Netzstecker	
proper ['prɒpə]	richtig	
working ['wɜːkɪŋ]	Funktionieren	
to keep [kiːp]	halten	
ventilation [ˌventɪ'leɪʃn]	Belüftung	
ventilation slot [ˌventɪ'leɪʃn slɒt]	Lüftungsschlitz	
in order to [ɪn 'ɔːdə tə]	um ... zu	
to avoid [ə'vɔɪd]	vermeiden, verhindern	
operational [ˌɒpə'reɪʃənl]	Bedienungs-, Betriebs-	
malfunction [ˌmæl'fʌŋkʃn]	Störung, Fehlfunktion	
operational malfunction [ˌɒpəˌreɪʃənl mæl'fʌŋkʃn]	Funktionsstörung	
to saw [sɔː]	sägen	
gypsum board ['dʒɪpsəm bɔːd]	Gipskarton	
overhead [ˌəʊvə'hed]	über Kopf	
condition [kən'dɪʃn]	Bedingung	
conductive [kən'dʌktɪv]	leitend, leitfähig	
dust [dʌst]	Staub	
to accumulate [ə'kjuːmjəleɪt]	sich ansammeln, sich absetzen	
interior [ɪn'tɪəriə]	das Innere	
protective [prə'tektɪv]	Schutz-	
insulation [ˌɪnsju'leɪʃn]	Isolierung	
to degrade [dɪ'greɪd]	zersetzen	
stationary ['steɪʃənri]	stationär	
extraction system [ɪk'strækʃn sɪstəm]	Absaugvorrichtung	
to recommend [ˌrekə'mend]	empfehlen	
case [keɪs]	Fall	
frequently ['friːkwəntli]	oft, häufig	
to blow out [ˌbləʊ 'aʊt]	ausblasen	
residual current device [rɪˌzɪdjuəl 'kʌrənt dɪvaɪs]	FI-Schutzschalter	
guide roller ['gaɪd rəʊlə]	Führungsrolle	
occasionally [ə'keɪʒənəli]	gelegentlich, ab und zu	
wear [weə]	Abnutzung(serscheinungen), Verschleiß	
to lubricate ['luːbrɪkeɪt]	schmieren	
drop [drɒp]	Tropfen	
oil [ɔɪl]	Öl	
worn [wɔːn]	abgenutzt	
to fail [feɪl]	ausfallen, versagen	
despite [dɪ'spaɪt]	trotz	
care [keə]	Sorgfalt	
procedure [prə'siːdʒə]	Verfahren	
repair [rɪ'peə]	Reparatur	
to carry out [ˌkæri 'aʊt]	ausführen	
after-sales service ['ɑːftəseɪlz sɜːvɪs]	Kundendienst	
power tool ['paʊə tuːl]	Elektrowerkzeug	
correspondence [ˌkɒrɪ'spɒndəns]	Schriftverkehr, Korrespondenz	
spare part [ˌspeə 'pɑːt]	Ersatzteil	
digit ['dɪdʒɪt]	Ziffer, Stelle	
nameplate ['neɪmpleɪt]	Typenschild	
20 bandsaw ['bændsɔː]	Bandsäge	
lathe [leɪð]	Drehbank, Drehmaschine	
centre lathe ['sentə leɪð]	Spitzendrehmaschine	
grinding machine ['graɪndɪŋ məʃiːn]	Schleifmaschine	
milling machine ['mɪlɪŋ məʃiːn]	Fräse	
off-hand grinder [ˌɒfhænd 'graɪndə]	Handschleifmaschine	

UNIT WORD LIST

power hacksaw ['paʊə hæksɔː]	Maschinenbügelsäge, Hubsäge
to turn [tɜːn]	drehen, drechseln
shaft [ʃɑːft]	Achse, Welle
operation [ˌɒpəˈreɪʃn]	Arbeitsgang, Tätigkeit
to face [feɪs]	plandrehen, querdrehen
to in-copy [ˌɪn ˈkɒpi]	kegeldrehen
to knurl [nɜːl]	rändeln
longitudinal turning [lɒndʒɪˌtjuːdɪnl ˈtɜːnɪŋ]	Längsdrehen
to out-copy [ˌaʊt ˈkɒpi]	kegeldrehen
to part-off [ˌpɑːt ˈɒf]	abstechen
to ream [riːm]	reiben
to thread [θred]	Gewinde drehen
21 bumper [ˈbʌmpə]	Stoßstange
loading platform [ˈləʊdɪŋ plætfɔːm]	Ladefläche, Pritsche
rear axle [ˌrɪər ˈæksl]	Hinterachse
rim [rɪm]	Rand, Fase
to clamp in [ˌklæmp ˈɪn]	einspannen
rod [rɒd]	Stab
degree [dɪˈgriː]	Grad
fraction [ˈfrækʃn]	Bruch
Watch out! [ˌwɒtʃ ˈaʊt]	Vorsicht!
supplier [səˈplaɪə]	Zulieferer, Lieferant/in
22 specifications [ˌspesɪfɪˈkeɪʃnz]	Technische Daten, Spezifikationen *P*
bar [bɑː]	Stange *P*
boring bar [ˈbɔːrɪŋ bɑː]	Innendrehmeißel *P*
provider [prəˈvaɪdə]	Anbieter/in *P*
depth [depθ]	Tiefe *P*
precise [prɪˈsaɪs]	genau, präzis, exakt *P*
cost-effective [ˌkɒst ɪˈfektɪv]	kostengünstig *P*
due to [ˈdjuː tə]	aufgrund *P*
multiple [ˈmʌltɪpl]	mehrfach *P*
to regrind [ˌriːˈgraɪnd]	nachschleifen *P*
cutting face [ˈkʌtɪŋ feɪs]	Schnittfläche *P*
roughing [ˈrʌfɪŋ]	Schruppen *P*
recessing [rɪˈsesɪŋ]	Einlassen, Absetzen *P*
internal thread [ɪnˌtɜːnl ˈθred]	Innengewinde *P*
shank [ʃæŋk]	Schaft *P*
to clarify [ˈklærəfaɪ]	klären
quantity [ˈkwɒntəti]	Menge
metric [ˈmetrɪk]	metrisch
quantity discount [ˌkwɒntəti ˈdɪskaʊnt]	Mengenrabatt
item [ˈaɪtəm]	Artikel *T*
to mind [maɪnd]	etwas dagegen haben *T*
at all [ət ˈɔːl]	überhaupt *T*
to hold on [ˌhəʊld ˈɒn]	warten *T*
to call up [ˌkɔːl ˈʌp]	aufrufen *T*
to be afraid [bi əˈfreɪd]	fürchten *T*
urgently [ˈɜːdʒəntli]	dringend *T*
to cancel [ˈkænsl]	stornieren *T*
unfortunately [ʌnˈfɔːtʃənətli]	leider *T*
in stock [ɪn ˈstɒk]	auf Lager, vorrätig *T*
to sort sth out [ˌsɔːt ˈaʊt]	etw in Ordnung bringen, etw klären *T*
delay [dɪˈleɪ]	Verzögerung *T*
delivery [dɪˈlɪvəri]	Lieferung *T*
23 chuck [tʃʌk]	Futter, Spann-Bohrfutter
three-jaw chuck [ˌθriː dʒɔː ˈtʃʌk]	Dreibackenfutter
to drill [drɪl]	bohren
drill bit [ˈdrɪl bɪt]	Bohrer
to fit [fɪt]	passen
reamer [ˈriːmə]	Reibahle
to carry on [ˌkæri ˈɒn]	weitermachen
24 measuring instrument [ˈmeʒərɪŋ ɪnstrəmənt]	Messinstrument
gauge [geɪdʒ]	Messgerät
depth gauge [ˈdepθ geɪdʒ]	Tiefenmessgerät
vernier calliper [ˈvɜːniə kælɪpə]	Messschieber
plug gauge [ˈplʌg geɪdʒ]	Grenzlehrdorn
snap gauge [ˈsnæp geɪdʒ]	Grenzrachenlehre
thread plug gauge [ˈθred plʌg geɪdʒ]	Gewinde-Grenzlehrdorn
inspection [ɪnˈspekʃn]	Überprüfung, Kontrolle, Inspektion
sheet [ʃiːt]	Blatt, Bogen
nominal [ˈnɒmɪnl]	nominell, Nenn-
tolerance [ˈtɒlərəns]	Toleranz
actual [ˈæktʃuəl]	tatsächlich
deviation [ˌdiːviˈeɪʃn]	Abweichung
device [dɪˈvaɪs]	Gerät, Instrument, Vorrichtung
25 radius [ˈreɪdiəs]	Radius
cylinder [ˈsɪlɪndə]	Zylinder
knurled [nɜːld]	gerändelt
height [haɪt]	Höhe
shoulder [ˈʃəʊldə]	Bund
bore [bɔː]	Zylindersenkung
control panel [kənˈtrəʊl pænl]	Steuerkonsole
coolant hose [ˈkuːlənt həʊz]	Kühlmittelschlauch
machine vice [məˈʃiːn vaɪs]	Maschinenschraubstock
milling cutter [ˌmɪlɪŋ ˈkʌtə]	Fräswerkzeug, Fräser
spray protection cabin [ˈspreɪ prətekʃn kæbɪn]	Maschinengehäuse
milling head [ˈmɪlɪŋ hed]	Fräskopf
vertical [ˈvɜːtɪkl]	senkrecht, vertikal
26 mediation [ˌmiːdiˈeɪʃn]	Vermittlung
summary [ˈsʌməri]	Zusammenfassung
to feed [fiːd]	führen, zuführen
past [pɑːst]	an … vorbei
tooth [tuːθ]	Zahn
cutter [ˈkʌtə]	Fräser
method [ˈmeθəd]	Art (und Weise), Methode
machining [məˈʃiːnɪŋ]	(maschinelle) Bearbeitung
to machine [məˈʃiːn]	(maschinell) bearbeiten
angular [ˈæŋgjələ]	eckig, kantig
curved [kɜːvd]	gewölbt, gekrümmt
to mill [mɪl]	fräsen
to rotate [rəʊˈteɪt]	drehen, sich drehen, rotieren
classification [ˌklæsɪfɪˈkeɪʃn]	Einteilung, Klassifizierung
face milling [ˈfeɪs mɪlɪŋ]	Messerkopf-Fräsen
spindle [ˈspɪndl]	Spindel

UNIT WORD LIST

axis ['æksɪs]	Achse	
rotation [rəʊ'teɪʃn]	Rotation	
perpendicular [ˌpɜːpən'dɪkjələ]	lotrecht, senkrecht	
to result [rɪ'zʌlt]	resultieren	
action ['ækʃn]	Arbeitsweise, Funktion	
cutting edge [ˌkʌtɪŋ 'edʒ]	Schneide	
located [ləʊ'keɪtɪd]	gelegen	
periphery [pə'rɪfəri]	Umfang	
face [feɪs]	Stirnseite	
end milling ['end mɪlɪŋ]	Stirnfräsen	
to tilt [tɪlt]	neigen	
tapered ['teɪpəd]	sich verjüngend, kegelig	
cutter body ['kʌtə bɒdi]	Fräserkörper	
peripheral milling [pə,rɪfərəl 'mɪlɪŋ]	Walzenfräsen	
slab milling ['slæb mɪlɪŋ]	Walzenfräsen	
parallel ['pærəlel]	parallel	
sketch [sketʃ]	Skizze	
arbor ['ɑːbə]	Achse	

27 sales representative ['seɪlz reprɪzentətɪv] — Vertreter/in, Vertriebsmitarbeiter/in
potential [pə'tenʃl] — potenziell
working range ['wɜːkɪŋ reɪndʒ] — Arbeitsbereich
longitudinal [ˌlɒndʒɪ'tjuːdɪnl] — längs
cross [krɒs] — quer
drive [draɪv] — Antrieb
speed range ['spiːd reɪndʒ] — Drehzahlbereich
rpm (revolutions per minute) [ˌɑː piː 'em] — U/min (Umdrehungen pro Minute)
taper ['teɪpə] — Kegel, *hier:* Kegelschaft
feed rate ['fiːd reɪt] — Vorschubgeschwindigkeit
rapid traverse [ˌræpɪd 'trævɜːs] — Schnellvorschub
contouring control [kɒn,tʊərɪŋ kən'trəʊl] — Maschinensteuerung
weight [weɪt] — Gewicht
approximately [ə'prɒksɪmətli] — ungefähr, zirka
clamping surface ['klæmpɪŋ sɜːfɪs] — Aufspannfläche, Spannfläche
loading ability ['ləʊdɪŋ əbɪləti] — maximale Last
decision [dɪ'sɪʒn] — Entscheidung *T*
energy consumption ['enədʒi kənsʌmpʃn] — Strom-/Energieverbrauch *T*
to require [rɪ'kwaɪə] — brauchen, benötigen *T*
revolution [ˌrevə'luːʃn] — Umdrehung *T*
That depends [ˌðæt dɪ'pendz] — Das kommt darauf an. *T*
according to [ə'kɔːdɪŋ tə] — gemäß, entsprechend, zufolge *T*
identical [aɪ'dentɪkl] — identisch *T*
controlling system [kən'trəʊlɪŋ sɪstəm] — Steuerungs- und Regelungssystem *T*
control [kən'trəʊl] — Steuerung, Regelung *T*
to weigh [weɪ] — wiegen *T*
similar ['sɪmələ] — ähnlich *T*
major ['meɪdʒə] — Haupt- *T*
size [saɪz] — Größe *T*

working area ['wɜːkɪŋ eəriə]	Arbeitsbereich *T*	
similarity [ˌsɪmə'lærəti]	Übereinstimmung, Ähnlichkeit	
to express [ɪk'spres]	ausdrücken	
angular table [ˌæŋgjələ 'teɪbl]	Schrägtisch	
rigid ['rɪdʒɪd]	starr	
slightly ['slaɪtli]	etwas, geringfügig	
light [laɪt]	leicht	
heavy ['hevi]	schwer	
loud [laʊd]	laut	
technical leaflet [ˌteknɪkl 'liːflət]	Datenblatt	
characteristics [ˌkærəktə'rɪstɪks]	Merkmale, Eigenschaften	

28 stable ['steɪbl] — stabil, robust
cast iron [ˌkɑːst 'aɪən] — Gusseisen
hardened ['hɑːdnd] — gehärtet
guideway ['gaɪdweɪ] — Führungsbahn
accuracy ['ækjərəsi] — Genauigkeit, Präzision
clamping ['klæmpɪŋ] — Einspannen
operational safety [ɒpə,reɪʃənl 'seɪfti] — Betriebssicherheit
stepless ['stepləs] — stufenlos
high-torque [ˌhaɪ 'tɔːk] — drehmomentstark
hydraulic [haɪ'drɔːlɪk] — hydraulisch
coolant fluid ['kuːlənt fluːɪd] — Kühlflüssigkeit
free-standing [ˌfriː 'stændɪŋ] — freistehend
capacity [kə'pæsəti] — Kapazität
splash-protection ['splæʃ prətekʃn] — Spritzschutz
processing cycle ['prəʊsesɪŋ saɪkl] — Prozessablaufsteuerung
digital readout [ˌdɪdʒɪtl 'riːdaʊt] — digitale Anzeige
lubrication [ˌluːbrɪ'keɪʃn] — Schmierung

29 trade fair ['treɪd feə] — (Handels-)Messe
to mediate ['miːdieɪt] — vermitteln
excerpt ['eksɜːpt] — Auszug, Ausschnitt
data sheet ['deɪtə ʃiːt] — Datenblatt

30 assembly group [ə'sembli gruːp] — Baugruppe
brief(ly) ['briːf] — kurz, knapp
to scan [skæn] — absuchen
review [rɪ'vjuː] — Zusammenfassung
to take sth into account [ˌteɪk ɪntu ə'kaʊnt] — etw berücksichtigen, auf etw achten
counterpart ['kaʊntəpɑːt] — Gegenstück
blunt [blʌnt] — stumpf
storeroom ['stɔːruːm] — Lagerraum
fit [fɪt] — Passung
wheelhousing ['wiːlhaʊsɪŋ] — Radkasten
lunch break ['lʌntʃ breɪk] — Mittagspause

31 axleguide ['ækslgaɪd] — Achshalter
cavity ['kævəti] — Hohlraum
indexable ['ɪndeksəbl] — *hier:* mit Wendeschneidplatten
swivel ['swɪvl] — Schwenk-
ball-nosed slot drill [ˌbɔːl nəʊzd 'slɒt drɪl] — Kugelkopffräser

UNIT WORD LIST

end mill stub ['end mɪl stʌb]	Fingerfräser
trapezoidal [ˌtræpiˈzɔɪdl]	trapezförmig
to fit sth together [ˌfɪt təˈgeðə]	etw zusammensetzen/-bauen
suitable [ˈsuːtəbl]	geeignet *T*
to swivel [ˈswɪvl]	schwenken *T*
miller [ˈmɪlə]	Fräsmaschine *T*
32 **to adjust** [əˈdʒʌst]	anpassen, ändern, einstellen
to be available [bi əˈveɪləbl]	zu sprechen sein
straightaway [ˌstreɪtəˈweɪ]	sofort
to examine [ɪgˈzæmɪn]	prüfen
previous [ˈpriːvɪəs]	vorherig
33 **water jet cutting machine** [ˌwɔːtə dʒet ˈkʌtɪŋ məʃiːn]	Wasserstrahl-Schneidemaschine
to depend on sb/sth [dɪˈpend ɒn]	von jdm/etw abhängen
angle piece [ˈæŋgl piːs]	Winkelstück
front [frʌnt]	Vorderseite
rear [rɪə]	Rückseite
34 **Allen set bolt** [ˈælən set bəʊlt]	Innensechskant-madenschraube
cylinder head bolt [ˈsɪlɪndə hed bəʊlt]	Zylinderschraube
countersunk bolt [ˈkaʊntəsʌŋk bəʊlt]	Senkschraube
cooling unit [ˈkuːlɪŋ juːnɪt]	Kühler
distance-piece [ˈdɪstəns piːs]	Abstandshalter
sheet steel [ˈʃiːt stiːl]	Stahlblech
underride guard [ˈʌndəraɪd gɑːd]	Unterfahrschutz
base part [ˈbeɪs pɑːt]	Unterteil
35 **fixing device** [ˈfɪksɪŋ dɪvaɪs]	Verbindungselement
wing screw [ˈwɪŋ skruː]	Flügelschraube
hexagon head bolt [ˌheksəgən ˈhed bəʊlt]	Sechskantschraube
slotted cheesehead bolt [ˌslɒtɪd ˈtʃiːzhed bəʊlt]	Zylinderkopfschraube abgerundet mit Querschlitz
slotted panhead bolt [ˌslɒtɪd ˈpænhed bəʊlt]	Halbrundkopfschraube mit Querschlitz
slotted countersunk bolt [ˌslɒtɪd ˈkaʊntəsʌŋk bəʊlt]	Senkkopfschraube mit Querschlitz
hexagon socket cap bolt [ˌheksəgən ˈsɒkɪt kæp bəʊlt]	Innensechskantschraube
round head screw [ˈraʊnd hed skruː]	Rundkopfschraube
Allen set screw [ˈælən set skruː]	Innensechskantgewindestift
wing nut [ˈwɪŋ nʌt]	Flügelmutter
plain flat washer [ˌpleɪn flæt ˈwɒʃə]	einfache flache Unterlegscheibe
spring washer [ˌsprɪŋ ˈwɒʃə]	Federscheibe
shakeproof washer [ˌʃeɪkpruːf ˈwɒʃə]	Zahnscheibe
panhead rivet [ˌpænhed ˈrɪvɪt]	Halbrundkopfniete
roundhead rivet [ˌraʊndhed ˈrɪvɪt]	Rundkopfniete
countersunk rivet [ˌkaʊntəsʌŋk ˈrɪvɪt]	Senkkopfniete
to fix [fɪks]	befestigen
to prevent [prɪˈvent]	verhindern, daran hindern
lawnmower [ˈlɔːnməʊə]	Rasenmäher
moveable [ˈmuːvəbl]	beweglich
hood [hʊd]	Schutzhaube
to fasten [ˈfɑːsn]	befestigen
wire [ˈwaɪə]	Kabel, Draht
plug [plʌg]	Stecker
36 **to join** [dʒɔɪn]	(miteinander) verbinden
detachable [dɪˈtætʃəbl]	abnehmbar, nicht fest verbunden
connection [kəˈnekʃn]	Verbindung
technique [tekˈniːk]	Methode, Technik
adhesive [ədˈhiːsɪv]	Klebstoff
permanent [ˈpɜːmənənt]	dauerhaft *T*
to take apart [ˌteɪk əˈpɑːt]	auseinandernehmen *T*
riveting [ˈrɪvɪtɪŋ]	Nieten, Vernieten *T*
bonding [ˈbɒndɪŋ]	Kleben *T*
soldering [ˈsəʊldərɪŋ]	Weichlöten *T*
welding [ˈweldɪŋ]	Schweißen *T*
thermoplastics [ˌθɜːməʊˈplæstɪks]	Thermoplaste
in contrast to [ɪn ˈkɒntrɑːst tə]	im Gegensatz zu
brazing [ˈbreɪzɪŋ]	Hartlöten
separate [ˈseprət]	separat, getrennt
to melt [melt]	schmelzen
joint [dʒɔɪnt]	Verbindung
filler material [ˈfɪlə mətɪərɪəl]	Zusatzwerkstoff
to add [æd]	hinzufügen
whilst [waɪlst]	während
to take place [ˌteɪk ˈpleɪs]	stattfinden, ablaufen
presence [ˈprezns]	Anwesenheit, Vorhandensein
inert [ɪˈnɜːt]	inert, chemisch inaktiv
inert gas [ɪˌnɜːt ˈgæs]	Schutzgas
semi-inert [ˌsemi ɪˈnɜːt]	teil-inert
shielding gas [ˈʃiːldɪŋ gæs]	Schutzgas
flux [flʌks]	Flussmittel
weakening [ˈwiːkənɪŋ]	Schwächung
arc [ɑːk]	Lichtbogen
electric arc welding [ɪˌlektrɪk ˈɑːk weldɪŋ]	Lichtbogenschweißen
to denote [dɪˈnəʊt]	bezeichnen
passing [ˈpɑːsɪŋ]	Fließen
current [ˈkʌrənt]	(elektrischer) Strom
base material [ˈbeɪs mətɪərɪəl]	Grundmaterial
variant [ˈveərɪənt]	Art
gas tungsten arc welding [ˌgæs tʌŋstən ˈɑːk weldɪŋ]	Wolframinertgasschweißen (WIG)
non-consumable [ˌnɒn kənˈsjuːməbl]	nichtabschmelzend
tungsten [ˈtʌŋstən]	Wolfram
particularly [pəˈtɪkjələli]	besonders
stainless steel [ˌsteɪnləs ˈstiːl]	Edelstahl

UNIT WORD LIST

shielded metal arc welding [ˈʃiːldɪd ˌmetl ˈɑːk weldɪŋ]	Lichtbogenhandschweißen
common [ˈkɒmən]	verbreitet
consumable [kənˈsjuːməbl]	abschmelzend
core [kɔː]	Kern
to act as [ˈækt əz]	fungieren als
gas metal arc welding [ˌgæs metl ˈɑːk weldɪŋ]	Metallinertgasschweißen (MIG), Metallaktivgasschweißen (MAG)
continuous [kənˈtɪnjuəs]	stetig, kontinuierlich
contamination [kənˌtæmɪˈneɪʃn]	Verunreinigung
commonly [ˈkɒmənli]	üblicherweise, im Allgemeinen
pipe [paɪp]	Rohr, Röhre
to undertake [ˌʌndəˈteɪk]	durchführen
resistance welding [rɪˈzɪstəns weldɪŋ]	Widerstandsschweißen
to involve [ɪnˈvɒlv]	mit sich bringen, einbeziehen, umfassen
molten [ˈməʊltən]	geschmolzen
pool [puːl]	Lache
to form [fɔːm]	sich bilden
weld area [ˈweld eəriə]	Schweißzone
resistance [rɪˈzɪstəns]	Widerstand
spot welding [ˈspɒt weldɪŋ]	Punktschweißen
principle [ˈprɪnsəpl]	Prinzip
overlapping [ˌəʊvəˈlæpɪŋ]	überlappend
sheet [ʃiːt]	Blech
simultaneous(ly) [ˌsɪmlˈteɪniəs]	gleichzeitig
to clamp [klæmp]	(ein-, fest-)klemmen
to secure [sɪˈkjʊə]	fixieren, festhalten
automated [ˈɔːtəmeɪtɪd]	automatisiert
likely [ˈlaɪkli]	wahrscheinlich
spot weld [ˈspɒt weld]	Schweißpunkt
chassis [ˈʃæsi]	Fahrgestell
energy-beam welding [ˈenədʒi biːm weldɪŋ]	Energiestrahlschweißen
laser-beam welding [ˈleɪzə biːm weldɪŋ]	Laserstrahlschweißen
to focus on sth [ˈfəʊkəs ɒn]	sich auf etw konzentrieren
high-powered [ˌhaɪˈpaʊəd]	Hochleistungs-
electron-beam welding [ɪˈlektrɒn biːm weldɪŋ]	Elektronenstrahlschweißen
vacuum [ˈvækjuəm]	Vakuum
laser-hybrid welding [ˈleɪzə haɪbrɪd weldɪŋ]	Laser-Hybrid-Schweißen
to combine [kəmˈbaɪn]	kombinieren
effective [ɪˈfektɪv]	effektiv
result [rɪˈzʌlt]	Ergebnis, Resultat
37 **word spider** [ˈwɜːd spaɪdə]	Wortnetz
38 **disadvantage** [ˌdɪsədˈvɑːntɪdʒ]	Nachteil
career [kəˈrɪə]	Karriere, Laufbahn
source [sɔːs]	Quelle
diode [ˈdaɪəʊd]	Diode
fibre [ˈfaɪbə]	Faser
disc laser [ˈdɪsk leɪzə]	Scheibenlaser
true [truː]	wahr, echt
to operate [ˈɒpəreɪt]	arbeiten, funktionieren
weld pool [ˈweld puːl]	Schmelzbad
to gain [geɪn]	erwerben, gewinnen
increasing [ɪnˈkriːsɪŋ]	zunehmend
acceptance [əkˈseptəns]	Akzeptanz
viable [ˈvaɪəbl]	brauchbar, durchführbar
shipbuilding [ˈʃɪpbɪldɪŋ]	Schiffbau
rail rolling stock [ˌreɪl ˈrəʊlɪŋ stɒk]	(Eisenbahn:) Rollmaterial
to implement [ˈɪmplɪmənt]	umsetzen, realisieren
customer-oriented [ˈkʌstəmər ɔːrɪəntɪd]	kundenorientiert
concept [ˈkɒnsept]	Konzept
application [ˌæplɪˈkeɪʃn]	Anwendung
benefit [ˈbenɪfɪt]	Nutzen, Vorteil
thick-walled [ˈθɪk wɔːld]	dickwandig
construction steel [kənˈstrʌkʃn stiːl]	Baustahl
penetration weld [ˌpenɪˈtreɪʃn weld]	Einschweißtiefe
comparable [ˈkɒmpərəbl]	vergleichbar
yet [jet]	*hier:* aber
improved [ɪmˈpruːvd]	besser
fit-up [ˈfɪtʌp]	Spaltüberbrückbarkeit
significant(ly) [sɪgˈnɪfɪkənt]	erheblich
to increase [ɪnˈkriːs]	erhöhen
stability [stəˈbɪləti]	Stabilität
compact [ˈkɒmpækt]	kompakt
unhindered [ˌʌnˈhɪndəd]	ungehindert
access [ˈækses]	Zugang, Zugriff
subassembly [ˌsʌbəˈsembli]	Unterbaugruppe
noticeably [ˈnəʊtɪsəbli]	deutlich
dependent on [dɪˈpendənt ɒn]	abhängig von
to bridge [brɪdʒ]	überbrücken
gap [gæp]	Lücke
seam [siːm]	(Schweiß-)Naht
to ensure [ɪnˈʃʊə]	gewährleisten, sicherstellen
increased [ɪnˈkriːst]	gesteigert
deformation [ˌdiːfɔːˈmeɪʃn]	Verformung
reworking [ˌriːˈwɜːkɪŋ]	Nachbearbeitung
weld penetration [ˈweld penɪtreɪʃn]	Einschweißtiefe
time-consuming [ˈtaɪm kənsjuːmɪŋ]	zeitraubend, zeitaufwändig
seam preparation [ˈsiːm prepəreɪʃn]	Schweißnahtvorbereitung
39 **batch production** [ˈbætʃ prədʌkʃn]	Serienfertigung
single-part production [ˌsɪŋgl pɑːt prəˈdʌkʃn]	Einzelfertigung
apron [ˈeɪprən]	Schlosskasten
bed [bed]	Maschinenbett, -führungsbahnen
controls [kənˈtrəʊlz]	Bedienelemente
feedshaft [ˈfiːdʃɑːft]	Zugspindel
footbrake [ˈfʊtbreɪk]	Fußhebel
gearbox [ˈgɪəbɒks]	Getriebe
head-end plinth [ˌhed end ˈplɪnθ]	Maschinengestell
headstock [ˈhedstɒk]	Spindelstock

UNIT WORD LIST

leadscrew ['liːdskruː]	Leitspindel
main spindle [,meɪn 'spɪndl]	Hauptspindel
saddle and slides [,sædl ən 'slaɪdz]	Support und Werkzeugschlitten
tail-end plinth [,teɪl end 'plɪnθ]	Maschinengestell
tailstock ['teɪlstɒk]	Reitstock
tool drawer ['tuːldrɔː]	Werkzeugschublade
40 drain screw ['dreɪn skruː]	Ablassschraube
filler screw ['fɪlə skruː]	Einfüllschraube
funnel ['fʌnl]	Trichter
headstock cover ['hedstɒk kʌvə]	Spindelstockabdeckung
operating manual ['ɒpəreɪtɪŋ mænjuəl]	Betriebsanleitung, Gebrauchsanweisung
power source ['paʊə sɔːs]	Stromquelle
store [stɔː]	Lager
waste oil [,weɪst 'ɔɪl]	Altöl
to make sure [,meɪk 'ʃʊə]	gewährleisten, sicherstellen
to disconnect [,dɪskə'nekt]	trennen
to remove [rɪ'muːv]	entfernen, ausbauen
to loosen ['luːsn]	lösen
to drain off [,dreɪn 'ɒf]	abfließen lassen
grade [greɪd]	Güteklasse
hazardous material [,hæzədəs mə'tɪəriəl]	Gefahrstoff
to pour [pɔː]	gießen
to replace [rɪ'pleɪs]	wieder einsetzen
to reconnect [,riːkə'nekt]	wieder verbinden
socket ['sɒkɪt]	Steckdose
to interrupt [,ɪntə'rʌpt]	unterbrechen
41 lubrication chart [,luːbrɪ'keɪʃn tʃɑːt]	Schmierplan
to oil [ɔɪl]	ölen
to grease [griːs]	schmieren
level ['levl]	Stand
to top up [,tɒp 'ʌp]	nachfüllen, auffüllen
bullet ['bʊlɪt]	Kugel, Punkt
donut ['dəʊnʌt]	Kringel
to hold the line [,həʊld ðə 'laɪn]	(Telefon:) am Apparat bleiben, dranbleiben T
to put sb through [,pʊt 'θruː]	(Telefon:) jdn durchstellen T
lid [lɪd]	Deckel, Klappe T
cover ['kʌvə]	Abdeckung, Deckel T
oiling point ['ɔɪlɪŋ pɔɪnt]	Schmiernippel T
sight glass ['saɪt glɑːs]	Schauglas T
rack [ræk]	Zahnstange T
bedslide ['bedslaɪd]	Maschinenführung T
cross-slide ['krɒsslaɪd]	Quersupport T
nipple ['nɪpl]	Schmiernippel T
bearing ['beərɪŋ]	Lager T
to spell [spel]	buchstabieren
42 gear oil ['gɪər ɔɪl]	Getriebeöl
canteen [kæn'tiːn]	Kantine
disposal [dɪ'spəʊzl]	Entsorgung
regulation [,regju'leɪʃn]	Vorschrift
environmental [ɪn,vaɪrən'mentl]	Umwelt-
drain [dreɪn]	Abfluss
to get rid of sth [,get 'rɪd əv]	etw loswerden
44 campaign [kæm'peɪn]	Kampagne, Aktion
to dispose of sth [dɪ'spəʊz əv]	etw entsorgen
waste [weɪst]	Alt-
engine ['endʒɪn]	Motor
engine oil ['endʒɪn ɔɪl]	Motoröl
visible ['vɪzəbl]	sichtbar
pollution [pə'luːʃn]	Verschmutzung
to cause [kɔːz]	verursachen
harm [hɑːm]	Schaden
to set up [,set 'ʌp]	einrichten. gründen
agency ['eɪdʒənsi]	Agentur
association [ə,səʊsi'eɪʃn]	Verbindung
to provide [prə'vaɪd]	bieten
guidance ['gaɪdəns]	Beratung, Anleitung
facility [fə'sɪləti]	Einrichtung
section ['sekʃn]	Abschnitt
note [nəʊt]	Anmerkung
storage ['stɔːrɪdʒ]	Lagerung
to accept [ək'sept]	akzeptieren
petrol ['petrəl]	Petroleum
thinner ['θɪnə]	Verdünnung
solvent ['sɒlvənt]	Lösungsmittel
cooking oil ['kʊkɪŋ ɔɪl]	Speiseöl
white spirit [,waɪt 'spɪrɪt]	Waschbenzin
enquiry [ɪn'kwaɪəri]	Anfrage, Erkundigung
45 circuit diagram ['sɜːkɪt daɪəgræm]	Schaltplan
resistor [rɪ'zɪstə]	Widerstand
transformer [træns'fɔːmə]	Transformator
fuse [fjuːz]	Sicherung
switch [swɪtʃ]	Schalter
earth [ɜːθ]	Erde
three-phase motor [,θriː feɪz 'məʊtə]	Drehstrommotor
relay ['riːleɪ]	Relais
three-phase switch [,θriː feɪz 'swɪtʃ]	Drehstromschalter
coolant overloads ['kuːlənt əʊvələʊdz]	Thermoschutzschalter
terminal block [,tɜːmɪnl 'blɒk]	Anschlussklemmen
to limit ['lɪmɪt]	begrenzen, beschränken
to regulate ['regjuleɪt]	regulieren
flow [fləʊ]	Fluss
excessive [ɪk'sesɪv]	übermäßig, zu hoch, zu viel
to conduct [kən'dʌkt]	leiten
direction [də'rekʃn]	Richtung
voltage ['vəʊltɪdʒ]	Spannung
electromagnet [ɪ,lektrəʊ'mægnət]	Elektromagnet
to operate ['ɒpəreɪt]	betätigen, steuern
mechanism ['mekənɪzəm]	Mechanismus
mechanical(ly) [mɪ'kænɪkl]	mechanisch
circuit ['sɜːkɪt]	Schaltkreis
incoming supply [,ɪnkʌmɪŋ sə'plaɪ]	Anschlussleitung
46 direction of rotation [də,rekʃn əv rəʊ'teɪʃn]	Drehrichtung P

UNIT WORD LIST

blackboard ['blækbɔːd]	(Wand-)Tafel *P*		**primary** ['praɪməri]	Primär-
rough [rʌf]	grob *P*		**submarine** [ˌsʌbməˈriːn]	U-Boot
accurate ['ækjərət]	genau, präzis *P*		**refrigerator** [rɪˈfrɪdʒəreɪtə]	Kühlschrank
mains [meɪnz]	Stromnetz		**furnace** ['fɜːnɪs]	Schmelzofen, Brennkammer
power supply ['paʊə səplaɪ]	Stromversorgung		**pellet furnace** ['pelɪt fɜːnɪs]	Pelletbrenner
separately-fused disconnect box [ˌseprətli fjuːzd dɪskəˈnekt bɒks]	abgesicherter Schaltkasten		**additional** [əˈdɪʃənl]	zusätzlich
			auxiliary [ɔːgˈzɪliəri]	Neben-, Hilfs-
			in reverse [ɪn rɪˈvɜːs]	umgekehrt
			to lower ['ləʊə]	senken
isolator switch ['aɪsəleɪtə swɪtʃ]	Trennschalter		**conjunction** [kənˈdʒʌŋkʃn]	Verbindung
electrical panel [ɪˌlektrɪkl 'pænl]	Schalttafel		**conventional** [kənˈvenʃənl]	herkömmlich, konventionell
			fuel cell ['fjuːəl sel]	Brennstoffzelle
input wire ['ɪnpʊt waɪə]	Zuleitung		**to power** ['paʊə]	antreiben, mit Energie versorgen
tray [treɪ]	Spanbehälter		**efficiency** [ɪˈfɪʃnsi]	Effizienz
to sheathe [ʃiːð]	ummanteln		**level of efficiency** [ˌlevl əv ɪˈfɪʃnsi]	Effizienzgrad
armoured cable [ˌɑːməd ˈkeɪbl]	Panzerkabel		**to utilize** ['juːtəlaɪz]	nutzen, verwerten
entry point ['entri pɔɪnt]	Zugang		**to operate** ['ɒpəreɪt]	betreiben
terminal ['tɜːmɪnl]	Klemme, Anschlussklemme	51	**sealed** [siːld]	luftdicht
change-gear guard [tʃeɪndʒ ˌgɪə ˈgɑːd]	Wechselradsicherung		**working gas** [ˌwɜːkɪŋ ˈgæs]	Arbeitsgas
			hydrogen ['haɪdrədʒən]	Wasserstoff
secure [sɪˈkjʊə]	sicher, gesichert		**to expand** [ɪkˈspænd]	sich ausdehnen
spindle nose ['spɪndl nəʊz]	Spindelkopf		**piston** ['pɪstən]	Kolben
obstruction [əbˈstrʌkʃn]	Blockierung		**to contract** [kənˈtrækt]	sich zusammenziehen
clear of obstruction [ˌklɪər əv əbˈstrʌkʃn]	frei		**pulse** [pʌls]	Impuls
			to enable [ɪˈneɪbl]	befähigen, ermöglichen, in die Lage versetzen
two-speed ['tuː spiːd]	Zweigang-			
lever ['liːvə]	Hebel		**smooth(ly)** [smuːð]	ruhig
to raise [reɪz]	anheben		**displacer** [dɪsˈpleɪsə]	Verdränger
anticlockwise [ˌæntiˈklɒkwaɪz]	gegen den Uhrzeigersinn		**to heat** [hiːt]	erhitzen
			to cool [kuːl]	kühlen
clockwise ['klɒkwaɪz]	im Uhrzeigersinn		**to displace** [dɪsˈpleɪs]	verdrängen
to interchange ['ɪntətʃeɪndʒ]	vertauschen		**crank shaft** ['kræŋk ʃɑːft]	Kurbelwelle
			flywheel ['flaɪwiːl]	Schwungrad
to isolate ['aɪsəleɪt]	trennen		**to exchange** [ɪksˈtʃeɪndʒ]	austauschen
to refer to sth [rɪˈfɜː tə]	sich auf etw beziehen	52	**to adhere to sth** [ədˈhɪə tə]	eine Sache befolgen, etw beachten
47 **competent** ['kɒmpɪtənt]	befähigt, kompetent			
to wire ['waɪə]	verkabeln		**to invent** [ɪnˈvent]	erfinden
suspect ['sʌspekt]	verdächtig		**to convert** [kənˈvɜːt]	umwandeln
faulty ['fɔːlti]	schadhaft, defekt		**to drive** [draɪv]	antreiben
to label ['leɪbl]	etikettieren		**to supply** [səˈplaɪ]	liefern
socket-outlet ['sɒkɪt aʊtlet]	Steckdose		**nitrogen oxide** [ˌnaɪtrədʒən ˈɒksaɪd]	Stickoxid
to unplug [ˌʌnˈplʌg]	(Stecker) ziehen			
adjustment [əˈdʒʌstmənt]	Änderung, Anpassung, Einstellung		**fuel** ['fjuːəl]	Brennstoff
			to burn [bɜːn]	verbrennen
alteration [ˌɔːltəˈreɪʃn]	Änderung, Umbau		**chlorofluorocarbon (CFC)** [ˌklɔːrəʊˌflʊərəʊˈkɑːbən]	Fluorchlorkohlenwasserstoff (FCKW)
to tackle ['tækl]	unternehmen, in Angriff nehmen			
			booklet ['bʊklət]	Broschüre
exposed [ɪkˈspəʊzd]	freiliegend, ungeschützt	54	**to market** ['mɑːkɪt]	vermarkten
live [laɪv]	unter Strom		**to impress** [ɪmˈpres]	beeindrucken
unless [ənˈles]	es sei denn, außer wenn		**CEO (Chief Executive Officer)** [ˌsiː iː ˈəʊ / ˌtʃiːf ɪgˈzekjətɪv ˈɒfɪsə]	Vorstandsvorsitzende/r, Geschäftsführer/in
unavoidable [ˌʌnəˈvɔɪdəbl]	unvermeidlich			
precaution [prɪˈkɔːʃn]	Vorsichtsmaßnahme, Vorkehrung			
			to show sb around [ˌʃəʊ əˈraʊnd]	jdn herumführen
injury ['ɪndʒəri]	Verletzung(en)			
safety ['seɪfti]	Sicherheit		**loading bay** ['ləʊdɪŋ beɪ]	Laderampe *T*
safety precautions ['seɪfti prɪkɔːʃnz]	Sicherheitsmaßnahmen		**to load** [ləʊd]	laden, beladen werden *T*
			until recently [ənˌtɪl ˈriːsntli]	bis vor kurzem *T*
50 **to be around** [bi əˈraʊnd]	es geben			
to function ['fʌŋkʃn]	funktionieren, laufen		**competition** [ˌkɒmpəˈtɪʃn]	Konkurrenz, Wettbewerb *T*

175

UNIT WORD LIST

fierce [fɪəs]	(Wettbewerb:) hart T	to multiply ['mʌltɪplaɪ]	multiplizieren, malnehmen
annex [ə'neks]	Anbau, Nebengebäude T	to divide by [dɪ'vaɪd baɪ]	teilen durch
to equip [ɪ'kwɪp]	ausrüsten, ausstatten T	squared [skweəd]	im Quadrat, hoch zwei
latest ['leɪtɪst]	neueste/r/s T	cubed [kju:bd]	hoch drei
guideline ['gaɪdlaɪn]	Richtlinie T	to the power of ['pauə əv]	hoch
lab [læb]	Labor T	square root ['skweə ru:t]	Quadratwurzel
guess [ges]	Vermutung T	to pronounce [prə'naʊns]	aussprechen
research [rɪ'sɜ:tʃ]	Forschung T	57 estimate ['estɪmət]	Schätzung
development [dɪ'veləpmənt]	Entwicklung T	prototype ['prəʊtətaɪp]	Prototyp
R & D [ˌɑ:r ən 'di: / rɪˌsɜ:tʃ ən dɪ'veləpmənt]	Forschung- und Entwicklungsabteilung T	rate [reɪt]	Preis, Satz
		overhead rate ['əʊvəhed reɪt]	Überschussrate
personnel [ˌpɜ:sə'nel]	Personal(abteilung) T	labour ['leɪbə]	Arbeit
purchasing ['pɜ:tʃəsɪŋ]	Einkauf(sabteilung) T	administrative overheads [ədˌmɪnɪstrətɪv 'əʊvəhedz]	Verwaltungskosten
sales [seɪlz]	Verkauf, Vertrieb T		
to take up [ˌteɪk 'ʌp]	einnehmen T	distribution overheads [dɪstrɪˌbju:ʃn 'əʊvəhedz]	Vertriebskosten
proud [praʊd]	stolz T		
sausage ['sɒsɪdʒ]	Würstchen T	sale price ['seɪl praɪs]	Verkaufspreis
bean [bi:n]	Bohne T	value added tax (VAT) [ˌvælju: 'ædɪd tæks]	Mehrwertsteuer
chips [tʃɪps]	Pommes frites T		
sophisticated [sə'fɪstɪkeɪtɪd]	anspruchsvoll T	retail price [ˌri:teɪl 'praɪs]	Einzelhandelspreis
		to calculate ['kælkjuleɪt]	berechnen
to invite [ɪn'vaɪt]	einladen T	to dictate [dɪk'teɪt]	diktieren
chef [ʃef]	Küchenchef/in T	58 drastic(ally) ['dræstɪk]	drastisch
excellent ['eksələnt]	hervorragend T	skill [skɪl]	Fähigkeit, Fertigkeit
mediterranean [ˌmedɪtə'reɪnɪən]	mediterran T	contract ['kɒntrækt]	Vertrag
dish [dɪʃ]	Gericht T	to cancel ['kænsl]	streichen
to look forward to sth [ˌlʊk 'fɔ:wəd tə]	sich auf etw freuen T	entire(ly) [ɪn'taɪə]	ganz
		profit margin ['prɒfɪt mɑ:dʒɪn]	Gewinnspanne
to sound [saʊnd]	klingen T		
organizational chart [ɔ:gənaɪˌzeɪʃənl 'tʃɑ:t]	Organigramm	to complain [kəm'pleɪn]	sich beschweren, sich beklagen
logistics [lə'dʒɪstɪks]	Logistik	overhead expenses [ˌəʊvəhed ɪk'spensɪz]	Gemeinkosten
financial department [faɪˌnænʃl dɪ'pɑ:tmənt]	Finanzabteilung		
		chargeable ['tʃɑ:dʒəbl]	zuweisbar, zuzuordnen
accounting [ə'kaʊntɪŋ]	Buchführung, Buchhaltung	to include [ɪn'klu:d]	umfassen, einschließen
vocational training [vəʊˌkeɪʃənl 'treɪnɪŋ]	Berufsausbildung	rent [rent]	Miete
		utilities [ju:'tɪlətiz]	Nebenkosten
55 reasonable ['ri:znəbl]	vernünftig	insurance [ɪn'ʃʊərəns]	Versicherung
to contact sb ['kɒntækt]	sich mit jdm in Verbindung setzen	fixed costs [ˌfɪkst 'kɒsts]	Fixkosten
		to distribute [dɪ'strɪbju:t]	verteilen, aufteilen
subdivision [ˌsʌbdɪ'vɪʒn]	Unterabteilung	equally ['i:kwəli]	gleich, gleichmäßig
records ['rekɔ:dz]	Daten, Aufzeichnungen	ongoing ['ɒngəʊɪŋ]	laufend
bill [bɪl]	Rechnung	to imagine [ɪ'mædʒɪn]	sich vorstellen
profit ['prɒfɪt]	Gewinn	convincing [kən'vɪnsɪŋ]	überzeugend
loss [lɒs]	Verlust	explanation [ˌeksplə'neɪʃn]	Erklärung
spreadsheet ['spredʃi:t]	Tabelle, Tabellenkalkulation(sbogen)	59 to select [sɪ'lekt]	auswählen, wählen
		to incorporate [ɪn'kɔ:pəreɪt]	einbeziehen
stage [steɪdʒ]	Schritt, Phase	regenerator [rɪ'dʒenəreɪtə]	Regenerator
to hire ['haɪə]	(Personal) einstellen	to improve [ɪm'pru:v]	verbessern
to fire ['faɪə]	entlassen, feuern	overall [ˌəʊvər'ɔ:l]	gesamt
thankfully ['θæŋkfəli]	Gott sei Dank, glücklicherweise	to expose sth to sth [ɪk'spəʊz tə]	etw einer Sache aussetzen
to expand [ɪk'spænd]	expandieren	contained [kən'teɪnd]	enthalten
to interview ['ɪntəvju:]	ein Vorstellungsgespräch führen	expansion [ɪk'spænʃn]	Ausdehnung
		conduit ['kɒndjuɪt]	Rohrleitung
applied [ə'plaɪd]	angewandt	to transfer ['trænsfɜ:]	weiterleiten, übertragen
psychology [saɪ'kɒlədʒi]	Psychologie	dominant ['dɒmɪnənt]	maßgeblich
measurement ['meʒəmənt]	Maß, Messung	to consider [kən'sɪdə]	berücksichtigen, bedenken, in Erwägung ziehen
reading ['ri:dɪŋ]	Messwert		
equals ['i:kwəlz]	ist gleich	simplicity [sɪm'plɪsəti]	Einfachheit

UNIT WORD LIST

demonstration tool [ˌdemənˈstreɪʃn tuːl]	Anschauungsmittel
ease of construction [ˌiːz əv kənˈstrʌkʃn]	Einfachheit der Konstruktion
durability [ˌdjʊərəˈbɪləti]	Haltbarkeit, Langlebigkeit
parabolic [ˌpærəˈbɒlɪk]	Parabol-
inexpensive [ˌɪnɪkˈspensɪv]	kostengünstig
to transmit [trænsˈmɪt]	übertragen
rod assembly [ˈrɒd əsembli]	Gestänge
to employ [ɪmˈplɔɪ]	anwenden
conduction [kənˈdʌkʃn]	Leitung
copper [ˈkɒpə]	Kupfer
to focus [ˈfəʊkəs]	sich konzentrieren
focal point [ˈfəʊkl pɔɪnt]	Brennpunkt
to attach [əˈtætʃ]	befestigen, anbringen
to pass through [ˈpɑːs θruː]	hindurchgehen
base [beɪs]	Sockel
enclosed [ɪnˈkləʊzd]	eingeschlossen
radiation [ˌreɪdiˈeɪʃn]	Strahlung
conducting rod [kənˈdʌktɪŋ rɒd]	Leiterstab
framework [ˈfreɪmwɜːk]	Gestell
sunlight [ˈsʌnlaɪt]	Sonnenlicht
to implement [ˈɪmplɪmənt]	einsetzen
60 scale [skeɪl]	Skala
fairly [ˈfeəli]	ziemlich
loose [luːs]	locker
tight [taɪt]	eng, stramm
pedal [ˈpedl]	Pedal
shock absorber [ˈʃɒk əbsɔːbə]	Stoßdämpfer
cogwheel [ˈkɒgwiːl]	Zahnrad
hinge [hɪndʒ]	Scharnier
DVD tray [ˌdiː viː ˈdiː treɪ]	DVD-Schublade
bowl [bəʊl]	Schüssel
pressure cooker [ˈpreʃə kʊkə]	Schnellkochtopf
radial bearing [ˌreɪdiəl ˈbeərɪŋ]	Radiallager
ball bearing [ˌbɔːl ˈbeərɪŋ]	Kugellager
roller [ˈrəʊlə]	Wälzkörper
roller bearing [ˌrəʊlə ˈbeərɪŋ]	Wälzlager
plain bearing [ˌpleɪn ˈbeərɪŋ]	Gleitlager
cage [keɪdʒ]	Käfig
inner race [ˌɪnə ˈreɪs]	Innenring
outer race [ˌaʊtə ˈreɪs]	Außenring
rolling ball [ˈrəʊlɪŋ bɔːl]	Kugellagerkugel
arrow [ˈærəʊ]	Pfeil
radial force [ˌreɪdiəl ˈfɔːs]	Radialkraft
axial force [ˌæksiəl ˈfɔːs]	Axialkraft
angular [ˈæŋgjələ]	schräg T
row [rəʊ]	Reihe T
to bear [beə]	tragen, aushalten T
loading capacity [ˈləʊdɪŋ kəpæsəti]	Traglast T
limited [ˈlɪmɪtɪd]	begrenzt T
ability [əˈbɪləti]	Fähigkeit T
self-aligning [ˌself əˈlaɪnɪŋ]	Selbstausrichtung T
to dismantle [dɪsˈmæntl]	demontieren, auseinanderbauen T
needle [ˈniːdl]	Nadel T
capacity [kəˈpæsəti]	Belastung T
to maintain [meɪnˈteɪn]	aufrecht erhalten T
condition [kənˈdɪʃn]	Bedingung, Umstand T
huge [hjuːdʒ]	groß, riesig T
spherical [ˈsferɪkl]	sphärisch, kugelförmig T
groove [gruːv]	Rille T
to compensate [ˈkɒmpenseɪt]	ausgleichen T
middle error [ˌmɪdl ˈerə]	Fluchtfehler T
housing [ˈhaʊzɪŋ]	Gehäuse T
barrel [ˈbærəl]	Tonne T
61 supporting plate [səˌpɔːtɪŋ ˈpleɪt]	Halteplatte
to press [pres]	drücken, pressen
clearance fit [ˈklɪərəns fɪt]	Abmaße
62 semi-locating bearing [semi ləʊˌkeɪtɪŋ ˈbeərɪŋ]	Stützlager P
full complement cylindrical roller bearing [fʊl ˌkɒmplɪmənt səˌlɪndrɪkl ˈrəʊlə beərɪŋ]	vollrolliges Zylinderrollenlager P
load rating [ˈləʊd reɪtɪŋ]	Last P
mass [mæs]	Masse P
gripper [ˈgrɪpə]	Greifer
63 mounting [ˈmaʊntɪŋ]	Montage
link [lɪŋk]	Verbindung
slide bearing [ˈslaɪd beərɪŋ]	Gleitlager
bearing pin [ˈbeərɪŋ pɪn]	Lagerstift
circlip [ˈsɜːklɪp]	Sprengring
crank [kræŋk]	Kurbel
counter plate [ˈkaʊntə pleɪt]	Befestigungsplatte
attachment [əˈtætʃmənt]	Befestigung
template [ˈtempleɪt]	Schablone
64 warranty [ˈwɒrənti]	Garantie, Gewährleistung
wholesaler [ˈhəʊlseɪlə]	Großhändler
aftermarket [ˈɑːftəmɑːkɪt]	Zubehörmarkt
wheel hub unit [ˈwiːl hʌb juːnɪt]	Radlager
user [ˈjuːzə]	Benutzer/in, Anwender/in
purchaser [ˈpɜːtʃəsə]	Käufer/in
defect [ˈdiːfekt]	Fehler
defect in workmanship [ˌdiːfekt ɪn ˈwɜːkmənʃɪp]	Verarbeitungsfehler
period [ˈpɪəriəd]	Zeitraum
malfunction [ˌmælˈfʌŋkʃn]	Defekt, Fehlfunktion
abuse [əˈbjuːs]	unsachgemäßer Gebrauch
accident [ˈæksɪdənt]	Unfall
misapplication [ˌmɪsæplɪˈkeɪʃn]	falsche Verwendung
improper [ɪmˈprɒpə]	falsch, unsachgemäß
removal [rɪˈmuːvl]	Ausbau
wear and tear [ˌweər ən ˈteə]	Abnutzung, Verschleiß
to cover [ˈkʌvə]	decken, abdecken
to fail sth [feɪl]	etw nicht erfüllen
fit [fɪt]	geeignet
intended [ɪnˈtendɪd]	beabsichtigt
purpose [ˈpɜːpəs]	Zweck

UNIT WORD LIST

attributable to [əˈtrɪbjətəbl tə]	bedingt durch, zurückzuführen auf	**cross connection** [ˌkrɒs kəˈnekʃn]	Querverbindung
to define [dɪˈfaɪn]	bestimmen, definieren	**shut-off valve** [ˌʃʌt ˈɒf vælv]	Sperrventil
warranty disclosure [ˈwɒrənti dɪsklˈəʊʒə]	Garantiebedingungen	**equivalent** [ɪˈkwɪvələnt]	Entsprechung
replacement [rɪˈpleɪsmənt]	Austausch	**plumber** [ˈplʌmə]	Klempner/in, Installateur/in
defective [dɪˈfektɪv]	fehlerhaft, defekt	**plumbing company** [ˈplʌmɪŋ kʌmpəni]	Klempnerei, Installationsbetrieb *T*
damage [ˈdæmɪdʒ]	Schaden	**foreman** [ˈfɔːmən]	Vorarbeiter *T*
consequential damages [ˌkɒnsɪˌkwənʃl ˈdæmɪdʒ]	Folgeschäden	**reservoir** [ˈrezəvwɑː]	Behälter *T*
wheel bearing module [ˈwiːl beərɪŋ mɒdjuːl]	Radlagermodul	**piping** [ˈpaɪpɪŋ]	Rohrleitungen *T*
		wallplug [ˈwɔːlplʌg]	Dübel *T*
		ceiling [ˈsiːlɪŋ]	Decke *T*
differential [ˌdɪfəˈrenʃl]	Differential	**beam** [biːm]	(Stahl-)Träger *T*
mileage [ˈmaɪlɪdʒ]	Kilometerstand	**clamp** [klæmp]	Schelle, Klemme *T*
wages [ˈweɪdʒɪz]	Lohn	**to clamp** [klæmp]	klemmen, befestigen *T*
further [ˈfɜːðə]	weitere/r/s	**commissioning** [kəˈmɪʃnɪŋ]	Inbetriebnahme *T*
hire car [ˈhaɪə kɑː]	Mietwagen	**to commission** [kəˈmɪʃn]	in Betrieb nehmen
breakdown [ˈbreɪkdaʊn]	Panne, Schaden	69 **distribution** [ˌdɪstrɪˈbjuːʃn]	Verteilung
66 **topic** [ˈtɒpɪk]	Thema	**installation instructions** [ˌɪnstəˈleɪʃn ɪnstrʌkʃnz]	Montageanleitung
subject line [ˈsʌbdʒɪkt laɪn]	Betreffzeile		
to mention [ˈmenʃn]	erwähnen, nennen	**plant** [plɑːnt]	Anlage
confirmation [ˌkɒnfəˈmeɪʃn]	Bestätigung	**pressure** [ˈpreʃə]	Druck
invoice [ˈɪnvɔɪs]	Rechnung	**line** [laɪn]	Leitung
involved in sth [ɪnˈvɒlvd ɪn]	in etw verwickelt, an etw beteiligt	**to lay** [leɪ]	(Leitung etc.) verlegen
		at a slope [ət ə ˈsləʊp]	mit Gefälle
to disassemble [ˌdɪsəˈsembl]	zerlegen, auseinanderbauen	**to drain** [dreɪn]	entwässern
		periodically [ˌpɪəriˈɒdɪkli]	regelmäßig
a. s. a. p. [ˌeɪ es eɪ ˈpiː]	so bald wie möglich	**treated air** [ˌtriːtɪd ˈeə]	aufbereitete Luft
complaint [kəmˈpleɪnt]	Reklamation, Beschwerde	**operating temperature** [ˈɒpəreɪtɪŋ temprətʃə]	Betriebstemperatur
67 **to set out** [ˌset ˈaʊt]	darlegen, darstellen		
dissatisfaction [ˌdɪsˌsætɪsˈfækʃn]	Unzufriedenheit	**otherwise** [ˈʌðəwaɪz]	sonst, ansonsten
		to condense [kənˈdens]	kondensieren
to expect [ɪkˈspekt]	erwarten	**supply-pressure line** [səˈplaɪ preʃə laɪn]	Versorgungsdruckleitung
damaged [ˈdæmɪdʒd]	beschädigt, schadhaft		
demand [dɪˈmɑːnd]	Forderung	**signal-pressure line** [ˈsɪgnəl preʃə laɪn]	Signaldruckleitung
expectation [ˌekspekˈteɪʃn]	Erwartung		
threat [θret]	Drohung	**polyethylene** [ˌpɒliˈeθəliːn]	Polethylen
refund [ˈriːfʌnd]	Rückerstattung	**polyamide** [ˌpɒliˈæmaɪd]	Polyamid
compensation [ˌkɒmpənˈseɪʃn]	Vergütung, Entschädigung	**soft copper** [ˌsɒft ˈkɒpə]	Weichkupfer
		tubing [ˈtjuːbɪŋ]	Rohre
inconvenience [ˌɪnkənˈviːniəns]	Unannehmlichkeit(en)	**requirement** [rɪˈkwaɪəmənt]	Vorschrift
		fire hazard [ˈfaɪə hæzəd]	Brandgefahr, Feuergefahr
account [əˈkaʊnt]	Konto	**rodent** [ˈrəʊdnt]	Nagetier
matter [ˈmætə]	Sache, Angelegenheit	**to observe** [əbˈzɜːv]	beachten
satisfaction [ˌsætɪsˈfækʃn]	Zufriedenheit	**manner** [ˈmænə]	Art (und Weise)
polite [pəˈlaɪt]	höflich	**force** [fɔːs]	Kraft
68 **pneumatics** [njuːˈmætɪks]	Pneumatik	**to act** [ækt]	ausüben
pneumatic [njuːˈmætɪk]	pneumatisch	**nipple** [ˈnɪpl]	Nippel
air pistol [ˈeə pɪstl]	Druckluftschrauber	**external** [ɪkˈstɜːnl]	Außen-
amount [əˈmaʊnt]	Menge	**throughput** [ˈθruːpʊt]	Durchsatz
compressed [kəmˈprest]	komprimiert	**pressure drop** [ˈpreʃə drɒp]	Druckabfall
compressed air [kəmˌprest ˈeə]	Druckluft	**to take into consideration** [ˌteɪk ɪntə kənˌsɪdəˈreɪʃn]	berücksichtigen
to generate [ˈdʒenəreɪt]	erzeugen	**screw-in nipple** [ˌskruː ɪn ˈnɪpl]	Einschraubnippel
currently [ˈkʌrəntli]	gegenwärtig, im Moment		
production area [prəˈdʌkʃn eəriə]	Produktionsfläche	**tape** [teɪp]	Band, Klebeband
		sealing stick [ˈsiːlɪŋ stɪk]	Dichtstift
interlinked [ɪntəˈlɪŋkt]	miteinander verbunden	**torque** [tɔːk]	Drehkraft, Drehmoment
to consist of [kənˈsɪst əv]	bestehen aus	**to apply** [əˈplaɪ]	anwenden
loop [luːp]	Ringleitung	**instead of** [ɪnˈsted əv]	anstatt

UNIT WORD LIST

tube remover ['tju:b rɪmu:və]	Abziehwerkzeug	
excessively [ɪk'sesɪvli]	übermäßig	
to widen ['waɪdn]	weiten	
sloped [sləʊpt]	mit Gefälle	
marten ['mɑ:tɪn]	Marder	
70 to monitor ['mɒnɪtə]	überwachen	
scaffolding ['skæfəldɪŋ]	Gerüst	
71 hose [həʊz]	Schlauch	
slack [slæk]	durchhängend, nicht gespannt	
to tear apart [ˌteər ə'pɑ:t]	auseinanderreißen	
sharp [ʃɑ:p]	scharf, hier: stark	
bend [bend]	Krümmung	
bending ['bendɪŋ]	Krümmung	
fitting piece ['fɪtɪŋ pi:s]	Anschlussstück	
hydraulics [haɪ'drɔ:lɪks]	Hydraulik	
to make sense [ˌmeɪk 'sens]	sinnvoll sein	
fast response [ˌfɑ:st rɪ'spɒns]	kurze Ansprech-/ Reaktionszeit(en) P	
fluid ['flu:ɪd]	Flüssigkeit P	
to leak out [ˌli:k 'aʊt]	austreten P	
flow [fləʊ]	Strom, Fluss P	
flammable ['flæməbl]	entflammbar P	
output force ['aʊtpʊt fɔ:s]	Nutzkraft P	
corrosion [kə'rəʊʒn]	Korrosion P	
transmission [trænsˈmɪʃn]	Übertragung P	
compressibility [kəmˌpresə'bɪləti]	Komprimierbarkeit P	
to occur [ə'kɜ:]	auftreten, vorkommen, geschehen P	
72 to ventilate ['ventɪleɪt]	entlüften	
73 safety sign ['seɪfti saɪn]	Sicherheitszeichen, -symbol	
to discover [dɪ'skʌvə]	entdecken	
fork-lift truck [ˌfɔ:klɪft 'trʌk]	Gabelstapler	
operation [ˌɒpə'reɪʃn]	Betrieb	
hazard ['hæzəd]	Gefahr	
no entry [nəʊ 'entri]	Eintritt verboten. Kein Zugang.	
naked light [ˌneɪkɪd 'laɪt]	offenes Licht	
ear protectors ['ɪə prətektəz]	Gehörschutz	
hard hat (AE) [ˌhɑ:d 'hæt]	Schutzhelm	
safety helmet ['seɪfti helmɪt]	Schutzhelm	
welding mask ['weldɪŋ mɑ:sk]	Schweißschutzmaske	
highly flammable [ˌhaɪli 'flæməbl]	leicht entflammbar	
high voltage [ˌhaɪ 'vəʊltɪdʒ]	Hochspannung	
protective footwear [prəˌtektɪv 'fʊtweə]	Sicherheitsschuhe	
glove [glʌv]	Handschuh	
hairnet ['heənet]	Haarnetz	
visor ['vaɪzə]	Schutzvisier	
to operate ['ɒpəreɪt]	bedienen	
74 to measure ['meʒə]	messen, vermessen	
supervision [ˌsu:pə'vɪʒn]	Überwachung, Beobachtung, Beaufsichtigung	
without supervision [wɪˌðaʊt su:pə'vɪʒn]	ohne Aufsicht	
scales [skeɪlz]	Waage	
to weigh [weɪ]	wiegen, abwiegen	
to try out [ˌtraɪ 'aʊt]	ausprobieren	
oscilloscope [ə'sɪləskəʊp]	Oszilloskop	
calculator ['kælkjuleɪtə]	(Taschen-)Rechner	
to tidy up [ˌtaɪdi 'ʌp]	aufräumen	
remedy ['remədi]	Abhilfe	
headline ['hedlaɪn]	Überschrift	
air powered ['eə paʊəd]	druckluftbetrieben	
to exceed [ɪk'si:d]	übertreffen	
rating ['reɪtɪŋ]	Auslegung, Herstellervorgabe	
to over-speed [ˌəʊvə'spi:d]	zu schnell laufen, zu hoch drehen	
hazardous ['hæzədəs]	gefährlich	
breakage ['breɪkɪdʒ]	Bruch	
to discharge [dɪs'tʃɑ:dʒ]	abgeben	
exhaust air [ɪgˌzɔ:st 'eə]	Abluft	
muffled ['mʌfld]	gedämpft	
noisy ['nɔɪzi]	laut	
prolonged [prə'lɒŋd]	fortdauernd	
exposure [ɪk'spəʊʒə]	Ausgesetztsein, Belastung	
hearing ['hɪərɪŋ]	Gehör	
to feed [fi:d]	versorgen	
antifreeze ['æntifri:z]	Frostschutzmittel	
contaminated [kən'tæmɪneɪtɪd]	kontaminiert	
environment [ɪn'vaɪrənmənt]	Umgebung	
to discharge [dɪs'tʃɑ:dʒ]	austreten	
to grip [grɪp]	greifen	
loss of grip [ˌlɒs əv 'grɪp]	Griffigkeitsverlust	
frostbite ['frɒstbaɪt]	Erfrierung	
to stiffen ['stɪfn]	versteifen, steif werden lassen	
grounded ['graʊndɪd]	geerdet	
to contact ['kɒntækt]	berühren	
severed ['sevəd]	abgetrennt, durchtrennt	
to whip around [ˌwɪp ə'raʊnd]	(wie eine Peitsche) um sich schlagen	
violent(ly) ['vaɪələnt]	heftig	
to shut off [ˌʃʌt 'ɒf]	absperren, abstellen	
particle ['pɑ:tɪkl]	Teilchen, Partikel	
chipping hammer ['tʃɪpɪŋ hæmə]	Schlaghammer	
rock drill ['rɒk drɪl]	Bohrhammer	
rotary drill [ˌrəʊtəri 'drɪl]	Bohrgerät	
sander ['sændə]	Schleifgerät	
75 fitting ['fɪtɪŋ]	Anschluss, Verbindungsstück	
male [meɪl]	männlich	
to wipe [waɪp]	abwischen	
to eliminate [ɪ'lɪmɪneɪt]	eliminieren, ausschließen	
to get caught up [get ˌkɔ:t 'ʌp]	sich verfangen	
reciprocating [rɪ'sɪprəkeɪtɪŋ]	hin- und hergehend	
muffler ['mʌflə]	Geräuschdämpfer	
exhaust [ɪg'zɔ:st]	Abluftrohr	
to take chances [ˌteɪk 'tʃɑ:nsɪz]	Risiken eingehen	

UNIT WORD LIST

precious ['preʃəs]	wertvoll	
eyesight ['aɪsaɪt]	Augenlicht	
kinked [kɪŋkt]	geknickt	
crushed [krʌʃt]	gequetscht	
rule [ruːl]	Vorschrift	

76
- to correspond [ˌkɒrɪ'spɒnd] — entsprechen
- life-span ['laɪfspæn] — Lebensdauer
- uncommon [ʌn'kɒmən] — ungewöhnlich
- to last [lɑːst] — dauern, Bestand haben, *hier:* laufen, in Betrieb sein
- initial cost [ɪˌnɪʃl 'kɒst] — Anschaffungskosten, Anlagekosten
- to bathe [beɪð] — baden, schwimmen
- coupler ['kʌplə] — Kupplung, Verbindungsstück
- confined space [kənˌfaɪnd 'speɪs] — geschlossener Raum
- poorly ventilated [ˌpʊəli 'ventɪleɪtɪd] — schlecht belüftet
- to freeze up [ˌfriːz 'ʌp] — einfrieren
- to become inoperable [bɪˌkʌm ɪn'ɒpərəbl] — ausfallen, versagen
- underwater [ˌʌndə'wɔːtə] — unter Wasser
- aside [ə'saɪd] — abgesehen von
- pressurized ['preʃəraɪzd] — unter Druck
- to compress [kəm'pres] — sich verdichten (lassen)
- liquid ['lɪkwɪd] — Flüssigkeit
- mess [mes] — Schweinerei, Chaos
- available [ə'veɪləbl] — erhältlich, verfügbar
- gallons per minute (gpm) [ˌgælənz pə 'mɪnɪt] — Gallonen (= 3,785 Liter) pro Minute
- trash pump ['træʃ pʌmp] — Abwasserpumpe
- sludge pump ['slʌdʒ pʌmp] — Schlammpumpe

77
- high-speed cutting [ˌhaɪ spiːd 'kʌtɪŋ] — Hochgeschwindigkeitszerspanung (HSC)
- variety [və'raɪəti] — Auswahl, Reihe
- a variety of [ə və'raɪəti əv] — verschiedene
- economic(ally) [ˌiːkə'nɒmɪk] — wirtschaftlich
- artificial [ˌɑːtɪ'fɪʃl] — künstlich
- hip joint ['hɪp dʒɔɪnt] — Hüftgelenk
- dental ['dentl] — Zahn-
- die making ['daɪ meɪkɪŋ] — Herstellung eines Spritzgusswerkzeugs
- impeller [ɪm'pelə] — Lüfterrad
- jet engine [ˌdʒet 'endʒɪn] — Düsentriebwerk
- artificial ventilation [ɑːtɪˌfɪʃl ventɪ'leɪʃn] — Belüftung
- stamping tool ['stæmpɪŋ tuːl] — Stanzwerkzeug
- wheel rim ['wiːl rɪm] — Felge
- aerospace industry ['eərəʊspeɪs ɪndəstri] — Luft- und Raumfahrtbranche
- dental equipment [ˌdentl ɪ'kwɪpmənt] — zahntechnische Aurüstung
- clockwork ['klɒkwɜːk] — Uhrwerk
- comparatively [kəm'pærətɪvli] — vergleichsweise

78
- machine operator [məˌʃiːn 'ɒpəreɪtə] — Maschinenführer/in
- highly accurate production [ˌhaɪli ˌækjərət prə'dʌkʃn] — Präzisionsfertigung

79
- precision [prɪ'sɪʒn] — Präzision
- dynamics [daɪ'næmɪks] — Dynamik
- unparalleled [ʌn'pærəleld] — unerreicht, einmalig
- foundation [faʊn'deɪʃn] — Grundlage
- outstanding [aʊt'stændɪŋ] — herausragend
- closed gantry [ˌkləʊzd 'gæntri] — geschlossene Portalausführung
- long-lasting [ˌlɒŋ 'lɑːstɪŋ] — lang anhaltend, dauerhaft
- acceleration [əkˌselə'reɪʃn] — Beschleunigung
- receiver [rɪ'siːvə] — Werkzeugaufnahme
- to withstand [wɪð'stænd] — aushalten, standhalten
- chipping-time volume ['tʃɪpɪŋ taɪm vɒljuːm] — Zerspanungsvolumen
- layer ['leɪə] — Schicht
- transfer rack ['trænsfɜː ræk] — Maschinenbett *(Führung der Werkzeugschlitten)*

80
- pallet exchange ['pælət ɪkstʃeɪndʒ] — Palettenwechsel
- pallet storage ['pælət stɔːrɪdʒ] — Palettenspeicher
- control pad [kən'trəʊl pæd] — Anzeige- und Bediengerät
- agreement key [ə'griːmənt kiː] — Bestätigungstaste
- emergency stop [ɪ'mɜːdʒənsi stɒp] — Notausschalter
- machine-specific [məˌʃiːn spə'sɪfɪk] — gerätespezifisch
- softkey ['sɒftkiː] — virtuelle Tasten auf dem Touchscreen
- operating panel ['ɒpəreɪtɪŋ pænl] — Bedienfeld

81
- utilization [ˌjuːtəlaɪ'zeɪʃn] — Gebrauch, Verwendung
- glass fibre [ˌglɑːs 'faɪbə] — Glasfaser
- reinforced [ˌriːɪn'fɔːst] — verstärkt
- intended for [ɪn'tendɪd fə] — geeignet für, gedacht für
- handling ['hændlɪŋ] — Einsatz von etw
- raw part [ˌrɔː 'pɑːt] — Rohling
- light metal [ˌlaɪt 'metl] — Leichtmetall
- maze [meɪz] — Labyrinth
- square [skweə] — *(Brettspiel:)* Feld
- stress [stres] — Betonung

82
- operating mode ['ɒpəreɪtɪŋ məʊd] — Betriebsart, Betriebsmodus
- selector switch [sɪ'lektə swɪtʃ] — Wahlschalter
- to appear [ə'pɪə] — erscheinen
- to indicate ['ɪndɪkeɪt] — anzeigen
- to insert [ɪn'sɜːt] — einsetzen, einstecken
- memory ['meməri] — Speicher
- authorization [ˌɔːθəraɪ'zeɪʃn] — Berechtigung, Autorisierung
- illuminated [ɪ'luːmɪneɪtɪd] — beleuchtet
- to apply [ə'plaɪ] — *(elektr. Spannung:)* anlegen
- supply voltage [sə'plaɪ vəʊltɪdʒ] — Versorgungsspannung
- desired [dɪ'zaɪəd] — gewünscht
- to remain [rɪ'meɪn] — bleiben
- unchanged [ʌn'tʃeɪndʒd] — unverändert

83
- selection [sɪ'lekʃn] — Wahl
- current(ly) ['kʌrənt] — aktuell
- to display [dɪ'spleɪ] — anzeigen

UNIT WORD LIST

to highlight	['haɪlaɪt]	hervorheben
84 to get mixed up	[ˌget ˌmɪkst 'ʌp]	durcheinandergeraten
fault message	['fɔːlt mesɪdʒ]	Fehlermeldung
cause	[kɔːz]	Ursache, Grund
e.g.	[ˌiː 'dʒiː]	z.B.
valid	['vælɪd]	gültig
appropriate	[ə'prəʊpriət]	entsprechend, passend, geeignet
error message	['erə mesɪdʒ]	Fehlermeldung T
permission	[pə'mɪʃn]	Erlaubnis, Genehmigung T
assistance	[ə'sɪstəns]	Hilfe T
probable	['prɒbəbl]	wahrscheinlich T
to act out	[ˌækt 'aʊt]	spielen
remaining	[rɪ'meɪnɪŋ]	übrige/r/s
88 brewery	['bruːəri]	Brauerei
beer	[bɪə]	Bier
to cope	[kəʊp]	zurechtkommen
increase	['ɪŋkriːs]	Steigerung
production plant	[prə'dʌkʃn plɑːnt]	Produktionsstätte, -anlage
supply	[sə'plaɪ]	Versorgung, Belieferung, Vorrat
raw material	[ˌrɔː mə'tɪəriəl]	Rohstoff
packaging	['pækɪdʒɪŋ]	Verpackung
deal	[diːl]	Geschäft, Abschluss, Vertrag
brand	[brænd]	Marke
tie-in deal	[ˌtaɪ 'ɪn diːl]	Vertragsbindung
lager	['lɑːɡə]	Pilsener
to anticipate	[æn'tɪsɪpeɪt]	erwarten, vorhersehen
89 to modernize	['mɒdənaɪz]	modernisieren
plant manager	['plɑːnt mænɪdʒə]	Werksleiter/in
module	['mɒdjuːl]	Modul
adaptable	[ə'dæptəbl]	variabel, vielseitig, anpassungsfähig
conveyor system	[kən'veɪə sɪstəm]	Fördersystem, -anlage
to take up	[ˌteɪk 'ʌp]	(Platz) einnehmen, benötigen
shop floor	[ˌʃɒp 'flɔː]	Fertigungsbereich, Produktionsbereich
versatility	[ˌvɜːsə'tɪləti]	Vielseitigkeit
to adapt	[ə'dæpt]	anpassen
palletising	['pælətaɪzɪŋ]	Palettieren
to increase	[ɪn'kriːs]	steigern
diagram	['daɪəɡræm]	Grafik, Skizze
conveyor lane	[kən'veɪə leɪn]	Fließband
to handle	['hændl]	handhaben, ausgelegt werden für
to pass	[pɑːs]	vorbeifahren, -laufen
portal	['pɔːtl]	portal
assembly	[ə'sembli]	Zusammenstellung
stage	[steɪdʒ]	Station
assembly stage	[ə'sembli steɪdʒ]	Zusammenstellungsstation
to grasp	[ɡrɑːsp]	greifen
to assemble	[ə'sembl]	zusammenstellen
to preselect	[ˌpriːsɪ'lekt]	vorwählen, vorher auswählen
guiding device	['ɡaɪdɪŋ dɪvaɪs]	Führungseinrichtung
complicated	['kɒmplɪkeɪtɪd]	kompliziert
disposable	[dɪ'spəʊzəbl]	Einweg-
to arrange	[ə'reɪndʒ]	anordnen
supplement	['sʌplɪmənt]	Ergänzung
shrink-wrapper	['ʃrɪŋkræpə]	Schrumpffolien-verpackungsmaschine
to wrap	[ræp]	wickeln
foil	[fɔɪl]	Folie
to shrink	[ʃrɪŋk]	schrumpfen
tight	[taɪt]	fest
fast	[fɑːst]	fest
capable of sth	['keɪpəbl əv]	zu etw fähig, imstande
90 accessible	[ək'sesəbl]	zugänglich
mounting	['maʊntɪŋ]	Montieren
fin	[fɪn]	hier: Nase
gentle	['dʒentl]	behutsam, sanft
to control	[kən'trəʊl]	steuern, regeln
to place	[pleɪs]	platzieren, setzen, stellen, legen
to convey	[kən'veɪ]	transportieren, befördern
distribution	[ˌdɪstrɪ'bjuːʃn]	Vertrieb
baggage claim	['bæɡɪdʒ kleɪm]	Gepäckausgabe
baggage trolley	['bæɡɪdʒ trɒli]	Gepäckwagen
currency	['kʌrənsi]	Währung
barber shop	['bɑːbə ʃɒp]	Friseur
first aid	[ˌfɜːst 'eɪd]	Erste Hilfe
left baggage	[ˌleft 'bæɡɪdʒ]	Gepäckaufbewahrung
lost property	[ˌlɒst 'prɒpəti]	Fundbüro
rental	['rentl]	Vermietung
to take turns	[ˌteɪk 'tɜːnz]	sich abwechseln
luggage	['lʌɡɪdʒ]	Gepäck
severe	[sɪ'vɪə]	stark, schwer
stomach pain(s)	['stʌmək peɪnz]	Bauchschmerzen
dizzy	['dɪzi]	schwindlig
91 tag	[tæɡ]	Anhänger, Etikett
identity card	[aɪ'dentəti kɑːd]	Personalausweis T
driving licence	['draɪvɪŋ laɪsns]	Führerschein T
to rent	[rent]	mieten T
not applicable	[ˌnɒt ə'plɪkəbl]	(in Formularen:) entfällt, keine Angabe T
hyphen	['haɪfn]	Trenn-/Bindestrich
underscore	[ˌʌndə'skɔː]	Unterstrich
receptionist	[rɪ'sepʃənɪst]	Empangsmitarbeiter/in
92 twin bed	[ˌtwɪn 'bed]	Einzelbett (in einem Zweibettzimmer)
double bed	[ˌdʌbl 'bed]	Doppelbett
registration	[ˌredʒɪ'streɪʃn]	Anmeldung
form	[fɔːm]	Formular
cash	[kæʃ]	Bargeld
debit card	['debɪt kɑːd]	Geldkarte
with en suite bathroom	[wɪð ˌswiːt 'bɑːθruːm]	(Zimmer) mit eigenem Bad
overlooking	[ˌəʊvə'lʊkɪŋ]	mit Blick auf
blanket	['blæŋkɪt]	Decke

UNIT WORD LIST

non-allergic [ˌnɒn ə'lɜːdʒɪk]	antiallergisch
pillow ['pɪləʊ]	Kopfkissen
to serve [sɜːv]	servieren
arrival [ə'raɪvl]	Ankunft, Eintreffen *P*
departure [dɪ'pɑːtʃə]	Abreise *P*
expiry date [ɪk'spaɪəri deɪt]	Verfallsdatum, *P*
sat nav ['sætnæv]	Satelliten-Navigationsgerät

93 **directions** [də'rekʃnz] — Wegbeschreibung
roadworks ['rəʊdwɜːks] — Straßenbauarbeiten
traffic jam ['træfɪk dʒæm] — Stau
to suggest [sə'dʒest] — vorschlagen
route [ruːt] — Weg, Route
to pick up [ˌpɪk 'ʌp] — abholen

94 **to give directions** [gɪv də'rekʃnz] — den Weg beschreiben
crossroads ['krɒsrəʊdz] — Straßenkreuzung
traffic lights ['træfɪk laɪts] — Ampel
road junction ['rəʊd dʒʌŋkʃn] — Straßenkreuzung
roundabout ['raʊndəbaʊt] — Kreisverkehr
monument ['mɒnjumənt] — Denkmal
to miss sth [mɪs] — etw verpassen
unexpected [ˌʌnɪk'spektɪd] — unerwartet
to be in place [bi ˌɪn 'pleɪs] — in Betrieb sein
valuable ['væljuəbl] — wertvoll
to integrate ['ɪntɪgreɪt] — integrieren
stand [stænd] — Ständer
relay controller ['riːleɪ kəntrəʊlə] — Relaissteuerung

95 **error log** ['erə lɒg] — Fehlerprotokoll
return [rɪ'tɜːn] — Rückkehr

96 **even(ly)** ['iːvn] — eben
smooth [smuːð] — glatt, problemlos
outdated [ˌaʊt'deɪtɪd] — veraltet
motor-circuit-breaker ['məʊtə sɜːkɪt breɪkə] — Motorschutzschalter
to jam [dʒæm] — sich stauen, blockieren

97 **stretch wrapper** ['stretʃ ræpə] — Dehnfolienumwicklungsmaschine
concurrent [kən'kʌrənt] — gleichzeitig, gleichlaufend
stretch wrapping ['stretʃ ræpɪŋ] — Dehnfolienumwicklung
high/low infeed [haɪ/ləʊ 'ɪnfiːd] — großer/kleiner Einlaufschacht
fully automated [ˌfʊli 'ɔːtəmeɪtɪd] — vollautomatisch
film [fɪlm] — Folie
grip [grɪp] — Greifen
wipe down [ˌwaɪp 'daʊn] — Abwischen
heavy duty [ˌhevi 'djuːti] — Hochleistungs-
turntable ['tɜːnteɪbl] — Drehscheibe
pre-stretch [ˌpriː'stretʃ] — Vordehnung
to impact sth ['ɪmpækt] — sich auf etw auswirken
layer build ['leɪə bɪld] — Lagenaufbau
load build ['ləʊd bɪld] — Zusammenstellung der zu verpackenden Einheiten
adjustable [ə'dʒʌstəbl] — regelbar, variabel
overlap [ˌəʊvə'læp] — Überlappung
top wrap ['tɒp ræp] — Wickellagen
tension ['tenʃn] — Spannung
layer head ['leɪə hed] — Sortiervorrichtung

continual [kən'tɪnjuəl]	kontinuierlich
to exit sth ['eksɪt]	etw verlassen
film carriage ['fɪlm kærɪdʒ]	Folienträger
safety relay ['seɪfti riːleɪ]	Sicherheitsschaltung
footprint ['fʊtprɪnt]	Grundfläche, Standfläche
to enclose [ɪn'kləʊz]	einschließen
enclosure [ɪn'kləʊʒə]	Gehäuse
fibre-optic cable [ˌfaɪbər ɒptɪk 'keɪbl]	Glasfaserkabel
exit ['eksɪt]	Ausgabe
curtain ['kɜːtn]	Vorhang, *hier:* Lichtschranke
blanking ['blæŋkɪŋ]	Abdunkelung
infeed conveyor ['ɪnfiːd kənveɪə]	Eingangsfließband
row pushing area ['rəʊ pʊʃɪŋ eəriə]	Reihensortierstation
control [kən'trəʊl]	Regler
to cycle ['saɪkl]	zyklisch betreiben
set-up ['setʌp]	Einrichtung
to clear [klɪə]	räumen, auflösen
compliant [kəm'plaɪənt]	konform
lockout ['lɒkaʊt]	Sperre
support [sə'pɔːt]	Trägerelement
light beam ['laɪt biːm]	Lichtstrahl
sensitive ['sensətɪv]	empfindlich
to register ['redʒɪstə]	wahrnehmen, registrieren
touch [tʌtʃ]	Berührung
industrial fair [ɪnˌdʌstrɪəl 'feə]	Gewerbemesse, Industriemesse

98 **ballpoint pen** [ˌbɔːlpɔɪnt 'pen] — Kugelschreiber
chromium-plated ['krəʊmɪəm pleɪtɪd] — verchromt
eloxated ['elɒkseɪtɪd] — eloxiert
gold-plated [ˌgəʊld 'pleɪtɪd] — vergoldet
rustfree [ˌrʌst 'friː] — rostfrei
luxurious [lʌg'ʒʊəriəs] — luxuriös
durable ['djʊərəbl] — langlebig, strapazierfähig
hard-wearing [ˌhɑːd'weərɪŋ] — strapazierfähig
small batch [ˌsmɔːl 'bætʃ] — Kleinserie
to label ['leɪbl] — bezeichnen
spring [sprɪŋ] — Feder
compression spring [kəm'preʃn sprɪŋ] — Druckfeder
handle piece ['hændl piːs] — Griffstück
rocker ['rɒkə] — Kipphebel
sleeve [sliːv] — Schaft
adaptor [ə'dæptə] — Adapter
cap [kæp] — Kappe
refill ['riːfɪl] — Mine
feed [fiːd] — Zuführung

99 **apparatus** [ˌæpə'reɪtəs] — Gerät, Maschine
to perform [pə'fɔːm] — (Handlung) ausführen
to fit [fɪt] — einpassen, einsetzen
to depress [dɪ'pres] — herunterdrücken
to disentangle [ˌdɪsɪn'tæŋl] — entwirren, voneinander lösen

100 **dutybook** ['djuːtibʊk] — Pflichtenheft
confused [kən'fjuːzd] — verwirrt
author ['ɔːθə] — Verfasser
respective [rɪ'spektɪv] — jeweilige/r/s

UNIT WORD LIST

	collecting arm [kəˈlektɪŋ ɑːm]	Aufnahmeköcher
	as opposed to [əz əˈpɒzd tə]	gegenüber, im Gegensatz zu
102	feeder [ˈfiːdə]	Zuführung
	commisioning certificate [kəˈmɪʃnɪŋ sətɪfɪkət]	Inbetriebnahmeanweisung
	to miss [mɪs]	unerwähnt lassen
	check [tʃek]	Test, Kontrolle T
	refill prism [ˈriːfɪl prɪzm]	Einfüllbehälter T
	mains box [ˈmeɪnz bɒks]	Stromversorgung T
	to align [əˈlaɪn]	ausrichten T
103	disentangler [ˌdɪsɪnˈtæŋglə]	Entwirrer
	drum [drʌm]	Trommel
	drum conveyor [ˈdrʌm kənveɪə]	Trommelförderer
	coil spring [ˈkɔɪl sprɪŋ]	Spiralfeder
	helical spring [ˌhelɪkl ˈsprɪŋ]	Schraubenfeder
	plate ring [ˈpleɪt rɪŋ]	Tellerfeder
	saw ring [ˈsɔː rɪŋ]	Zahnscheibe
	snap ring [ˈsnæp rɪŋ]	Sprengring
	tension spring [ˈtenʃn sprɪŋ]	Sicherungsring
	loop [luːp]	Öse
	to guide [gaɪd]	führen
	hard-to-disentangle [ˌhɑːd tə dɪsɪnˈtæŋgl]	schwer entwirrbar
	processing [ˈprəʊsesɪŋ]	(Weiter-)Verarbeitung
	to automate [ˈɔːtəmeɪt]	automatisieren
	bulk goods [ˈbʌlk gʊdz]	Schüttgut
	interlocked [ˈɪntəlɒkt]	verhakt
	to separate [ˈseprət]	trennen, separieren
	to accelerate [əkˈseləreɪt]	beschleunigen
	low-voltage [ˌləʊ ˈvəʊltɪdʒ]	Niederspannung
	squirrel cage motor [ˈskwɪrəl keɪdʒ məʊtə]	Käfigläufermotor
	slip-ring motor [ˈslɪp rɪŋ məʊtə]	Schleifringläufermotor
	direct current motor [ˈdərekt kʌrənt məʊtə]	Gleichstrommotor
	stepper motor [ˈstepə məʊtə]	Schrittmotor
104	to arise [əˈraɪz]	(Problem:) auftreten
	to solve [sɒlv]	lösen
	machine fault chart [məˈʃiːn fɔːlt tʃɑːt]	Fehlersuchplan
	cable break [ˈkeɪbl breɪk]	Kabelbruch
	line protection [ˈlaɪn prətekʃn]	Leitungsschutz
	winding [ˈwaɪndɪŋ]	Wicklung
	load [ləʊd]	Last
	spark [spɑːk]	Funken
	jerkily [ˈdʒɜːkɪli]	ruckelnd
105	to engrave [ɪnˈgreɪv]	gravieren
	barrel [ˈbærəl]	Schaft, Zylinder, Rolle
	gift [gɪft]	Geschenk
	collector's item [kəˈlektəz aɪtəm]	Sammlerstück
	impressive [ɪmˈpresɪv]	eindrucksvoll
	appearance [əˈpɪərəns]	Aussehen, Erscheinungsbild
	superb [suːˈpɜːb]	grandios, prachtvoll
	to quote a price [ˌkwəʊt ə ˈpraɪs]	einen Preis nennen, ein Angebot machen
106	developing country [dɪˌveləpɪŋ ˈkʌntri]	Entwicklungsland
	scratch [skrætʃ]	Kratzer
	burr [bɜː]	Grat
	arrangement [əˈreɪndʒmənt]	Anordnung
107	customer satisfaction [ˌkʌstəmə ˌsætɪsˈfækʃn]	Kundenzufriedenheit
	the former [ðə ˈfɔːmə]	der/die/das erste
	to concern [kənˈsɜːn]	betreffen
	fitness [ˈfɪtnəs]	Eignung, Tauglichkeit
	the latter [ðə ˈlætə]	der/die/das zweite
	supporter [səˈpɔːtə]	Befürworter, Unterstützer
	to characterise [ˈkærəktəraɪz]	charakterisieren
	succinctly [səkˈsɪŋktli]	(kurz und) bündig
	to associate [əˈsəʊsieɪt]	verbinden, assoziieren
	sample test [ˈsɑːmpl test]	Stichprobenkontrolle
	stress testing [ˈstres testɪŋ]	Belastungstest
	to structure [ˈstrʌktʃə]	strukturieren
	quality assurance manual [ˈkwɒləti əʃʊərəns mænjuəl]	Qualitätsmanagementshandbuch T
	strict [strɪkt]	streng T
	intertwining [ˌɪntəˈtwaɪnɪŋ]	Verflechtung T
	product liability [ˌprɒdʌkt ˌlaɪəˈbɪləti]	Produkthaftung T
	environmental compatibility [ɪnvaɪrənˌmentl kəmpætəˈbɪləti]	Umweltverträglichkeit T
	ground [graʊnd]	Erdboden T
	plant [plɑːnt]	Pflanze T
	usage [ˈjuːsɪdʒ]	Gebrauch, Verwendung T
	to sum up [ˌsʌm ˈʌp]	zusammenfassen T
	owner [ˈəʊnə]	Besitzer/in, Inhaber/in T
	society [səˈsaɪəti]	Gesellschaft T
	frequent [ˈfriːkwənt]	häufig T
	periodical [ˌpɪəriˈɒdɪkl]	regelmäßig T
	examination [ɪgˌzæmɪˈneɪʃn]	Untersuchung T
	authorized [ˈɔːθəraɪzd]	befugt, autorisiert T
	to fulfil [fʊlˈfɪl]	erfüllen T
	steady [ˈstedi]	gleichbleibend, stabil, solide T
108	industrial safety [ɪnˌdʌstriəl ˈseɪfti]	Arbeitsschutz, Arbeitssicherheit
	occupational safety [ɒkjuˌpeɪʃnəl ˈseɪfti]	Arbeitsschutz, Arbeitssicherheit
	to publish [ˈpʌblɪʃ]	veröffentlichen, publizieren
	to promote [prəˈməʊt]	fördern
	to be an asset to sth [bi ən ˈæset tə]	wertvoll, eine Bereicherung für etw sein
	workforce [ˈwɜːkfɔːs]	Belegschaft
	enthusiastic [ɪnˌθjuːziˈæstɪk]	begeisterungsfähig
	eager to learn [ˌiːgə tə ˈlɜːn]	lernwillig
	inexperienced [ˌɪnɪkˈspɪəriənst]	unerfahren

UNIT WORD LIST

to injure ['ɪndʒə]	verletzen	
adequate ['ædɪkwət]	angemessen	
lifelong ['laɪflɒŋ]	lebenslang	
impact ['ɪmpækt]	Auswirkung, Einfluss	
fatal ['feɪtl]	tödlich	
furthermore [,fɜ:ðə'mɔ:]	außerdem, darüber hinaus	
costly ['kɒstli]	teuer, kostenintensiv	
to get hurt [get 'hɜ:t]	sich verletzten	
to take sth on [,teɪk 'ɒn]	etw übernehmen	
construction site [kən'strʌkʃn saɪt]	Baustelle	
construction industry [kən'strʌkʃn ɪndəstri]	Baubranche	
to rank third [,ræŋk 'θɜ:d]	auf dem dritten Platz stehen	
fatality [fə'tæləti]	Unfall mit Todesfolge	
occupational death [ɒkju,peɪʃənl 'deθ]	Arbeitsunfall mit Todesfolge	
law [lɔ:]	Gesetz	
to demonstrate ['demənstreɪt]	zeigen, vorführen	
to assume [ə'sju:m]	davon ausgehen, annehmen	
firm rule [,fɜ:m 'ru:l]	bindende Vorschrift	
to stress [stres]	betonen	
legal(ly) ['li:gl]	legal, vorschriftsgemäß	

109
to treat [tri:t]	behandeln	
patient ['peɪʃnt]	Patient/in	
company doctor [,kʌmpəni 'dɒktə]	Betriebsarzt/-ärztin	
illness ['ɪlnəs]	Krankheit	
wounded ['wu:ndɪd]	verwundet, verletzt	
forehead ['fɔ:hed]	Stirn	
bleeding nose [,bli:dɪŋ 'nəʊz]	blutende Nase, Nasenbluten	
back [bæk]	Rücken	
bruised [bru:zd]	geprellt	
chest [tʃest]	Brust	
stomach ['stʌmək]	Magen, Bauch	
upset stomach [,ʌpset 'stʌmək]	Magenverstimmung, Bauchweh	
sprained [spreɪnd]	verstaucht	
ankle ['æŋkl]	Knöchel, Sprunggelenk	
toe [təʊ]	Zeh	
cough [kɒf]	Husten	
cold [kəʊld]	Erkältung	
sore throat [,sɔ: 'θrəʊt]	Halsschmerzen, Rachenentründung	
flu [flu:]	Grippe	
redness ['rednəs]	Rötung	
pain [peɪn]	Schmerz(en)	
itching ['ɪtʃɪŋ]	Jucken	
bowel ['baʊəl]	Darm	
nose bleed ['nəʊz bli:d]	Nasenbluten	
nausea ['nɔ:ziə]	Übelkeit	
diarrhoea [,daɪə'rɪə]	Durchfall	
toothache ['tu:θeɪk]	Zahnschmerzen	
to lay sb down [,leɪ 'daʊn]	jdn hinlegen T	
bed [bed]	Liege T	
bleeding ['bli:dɪŋ]	Blutung T	
to fall over sth ['fɔ:l əʊvə]	über etw stolpern T	
nasty ['nɑ:sti]	schlimm, böse T	
rusty ['rʌsti]	rostig T	

bottling factory ['bɒtlɪŋ fæktəri]	Abfüllbetrieb T	
injection [ɪn'dʒekʃn]	Spritze, Injektion T	
to anaesthetize [ə'ni:sθətaɪz]	betäuben T	
to suture ['su:tʃə]	nähen T	
wound [wu:nd]	Wunde T	
to hurt [hɜ:t]	wehtun T	
X-ray ['eksreɪ]	Röntgenbild, -untersuchung T	
tiger balm ['taɪgə bɑ:m]	Tigerbalsam T	
ice-pack ['aɪspæk]	Kühlpackung T	
to recall sth [rɪ'kɔ:l]	sich an etw erinnern	
childhood ['tʃaɪldhʊd]	Kindheit	
medical ['medɪkl]	medizinisch, Medizin-	
first-aid kit [,fɜ:st'eɪd kɪt]	Erste-Hilfe-Kasten	
antiseptic [,ænti'septɪk]	antiseptisch	
ointment ['ɔɪntmənt]	Salbe	
bandage ['bændɪdʒ]	Verband	
basin ['beɪsn]	Schale	
blood pressure monitor ['blʌd preʃə mɒnɪtə]	Blutdruckmess-/ überwachungsgerät	
eye pad ['aɪ pæd]	Augenpad	
inhaler [ɪn'heɪlə]	Inhalator	
safety pin ['seɪfti pɪn]	Sicherheitsnadel	
scalpel ['skælpəl]	Skalpell	
stretcher ['stretʃə]	Trage	
syringe [sɪ'rɪndʒ]	Spritze	

110
acute [ə'kju:t]	scharf, akut	
bleary ['blɪəri]	verschwommen, trüb	
burning ['bɜ:nɪŋ]	brennend	
dislocated ['dɪsləkeɪtɪd]	ausgerenkt, ausgekugelt	
giddy ['gɪdi]	schwindlig	
painful ['peɪnfl]	schmerzhaft	
stiff [stɪf]	steif	
shooting ['ʃu:tɪŋ]	(Schmerz:) stechend	
stabbing ['stæbɪŋ]	(Schmerz:) stechend	
unclear [,ʌn'klɪə]	unklar	
unfocussed [ʌn'fəʊkəst]	verschwommen	
vision ['vɪʒn]	Sehvermögen	
joint [dʒɔɪnt]	Gelenk	
to instruct sb [ɪn'strʌkt]	jdm Anweisungen erteilen	
protective equipment [prə,tektɪv ɪ'kwɪpmənt]	Schutzausrüstung	
replica ['replɪkə]	Kopie, Reproduktion	
metalworker ['metlwɜ:kə]	Metallarbeiter/in	

111
surgery ['sɜ:dʒəri]	(Arzt-)Praxis	
health insurance ['helθ ɪnʃʊərəns]	Krankenversicherung	
health insurance card ['helθ ɪnʃʊərəns kɑ:d]	Versichertenkarte	
to itch [ɪtʃ]	jucken	
to scratch [skrætʃ]	kratzen	
medication [,medɪ'keɪʃn]	Medikamente	
to take sb's blood pressure [,teɪk sʌmbədiz 'blʌd preʃə]	jds Blutdruck messen	
sleeve [sli:v]	Ärmel	
to slip [slɪp]	ausrutschen, abrutschen	
stain [steɪn]	Fleck	
appointment [ə'pɔɪntmənt]	Termin	

UNIT WORD LIST

112	**to file** [faɪl]	einreichen	**stead(il)y** ['stedi]	gleichmäßig
	exchange [ɪksˈtʃeɪndʒ]	Austausch	**115 structural steel**	Baustahl
	day before yesterday	vorgestern	[ˌstrʌktʃərəl ˈstiːl]	
	[deɪ bɪˌfɔː ˈjestədeɪ]		**alloyed steel** [ˈælɔɪd stiːl]	legierter Stahl
	to be caught [bɪ ˈkɔːt]	sich verfangen	**tensile test** [ˈtensaɪl test]	Zugversuch T
	to undergo sth [ˌʌndəˈgəʊ]	sich einer Sache unterziehen	**stress-strain diagram**	Spannungs-Dehnungs-
	ligament [ˈlɪgəmənt]	Band	[ˈstres streɪn daɪəgræm]	Diagramm T
	disease [dɪˈziːz]	Krankheit	**extension level**	Dehnungsgrad T
	occurrence [əˈkʌrəns]	Vorkommnis	[ɪkˈstenʃn levl]	
	major [ˈmeɪdʒə]	größere/r/s	**in terms of ...**	was ... betrifft T
	for instance [fəˈr ɪnstəns]	zum Beispiel	[ɪn ˈtɜːmz əv]	
	substance [ˈsʌbstəns]	Substanz	**116 computerised**	computergesteuert
	incident [ˈɪnsɪdənt]	Zwischenfall, Vorfall	[kəmˈpjuːtəraɪzd]	
113	**to apply for a job**	sich um eine Stelle	**universal testing machine**	Universalprüfmaschine
	[əˌplaɪ fər ə ˈdʒɒb]	bewerben	[juːnɪˌvɜːsl ˈtestɪŋ məʃiːn]	
	materials testing	Materialprüfung	**tensile stress**	Zugbelastung
	[məˈtɪərɪəlz testɪŋ]		[ˌtensaɪl ˈstres]	
	giant [ˈdʒaɪənt]	Riese, Riesen-	**compressive stress**	Druckbelastung
	dumper [ˈdʌmpə]	Muldenkipper	[kəmˌpresɪv ˈstres]	
	quarry [ˈkwɒri]	Steinbruch	**embedded** [ɪmˈbedɪd]	eingebettet
	to be up to sth [bɪ ˈʌp tə]	einer Sache genügen, entsprechen	**to conduct** [kənˈdʌkt]	durchführen
			peel test [ˈpiːl test]	Abschältest
	destructive testing	zerstörende Prüfung,	**bond test** [ˈbɒnd test]	Hafttest
	[dɪˌstrʌktɪv ˈtestɪŋ]	zerstörendes Prüfverfahren	**friction test** [ˈfrɪkʃn test]	Reibungsprüfung
	non-destructive testing	zerstörungsfreies	**fixture** [ˈfɪkstʃə]	Zubehörteil
	[ˌnɒn dɪˌstrʌktɪv ˈtestɪŋ]	Prüfverfahren	**cross travel** [ˈkrɒs trævl]	Durchgangshöhe
	ultrasonic [ˌʌltrəˈsɒnɪk]	Ultraschall-	**powder coated**	pulverbeschichtet
	magnetic-particle test	Magnetpulverrissprüfung	[ˈpaʊdə kəʊtɪd]	
	[mægˌnetɪk ˈpɑːtɪkl test]		**single phase** [ˌsɪŋgl ˈfeɪs]	einphasig
	tension test [ˈtenʃn test]	Zugversuch	**material sample**	Materialprobe
	pressure test [ˈpreʃə test]	Druckprüfung	[məˈtɪərɪəl sɑːmpl]	
	vibration test	Schwingungsprüfung	**width** [wɪdθ]	Breite
	[vaɪˈbreɪʃn test]		**117 testing procedure**	Prüfverfahren
	hardness test [ˈhɑːdnəs test]	Härteprüfung	[ˈtestɪŋ prəsiːdʒə]	
	toughness [ˈtʌfnəs]	Festigkeit	**to harden** [ˈhɑːdn]	härten
	imperfection [ˌɪmpəˈfekʃn]	Mangel	**to alloy** [ˈælɔɪ]	legieren
	discontinuity	Unterbrechung	**cut** [kʌt]	Schnittverletzung
	[ˌdɪskɒntɪnˈjuːəti]		**to bleed** [bliːd]	bluten
114	**extension** [ɪkˈstenʃn]	Dehnung	**beer mat** [ˈbɪəmæt]	Bierdeckel
	lower yield point	untere Streckgrenze	**118 advert** [ˈædvɜːt]	Anzeige, Inserat
	[ˌləʊə ˈjiːld pɔɪnt]		**to advertise** [ˈædvətaɪz]	inserieren
	stress [stres]	Belastung	**job advert** [ˈdʒɒb ædvɜːt]	Stellenanzeige
	failure [ˈfeɪljə]	Bruch	**to recruit** [rɪˈkruːt]	einstellen
	ultimate stress	Zugfestigkeit	**multi-skilled** [ˌmʌlti ˈskɪld]	vielseitig ausgebildet
	[ˌʌltɪmət ˈstres]		**bias** [ˈbaɪəs]	Ausrichtung, Vorliebe
	upper yield point	obere Streckgrenze	**reliability** [rɪˌlaɪəˈbɪləti]	Zuverlässigkeit
	[ˌʌpə ˈjiːld pɔɪnt]		**downtime** [ˈdaʊntaɪm]	Stillstandzeit
	graph [grɑːf]	Kurve, Diagramm	**preventive** [prɪˈventɪv]	vorbeugend
	velocity [vəˈlɒsəti]	Geschwindigkeit	**to rectify** [ˈrektɪfaɪ]	(Fehler) beheben
	to drop [drɒp]	sinken	**breakdown** [ˈbreɪkdaʊn]	Ausfall, Störung
	to flatten out [ˌflætn ˈaʊt]	sich verflachen	**vitally important**	von entscheidender
	to fluctuate [ˈflʌktʃueɪt]	schwanken, pendeln	[ˌvaɪtli ɪmˈpɔːtnt]	Bedeutung
	to hit a maximum	einen Maximalwert erreichen	**proven** [ˈpruːvn]	nachgewiesen
	[hɪt ə ˈmæksɪməm]		**hands-on experience**	praktische Erfahrung
	to level off [ˌlevl ˈɒf]	sich stabilisieren, sich einpendeln (bei)	[hændz ˌɒn ɪkˈspɪərɪəns]	
			119 application [ˌæplɪˈkeɪʃn]	Bewerbung
	to peak [piːk]	einen Spitzenwert erreichen	**precision mechanic**	Feinmechaniker/in
	to plunge [plʌndʒ]	schnell absinken, steil abfallen	[prɪˈsɪʒn mɪkænɪk]	
			higher vocational course	weiterführende Ausbildung
	to shoot up [ˌʃuːt ˈʌp]	in die Höhe schnellen	[ˌhaɪə vəʊˌkeɪʃənl ˈkɔːs]	
	gradually [ˈgrædʒuəli]	allmählich	**attention** [əˈtenʃn]	Aufmerksamkeit

UNIT WORD LIST

challenge ['tʃælɪndʒ]	Herausforderung, Aufgabe	
Yours faithfully, [jɔːz 'feɪθfəli]	Mit freundlichen Grüßen	
grateful ['greɪtfl]	dankbar	
vacancy ['veɪkənsi]	offene Stelle	
appliance [ə'plaɪəns]	Gerät, Vorrichtung	
operative ['ɒpərətɪv]	Mitarbeiter/in	
to expand [ɪk'spænd]	erweitern	
interview ['ɪntəvjuː]	Vorstellungsgespräch	
enclosure [ɪn'kləʊʒə]	(Brief:) Anlage	
120 post [pəʊst]	Stelle, Posten	
to specialize ['speʃəlaɪz]	sich spezialisieren	
at present [ət 'preznt]	gegenwärtig, im Moment	
to seek [siːk]	suchen	
enthusiasm [ɪn'θjuːziæzəm]	Begeisterung	
adaptability [əˌdæptə'bɪləti]	Anpassungsfähigkeit	
enclosed [ɪn'kləʊzd]	beigefügt	
curriculum vitae (CV) (BE) [kəˌrɪkjələm 'viːtaɪ]	Lebenslauf	
121 résumé (AE) ['rezjumeɪ]	Lebenslauf	
subheading ['sʌbhedɪŋ]	Zwischenüberschrift	
gender ['dʒendə]	Geschlecht	
mother tongue ['mʌðə tʌŋ]	Muttersprache	
occupation [ˌɒkju'peɪʃn]	Beschäftigung, Anstellung	
exam [ɪg'zæm]	Prüfung	
template ['templeɪt]	Vorlage, Muster	
122 female ['fiːmeɪl]	weiblich	
voluntary ['vɒləntri]	freiwillig	
qualification [ˌkwɒlɪfɪ'keɪʃn]	Abschluss, Qualifikation	
to award [ə'wɔːd]	zuerkennen, erteilen	
work placement ['wɜːk pleɪsmənt]	Praktikum	
123 self-assessment [ˌself ə'sesmənt]	Selbsteinschätzung	
framework ['freɪmwɜːk]	Rahmen, Bezugsrahmen	
artistic [ɑː'tɪstɪk]	künstlerisch	
motorcycle ['məʊtəsaɪkl]	Motorrad	
disaster relief [dɪ'zɑːstə rɪliːf]	Katastrophenhilfe	
to specify ['spesɪfaɪ]	(genau) angeben	
draft [drɑːft]	Entwurf	
library ['laɪbrəri]	Bibltiothek	
to suit [suːt]	passen	
ink [ɪŋk]	Tinte	
immeasurably [ɪ'meʒərəbli]	unermesslich, unendlich	
124 advice [əd'vaɪs]	Rat, Ratschläge	
usefulness ['juːsfəlnəs]	Nützlichkeit	
awake [ə'weɪk]	wach	
to practise ['præktɪs]	üben, proben	
duty ['djuːti]	Aufgabe, Pflicht	
strength [streŋθ]	Stärke	
weakness ['wiːknəs]	Schwäche	
interviewee [ˌɪntəvjuː'iː]	Person, mit der ein Vorstellungsgespräch geführt wird	
125 to evaluate [ɪ'væljueɪt]	bewerten, auswerten, einstufen	
journey ['dʒɜːni]	Fahrt, Anreise *T*	
blow-up ['bləʊ ʌp]	aufblasbar *T*	
workmate ['wɜːkmeɪt]	Kollege/-in *T*	
to smell of sth ['smel əv]	nach etw riechen *T*	
garlic ['gɑːlɪk]	Knoblauch *T*	
unpleasant [ʌn'pleznt]	unangenehm *T*	
habit ['hæbɪt]	Gewohnheit *T*	
to spit [spɪt]	spucken *T*	
disgusting [dɪs'gʌstɪŋ]	eklig *T*	
to appreciate [ə'priːʃieɪt]	verstehen, einsehen *T*	
applicant ['æplɪkənt]	Bewerber/in *T*	
individuality [ˌɪndɪˌvɪdʒu'æləti]	Individualität	
to achieve [ə'tʃiːv]	erreichen	
committee [kə'mɪti]	Ausschuss, Komitee	
to stifle ['staɪfl]	ersticken, unterdrücken	
individual [ˌɪndɪ'vɪdʒuəl]	Einzelne/r, Einzelperson	
to think out of the box [θɪŋk ˌaʊt əv ðə 'bɒks]	unkonventionell denken	
128 automation [ˌɔːtə'meɪʃn]	Automatisierung, Automation	
PLC (programmable logic controller) [ˌpiː el 'siː]	Speicherprogrammierbare Steuerung (SPS)	
mechatronics technician [ˌmekə'trɒnɪks teknɪʃn]	Mechatroniker/in	
production line [prə'dʌkʃn laɪn]	Fertigungsstraße	
expenses [ɪk'spensɪz]	Kosten	
as time goes by [əz ˌtaɪm gəʊz 'baɪ]	im Lauf der Zeit	
handling robot ['hændlɪŋ rəʊbɒt]	Handhabungsroboter	
magazine [ˌmægə'ziːn]	Magazin	
to pass sth [pɑːs]	etw weiterbefördern, weiterreichen *T*	
sheet metal ['ʃiːt metl]	Blech(e) *T*	
vehicle body ['viːəkl bɒdi]	Fahrzeugkarrosserie, -chassis *T*	
light barrier ['laɪt bæriə]	Lichtschranke *T*	
power cable ['paʊə keɪbl]	Stromkabel *T*	
control cable [kən'trəʊl keɪbl]	Steuerleitung *T*	
push button ['pʊʃ bʌtn]	Druckknopf *T*	
signal lamp ['sɪgnəl læmp]	Anzeige-, Signallampe *T*	
activator ['æktɪveɪtə]	Startknopf *T*	
representative [ˌreprɪ'zentətɪv]	Vertreter/in	
129 automotive industry [ˌɔːtəˌməʊtɪv 'ɪndəstri]	Automobilbranche	
expansion [ɪk'spænʃn]	Erweiterung	
to consider sth sth [kən'sɪdə]	etw für etw halten, als etw ansehen *T*	
benchmark ['bentʃmɑːk]	Maßstab, Richtgröße *T*	
synonymous [sɪ'nɒnɪməs]	gleichbedeutend *T*	
especially [ɪ'speʃəli]	eigens, speziell *T*	
to iron out [ˌaɪən 'aʊt]	(Fehler) ausmerzen, beheben *T*	
honest(ly) ['ɒnɪst]	ehrlich *T*	
to claim [kleɪm]	behaupten *T*	
humanly possible [ˌhjuːmənli 'pɒsəbl]	nach menschlichem Ermessen möglich *T*	
operational life [ɒpəˌreɪʃənl 'laɪf]	Lebensdauer *T*	
expandable [ɪkˌspændəbl]	erweiterbar *T*	

UNIT WORD LIST

maintenance-free ['meɪntənəns friː]	wartungsfrei T	non-volatile memory [nɒn ˌvɒlətaɪl 'memərɪ]	nicht-flüchtiger Speicher
pluggable ['plʌgəbl]	Steck- T	circuitry ['sɜːkɪtrɪ]	Schaltung
tailored ['teɪləd]	maßgeschneidert T	output actuator ['aʊtpʊt æktʃueɪtə]	Aktor, Stellglied
particular [pə'tɪkjələ]	spezielle/r/s T	starter motor ['stɑːtə məʊtə]	Starter
131 utility building [juː'tɪlətɪ bɪldɪŋ]	technische Gebäudeausrüstung	solenoid ['sɒlənɔɪd]	Magnetspule
switchgear ['swɪtʃgɪə]	Schaltanlage	to yield [jiːld]	liefern
scalable ['skeɪləbl]	anpassbar, erweiterbar	state [steɪt]	Zustand
closed-loop control [ˌkləʊzd luːp kən'trəʊl]	Regelung	volume ['vɒljuːm]	Lautstärke
motion control ['məʊʃn kəntrəʊl]	Ablaufsteuerung	floating point value ['fləʊtɪŋ pɔɪnt væljuː]	Gleitkommazahl
local intelligence [ˌləʊkl ɪn'telɪdʒəns]	intelligentes Schnittstellensystem	SCADA system ['skɑːdə sɪstəm]	elektrisches Überwachungs-, Steuer- und Datenaufnahmesystem
data retentivity [ˌdeɪtə rɪten'tɪvətɪ]	Datenerhaltung	hard-wired relay [hɑːd ˌwaɪəd 'riːleɪ]	festverdrahtete Schaltung
isochronous mode [aɪ'zɒkrənəs məʊd]	isochrone Datenübertragung (mit konstanter Datenrate)	to represent [ˌreprɪ'zent]	darstellen
process industry [ˌprəʊses 'ɪndəstrɪ]	verarbeitende Industrie	integer ['ɪntɪdʒə]	ganze Zahl
		to substitute ['sʌbstɪtjuːt]	ersetzen
132 custom manufacture ['kʌstəm mænjufæktʃə]	Sonderanfertigung	136 wining and dining [ˌwaɪnɪŋ ən 'daɪnɪŋ]	Bewirten (von Gästen)
power generation ['paʊə dʒenəreɪʃn]	Stromerzeugung	appetizer ['æpɪtaɪzə]	Vorspeise
woodworking ['wʊdwɜːkɪŋ]	Holzverarbeitung	slice [slaɪs]	Scheibe, Schnitte
beverage ['bevərɪdʒ]	Getränk	turkey ['tɜːkɪ]	Truthahn
process engineering [ˌprəʊses endʒɪ'nɪərɪŋ]	Verfahrenstechnik	beef [biːf]	Rindfleisch
water utility ['wɔːtə juːtɪlətɪ]	Wasserversorgung(sunternehmen)	pork [pɔːk]	Schweinefleisch
		pulled pork [ˌpʊld 'pɔːk]	Streifen von Schweinebraten
wastewater [ˌweɪst'wɔːtə]	Abwasser	mustard ['mʌstəd]	Senf
petrochemicals [ˌpetrəʊ'kemɪklz]	Petrochemie (Erdöl- bzw. Erdgasverarbeitung)	cream [kriːm]	Sahne, Creme
		shrimp [ʃrɪmp]	Garnele, Krabbe
133 to apply [ə'plaɪ]	einsetzen	spiced [spaɪst]	würzig, (scharf) gewürzt
134 robustness [rəʊ'bʌstnəs]	Robustheit	poached [pəʊtʃt]	pochiert
suitability [ˌsuːtə'bɪlətɪ]	Eignung	blue cheese [ˌbluː 'tʃiːz]	Blauschimmelkäse
certified ['sɜːtɪfaɪd]	zertifiziert	carrot ['kærət]	Möhre, Karotte
accordingly [ə'kɔːdɪŋlɪ]	entsprechend	celery ['selərɪ]	Sellerie
range [reɪndʒ]	Bereich, Spanne	bell pepper ['bel pepə]	Paprika
shock [ʃɒk]	Stoß, Erschütterung	onion ['ʌnjən]	Zwiebel
dustproof ['dʌstpruːf]	staubdicht	lettuce ['letɪs]	Salat
temporary ['temprərɪ]	vorübergehend, zeitweilig	cucumber ['kjuːkʌmbə]	Gurke
submersion [səb'mɜːʃn]	Untertauchen	bacon ['beɪkən]	Speck
operating conditions ['ɒpəreɪtɪŋ kəndɪʃnz]	Betriebsbedingungen	bit [bɪt]	Stück, Stückchen
		pickled ['pɪkld]	sauer eingelegt
expanded [ɪk'spændɪd]	weit	shallot [ʃə'lɒt]	Lauchzwiebel
ambient temperature [ˌæmbɪənt 'temprətʃə]	Umgebungstemperatur	radish ['rædɪʃ]	Rettich
		melted ['meltɪd]	geschmolzen
corrosive [kə'rəʊsɪv]	korrosionsfördernd	cheddar ['tʃedə]	Cheddar-Käse
salty ['sɔːltɪ]	salzhaltig, salzig	secret ['siːkrɪt]	Geheim-
ambient air [ˌæmbɪənt 'eə]	Außenluft, Umgebungsluft	French fries [ˌfrentʃ 'fraɪz]	Pommes frites
deposit [dɪ'pɒzɪt]	Ablagerung	smokey ['sməʊkɪ]	rauchig, Räucher-
harsh [hɑːʃ]	rau	ham [hæm]	Schinken
rough [rʌf]	rau	entree ['ɒntreɪ]	Hauptgericht, Hauptgang
field device ['fiːld dɪvaɪs]	Feldgerät (in direkter Beziehung zum Produktionsprozess)	smoked [sməʊkt]	geräuchert
		roasted ['rəʊstɪd]	gebraten
		root vegetables [ˌruːt 'vedʒtəblz]	Wurzelgemüse
coastal ['kəʊstl]	Küsten-	meatloaf [ˌmiːt'ləʊf]	Hackbraten, Fleischkäse
135 typically ['tɪpɪklɪ]	normalerweise, üblicherweise	mashed potatoes [ˌmæʃt pə'teɪtəʊz]	Kartoffelbrei
to store [stɔː]	(Daten) speichern	beer battered ['bɪə bætəd]	im Bierteig

187

UNIT WORD LIST

malt vinegar [ˌmɔːlt 'vɪnɪgə]	Malzessig
pot roast ['pɒt rəʊst]	Schmorbraten
sautéd ['səʊteɪd]	sautiert, geschmort
dessert [dɪ'zɜːt]	Nachspeise, Dessert
oatmeal ['əʊtmiːl]	Hafer
whipped cream [ˌwɪpt 'kriːm]	Schlagsahne
wine list ['waɪn lɪst]	Weinkarte

137 milking machine ['mɪlkɪŋ məʃiːn] — Melkmaschine
oat crusher ['əʊt krʌʃə] — Haferquetsche
tractor ['træktə] — Traktor
chainsaw ['tʃeɪnsɔː] — Kettensäge
forestry harvester ['fɒrɪstri hɑːvɪstə] — Holzerntemaschine
oats [əʊts] — Hafer
to grind [graɪnd] — mahlen
to crush [krʌʃ] — quetschen
stable ['steɪbl] — Stall
livery stable ['lɪvəri ˌsteɪbl] — Reitstall, Mietstall
cereal ['sɪəriəl] — Getreide
cereals ['sɪəriəlz] — Getreidenahrung, -futter
work breakdown structure (WBS) [ˌwɜːk 'breɪkdaʊn strʌktʃə] — Projektstrukturplan

138 gearwheel ['gɪə wiːl] — Zahnrad, Getrieberad
belt [belt] — Riemen
toothed belt [ˌtuːθ 'belt] — Zahnriemen
drafting ['drɑːftɪŋ] — Zeichnungserstellung
dimensioning [dɪ'menʃnɪŋ] — Auslegung, Dimensionierung

139 hopper ['hɒpə] — Einfülltrichter
bin [bɪn] — Tonne

140 rectangle ['rektæŋgl] — Rechteck
rectangular [rek'tæŋgjələ] — rechteckig
triangle ['traɪæŋgl] — Dreieck
triangular [traɪ'æŋgjələ] — dreieckig
circular ['sɜːkjələ] — kreisförmig, rund
semi-circle ['semisɜːkl] — Halbkreis
semi-circular [ˌsemi'sɜːkjələ] — halbkreisförmig
convex ['kɒnveks] — konvex
concave [kɒn'keɪv] — konkav
cube [kjuːb] — Würfel
cubic ['kjuːbɪk] — würfelförmig
rectangular solid [rekˌtæŋgjələ 'sɒlɪd] — Quader
rectangular [rek'tæŋgjələ] — quaderförmig
sphere [sfɪə] — Kugel
hemisphere ['hemɪsfɪə] — Halbkugel
hemispherical [ˌhemɪ'sferɪkl] — halbkugelförmig
cone [kəʊn] — Kegel, Konus

141 technical term [ˌteknɪkl 'fɜːm] — Fachbegriff
roller ['rəʊlə] — Walze
belt drive ['belt draɪv] — Riemenantrieb
handwheel ['hændwiːl] — Handrad
brackets ['brækɪts] — Halterung
to slip [slɪp] — abrutschen
covering ['kʌvərɪŋ] — Abdeckung
grain [greɪn] — Korn

to force [fɔːs] — zwängen

142 to assess [ə'ses] — einschätzen, bewerten
slide [slaɪd] — Dia, Slide
talk [tɔːk] — Vortrag
to clap [klæp] — klatschen
bullet ['bʊlɪt] — Aufzählungspunkt
to memorize ['meməraɪz] — sich merken, auswendig lernen
to point to sth ['pɔɪnt tə] — auf etw zeigen
to wave sth about [ˌweɪv ə'baʊt] — mit etw herumwedeln
to gesture ['dʒestʃə] — gestikulieren
to shout [ʃaʊt] — schreien
confidently ['kɒnfɪdəntli] — (selbst-)bewusst
overly ['əʊvəli] — zu (sehr)

143 to revise [rɪ'vaɪz] — überarbeiten
slip [slɪp] — Abrutschen

144 cloth [klɒθ] — Tuch
impurity [ɪm'pjʊərəti] — Verunreinigung
foreign bodies [ˌfɒrən 'bɒdiz] — Fremdkörper
grit [grɪt] — Splitt, Kies
abrasive [ə'breɪsɪv] — scheuernd
cleaner ['kliːnə] — Reinigungsmittel
inappropriate [ˌɪnə'prəʊpriət] — unsachgemäß
to invalidate [ɪn'vælɪdeɪt] — außer Kraft setzen
crate [kreɪt] — Kiste
to misuse [mɪs'juːs] — falsch verwenden, missbräuchlich verwenden
padding ['pædɪŋ] — Polsterung, Füllung
prepaid [ˌpriː'peɪd] — im Voraus bezahlt
at sb's expense [ət ˌsʌmbədɪz ɪk'spens] — auf jds Kosten
provided [prə'vaɪdɪd] — unter der Voraussetzung, dass
non-transferable [ˌnɒn træns'fɜːrəbl] — nicht übertragbar
to apply [ə'plaɪ] — gelten
to incur [ɪn'kɜː] — vorkommen, hier: verursachen
negligence ['neglɪdʒəns] — Fahrlässigkeit
mishandling [ˌmɪs'hændlɪŋ] — fehlerhafte Handhabung
transit ['trænzɪt] — Transport
carrier ['kæriə] — Frachtführer, Spedition
to report [rɪ'pɔːt] — melden
receipt [rɪ'siːt] — Erhalt
to expire [ɪk'spaɪə] — verfallen
sufficient [sə'fɪʃnt] — ausreichend
to quote [kwəʊt] — angeben, nennen
purchase ['pɜːtʃəs] — Kauf
note [nəʊt] — Vermerk

145 initial [ɪ'nɪʃl] — erste/r/s, Anfangs-

146 guiding slide ['gaɪdɪŋ slaɪd] — Führungsschlitten
slackness ['slæknəs] — Spiel
excentric [ɪk'sentrɪk] — exzentrisch
insensitive to [ɪn'sensətɪv tə] — unempfindlich gegen
gear drive ['gɪə draɪv] — Getriebe
prefabricated [ˌpriː'fæbrɪkeɪtɪd] — vorgefertigt

UNIT WORD LIST

	gear [gɪə]	Gang
	reverse [rɪˈvɜːs]	Rückwärtsgang
	reversion [rɪˈvɜːʃn]	Umkehr
	belt tightener [ˈbelt taɪtnə]	Riemenspanner
	guard [gɑːd]	Gehäuse, Abdeckung
	lightweight [ˈlaɪtweɪt]	leicht
	trade off [ˈtreɪdɒf]	Kompromiss
	competing [kəmˈpiːtɪŋ]	konkurrierend
	ease of operation [ˌiːz əv ɒpəˈreɪʃn]	Bedienungsfreundlichkeit
147	safety sticker [ˈseɪfti stɪkə]	Aufkleber mit Sicherheitssymbolen
	to apply sth to sth [əˈplaɪ tə]	etw an etw anbringen
	plate [pleɪt]	Plakette, Schild
	final time schedule [ˌfaɪnl ˈtaɪm ʃedjuːl]	Fertigungszeitplanung
	to estimate [ˈestɪmeɪt]	schätzen
	reasonably [ˈriːznəbli]	ziemlich, halbwegs
	inaccurate [ɪnˈækjərət]	ungenau
149	equine [ˈekwaɪn]	Pferde-
	animal [ˈænɪml]	Tier-
	saddlery [ˈsædləri]	Sattelzeug, Sattlereiwaren
	compound feed [ˌkɒmpaʊnd ˈfiːd]	Mischfutter
	sized [saɪzd]	in verschiedenen Größen
	bruising [ˈbruːzɪŋ]	Quetschen
	adjuster [əˈdʒʌstə]	Versteller
	patented [ˈpeɪtəntɪd]	patentiert
	ammeter [ˈæmiːtə]	Amperemeter
	overload [ˈəʊvələʊd]	Überspannung
150	cheers [tʃɪəz]	Danke
	barley [ˈbɑːli]	Gerste
	wheat [wiːt]	Weizen
152	riding [ˈraɪdɪŋ]	Reiten
	accommodation [əˌkɒməˈdeɪʃn]	Unterkunft
	hospitality [ˌhɒspɪˈtæləti]	Gastfreundschaft
	stay [steɪ]	Aufenthalt
	throughout your stay [θruːˌaʊt jɔː ˈsteɪ]	während Ihres gesamten Aufenthalts
	in style [ɪn ˈstaɪl]	stilvoll
	party [ˈpɑːti]	Gruppe
	rider [ˈraɪdə]	Reiter/in
	to explore [ɪkˈsplɔː]	erkunden
	undiscovered [ˌʌndɪˈskʌvəd]	unentdeckt
	relative [ˈrelətɪv]	Verwandte/r
	to stop off [ˌstɒp ˈɒf]	Station machen, einkehren
	cliff [klɪf]	Klippe, Fels
	ride [raɪd]	Ausritt
	to break [breɪk]	eine Pause einlegen
	terrain [təˈreɪn]	Umgebung, Landschaft
	breathtaking [ˈbreθteɪkɪŋ]	atemberaubend
	wealth [welθ]	Reichtum
	to alter [ˈɔːltə]	ändern, anpassen
	pace [peɪs]	Tempo
	to walk [wɔːk]	(Gangart:) Schritt gehen
	to trot [trɒt]	(Gangart:) traben
	to canter [ˈkæntə]	(Gangart:) leicht galoppieren
	to gallop [ˈgæləp]	galoppieren
	cross-country [ˌkrɒs ˈkʌntri]	querfeldein
	en-route [ˌɒn ˈruːt]	unterwegs
	excitement [ɪkˈsaɪtmənt]	Aufregung, Spannung
	departure [dɪˈpɑːtʃə]	Abreise, Aufbruch
	course [kɔːs]	(Menü:) Gang
	host [həʊst]	Gastgeber/in
	produce [ˈprɒdjuːs]	landwirtschaftliche Erzeugnisse
	second to none [ˌsekənd tə ˈnʌn]	absolute Spitze
	spacious [ˈspeɪʃəs]	geräumig
	to comprise [kəmˈpraɪz]	umfassen
	adjacent [əˈdʒeɪsnt]	angrenzend, angeschlossen
	genuine [ˈdʒenjuɪn]	echt, authentisch
	estate [ɪˈsteɪt]	Gut, Landgut
	bay [beɪ]	Bucht
	oasis [əʊˈeɪsɪs]	Oase
	availability [əˌveɪləˈbɪləti]	Verfügbarkeit

A–Z word list

Diese Liste enthält alle Wörter in alphabtischer Reihenfolge. Nicht aufgeführt sind die Wörter aus der Liste des Grundwortschatzes (Basic word list). Die Zahl nach dem Stichwort bezieht sich uf die Seite, auf der das Wort zum ersten Mal erscheint.
T = das Wort befindet sich in den *Transcripts* (Hörverständnistexte).
P = Das Wort befinder sich in den *Pairwork files*.

A

a. s. a. p. so bald wie möglich 66
ability Fähigkeit 60T
abrasive scheuernd 144
abuse unsachgemäßer Gebrauch 64
to accelerate beschleunigen 103
acceleration Beschleunigung 79
to accept akzeptieren 44
acceptance Akzeptanz 38
access Zugang, Zugriff 38
accessible zugänglich 90
accident Unfall 64
accommodation Unterkunft 152
according to gemäß, entsprechend, zufolge 27T
accordingly entsprechend 134
account Konto 67; **to take sth into ~** etw berücksichtigen 30
accounting Buchführung, Buchhaltung 54
to accumulate sich ansammeln, sich absetzen 19
accuracy Genauigkeit, Präzision 28
accurate genau, präzis 46P
to achieve erreichen 125
to act ausüben 69; **~ as** fungieren als 36; **~ out** spielen 84
action Arbeitsweise, Funktion 26
activator Startknopf 128T
actual tatsächlich 24
acute scharf, akut 110
to adapt anpassen 89
adaptability Anpassungsfähigkeit 120
adaptable variabel, vielseitig, anpassungsfähig 89
adaptor Adapter 98
to add hinzufügen 36
addition, in ~ to zusätzlich 13
additional zusätzlich 50
adequate angemessen 108
to adhere to sth eine Sache befolgen, etw beachten 52
adhesive Klebstoff 26
adjacent angrenzend, angeschlossen 152
to adjust anpassen, ändern, einstellen 32
adjustable regelbar, variabel 97
adjuster Versteller 149
adjustment Änderung, Anpassung, Einstellung 47
administrative overheads Verwaltungskosten 57
advert Anzeige, Inserat 118
to advertise inserieren 118
advice Rat, Ratschläge 124
aerospace industry Luft- und Raumfahrtbranche 77

afraid, to be ~ fürchten 22T
aftermarket Zubehörmarkt 64
after-sales service Kundendienst 19
agency Agentur 44
agreement key Bestätigungstaste 80
air conditioning Klimatisierung, Klimaanlage(n) 8
air pistol Druckluftschrauber 68
air powered druckluftbetrieben 74
to align ausrichten 102T
all, at ~ überhaupt 22T
Allen: ~ key Innensechskantschlüssel 16; **~ set bolt** Innensechskantmadenschraube 34; **~ set screw** Innensechskantgewindestift 35; **~-head screw** Innensechskantschraube 12
to alloy legieren 117
alloyed steel legierter Stahl 115
to alter ändern, anpassen 152
alteration Änderung, Umbau 47
ambient: ~ air Außenluft, Umgebungsluft 134; **~ temperature** Umgebungstemperatur 134
ammeter Amperemeter 149
amount Menge 68
to anaesthetize betäuben 109T
angle Winkel 13; **~ grinder** Winkelschleifer 11; **~ piece** Winkelstück 33
angular eckig, kantig 26; schräg 60T; **~ table** Schrägtisch 27
animal Tier- 149
ankle Knöchel, Sprunggelenk 109
annex Anbau, Nebengebäude 54T
to anticipate erwarten, vorhersehen 88
anticlockwise gegen den Uhrzeigersinn 46
antifreeze Frostschutzmittel 74
antiseptic antiseptisch 109
apart (voneinander) entfernt, auseinander 14T
apparatus Gerät, Maschine 99
to appear erscheinen 82
appearance Aussehen, Erscheinungsbild 105
appetizer Vorspeise 136
appliance Gerät, Vorrichtung 119
applicable, not ~ (in Formularen:) entfällt, keine Angabe 91T
applicant Bewerber/in 125T
application Anwendung 38; Bewerbung 119
applied angewandt 55
to apply anwenden 69; (elektr. Spannung:) anlegen 82; einsetzen 133;

gelten 144; **~ for a job** sich um eine Stelle bewerben 113; **~ sth to sth** etw an etw anbringen 147
appointment Termin 111
to appreciate verstehen, einsehen 125T
apprenticeship Lehre, Ausbildung 12
appropriate entsprechend, passend, geeignet 84
approximately ungefähr, zirka 27
apron Schlosskasten 39
arbor Achse 26
arc Lichtbogen 36
to arise (Problem:) auftreten 104
armoured cable Panzerkabel 46
around, to be ~ es geben 50
to arrange anordnen 89
arrangement Anordnung 106
arrival Ankunft, Eintreffen 92P
arrow Pfeil 60
artificial künstlich 77
artistic künstlerisch 123
aside abgesehen von 76
to assemble zusammenbauen, montieren 8; zusammenstellen 89
assembly Montage 16; Zusammenstellung 89; **~ group** Baugruppe 30; **~ line** Montagestraße, Fertigungslinie, Fließband 17; **~ stage** Zusammenstellungsstation 89
to assess einschätzen, bewerten 142
asset, to be an ~ to sth wertvoll, eine Bereicherung für etw sein 108
assistance Hilfe 84T
to associate verbinden, assoziieren 107
association Verbindung 44
to assume davon ausgehen, annehmen 108
to attach befestigen, anbringen 59
attachment Befestigung 63
attention Aufmerksamkeit 119
attributable to bedingt durch, zurückzuführen auf 64
author Verfasser 100
authorization Berechtigung, Autorisierung 82
authorized befugt, autorisiert 107T
to automate automatisieren 103
automated automatisiert 36; **fully ~** vollautomatisch 97
automation Automatisierung, Automation 128
to automatize automatisieren 8
automobile Auto, Automobil- 6
automotive Automobil- 6; **~ industry** Automobilbranche 129

190

A–Z WORD LIST

auxiliary Neben-, Hilfs- *50*
availability Verfügbarkeit *152*
available erhältlich, verfügbar *76*; **to be ~** zu sprechen sein *32*
to avoid vermeiden, verhindern *19*
awake wach *124*
to award zuerkennen, erteilen *122*
axial force Axialkraft *60*
axis Achse *26*
axleguide Achshalter *31*

B

back Rücken *109*
bacon Speck *136*
baggage: ~ claim Gepäckausgabe *90*; **~ trolley** Gepäckwagen *90*; **left ~** Gepäckaufbewahrung *90*
ball bearing Kugellager *60*
ball-nosed slot drill Kugelkopffräser *31*
ballpoint pen Kugelschreiber *98*
bandage Verband *109*
bandsaw Bandsäge *20*
bar Stange *22P*
barber shop Friseur *90*
barley Gerste *150*
barrel Tonne *60T*; Schaft, Zylinder *105*
base Sockel *59*
base material Grundmaterial *36*
base part Unterteil *34*
basin Schale *109*
batch production Serienfertigung *39*
to bathe baden, schwimmen *76*
bay Bucht *152*
beam (Stahl-)Träger *68T*
bean Bohne *54T*
to bear tragen, aushalten *60T*
bearing Lager *41T*; **ball ~** Kugellager *60*; **full complement cylindrical roller ~** vollrolliges Zylinderrollenlager *62P*; **~ pin** Lagerstift *63*; **plain ~** Gleitlager *60*; **radial ~** Radiallager *60*; **roller ~** Wälzlager *60*; **semi-locating ~** Stützlager *62P*; **slide ~** Gleitlager *63*
bed Maschinenbett, -führungsbahnen *39*; Liege *109T*
bedslide Maschinenführung *41T*
beef Rindfleisch *136*
beer Bier *88*; **~ mat** Bierdeckel *117*; **~ battered** im Bierteig *136*
bell pepper Paprika *8*
belt Riemen *138*; **~ drive** Riemenantrieb *141*; **~ tightener** Riemenspanner *146*
benchmark Maßstab, Richtgröße *129T*
bend Krümmung *71*
bending Krümmung *71*
benefit Nutzen, Vorteil *38*
beverage Getränk *132*
bias Ausrichtung, Vorliebe *118*
bill Rechnung *55*
bin Tonne *139*
bit Stück, Stückchen *136*
blackboard (Wand-)Tafel *46P*
blanket Decke *92*

blanking Abdunkelung *97*
bleary verschwommen, trüb *110*
to bleed bluten *117*
bleed: nose ~ Nasenbluten *109*
bleeding Blutung *109T*; **~ nose** blutende Nase, Nasenbluten *109*
blood pressure: ~ monitor Blutdruckmess-/-überwachungsgerät *109*; **to take sb's ~** jds Blutdruck messen *111*
to blow out ausblasen *19*
blow-up aufblasbar *125T*
blue cheese Blauschimmelkäse *136*
blunt stumpf *30*
bolt Schraube *12*; **countersunk ~** Senkschraube *34*; **hexagon socket cap ~** Innensechskantschraube *35*; **hexagonal head ~** Sechskantschraube *12*; **slotted cheesehead ~** Zylinderkopfschraube abgerundet mit Querschlitz *35*; **slotted countersunk ~** Senkschraube mit Querschlitz *35*; **slotted panhead ~** Halbrundkopfschraube mit Querschlitz *35*
bond test Hafttest *116*
bonding Kleben *36T*
booklet Broschüre *52*
bore Zylindersenkung *25*
to bore bohren *12*
borehole Bohrloch *13*
boring bar Innendrehmeißel *22P*
bottling factory Abfüllbetrieb *109T*
bowel Darm *109*
bowl Schüssel *60*
brackets Halterung *141*
brand Marke *88*
brazing Hartlöten *36*
to break eine Pause einlegen *152*
breakage Bruch *74*
breakdown Panne, Schaden *64*; Ausfall, Störung *118*
to break down kaputtgehen *7T*
breathtaking atemberaubend *152*
brewery Brauerei *88*
to bridge überbrücken *38*
brief(ly) kurz, knapp *30*
broken kaputt *8*
bruised geprellt *109*
bruising Quetschen *149*
brush Bürste *16*
bulk goods Schüttgut *103*
bullet Kugel, Punkt *41*; Aufzählungspunkt *142*
bumper Stoßstange *21*
to burn verbrennen *52*
burning brennend *110*
burr Grat *106*

C

cable, armoured ~ Panzerkabel *46*; **~ break** Kabelbruch *104*
CAD engineer Technische/r Zeichner/in *7*
cage Käfig *60*
to calculate berechnen *57*
calculator (Taschen-)Rechner *74*

to call up aufrufen *22T*
calliper Messschieber *14T*
campaign Kampagne, Aktion *44*
to cancel stornieren *22T*; streichen *58*
canteen Kantine *43*
to canter leicht galoppieren *152*
cap Kappe *98*
capable of sth zu etw fähig, imstande *89*
capacity Kapazität *28*; Belastung *60T*
care Sorgfalt *19*
career Karriere, Laufbahn *38*
carrier Frachtführer, Spedition *144*
carrot Möhre, Karotte *136*
to carry on weitermachen *23*
to carry out ausführen *19*
case Kasten, Koffer *16*; Fall *19*
cash Bargeld *27*
cast iron Gusseisen *28*
catalogue Katalog *16*
caught, to be ~ sich verfangen *112*; **to get ~ up** sich verfangen *75*
cause Ursache, Grund *84*
to cause verursachen *44*
cavity Hohlraum *31*
ceiling Decke *68T*
celery Sellerie *136*
centre lathe Spitzendrehmaschine *20*
centre line Symmetrieachse *13*
centre punch Körner *11*
CEO (Chief Executive Officer) Vorstandsvorsitzende/r, Geschäftsführer/in *54*
cereal Getreide *137*
cereals Getreidenahrung, -futter *137*
certified zertifiziert *134*
chainsaw Kettensäge *137*
challenge Herausforderung, Aufgabe *119*
chamfer Fase *13*
to chamfer (an)fasen *13*
change-gear guard Wechselradsicherung *46*
to characterise charakterisieren *107*
characteristics Merkmale, Eigenschaften *27*
chargeable zuweisbar, zuzuordnen *58*
chassis Fahrgestell *36*
check Kontrolle, Überprüfung *102T*
cheddar Cheddar-Käse *136*
cheers Danke *150*
chef Küchenchef/in *54T*
chest Brust *109*
childhood Kindheit *109*
chip Span *12*
chipping hammer Schlaghammer *74*
chipping-time volume Zerspanungsvolumen *79*
chips Pommes frites *54T*
chisel Meißel *11*
chlorofluorocarbon (CFC) Fluorchlorkohlenwasserstoff (FCKW) *52*
chromium-plated verchromt *98*
chuck Futter, Spann-Bohrfutter *23*
circlip Sprengring *63*
circuit Schaltkreis *45*; **~ diagram** Schaltplan *45*

A–Z WORD LIST

circuitry Schaltung *135*
circular kreisförmig, rund *140*
to claim behaupten *129T*
clamp Schelle, Klemme *68T*
to clamp (ein-, fest-)klemmen *36*; klemmen, befestigen *68T*; ~ **in** einspannen *21*
clamping Einspannen *28*; ~ **surface** Aufspannfläche, Spannfläche *27*
to clap klatschen *142*
to clarify klären *22*
classification Klassifizierung *26*
cleaner Reinigungsmittel *144*
cleaning Reinigung *19*
to clear räumen, auflösen *97*
clear of obstruction frei *46*
clearance fit Abmaße *61*
cliff Klippe, Fels *152*
clockwise im Uhrzeigersinn *46*
clockwork Uhrwerk *77*
closed gantry geschlossene Portalausführung *79*
closed-loop control Regelung *131*
cloth Tuch *144*
coastal Küsten- *134*
cogwheel Zahnrad *60*
coil spring Spiralfeder *103*
cold Erkältung *109*
colleague Kollege/-in *9*
collecting arm Aufnahmeköcher *100*
collector's item Sammlerstück *105*
combination pliers Kombizange *16*
to combine kombinieren *36*
to commission in Betrieb nehmen *68*
commissioning Inbetriebnahme *68T*; ~ **certificate** Inbetriebnahmeanweisung *102*
committee Ausschuss, Komitee *125*
common verbreitet *36*;
commonly üblicherweise, im Allgemeinen *36*
communications Kommunikation *8*
compact kompakt *38*
company doctor Betriebsarzt/-ärztin *109*
comparable vergleichbar *38*
comparatively vergleichsweise *78*
to compensate ausgleichen *60T*
compensation Vergütung, Entschädigung *67*
competent befähigt, kompetent *47*
competing konkurrierend *146*
competition Konkurrenz, Wettbewerb *54T*
to complain sich beschweren, sich beklagen *58*
complaint Reklamation, Beschwerde *66*
compliant konform *97*
complicated kompliziert *89*
component Bauteil, Element *6*
compound feed Mischfutter *149*
to compress sich verdichten (lassen) *76*
compressed komprimiert *68*
compressed air Druckluft *68*
compressibility Komprimierbarkeit *71P*
compression spring Druckfeder *98*

compressive stress Druckbelastung *116*
to comprise umfassen *152*
computerised computergesteuert *116*
computing Computer(wesen) *7*
concave konkav *140*
concept Konzept *38*
to concern betreffen *107*
concurrent gleichzeitig *97*
to condense kondensieren *69*
condition Bedingung *19*; Umstand *60T*
to conduct leiten *45*; durchführen *116*
conducting rod Leiterstab *59*
conduction Leitung *59*
conductive leitend, leitfähig *19*
conduit Rohrleitung *59*
cone Kegel, Konus *140*
confidently (selbst-)bewusst *142*
confined space geschlossener Raum *76*
to confirm bestätigen *15*
confirmation Bestätigung *66*
confused verwirrt *100*
conical kegelförmig, konisch *12*
conjunction Verbindung *50*
connection Verbindung *36*
consequential damages Folgeschäden *64*
to consider berücksichtigen, bedenken, in Erwägung ziehen *59*; ~ **sth sth** etw für etw halten, als etw ansehen *129T*
to consist of bestehen aus *68*
construction Konstruktion(sabteilung) *18*; ~ **industry** Baubranche *108*; ~ **site** Baustelle *108*; ~ **steel** Baustahl *38*
consumable abschmelzend *36*
to contact berühren *74*; ~ **sb** sich mit jdm in Verbindung setzen *55*
contained enthalten *59*
contaminated kontaminiert *74*
contamination Verunreinigung *36*
continual kontinuierlich *97*
to continue fortführen, weiterführen *12*
continuous stetig, kontinuierlich *36*
contouring control Maschinensteuerung *27*
contract Vertrag *58*
to contract sich zusammenziehen *51*
contrast, in ~ to im Gegensatz zu *36*
to contribute to sth zu etw einen Beitrag leisten *6*
control Steuerung, Regelung *27T*; Regler *97*; ~ **cable** Steuerleitung *128T*; ~ **pad** Anzeige- und Bediengerät *80*; ~ **panel** Steuerkonsole *25*
to control steuern, regeln *90*
controlling system Steuerungs- und Regelungssystem *27T*
controls Bedienelemente *39*
conventional herkömmlich, konventionell *50*
to convert umwandeln *52*
convex konvex *140*
to convey transportieren, befördern *90*
conveyor lane Fließband *89*
conveyor system Fördersystem, -anlage *89*

convincing überzeugend *58*
cooking oil Speiseöl *44*
to cool kühlen *51*
coolant: ~ **fluid** Kühlflüssigkeit *28*; ~ **hose** Kühlmittelschlauch *25*; ~ **overloads** Thermoschutzschalter *45*
cooling unit Kühler *34*
to cope zurechtkommen *88*
copper Kupfer *59*; **soft** ~ Weichkupfer *69*
core Kern *36*
to correspond entsprechen *76*
correspondence Schriftverkehr, Korrespondenz *19*
corresponding entsprechend *6*
corridor Flur, Gang *18*
corrosion Korrosion *71P*
corrosive korrosionsfördernd *134*
cost-effective kostengünstig *22P*
costly teuer, kostenintensiv *108*
cough Husten *109*
counter plate Befestigungsplatte *63*
counterbore Zapfensenker *11*; Stirnsenkung *13*
counterpart Gegenstück *30*
countersink Spitzsenker *11*; Spitzsenkung *13*
countersunk bolt Senkschraube *34*
countersunk rivet Senkkopfniete *35*
coupler Kupplung, Verbindungsstück *76*
course *(Menü:)* Gang *157*
cover Abdeckung, Deckel *41T*
to cover decken, abdecken *64*
covering Abdeckung *141*
craftsman Handwerker *8*
crank Kurbel *63*
crank shaft Kurbelwelle *51*
crate Kiste *144*
cream Sahne, Creme *136*
cross quer *27*
cross connection Querverbindung *68*
cross travel Durchgangshöhe *116*
cross-country querfeldein *152*
cross-headed screw Kreuzschlitzschraube *12*
crossroads Straßenkreuzung *94*
cross-slide Quersupport *41T*
to crush quetschen *137*
crushed gequetscht *75*
cube Würfel *140*
cubed hoch drei *56*
cubic würfelförmig *140*
cucumber Gurke *136*
currency Währung *90*
current (elektrischer) Strom *36*
current(ly) gegenwärtig, im Moment *68*; aktuell *83*
curriculum vitae (CV) *(BE)* Lebenslauf *120*
curtain Vorhang, *hier:* Lichtschranke *97*
curved gewölbt, gekrümmt *26*
custom manufacture Sonderanfertigung *132*
customer Kunde/-in *10*; ~ **satisfaction** Kundenzufriedenheit *107*; ~**-oriented**

A–Z WORD LIST

kundenorientiert *38*
cut Schnittverletzung *117*
cutter Fräser *26*; ~ **body** Fräserkörper *26*
cutting, high-speed ~ Hochgeschwindigkeitszerspanung (HSC) *77*; ~ **edge** Schneide *26*; ~ **face** Schnittfläche *22P*
to cycle zyklisch betreiben *97*
cylinder Zylinder *25*
cylinder head bolt Zylinderschraube *34*
cylindrical zylindrisch *12*

D

damage Schaden *64*
damaged beschädigt, schadhaft *67*
data retentiviy Datenerhaltung *131*
data sheet Datenblatt *29*
day before yesterday vorgestern *112*
deal Geschäft, Abschluss, Vertrag *88*
debit card Geldkarte *92*
decision Entscheidung *27T*
defect Fehler *64*; ~ **in workmanship** Verarbeitungsfehler *64*
defective fehlerhaft, defekt *64*
to define bestimmen, definieren *64*
deformation Verformung *38*
to degrade zersetzen *19*
degree Grad *21*
delay Verzögerung *22T*
delivery Lieferung *22T*
demand Forderung *67*
to demonstrate zeigen, vorführen *108*
demonstration tool Anschauungsmittel *59*
to denote bezeichnen *36*
dental Zahn- *77*; ~ **equipment** zahntechnische Aurüstung *77*
department Abteilung *18*
departure Abreise *92P*; Aufbruch *152*
to depend on sb/sth von jdm/etw abhängen *33*; **That ~s.** Das kommt darauf an. *27T*
dependent on abhängig von *38*
deposit *134*
to depress herunterdrücken *99*
depth Tiefe *22P*; ~ **gauge** Tiefenmessgerät *24*
desired gewünscht *82*
despite trotz *19*
dessert Nachspeise, Dessert *136*
destructive testing zerstörende Prüfung, zerstörendes Prüfverfahren *113*
detachable abnehmbar, nicht fest verbunden *36*
developing country Entwicklungsland *106*
development Entwicklung *54T*
deviation Abweichung *24*
device Gerät, Instrument, Vorrichtung *24*
diagram Grafik, Skizze *89*
diameter Durchmesser *13*
diarrhoea Durchfall *109*
to dictate diktieren *57*
die making Herstellung eines Spritzgusswerkzeugs *77*
differential Differential *64*

digit Ziffer, Stelle *19*
digital readout digitale Anzeige *28*
dimensioning Auslegung, Dimensionierung *138*
dimensions Abmessungen, Dimensionen *13*
diode Diode *38*
direct current motor Gleichstrommotor *103*
direction Richtung *45*; ~ **of rotation** Drehrichtung *46P*
directions Wegbeschreibung *93*; **to give ~** den Weg beschreiben *94*
disadvantage Nachteil *38*
to disassemble zerlegen, auseinanderbauen *66*
disaster relief Katastrophenhilfe *123*
to discharge abgeben *74*; austreten *74*
disc laser Scheibenlaser *38*
to disconnect trennen *40*
disconnect box, separately-fused ~ abgesicherter Schaltkasten *46*
discontinuity Unterbrechung *113*
to discover entdecken *73*
to discuss besprechen *7T*
disease Krankheit *112*
to disentangle entwirren, voneinander lösen *99*; **hard-to-~** schwer entwirrbar *103*
disentangler Entwirrer *103*
disgusting eklig *125T*
dish Gericht *54T*
dislocated ausgerenkt, ausgekugelt *110*
to dismantle demontieren, auseinanderbauen *60T*
to displace verdrängen *51*
displacer Verdränger *51*
to display anzeigen *83*
disposable Einweg- *89*
disposal Entsorgung *43*
to dispose of sth etw entsorgen *44*
dissatisfaction Unzufriedenheit *67*
distance Abstand *14T*; ~**-piece** Abstandshalter *34*
distinct unterschiedlich, verschieden *17*
to distribute verteilen, aufteilen *58*
distribution Verteilung *69*; Vertrieb *90*; ~ **overheads** Vertriebskosten *57*
to divide by teilen durch *56*
dizzy schwindlig *90*
dominant maßgeblich *59*
donut Kringel *41*
double bed Doppelbett *92*
downtime Stillstandzeit *118*
draft Entwurf *123*
drafting Zeichnungserstellung *138*
drain Abfluss *43*; ~ **screw** Ablassschraube *40*
to drain entwässern *69*; ~ **off** abfließen lassen *40*
drastic(ally) drastisch *58*
drill Bohrmaschine *11*; ~ **bit** Bohrer *23*
to drill bohren *23*
drilling machine Bohrmaschine *18*

drive Antrieb *27*
to drive treiben, schlagen *12*; antreiben *52*
driver's cab Fahrerhaus *17*
driving licence Führerschein *91T*
drop Tropfen *19*
to drop sinken *114*
drum Trommel *103*; ~ **conveyor** Trommelförderer *103*
drums Schlagzeug *7*
due to aufgrund *22P*
dumper Muldenkipper *113*
durability Haltbarkeit, Langlebigkeit *59*
durable langlebig, strapazierfähig *98*
dust Staub *19*
dustproof staubdicht *134*
duty Aufgabe, Pflicht *124*
dutybook Pflichtenheft *100*
DVD tray DVD-Schublade *60*
dynamics Dynamik *79*

E

e.g. z.B. *84*
eager to learn lernwillig *108*
ear protectors Gehörschutz *73*
earth Erde *45*
ease of construction Einfachheit der Konstruktion *59*
ease of operation Bedienungsfreundlichkeit *146*
economic(ally) wirtschaftlich *77*
edge Kante *13*
effective effektiv *36*
efficiency Effizienz *50*; **level of ~** Effizienzgrad *50*
electric arc welding Lichtbogenschweißen *36*
electric drill Elektrobohrmaschine *11*
electrical elektrisch *6*
electrical panel Schalttafel *46*
electricity Strom, Elektrizität *8*
electromagnet Elektromagnet *45*
electron-beam welding Elektronenstrahlschweißen *36*
to eliminate eliminieren, ausschließen *75*
eloxated eloxiert *98*
embedded eingebettet *116*
emergency stop Notausschalter *80*
to employ anwenden *59*
en suite, with ~ bathroom *(Zimmer)* mit eigenem Bad *92*
to enable befähigen, ermöglichen, in die Lage versetzen *51*
to enclose einschließen *97*
enclosed eingeschlossen *59*; beigefügt *120*
enclosure Gehäuse *97*; *(Brief:)* Anlage *119*
end mill stub Fingerfräser *31*
end milling Stirnfräsen *26*
energy consumption Strom-/Energieverbrauch *27T*
energy-beam welding Energiestrahl-

193

schweißen 36
engine Motor 44; ~ oil Motoröl 44
engineer Ingenieur/in, Techniker/in 7
to engrave gravieren 105
to enjoy sich erfreuen, genießen 6; ~ doing sth etw gern tun 7
enquiry Anfrage, Erkundigung 44
en-route unterwegs 152
to ensure gewährleisten, sicherstellen 38
enthusiasm Begeisterung 120
enthusiastic begeisterungsfähig 108
entire(ly) ganz 58
entree Hauptgericht, Hauptgang 136
entry, no ~ Eintritt verboten. Kein Zugang. 73; ~ point Zugang 46
environment Umgebung 74
environmental Umwelt- 43; ~ compatibility Umweltverträglichkeit 107T
equally gleich, gleichmäßig 58
equals ist gleich 56
equine Pferde- 149
to equip ausrüsten, ausstatten 54T
equipment Geräte 7T
equivalent Entsprechung 68
error log Fehlerprotokoll 95
error message Fehlermeldung 84T
especially eigens, speziell 129T
estate Gut, Landgut 152
estimate Schätzung 57
to estimate schätzen 147
to evaluate bewerten, auswerten, einstufen 125
even(ly) eben 96
exam Prüfung 121
examination Untersuchung 107T
to examine prüfen 32
to exceed übertreffen 74
excellence ausgezeichnete Qualität, hohes Niveau 6
excellent hervorragend 54T
excentric exzentrisch 146
excerpt Auszug, Ausschnitt 29
excessive übermäßig, zu hoch, zu viel 45
exchange Austausch 112
to exchange austauschen 51
excitement Aufregung, Spannung 152
exhaust Abluftrohr 75
exhaust air Abluft 74
exit Ausgabe 97
to exit sth etw verlassen 97
to expand sich ausdehnen 51; expandieren 55; erweitern 119
expandable erweiterbar 129T
expanded weit 134
expansion Ausdehnung 59; Erweiterung 129
to expect erwarten 67
expectation Erwartung 67
expense, at sb's ~ auf jds Kosten 144
expenses Kosten 128
expertise Fachwissen, Know-how 6
to expire verfallen 144
expiry date Verfallsdatum, 92P
explanation Erklärung 58
to explore erkunden 152

to expose sth to sth etw einer Sache aussetzen 59
exposed freiliegend, ungeschützt 47
exposure Ausgesetztsein, Belastung 74
to express ausdrücken 27
expression Ausdruck 6
extension Dehnung 114; ~ level Dehnungsgrad 115T
external Außen- 69
extraction system Absaugvorrichtung 19
eye pad Augenpad 109
eyesight Augenlicht 75

F

face Stirnseite 26; ~ milling Messerkopf-Fräsen 26
to face plandrehen, querdrehen 20
facility Einrichtung 44
factory Fabrik, Werk 18
to fail ausfallen, versagen 19; ~ sth etw nicht erfüllen 64
failure Bruch 114
fairly ziemlich 60
to fall over sth über etw stolpern 109T
fast fest 89
fast response kurze Ansprech-/Reaktionszeit(en) 71P
to fasten befestigen 35
fatal tödlich 108
fatality Unfall mit Todesfolge 108
fault message Fehlermeldung 84
faulty schadhaft, defekt 47
feature Merkmal, Eigenschaft 6
feed Zuführung 98; ~ rate Vorschubgeschwindigkeit 27
to feed (zu)führen 26; versorgen 74
feeder Zuführung 102
feedshaft Zugspindel 39
female weiblich 122
fibre Faser 38
fibre-optic cable Glasfaserkabel 97
field device Feldgerät 134
fierce (Wettbewerb:) hart 54T
file Feile 16; ~ brush Feilenbürste 16
to file einreichen 112
to fill in eintragen 14T
filler material Zusatzwerkstoff 36
filler screw Einfüllschraube 40
film Folie 97; ~ carriage Folienträger 97
fin Nase 90
final time schedule Fertigungszeitplanung 147
financial department Finanzabteilung 54
fine, I'm ~. Mir geht es gut. 9
to finish polieren 13
to fire entlassen, feuern 55
fire hazard Brandgefahr, Feuergefahr 75
firm rule bindende Vorschrift 108
first aid Erste Hilfe 90; ~ kit Erste-Hilfe-Kasten 109
fit Passung 30; geeignet 64
to fit passen 23; einpassen, einsetzen 99; ~ sth together etw zusammensetzen/-bauen 31

fitness Eignung, Tauglichkeit 107
fitting Anschluss, Verbindungsstück 75; ~ piece Anschlussstück 71
fit-up Spaltüberbrückbarkeit 38
to fix befestigen 35
fixed costs Fixkosten 58
fixing device Verbindungselement 35
fixture Zubehörteil 116
flammable entflammbar 71P; highly ~ leicht entflammbar 73
flat flach, eben 16
to flatten out sich verflachen 114
floating point value Gleitkommazahl 135
flow Fluss 45; Strom 71P
flu Grippe 109
to fluctuate schwanken, pendeln 114
fluid Flüssigkeit 71P
flux Flussmittel 36
flywheel Schwungrad 51
focal point Brennpunkt 59
to focus (on sth) sich (auf etw) konzentrieren 36
foil Folie 89
following folgende/r/s 8
footbrake Fußhebel 39
footprint Grundfläche, Standfläche 97
force Kraft 69
to force zwängen 141
forehead Stirn 109
foreign bodies Fremdkörper 144
foreman Vorarbeiter 68T
forestry harvester Holzerntemaschine 137
fork-lift truck Gabelstapler 73
form Formular 92
to form sich bilden 36
(the) former der/die/das erste 107
foundation Grundlage 79
fraction Bruch 21
frame plate Rahmenplatte 12
framework Gestell 59; Rahmen, Bezugsrahmen 123
free-standing freistehend 28
to freeze up einfrieren 76
French fries Pommes frites 136
frequent oft, häufig 19
friction test Reibungsprüfung 116
front Vorderseite 33; ~ view Ansicht von vorn 134
frostbite Erfrierung 74
fuel Brennstoff 52
fuel cell Brennstoffzelle 50
to fulfil erfüllen 107T
full complement cylindrical roller bearing vollrolliges Zylinderrollenlager 62P
fully automated vollautomatisch 97
to function funktionieren, laufen 50
functional(ly) funktional 6
funnel Trichter 40
furnace Schmelzofen, Brennkammer 50
further weitere/r/s 64
furthermore außerdem, darüber hinaus 108
fuse Sicherung 45

G

to gain erwerben, gewinnen *38*
gallons per minute (gpm) Gallonen *(= 3,785 Liter)* pro Minute *76*
to gallop galoppieren *152*
gantry, closed ~ geschlossene Portalausführung
gap Lücke *38*
garlic Knoblauch *125T*
gas, inert ~ Schutzgas *36*; **~ metal arc welding** Metallinertgasschweißen (MIG), Metallaktivgasschweißen (MAG) *36*; **~ tungsten arc welding** Wolframinertgasschweißen (WIG) *36*
gauge Messgerät *24*; **depth ~** Tiefenmessgerät *24*; **height ~** Höhenanreißgerät *11*; **plug ~** Grenzlehrdorn *24*; **snap ~** Grenzrachenlehre *24*; **thread plug ~** Gewinde-Grenzlehrdorn *24*
gear Gang *146*; **~box** Getriebe *39*; **~ drive** Getriebe *146*; **~ oil** Getriebeöl *42*
gearwheel Zahnrad, Getrieberad *138*
gender Geschlecht *121*
to generate erzeugen *68*
gentle behutsam, sanft *90*
genuine echt, authentisch *152*
to gesture gestikulieren *142*
giant Riese, Riesen- *113*
giddy schwindlig *110*
gift Geschenk *105*
glass fibre Glasfaser *81*
glove Handschuh *73*
gold-plated vergoldet *98*
grade Güteklasse *40*
gradually allmählich *114*
grain Korn *141*
graph Kurve, Diagramm *114*
to grasp greifen *89*
grateful dankbar *119*
to grease schmieren *41*
to grind schleifen, abschleifen *12*; mahlen *137*
grinder, angle ~ Winkelschleifer *11*; **off-hand ~** Handschleifmaschine *20*
grinding machine Schleifmaschine *20*
grip Greifen *97*
to grip greifen *74*
gripper Greifer *62*
grit Splitt, Kies *144*
groove Rille *60T*
ground Erdboden *107T*
grounded geerdet *74*
guard Gehäuse, Abdeckung *146*
guess Vermutung *54T*
guidance Beratung, Anleitung *44*
to guide führen *103*
guideline Richtlinie *54T*
guide roller Führungsrolle *19*
guideway Führungsbahn *28*
guiding device Führungseinrichtung *89*
guiding slide Führungsschlitten *146*
gypsum board Gipskarton *19*

H

habit Gewohnheit *125T*
hacksaw Bügelsäge *11*
hairnet Haarnetz *73*
ham Schinken *136*
hammer Hammer *11*
handfile Handfeile *11*
hand-held tool Handwerkzeug *11*
to handle handhaben, ausgelegt werden für *89*
handle piece Griffstück *98*
handling Einsatz von etw *81*
handling robot Handhabungsroboter *128*
hands-on experience praktische Erfahrung *118*
handwheel Handrad *141*
hard hat *(AE)* Schutzhelm *73*
to harden härten *117*
hardened gehärtet *28*
hardness test Härteprüfung *113*
hard-wearing strapazierfähig *98*
hard-wired relay festverdrahtete Schaltung *135*
harm Schaden *44*
harsh rau *134*
hazard Gefahr *73*
hazardous gefährlich *74*; **~ material** Gefahrstoff *40*
head-end plinth Maschinengestell *39*
headline Überschrift *74*
headquarters Zentrale *6*
headstock Spindelstock *39*; **~ cover** Spindelstockabdeckung *40*
health insurance Krankenversicherung *111*; **~ card** Versichertenkarte *111*
hearing Gehör *74*
to heat erhitzen *51*
heating Heizung *8*
heavy schwer *27*
heavy duty Hochleistungs- *97*
height Höhe *25*; **~ gauge** Höhenanreißgerät *11*
helical spring Schraubenfeder *103*
hemisphere Halbkugel *140*
hemispherical halbkugelförmig *140*
hex key Innensechskantschlüssel *11*
hexagon socket cap bolt Innensechskantschraube *35*
hexagonal sechseckig *12*; **~ head bolt** Sechskantschraube *12*
high voltage Hochspannung *73*
higher vocational course weiterführende Ausbildung *119*
to highlight hervorheben *83*
highly accurate production Präzisionsfertigung *78*
highly flammable leicht entflammbar *73*
high-powered Hochleistungs- *36*
high-speed cutting Hochgeschwindigkeitszerspanung (HSC) *77*
high-torque drehmomentstark *28*
hinge Scharnier *60*
hip joint Hüftgelenk *77*
to hire *(Personal)* einstellen *55*
hire car Mietwagen *64*
to hold on warten *22T*
to hold the line *(Telefon:)* am Apparat bleiben, dranbleiben *41T*
honest(ly) ehrlich *129T*
hood Schutzhaube *35*
hopper Einfülltrichter *139*
hose Schlauch *71*
hospitality Gastfreundschaft *152*
host Gastgeber/in *152*
housing Gehäuse *60T*
huge groß, riesig *60T*
humanly possible nach menschlichem Ermessen möglich *129T*
hurt, to get ~ sich verletzten *108*
to hurt wehtun *109T*
hydraulic hydraulisch *28*
hydraulics Hydraulik *71*
hydrogen Wasserstoff *51*
hyphen Trenn-/Bindestrich *91*

I

ice-pack Kühlpackung *109T*
identical identisch *27T*
to identify bestimmen, identifizieren *11*
identity card Personalausweis *91T*
illness Krankheit *109*
illuminated beleuchtet *82*
to imagine sich vorstellen *58*
immeasurably unermesslich, unendlich *123*
impact Auswirkung, Einfluss *108*
to impact sth sich auf etw auswirken *97*
impeller Lüfterrad *77*
imperfection Mangel *113*
to implement umsetzen, realisieren *38*; einsetzen *59*
to impress beeindrucken *54*
impressive eindrucksvoll *105*
improper falsch, unsachgemäß *64*
to improve verbessern *59*
improved besser *38*
impurity Verunreinigung *144*
inaccurate ungenau *147*
inappropriate unsachgemäß *144*
incident Zwischenfall, Vorfall *112*
to include einschließen, umfassen, einbeziehen *6*; umfassen *58*
incoming supply Anschlussleitung *45*
inconvenience Unannehmlichkeit(en) *67*
to in-copy kegeldrehen *20*
to incorporate einbeziehen *59*
increase Steigerung *88*
to increase erhöhen *38*; steigern *89*
increased gesteigert *38*
increasing zunehmend *38*
to incur vorkommen, *hier:* verursachen *144*
independent unabhängig *6*
indexable *hier:* mit Wendeschneidplatten *31*
to indicate anzeigen *82*
individual Einzelne/r, Einzelperson *125*
individuality Individualität *125*

A–Z WORD LIST

industrial fair Gewerbemesse, Industriemesse *97*
industrial safety Arbeitsschutz, Arbeitssicherheit *108*
inert inert, chemisch inaktiv *36*; ~ **gas** Schutzgas *36*
inexpensive kostengünstig *59*
inexperienced unerfahren *108*
infeed, high/low ~ großer/kleiner Einlaufschacht *97*; ~ **conveyor** Eingangsfließband *97*
inhaler Inhalator *109*
initial erste/r/s, Anfangs- *145*
initial cost Anschaffungskosten, Anlagekosten *76*
injection Spritze, Injektion *109T*
to injure verletzen *108*
injury Verletzung(en) *47*
ink Tinte *123*
inner race Innenring *60*
inoperable, to become ~ ausfallen, versagen *76*
input wire Zuleitung *46*
insensitive to unempfindlich gegen *146*
to insert einsetzen, einstecken *82*
inspection Überprüfung, Kontrolle, Inspektion *24*
to install installieren *18*
installation instructions Montageanleitung *69*
instance, for ~ zum Beispiel *112*
instead of anstatt *69*
to instruct sb jdm Anweisungen erteilen *110*
instructor Ausbilder/in *14*
insulation Isolierung *19*
insurance Versicherung *58*
integer ganze Zahl *135*
to integrate integrieren *94*
integrated integriert *6*
intended beabsichtigt *64*
intended for geeignet für, gedacht für *81*
to interchange vertauschen *46*
interior das Innere *19*
interior Innen-, Inneneinrichtungs- *6*
interlinked miteinander verbunden *68*
interlocked verhakt *103*
internal thread Innengewinde *22P*
to interrupt unterbrechen *40*
intertwining Verflechtung *107T*
interview Vorstellungsgespräch *119*
to interview ein Vorstellungsgespräch führen *55*
interviewee *Person, mit der ein Vorstellungsgespräch geführt wird* *124*
to introduce vorstellen, bekannt machen *7T*
to invalidate außer Kraft setzen *144*
to invent erfinden *52*
to invite einladen *54T*
invoice Rechnung *66*
to involve mit sich bringen, einbeziehen, umfassen *36*
involved in sth in etw verwickelt, an etw beteiligt *66*

iron, cast ~ Gusseisen *28*
to iron out *(Fehler)* ausmerzen, beheben *129T*
isochronous mode isochrone Datenübertragung *(mit konstanter Datenrate)* *131*
to isolate trennen *46*
isolator switch Trennschalter *46*
to itch jucken *111*
itching Jucken *109*
item Artikel *22T*

J

to jam sich stauen, blockieren *96*
jerkily ruckelnd *104*
jet engine Düsentriebwerk *77*
jigsaw Stichsäge *11*
job advert Stellenanzeige *118*
to join (miteinander) verbinden *36*
joint Verbindung *36*; Gelenk *110*
journey Fahrt, Anreise *125T*

K

to keep aufbewahren *18*; halten *19*
kinked geknickt *75*
to knurl rändeln *20*
knurled gerändelt *25*

L

lab Labor *54T*
to label etikettieren *47*; bezeichnen *98*
labour Arbeit *57*
lager Pilsener *88*
laser-beam welding Laserstrahlschweißen *36*
laser-hybrid welding Laser-Hybrid-Schweißen *36*
to last dauern, Bestand haben, *hier:* laufen, in Betrieb sein *76*
latest neueste/r/s *54T*
lathe Drehbank, Drehmaschine *20*; **centre** ~ Spitzendrehmaschine *20*
(the) latter der/die/das zweite *107*
law Gesetz *108*
lawnmower Rasenmäher *35*
to lay *(Leitung etc.)* verlegen *69*; ~ **sb down** jdn hinlegen *109T*
layer Schicht *79*; ~ **build** Lagenaufbau *97*; ~ **head** Sortiervorrichtung *97*
leadscrew Leitspindel *39*
to leak out austreten *71P*
leather Leder *6*
left baggage Gepäckaufbewahrung *90*
legal(ly) legal, vorschriftsgemäß *108*
lettuce Salat *136*
level Stand *41*; ~ **of efficiency** Effizienzgrad *50*
to level off sich stabilisieren, sich einpendeln (bei) *114*
lever Hebel *46*
library Bibltiothek *123*
lid Deckel, Klappe *41T*

lifelong lebenslang *108*
life-span Lebensdauer *76*
ligament Band *112*
light leicht *27*; ~ **barrier** Lichtschranke *128T*; ~ **beam** Lichtstrahl *97*; ~ **metal** Leichtmetall *81*
lightweight leicht *146*
likely wahrscheinlich *36*
to limit begrenzen, beschränken *45*
limited begrenzt *60T*
line Leitung *69*
line protection Leitungsschutz *104*
link Verbindung *63*
liquid Flüssigkeit *76*
live unter Strom *47*
livery stable Reitstall, Mietstall *137*
load Last *104*; ~ **build** Zusammenstellung der zu verpackenden Einheiten *97*; ~ **rating** Last *62P*
to load laden *18*; beladen werden *54T*
loading: ~ **ability** maximale Last *27*; ~ **bay** Laderampe *54T*; ~ **capacity** Traglast *60T*; ~ **platform** Ladefläche, Pritsche *21*
local intelligence intelligentes Schnittstellensystem *131*
located gelegen *26*
lockout Sperre *97*
logistics Logistik *54*
longitudinal längs *27*; ~ **turning** Längsdrehen *20*
long-lasting lang anhaltend, dauerhaft *79*
to look forward to sth sich auf etw freuen *54T*
loop Ringleitung *68*; Öse *103*
loose locker *60*
to loosen lösen *40*
lorry Lastwagen *12*
loss Verlust *55*
loss of grip Griffkeitsverlust *74*
lost property Fundbüro *90*
loud laut *27*
to lower senken *50*
lower yield point untere Streckgrenze *114*
low-voltage Niederspannung *103*
to lubricate schmieren *19*
lubrication Schmierung *28*; ~ **chart** Schmierplan *41*
luggage Gepäck *90*
lunch break Mittagspause *30*
luxurious luxuriös *98*

M

machine: ~ **fault chart** Fehlersuchplan *104*; ~ **operator** Maschinenführer/in *78*; ~-**specific** gerätespezifisch *80*; ~ **tool** Werkzeugmaschine *8*; ~ **vice** Maschinenschraubstock *25*
to machine maschinell bearbeiten *26*
machining maschinelle Bearbeitung *26*
magazine Magazin *128*
magnetic-particle test Magnetpulverrissprüfung *113*

A–Z WORD LIST

mains Stromnetz *46*; **~ box** Stromversorgung *102T*; **~ plug** Netzstecker *19*
to maintain aufrecht erhalten *60T*
maintenance Wartung, Instandhaltung *7*; **~-free** wartungsfrei *129T*
major Haupt- *27T*; größere/r/s *112*
to make sense sinnvoll sein *71*
to make sure gewährleisten, sicherstellen *40*
male männlich *75*
malfunction Störung, Fehlfunktion *19*; Defekt *64*
malt vinegar Malzessig *136*
management system Steuerungs- und Regelungssystem *6*
manner Art (und Weise) *69*
manual Hand- *12*
to manufacture herstellen, fertigen *14*
manufacturer Hersteller *6*
to mark off anzeichnen, anreißen *12*
to market vermarkten *54*
marriage Verbindung *6*
marten Marder *69*
mashed potatoes Kartoffelbrei *136*
mass Masse *62P*
material sample Materialprobe *116*
materials testing Materialprüfung *113*
matter Sache, Angelegenheit *67*
maximum, to hit a ~ einen Maximalwert erreichen *114*
maze Labyrinth *81*
to measure messen, vermessen *74*
measurement Maß, Messung *56*
measuring instrument Messinstrument *24*
meatloaf Hackbraten, Fleischkäse *136*
mechanic Mechaniker/in *8*
mechanical(ly) mechanisch *45*
mechanical engineering Maschinenbau *7T*
mechanism Mechanismus *45*
mechatronics technician Mechatroniker/in *128*
to mediate vermitteln *29*
mediation Vermittlung *26*
medical medizinisch, Medizin- *109*
medication Medikamente *111*
mediterranean mediterran *54T*
meeting Besprechung *18*
to melt schmelzen *36*
melted geschmolzen *136*
to memorize sich merken, auswendig lernen *142*
memory Speicher *82*
to mention erwähnen, nennen *66*
mess Schweinerei, Chaos *76*
metalworker Metallarbeiter/in *110*
metalworking metallverarbeitend, in der Metallverarbeitung *8*
method Art (und Weise), Methode *26*
metric metrisch *22*
micrometer Messschraube *14T*
middle error Fluchtfehler *60T*
mileage Kilometerstand *64*
milking machine Melkmaschine *137*

to mill fräsen *26*
miller Fräsmaschine *31T*
milling: ~ cutter Fräswerkzeug, Fräser *25*; **end ~** Stirnfräsen *26*; **face ~** Messerkopf-Fräsen *26*; **~ head** Fräskopf *25*; **~ machine** Fräse *20*; **peripheral ~** Walzenfräsen *26*; **slab ~** Walzenfräsen *26*
to mind etwas dagegen haben *22T*
misapplication falsche Verwendung *64*
mishandling fehlerhafte Handhabung *144*
to miss unerwähnt lassen *102*; **~ sth** etw verpassen *94*
to misuse falsch verwenden, missbräuchlich verwenden *144*
mixed up, to get ~ durcheinandergeraten *84*
to modernize modernisieren *89*
module Modul *89*
molten geschmolzen *36*
to monitor überwachen *70*
monument Denkmal *94*
mother tongue Muttersprache *121*
motion control Ablaufsteuerung *131*
motor-circuit-breaker Motorschutzschalter *96*
motorcycle Motorrad *123*
motorcycling Motorradfahren *7T*
to mount montieren *17*
mounting Montage *63*; Montieren *90*
moveable beweglich *35*
muffled gedämpft *74*
muffler Geräuschdämpfer *75*
multiple mehrfach *22P*
to multiply multiplizieren *56*
multi-skilled vielseitig ausgebildet *118*
mustard Senf *136*

N

nail Nagel *12*
naked light offenes Licht *73*
nameplate Typenschild *19*
nasty schlimm, böse *109T*
nausea Übelkeit *109*
needle Nadel *60T*
negligence Fahrlässigkeit *144*
nipple Nippel *69*; Schmiernippel *41T*
nitrogen oxide Stickoxid *52*
no entry Eintritt verboten. Kein Zugang. *73*
noisy laut *74*
nominal nominell, Nenn- *24*
non-allergic antiallergisch *92*
non-consumable nichtabschmelzend *36*
non-destructive testing zerstörungsfreies Prüfverfahren *113*
non-transferable nicht übertragbar *144*
non-volatile memory nicht-flüchtiger Speicher *135*
nose bleed Nasenbluten *109*
not applicable *(in Formularen:)* entfällt, keine Angabe *91T*
note Anmerkung *44*; Vermerk *144*

noticeably deutlich *38*
nut Mutter *15*

O

oasis Oase *152*
oat crusher Haferquetsche *137*
oatmeal Hafer *136*
oats Hafer *137*
object Gegenstand, Ding, Objekt *8*
to observe beachten *69*
obstruction Blockierung *46*; **clear of ~** frei *46*
occasionally gelegentlich, ab und zu *19*
occupation Beschäftigung, Anstellung *121*
occupational death Arbeitsunfall mit Todesfolge *108*
occupational safety Arbeitsschutz, Arbeitssicherheit *108*
to occur auftreten, vorkommen, geschehen *71P*
occurrence Vorkommnis *112*
off-hand grinder Handschleifmaschine *20*
oil Öl *19*
to oil ölen *41*
oiling point Schmiernippel *41T*
ointment Salbe *109*
ongoing laufend *58*
onion Zwiebel *136*
open-ended spanner Maulschlüssel, Gabelschlüssel *11*
to operate arbeiten, funktionieren *38*; betätigen, steuern *45*; betreiben *50*; bedienen *73*
operating: ~ conditions Betriebsbedingungen *134*; **~ manual** Betriebsanleitung, Gebrauchsanweisung *40*; **~ mode** Betriebsart, Betriebsmodus *82*; **~ panel** Bedienfeld *80*; **~ temperature** Betriebstemperatur *69*
operation Arbeitsgang, Tätigkeit *20*; Betrieb *73*; **ease of ~** Bedienungsfreundlichkeit *146*
operational Bedienungs-, Betriebs- *19*; **~ life** Lebensdauer *129T*; **~ malfunction** Funktionsstörung *19*; **~ safety** Betriebssicherheit *28*
operative Mitarbeiter/in *119*
opportunity Gelegenheit *7*
opposed, as ~ to gegenüber, im Gegensatz zu *100*
order Reihenfolge *9*; Auftrag, Bestellung *15*
order, in ~ to um ... zu *19*
to order bestellen *15*
organizational chart Organigramm *54*
oscilloscope Oszilloskop *74*
otherwise sonst, ansonsten *69*
to out-copy kegeldrehen *20*
outdated veraltet *96*
outer race Außenring *60*
output actuator Aktor, Stellglied *135*
output force Nutzkraft *71P*
outstanding herausragend *79*

197

A–Z WORD LIST

overall Gesamt- *14T*; gesamt *59*
overhead über Kopf *19*; ~ **expenses** Gemeinkosten *58*; ~ **rate** Überschussrate *57*; **administrative ~s** Verwaltungskosten *57*
overlap Überlappung *97*
overlapping überlappend *36*
overload Überspannung *149*
overlooking mit Blick auf *92*
overly zu (sehr) *142*
to over-speed zu schnell laufen, zu hoch drehen *74*
owner Besitzer/in, Inhaber/in *107T*

P

pace Tempo *152*
packaging Verpackung *88*
padding Polsterung, Füllung *144*
pain Schmerz(en) *109*
painful schmerzhaft *110*
pallet exchange Palettenwechsel *80*
pallet storage Palettenspeicher *80*
palletising Palettieren *89*
panhead rivet Halbrundkopfniete *35*
parabolic Parabol- *59*
parallel parallel *26*
particle Teilchen, Partikel *74*
particular spezielle/r/s *129T*
particularly besonders *36*
to part-off abstechen *20*
party Gruppe *152*
to pass reichen *17*; vorbeifahren, -laufen *89*; ~ **sth** etw weiterbefördern, weiterreichen *128T*; ~ **through** hindurchgehen *59*
passing Fließen *36*
past an … vorbei *26*
patented patentiert *149*
patient Patient/in *109*
to peak einen Spitzenwert erreichen *114*
pedal Pedal *60*
peel test Abschältest *116*
pellet furnace Pelletbrenner *50*
penetration weld Einschweißtiefe *38*
to perform *(Handlung)* ausführen *99*
period Zeitraum *64*
periodical(ly) regelmäßig *69*
peripheral milling Walzenfräsen *26*
periphery Umfang *26*
permanent dauerhaft *36T*
permission Erlaubnis, Genehmigung *84T*
perpendicular lotrecht, senkrecht *26*
personnel Personal(abteilung) *54T*
petrochemicals Petrochemie *132*
petrol Petroleum *44*
Phillips screw(driver) Kreuzschlitzschraube(ndreher) *11*
phrase (Rede-)Wendung, Satz *12*
to pick up abholen *93*
pickled sauer eingelegt *136*
pillow Kopfkissen *92*
pin punch Schlagdorn *16*
pincers Pinzette, Zange *17*
pipe Rohr, Röhre *36*

piping Rohrleitungen *68T*
piston Kolben *51*
place, to be in ~ in Betrieb sein *94*
to place platzieren, setzen, stellen, legen *90*; ~ **an order** einen Auftrag erteilen, eine Bestellung aufgeben *15*
plain bearing Gleitlager *60*
plain flat washer Unterlegscheibe *35*
plant Anlage *69*; Pflanze *107T*; ~ **manager** Werksleiter/in *89*
plastics Plastik *8*
plate Plakette, Schild *147*
plate ring Tellerfeder *103*
PLC (programmable logic controller) Speicherprogrammierbare Steuerung (SPS) *128*
Pleased to meet you. Schön, Sie kennen zu lernen. *9*
pliers Zange *16*; **combination ~** Kombizange *16*; **waterpump ~** Wasserpumpenzange *16*
plug Stecker *35*; ~ **gauge** Grenzlehrdorn *24*
to plug sth in etw einstecken, anschließen *8*
pluggable Steck- *129T*
plumber Klempner/in, Installateur/in *68*
plumbing company Klempnerei, Installationsbetrieb *68T*
to plunge schnell absinken, steil abfallen *114*
pneumatic pneumatisch *68*
pneumatics Pneumatik *68*
poached pochiert *136*
point Komma *14T*
to point to sth auf etw zeigen *142*
polite höflich *67*
pollution Verschmutzung *44*
polyamide Polyamid *69*
polyethylene Polethylen *69*
pool Lache *36*
poorly ventilated schlecht belüftet *76*
pork Schweinefleisch *136*
portal portal *89*
post Stelle, Posten *120*
pot roast Schmorbraten *136*
potential potenziell *27*
to pour gießen *40*
powder coated pulverbeschichtet *116*
power: ~ **cable** Stromkabel *128T*; ~ **generation** Stromerzeugung *132*; ~ **hacksaw** Maschinenbügelsäge, Hubsäge *20*; ~ **source** Stromquelle, Stromversorgung *40*; ~ **supply** Stromversorgung *46*; ~ **tool** Elektrowerkzeug *19*; **to the ~ of** hoch *56*
to power antreiben, mit Energie versorgen *50*
pozidriv screw(driver) Pozidriv-Schraube(ndreher) *11*
to practise üben, proben *124*
precaution Vorsichtsmaßnahme, Vorkehrung *47*
precious wertvoll *75*
precise genau, präzis, exakt *22P*

precision Präzision *79*; ~ **mechanic** Feinmechaniker/in *119*
prefabricated vorgefertigt *146*
prepaid im Voraus bezahlt *144*
to prepare vorbereiten *12*
to preselect vorwählen, vorher auswählen *89*
presence Anwesenheit, Vorhandensein *36*
present, at ~ gegenwärtig *120*
to press drücken, pressen *61*
pressure Druck *69*; ~ **cooker** Schnellkochtopf *60*; ~ **drop** Druckabfall *69*; ~ **test** Druckprüfung *113*
pressurized unter Druck *76*
pre-stretch Vordehnung *97*
pretty ziemlich *9*
to prevent verhindern *35*
preventive vorbeugend *118*
previous vorherig *32*
primary Primär- *50*
principle Prinzip *36*
probable wahrscheinlich *84T*
procedure Verfahren *19*
process engineering Verfahrenstechnik *132*
process industry verarbeitende Industrie *131*
processing (Weiter-)Verarbeitung *103*; ~ **cycle** Prozessablaufsteuerung *28*
produce landwirtschaftliche Erzeugnisse *152*
product liability Produkthaftung *107T*
production area Produktionsfläche *68*
production line Fertigungsstraße *128*
production plant Produktionsstätte, -anlage *88*
profile Profil, Beschreibung, Porträt *7*
profit Gewinn *55*; ~ **margin** Gewinnspanne *58*
prolonged fortdauernd *74*
to promote fördern *108*
to pronounce aussprechen *56*
proof Nachweis, Beweis *6*
proper richtig *17*
protective Schutz- *19*; ~ **equipment** Schutzausrüstung *110*; ~ **footwear** Sicherheitsschuhe *73*
prototype Prototyp *57*
proud stolz *54T*
proven nachgewiesen *118*
to provide bieten *44*
provided unter der Voraussetzung, dass *144*
provider Anbieter/in *22P*
psychology Psychologie *55*
to publish veröffentlichen, publizieren *108*
pulled pork Streifen von Schweinebraten *136*
pulse Impuls *51*
pump Pumpe *17*
punch, centre ~ Körner *11*
to punch mark ankörnen *12*
purchase Kauf *144*
purchaser Käufer/in *64*

A–Z WORD LIST

purchasing Einkauf(sabteilung) *54T*
purpose Zweck *64*
push button Druckknopf *128T*
to put sb through *(Telefon:)* jdn durchstellen *41T*

Q

qualification Abschluss, Qualifikation *122*
quality assurance manual Qualitätsmanagementshandbuch *107T*
quantity Menge *22*; ~ **discount** Mengenrabatt *22*
quarry Steinbruch *113*
to quote angeben, nennen *144*; ~ a **price** einen Preis nennen, ein Angebot machen *105*

R

R & D Forschung- und Entwicklungsabteilung *54T*
race, inner ~ Innenring *60*; **outer** ~ Außenring *60*
rack Zahnstange *41T*
radial bearing Radiallager *60*
radial force Radialkraft *60*
radiation Strahlung *59*
radish Rettich *136*
radius Radius *25*
rail rolling stock *(Eisenbahn:)* Rollmaterial *38*
to raise anheben *46*
range Bereich, Spanne *134*; **a broad ~ of** eine große Auswahl von *17*
to rank third auf dem dritten Platz stehen *108*
rapid traverse Schnellvorschub *27*
rate Preis, Satz *57*
rating Auslegung, Herstellervorgabe *74*
raw material Rohstoff *88*
raw part Rohling *81*
reading Messwert *56*
to ream reiben *20*
reamer Reibahle *23*
rear Rückseite *33*
rear axle Hinterachse *21*
reasonable vernünftig *55*
reasonably ziemlich, halbwegs *147*
to recall sth sich an etw erinnern *109*
receipt Erhalt *144*
receiver Werkzeugaufnahme *79*
receptionist Empangsmitarbeiter/in *91*
recess Aussparung *12*
recessing Einlassen, Absetzen *22P*
reciprocating hin- und hergehend *75*
to recommend empfehlen *19*
to reconnect wieder verbinden *40*
records Daten, Aufzeichnungen *55*
to recruit einstellen *118*
rectangle Rechteck *140*
rectangular quaderförmig *140*; rechteckig *140*; ~ **solid** Quader *140*
to rectify *(Fehler)* beheben *118*

redness Rötung *109*
to reduce senken, reduzieren, verringern, *8*
to refer to sth sich auf etw beziehen *46*
refill Mine *98*
refill prism Einfüllbehälter *102T*
refrigerator Kühlschrank *50*
refund Rückerstattung *67*
regenerator Regenerator *59*
to register wahrnehmen, registrieren *97*
registration Anmeldung *92*
to regrind nachschleifen *22P*
to regulate regulieren *45*
regulation Vorschrift *43*
reinforced verstärkt *81*
relative Verwandte/r *152*
relay Relais *45*; ~ **controller** Relaissteuerung *94*; **hard-wired** ~ festverdrahtete Schaltung *135*
reliability Zuverlässigkeit *118*
reliable zuverlässig *6*
to remain bleiben *82*
remaining übrige/r/s *84*
remedy Abhilfe *74*
removal Ausbau *64*
to remove entfernen, ausbauen *40*
renowned bekannt, renommiert *6*
rent Miete *58*
to rent mieten *91T*
rental Vermietung *90*
repair Reparatur *19*
to repair reparieren *7T*
to replace ersetzen, austauschen *7T*; wieder einsetzen *40*
replacement Austausch *64*
replica Kopie, Reproduktion *110*
to report melden *144*
to represent darstellen *135*
representative Vertreter/in *129*
reputation Ruf *6*
to require brauchen, benötigen *27T*
requirement Vorschrift *69*
research Forschung *54T*
reservoir Behälter *68T*
residual current device FI-Schutzschalter *19*
resistance Widerstand *36*; ~ **welding** Widerstandsschweißen *36*
resistor Widerstand *45*
to respect schätzen, respektieren *6*
respective jeweilige/r/s *100*
response, fast ~ kurze Ansprech-/Reaktionszeit(en) *71P*
responsible for verantwortlich für, zuständig für *8*
result Ergebnis, Resultat *36*
to result resultieren *26*
résumé *(AE)* Lebenslauf *121*
retail price Einzelhandelspreis *57*
retentivity, data ~ Datenerhaltung *131*
return Rückkehr *95*
reverse Rückwärtsgang *146*; **in** ~ umgekehrt *50*
reversion Umkehr *146*
review Zusammenfassung *30*

to revise überarbeiten *143*
revolution Umdrehung *27T*
reworking Nachbearbeitung *38*
rid, to get ~ **of sth** etw loswerden *43*
ride Ausritt *152*
rider Reiter/in *152*
riding Reiten *152*
rigid starr *27*
rim Rand, Fase *21*
rivet, countersunk ~ Senkkopfniete *35*; **panhead** ~ Halbrundkopfniete *35*; **roundhead** ~ Rundkopfniete *35*
riveting Nieten, Vernieten *36T*
road junction Straßenkreuzung *94*
roadworks Straßenbauarbeiten *93*
roasted gebraten *136*
robustness Robustheit *134*
rock drill Bohrhammer *74*
rocker Kipphebel *98*
rod Stab *21*
rod assembly Gestänge *59*
rodent Nagetier *69*
roller Wälzkörper *60*; Walze *141*; ~ **bearing** Wälzlager *60*
rolling ball Kugellagerkugel *60*
root vegetables Wurzelgemüse *136*
rotary drill Bohrgerät *74*
to rotate sich drehen, rotieren *26*
rotation Rotation *26*
rough grob *46P*; rau *134*
roughing Schruppen *22P*
round head screw Rundkopfschraube *35*
roundabout Kreisverkehr *94*
roundhead rivet Rundkopfniete *35*
route Weg, Route *93*
row Reihe *60T*
row pushing area Reihensortierstation *97*
rpm (revolutions per minute) U/min (Umdrehungen pro Minute) *27*
rule Lineal *16*; Vorschrift *75*
rustfree rostfrei *98*
rusty rostig *109T*

S

saddle and slides Support und Werkzeugschlitten *39*
saddlery Sattelzeug, Sattlereiwaren *149*
safety Sicherheit *47*; ~ **goggles** Schutzbrille *16*; ~ **helmet** Schutzhelm *73*; ~ **pin** Sicherheitsnadel *109*; ~ **precautions** Sicherheitsmaßnahmen *47*; ~ **relay** Sicherheitsschaltung *97*; ~ **sign** Sicherheitszeichen, -symbol *73*; ~ **sticker** Aufkleber mit Sicherheitssymbolen *147*
sale price Verkaufspreis *57*
sales Verkauf, Vertrieb *54T*; ~ **representative** Vertreter/in, Vertriebsmitarbeiter/in *27*
salty salzhaltig, salzig *134*
sample test Stichprobenkontrolle *107*
sander Schleifgerät *74*
sat nav Satelliten-Navigationsgerät *92*
satisfaction Zufriedenheit *67*

199

A–Z WORD LIST

sausage Würstchen *54T*
sautéd sautiert, geschmort *136*
to saw sägen *19*
saw ring Zahnscheibe *103*
SCADA system elektrisches Überwachungs-, Steuer- und Datenaufnahmesystem *135*
scaffolding Gerüst *70*
scalable anpassbar, erweiterbar *131*
scale Skala *60*
scales Waage *74*
scalpel Skalpell *109*
to scan absuchen *30*
schedule (Termin-)Plan *18*; **final time ~** Fertigungszeitplanung *147*
scissors Schere *17*
scratch Kratzer *106*
to scratch kratzen *111*
screw, Allen-head ~ Innensechskantschraube *12*; **cross-headed ~** Kreuzschlitzschraube *12*; **~ head** Schraubenkopf *12*; **Phillips ~** Kreuzschlitzschraube *11*; **pozidriv ~** Pozidriv-Schraube *11*; **round head ~** Rundkopfschraube *35*; **slot-headed ~** Schlitzschraube *12*; **slotted ~** Schlitzschraube *11*; **wing ~** Flügelschraube *35*
screw-in nipple Einschraubnippel *69*
sealed luftdicht *51*
sealing stick Dichtstift *69*
seam (Schweiß-)Naht *38*; **~ preparation** Schweißnahtvorbereitung *38*
second to none absolute Spitze *152*
secret Geheim- *136*
section Abschnitt *44*
secure sicher, gesichert *46*
to secure fixieren, festhalten *36*
security Sicherheit *15*
to seek suchen *120*
to select auswählen, wählen *59*
selection Wahl *83*
selector switch Wahlschalter *82*
self-aligning Selbstausrichtung *60T*
self-assessment Selbsteinschätzung *123*
semi-circle Halbkreis *140*
semicircular halbrund *16*; halbkreisförmig *140*
semi-inert teil-inert *36*
semi-locating bearing Stützlager *62P*
sensitive empfindlich *97*
separate separat, getrennt *36*
to separate trennen, separieren *103*
separately-fused disconnect box abgesicherter Schaltkasten *46*
to serve servieren *92*
to service sth etw warten *17*
to set out darlegen, darstellen *67*
set-up Einrichtung *97*
to set up einrichten. gründen *44*
severe stark, schwer *90*
severed abgetrennt, durchtrennt *74*
shaft Achse, Welle *20*
shakeproof washer Zahnscheibe *35*
shallot Lauchzwiebel *136*
shank Schaft *22P*

shape Form *12*
to shape formen *12*
sharp scharf, *hier:* stark *71*
shears Schere *17*
to sheathe ummanteln *46*
sheet Blatt, Bogen *24*; Blech *36*; **~ metal** Blech(e) *128T*; **~ steel** Stahlblech *34*
shielded metal arc welding Lichtbogenhandschweißen *36*
shielding gas Schutzgas *36*
shipbuilding Schiffbau *38*
shock Stoß, Erschütterung *134*
shock absorber Stoßdämpfer *60*
to shoot up in die Höhe schnellen *114*
shooting *(Schmerz:)* stechend *110*
shop floor Fertigungsbereich, Produktionsbereich *89*
shoulder Bund *25*
to shout schreien *142*
to show sb around jdn herumführen *54*
shrimp Garnele, Krabbe *136*
to shrink schrumpfen *89*
shrink-wrapper Schrumpffolienverpackungsmaschine *89*
to shut off absperren, abstellen *74*
shut-off valve Sperrventil *68*
side view Seitenansicht *13*
sight glass Schauglas *41T*
signal lamp Anzeige-, Signallampe *128T*
signal-pressure line Signaldruckleitung *69*
significant(ly) erheblich *38*
similar ähnlich *27T*
similarity Übereinstimmung, Ähnlichkeit *27*
simplicity Einfachheit *59*
simultaneous(ly) gleichzeitig *36*
single phase einphasig *116*
single-part production Einzelfertigung *39*
size Größe *27T*
sized in verschiedenen Größen *149*
sketch Skizze *26*
skill Fähigkeit, Fertigkeit *58*
skilled worker Facharbeiter/in *7*
slab milling Walzenfräsen *26*
slack durchhängend, nicht gespannt *71*
slackness Spiel *146*
sleeve Schaft *98*; Ärmel *111*
slice Scheibe, Schnitte *136*
slide Dia, Slide *142*
slide bearing Gleitlager *63*
slightly etwas, geringfügig *27*
slip Abrutschen *143*
to slip ausrutschen *111*; abrutschen *141*
slip-ring motor Schleifringläufermotor *103*
slope, at a ~ mit Gefälle *69*
sloped mit Gefälle *69*
slot-headed screw Schlitzschraube *12*
slotted geschlitzt, Schlitz- *15*; **~ cheesehead bolt** Zylinderkopfschraube abgerundet mit Querschlitz *35*; **~**

countersunk bolt Senkkopfschraube mit Querschlitz *35*; **~ panhead bolt** Halbrundkopfschraube mit Querschlitz *35*; **~ screw(driver)** Schlitzschraube(ndreher) *11*
sludge pump Schlammpumpe *76*
small batch Kleinserie *98*
to smell of sth nach etw riechen *125T*
smoked geräuchert *136*
smokey rauchig, Räucher- *136*
smooth glatt, problemlos *96*
smooth(ly) ruhig *51*
snap gauge Grenzrachenlehre *24*
snap ring Sprengring *103*
snipe nose pliers Flachrundzange *17*
to socialize with sb sich mit jdm treffen *7T*
socializing Ausgehen, unter Leute gehen *7*
society Gesellschaft *107T*
socket Steckdose *40*
socket-outlet Steckdose *47*
soft copper Weichkupfer *69*
softkey virtuelle Tasten auf dem Touchscreen *80*
soldering Weichlöten *36T*
solenoid Magnetspule *135*
solution Lösung *9*
to solve lösen *104*
solvent Lösungsmittel *44*
sophisticated anspruchsvoll *54T*
sore throat Halsschmerzen, Rachenentründung *109*
to sort sortieren *12*; **~ sth out** etw in Ordnung bringen, etw klären *22T*
sound Klang, Geräusch *11*
to sound klingen *54T*
source Quelle *38*
spacious geräumig *152*
spare part Ersatzteil *19*
spare time Freizeit *7T*
spark Funken *104*
specialist Spezial- *17*
to specialize sich spezialisieren *120*
specifications Technische Daten, Spezifikationen *22P*
to specify (genau) angeben *123*
speed range Drehzahlbereich *27*
to spell buchstabieren *41*
sphere Kugel *140*
spherical sphärisch, kugelförmig *60T*
spiced würzig, (scharf) gewürzt *136*
spindle Spindel *26*; **main ~** Hauptspindel *39*; **~ nose** Spindelkopf *46*
to spit spucken *125T*
splash-protection Spritzschutz *28*
spot weld Schweißpunkt *36*
spot welding Punktschweißen *36*
sprained verstaucht *109*
spray protection cabin Maschinengehäuse *25*
spreadsheet Tabelle, Tabellenkalkulation(sbogen) *55*
spring Feder *98*; **coil ~** Spiralfeder *103*; **compression ~** Druckfeder *98*;

helical ~ Schraubenfeder *103*
spring washer Federscheibe *35*
square *(Brettspiel:)* Feld *81*
square root Quadratwurzel *56*
squared im Quadrat, hoch zwei *56*
squirrel cage motor Käfigläufer-motor *103*
stabbing *(Schmerz:)* stechend *110*
stability Stabilität *38*
stable stabil, robust *28*; Stall *137*
staff Personal, Belegschaft *7*
stage Schritt, Phase *55*; Station *89*
stain Fleck *111*
stainless steel Edelstahl *36*
stamping tool Stanzwerkzeug *77*
stand Ständer *94*
star-shaped sternförmig *15*
starter motor Starter *135*
state Zustand *135*
stationary stationär *19*
stay Aufenthalt *152*
stead(il)y gleichmäßig *114*
steady gleichbleibend, stabil, solide *107T*
steel Stahl *8*; **alloyed ~** legierter Stahl *115*; **construction ~** Baustahl *38*; **stainless ~** Edelstahl *36*; **structural ~** Baustahl *115*
stepless stufenlos *28*
stepper motor Schrittmotor *103*
stiff steif *110*
to stiffen versteifen, steif werden lassen *74*
to stifle ersticken, unterdrücken *125*
stock, in ~ auf Lager, vorrätig *22T*
stomach Magen, Bauch *109*; ~ **pain(s)** Bauchschmerzen *90*
stone Stein *6*
to stop off Station machen, einkehren *152*
storage Lagerung *44*
store Lager *40*
to store *(Daten)* speichern *135*
storeroom Lagerraum *30*
straightaway sofort *32*
strength Stärke *124*
stress Betonung *81*; Belastung *114*; ~ **testing** Belastungstest *107*; **~-strain diagram** Spannungs-Dehnungs-Diagramm *115T*
to stress betonen *108*
stretch wrapper Dehnfolienumwicklungsmaschine *97*
stretch wrapping Dehnfolienumwicklung *97*
stretcher Trage *109*
strict streng *107T*
to strip abziehen *17*
structural steel Baustahl *115*
to structure strukturieren *107*
style, in ~ stilvoll *152*
subassembly Unterbaugruppe *38*
subdivision Unterabteilung *55*
subheading Zwischenüberschrift *121*
subject line Betreffzeile *66*
submarine U-Boot *50*

submersion Untertauchen *134*
subsidiary Niederlassung *6*
substance Substanz *112*
to substitute ersetzen *135*
succinctly (kurz und) bündig *107*
sufficient ausreichend *144*
to suggest vorschlagen *93*
suitability Eignung *134*
to suit passen *123*
suitable geeignet *31T*
to sum up zusammenfassen *107T*
summary Zusammenfassung *26*
sunlight Sonnenlicht *59*
superb grandios, prachtvoll *105*
supervision Überwachung, Beobachtung, Beaufsichtigung *74*
supplement Ergänzung *89*
supplier Zulieferer, Lieferant/in *21*
supply Versorgung, Belieferung, Vorrat *88*; **~ voltage** Versorgungsspannung *82*; **~-pressure line** Versorgungsdruckleitung *69*
to supply liefern *52*
support Trägerelement *97*
supporter Befürworter, Unterstützer *107*
supporting plate Halteplatte *61*
surface Oberfläche *12*
surgery (Arzt-)Praxis *111*
suspect verdächtig *47*
to suture nähen *109T*
to swap tauschen *10*
switch Schalter *45*
switchgear Schaltanlage *131*
swivel Schwenk- *31*
to swivel schwenken *31T*
synonymous gleichbedeutend *129T*
syringe Spritze *109*

T

to tackle unternehmen, in Angriff nehmen *47*
tag Anhänger, Etikett *91*
tail-end plinth Maschinengestell *39*
tailored maßgeschneidert *129T*
tailstock Reitstock *39*
to take a look around sich umsehen *9*
to take apart auseinandernehmen *36T*
to take care aufpassen *14T*; ~ **of sth** sich um etw kümmern *14*
to take chances Risiken eingehen *75*
to take place stattfinden, ablaufen *36*
to take sth on etw übernehmen *108*
to take turns sich abwechseln *90*
to take up einnehmen *54T*; *(Platz)* einnehmen, benötigen *89*
talk Vortrag *142*
tap Gewindebohrer *11*
tape Band, Klebeband *69*
taper Kegel, *hier:* Kegelschaft *27*
tapered sich verjüngend, kegelig *26*
task Aufgabe, Auftrag *12*
to tear apart auseinanderreißen *71*
technical leaflet Datenblatt *27*
technical term Fachbegriff *141*

technician Techniker/in *7*
technique Methode, Technik *36*
technology Technik, Technologie *8*
template Schablone *63*; Vorlage, *121*
temporary vorübergehend, zeitweilig *134*
tensile stress Zugbelastung *116*
tensile test Zugversuch *115T*
tension Spannung *97*
tension spring Sicherungsring *103*
tension test Zugversuch *113*
term Begriff *15*
terms, in ~ of ... was ... betrifft *115T*
terminal Klemme, Anschlussklemme *46*
terminal block Anschlussklemmen *45*
terrain Umgebung, Landschaft *152*
test, bond ~ Hafttest *116*; **friction ~** Reibungsprüfung *116*; **hardness ~** Härteprüfung *113*; **magnetic-particle ~** Magnetpulverrissprüfung *113*; **peel ~** Abschältest *116*; **pressure ~** Druckprüfung *113*; **tensile ~** Zugversuch *115T*; **tension ~** Zugversuch *113*; **vibration ~** Schwingungsprüfung *113*
testing procedure Prüfverfahren *117*
thankfully Gott sei Dank, glücklicherweise *55*
thermoplastics Thermoplaste *36*
thickness Stärke, Dicke *13*
thick-walled dickwandig *38*
to think about sth über etw nachdenken *8*
to think out of the box unkonventionell denken *125*
thinner Verdünnung *44*
thread Gewinde *12*; **internal ~** Innengewinde *22P*; ~ **plug gauge** Gewinde-Grenzlehrdorn *23*
to thread Gewinde drehen *20*
threat Drohung *67*
three-jaw chuck Dreibackenfutter *23*
three-phase motor Drehstrommotor *45*
three-phase switch Drehstromschalter *45*
throughput Durchsatz *69*
to tidy up aufräumen *74*
tie-in deal Vertragsbindung *88*
tiger balm Tigerbalsam *109T*
tight eng, stramm *60*; fest *89*
to tilt neigen *26*
time, as ~ goes by im Lauf der Zeit *128*; **~-consuming** zeitraubend, zeitaufwändig *38*
toe Zeh *109*
tolerance Toleranz *24*
tool Werkzeug *11*
toolbox Werkzeugkasten *16*
tool drawer Werkzeugschublade *39*
tooth Zahn *26*
toothache Zahnschmerzen *109*
toothed belt Zahnriemen *138*
to top up nachfüllen, auffüllen *41*
top view Ansicht von oben *13*
top wrap Wickellagen *97*
topic Thema *66*
torque Drehkraft, Drehmoment *69*
torque, high-~ drehmomentstark *28*

A–Z WORD LIST

touch Berührung *97*
toughness Festigkeit *113*
tractor Traktor *137*
trade fair (Handels-)Messe *29*
trade off Kompromiss *146*
traffic jam Stau *93*
traffic lights Ampel *94*
to train to be eine Ausbildung zum/r ... machen *7*
training supervisor Ausbilder/in *7*
to transfer weiterleiten, übertragen *59*
transfer rack Maschinenbett *(Führung der Werkzeugschlitten) 79*
transformer Transformator *45*
transit Transport *145*
transmission übertragung *71P*
to transmit übertragen *59*
trapezoidal trapezförmig *31*
trash pump Abwasserpumpe *76*
travel, cross ~ Durchgangshöhe *116*
travelling Reisen *7*
tray Spanbehälter *46*
to treat behandeln *109*
treated air aufbereitete Luft *69*
triangle Dreieck *140*
triangular dreikantig *16*; dreieckig *140*
to trot traben *152*
true wahr, echt *38*
to try out ausprobieren *74*
tube remover Abziehwerkzeug *69*
tubing Rohre *69*
tungsten Wolfram *36*
turkey Truthahn *136*
turn, to be one's ~ an der Reihe sein, dran sein *7T*; **to take** ~**s** sich abwechseln *90*
to turn drehen, drechseln *20*
turning, longitudinal ~ Längsdrehen *20*
turntable Drehscheibe *97*
twin bed Einzelbett *(in einem Zweibettzimmer) 92*
to twist drehen, verdrehen, verdrillen *17*
two-speed Zweigang- *46*
typically normalerweise, üblicherweise *135*

U

ultimate stress Zugfestigkeit *114*
ultrasonic Ultraschall- *113*
unavoidable unvermeidlich *47*
unchanged unverändert *82*
unclear unklar *110*
uncommon ungewöhnlich *76*
to undergo sth sich einer Sache unterziehen *112*
underride guard Unterfahrschutz *34*
underscore Unterstrich *91*
to undertake durchführen *36*
underwater unter Wasser *76*
undiscovered unentdeckt *152*
unexpected unerwartet *94*
unfocussed verschwommen *110*
unfortunately leider *22T*
unhindered ungehindert *38*

unique einzigartig, einmalig *6*
universal testing machine Universalprüfmaschine *116*
unless es sei denn, außer wenn *47*
unparalleled unerreicht, einmalig *79*
unpleasant unangenehm *125T*
to unplug *(Stecker)* ziehen *47*
until recently bis vor kurzem *54T*
up, to be ~ **to sth** einer Sache genügen, entsprechen *113*
upper yield point obere Streckgrenze *114*
upset stomach Magenverstimmung, Bauchweh *109*
urgently dringend *22T*
usage Gebrauch, Verwendung *107T*
usefulness Nützlichkeit *124*
user Benutzer/in, Anwender/in *64*
usually normalerweise *7T*
utilities Nebenkosten *58*
utility building technische Gebäudeausrüstung *131*
utilization Gebrauch, Verwendung *81*
to utilize nutzen, verwerten *50*

V

vacancy offene Stelle *119*
vacuum Vakuum *36*
valid gültig *84*
valuable wertvoll *94*
value added tax (VAT) Mehrwertsteuer *57*
variant Art *36*
variety Auswahl, Reihe *77*; **a** ~ **of** verschiedene *77*
vehicle Fahrzeug *6*
vehicle body Fahrzeugkarrosserie, -chassis *128T*
velocity Geschwindigkeit *114*
to ventilate entlüften *72*
ventilation Belüftung *19*; ~ **slot** Lüftungsschlitz *19*
vernier calliper Messschieber *24*
versatility Vielseitigkeit *89*
vertical senkrecht, vertikal *25*
viable brauchbar, durchführbar *38*
vibration test Schwingungsprüfung *113*
view Ansicht *13*
violent(ly) heftig *74*
virtual virtuell *8*
visible sichtbar *44*
vision Sehvermögen *110*
visit Besuch *10*
visitor Besucher/in *10*
visor Schutzvisier *73*
vitally important von entscheidender Bedeutung *118*
vocational, higher ~ **course** weiterführende Ausbildung *119*; ~ **training** Berufsausbildung *54*
voltage Spannung *45*; **high** ~ Hochspannung *73*
volume Lautstärke *135*
voluntary freiwillig *122*

W

wages Lohn *64*
to walk Schritt gehen *152*
wallplug Dübel *68T*
warranty Garantie, Gewährleistung *64*
warranty disclosure Garantiebedingungen *64*
waste Alt- *44*
waste oil Altöl *40*
wastewater Abwasser *132*
Watch out! Vorsicht! *21*
water jet cutting machine Wasserstrahl-Schneidemaschine *33*
water utility Wasserversorgung(sunternehmen) *132*
waterpump pliers Wasserpumpenzange *16*
to wave sth about mit etw herumwedeln *142*
weakening Schwächung *36*
weakness Schwäche *124*
wealth Reichtum *152*
wear Abnutzung(serscheinungen), Verschleiß *19*
wear and tear Abnutzung, Verschleiß *64*
to weigh wiegen *27T*; abwiegen *74*
weight Gewicht *27*
weld area Schweißzone *36*
weld penetration Einschweißtiefe *38*
weld pool Schmelzbad *38*
welding Schweißen *36T*; **electric arc** ~ Lichtbogenschweißen *36*; **electron-beam** ~ Elektronenstrahlschweißen *36*; **energy-beam** ~ Energiestrahlschweißen *36*; **gas metal arc** ~ Metallinertgasschweißen (MIG), Metallaktivgasschweißen (MAG) *36*; **gas tungsten arc** ~ Wolframinertgasschweißen (WIG) *36*; **laser-beam** ~ Laserstrahlschweißen *36*; **laser-hybrid** ~ Laser-Hybrid-Schweißen *36*; **resistance** ~ Widerstandsschweißen *36*; **shielded metal arc** ~ Lichtbogenhandschweißen *36*; **spot** ~ Punktschweißen *36*
welding mask Schweißschutzmaske *73*
wheat Weizen *150*
wheel bearing module Radlagermodul *64*
wheel hub unit Radlager *64*
wheel rim Felge *77*
wheelhousing Radkasten *30*
whilst während *36*
to whip around (wie eine Peitsche) um sich schlagen *74*
whipped cream Schlagsahne *136*
white spirit Waschbenzin *44*
wholesaler Großhändler *64*
wide breit *12*
to widen weiten *69*
width Breite *116*
winding Wicklung *104*
wine list Weinkarte *136*
wing nut Flügelmutter *35*
wing screw Flügelschraube *35*
wining and dining Bewirten *(von Gästen) 136*

to wipe abwischen *75*
wipe down Abwischen *97*
wire Kabel, Draht *35*; ~ **brush** Drahtbürste *16*
to wire verkabeln *47*
wiring harness Kabelbaum, Kabelstrang *6*
without supervision ohne Aufsicht *74*
to withstand aushalten, standhalten *79*
wood Holz *6*
woodworking Holzverarbeitung *132*
word spider Wortnetz *37*
work breakdown structure (WBS) Projektstrukturplan *137*

work placement Praktikum *122*
workforce Belegschaft *108*
working Funktionieren *19*; ~ **area** Arbeitsbereich *27T*; ~ **gas** Arbeitsgas *51*; ~ **range** Arbeitsbereich *27*
workmate Kollege/-in *125T*
workpiece Werkstück *8*
workplace Arbeitsplatz *6*
workshop Werkstatt *12*
worn abgenutzt *19*
wound Wunde *109T*
wounded verwundet, verletzt *109*
to wrap wickeln *89*

XY

X-ray Röntgenbild, -untersuchung *109T*
yet aber *38*
yield, lower ~ point untere Streckgrenze *114*; **upper ~ point** obere Streckgrenze *114*
to yield liefern *135*
Yours faithfully, Mit freundlichen Grüßen *119*

Basic technical vocabulary

German - English

Berufe – jobs

Ausbilder/in	training supervisor
Auszubildender/in	apprentice, trainee
Dreher/in	turner
Elektriker/in	electrician, electrical engineer
Facharbeiter/in	skilled worker
Feinwerkmechaniker/in	precision mechanic
Konstruktionsmechaniker/in	construction mechanic
Machinenbauer/in	machine builder
Mechatroniker/in	mechatronic systems engineer
Meister/in	foreman
Schneidwerkzeug-mechaniker/in/in	cutting tool mechanic
Techniker/in	state-certified engineer
Technischer Zeichner/in	CAD engineer
Teilezurichter/in	metal dresser
Werkstattleiter/in	workshop manager
Werkzeugmacher/in	toolmaker

Handwerkzeuge – hand-held tools

Bandsäge	bandsaw
Bügelsäge	hacksaw
Elektrobohrmaschine	electric drill
Feile	file
Flachrundzange	snipe-nose pliers
Gewindebohrer	tap
Hammer	hammer
Innensechskantschlüssel	hex key
Körner	centre punch
Maulschlüssel	open-ended spanner
Meißel	chisel
Schlagdorn	pin punch
Schraubendreher	screwdriver
Spitzsenker	countersink
Stichsäge	jigsaw
Wasserpumpenzange	waterpump pliers
Zapfensenker	counterbore

Werkzeugmaschinen – machine tools

Bohrmaschine	drilling machine
Fräsmaschine	milling machine
Hubsäge	power hacksaw
Schleifmaschine	grinding machine
Drehmaschine	lathe
Winkelschleifer	angle grinder

Messintrumente – measuring instruments

Gewinde-Grenzlehrdorn	thread plug gauge
Grenzlehrdorn	plug gauge
Grenzrachenlehre	snap gauge
Lineal	rule
Messgerät	gauge
Messschieber	vernier calliper
Tiefenmessgerät	depth gauge

Verbindungselemente – fixing devices

einfache flache Unterlegscheibe	plain flat washer
Federscheibe	spring washer
Flügelmutter	wing nut
Flügelschraube	wing screw
Halbrundkopfniete	panhead rivet
Halbrundkopfschraube mit Querschlitz	slotted panhead bolt
Innensechskant-geschwindestift	Allen set screw
Innensechskantschraube	hexagon socket cap bolt
Nagel	nail
Rundkopfniete	round head rivet
Rundkopfschraube	round head screw
Sechskantschraube	hexagon head bolt
Senkkopfniete	countersunk rivet
Senkkopfschraube mit Querschlitz	slotted countersunk bolt
Zahnscheibe	shakeproof washer
Zylinderkopfschraube	slotted cheesehead bolt

Aktionen – actions

(ab)schleifen	to grind
(an)fasen	to chamfer
befestigen	to fasten, fix
biegen	to bend
bohren	to bore, drill
drehen	to turn
ersetzen	to replace
formen	to shape
fräsen	to mill
hartlöten	to braze
lösen	to loosen
montieren	to assemble
nachfüllen	to refill
ölen	to oil
polieren	to finish
rändeln	to knurl
reparieren	to repair
schmieren	to grease
schweißen	to weld
weichlöten	to solder

Talking about numbers

Cardinal numbers

0	oh/nought/null (AE) zero
1	one
2	two
3	three
4	four
5	five
6	six
7	seven
8	eight
9	nine
10	ten
11	eleven
12	twelve
13	thirteen
14	fourteen
15	fifteen
16	sixteen
17	seventeen
18	eighteen
19	nineteen
20	twenty
21	twenty-one
22	twenty-two
23	twenty-three
24	twenty-four
30	thirty
40	forty
50	fifty
60	sixty
70	seventy
80	eighty
90	ninety
100	one hundred

In English you say:
101	one hundred **and** one
235	two hundred **and** thirty-five
1,563,765	one million, five hundred **and** sixty-three thousand, seven hundred **and** sixty-five
1 563 765	

You use commas or spaces (and not a point) after the thousands (or millions) in large numbers.

Ordinal numbers

1st	first
2nd	second
3rd	third
4th	fourth
5th	fifth
6th	sixth
7th	seventh
8th	eighth
9th	ninth
10th	tenth
11th	eleventh
12th	twelfth
13th	thirteenth
14th	fourteenth
15th	fifteenth
16th	sixteenth
17th	seventeenth
18th	eighteenth
19th	nineteenth
20th	twentieth
21st	twenty-first
22nd	twenty-second
23rd	twenty-third
24th	twenty-fourth
30th	thirtieth
40th	fortieth
50th	fiftieth
60th	sixtieth
70th	seventieth
80th	eightieth
90th	ninetieth
100th	one hundredth

Decimals

In English, you write decimals with a point, not a comma.

0.25	oh/nought point two five (BE) zero point two five (AE)
3.76	three point seven six
55.37	fifty-five point three seven
1.585	one point five eight five

Fractions

$1/4$	a/one quarter
$1/3$	a/one third
$1/2$	a/one half
$2/3$	two-thirds
$3/4$	three-quarters
$5/16$	five sixteenths
$1 1/2$	one and a half

$1\,m^2$	one **square** metre
$1\,m^3$	one **cubic** metre
5^2	five **squared**
10^4	ten **to the power** of four
+	plus
−	minus
×	times/multiply by
÷	divide by

Symbols

+	plus/and
−	minus
±	plus or minus
×	multiplied by/times by (6 mm × 2 mm)
÷	divided by
=	is equal to/equals
≠	isn't equal to/doesn't equal
≈	is approximately equal to
<	is less than
>	is greater/more than
μ	micro- (one millionth)
%	per cent (*auch:* percent)
°	degree

205

Talking about measurements

Conversion tables

Length:

1 inch	=	2.54 cm
1 foot	=	30.48 cm
1 yard	=	91.44 cm
1 mile	=	1.609 km
1 cm	=	0.3937 inches
1 m	=	39.37 inches
1 km	=	0.62137 miles

Area:

1 square inch (in²)	=	6.45 cm²
1 square foot (ft²)	=	0.093 m²
1 square mile (m²)	=	2.59 km²
1 cm²	=	0.155 square inches
1 m²	=	10.764 square feet
1 km²	=	0.3861 square miles

Volume:

1 cubic inch (in³)	=	16.387 cm³
20 fluid ounces	=	0.57 l
1 pint (pt.)	=	0.57 l
1 gallon (gal.)	=	4.546 l
1 US gallon	=	3.785 l
1 cm³	=	0.061 cubic inch
1 m³	=	35.315 cubic feet
1 litre (l)	=	1.76 pints
1 litre (l)	=	0.22 gallons

Mass:

1 pound (lb)	=	0.453 kg
1 long ton	=	1016 kg
1 short ton	=	907.18 kg
1 tonne	=	1000 kg
1 kilogram (kg)	=	2.2046 pounds

Temperature:

Degrees Celsius		Degrees Fahrenheit
−17.8 °C	=	0 °F
−12.2 °C	=	10 °F
−6.7 °C	=	20 °F
−1.1 °C	=	30 °F
0 °C	=	32 °F
4.4 °C	=	40 °F
10 °C	=	50 °F
20 °C	=	68 °F
30 °C	=	86 °F
40 °C	=	104 °F
50 °C	=	122 °F

Absolute zero = −273.15 °C

You say: −5 °C   minus five degrees Celsius
         −25.5 °C   minus twenty-five point five degrees Celsius

Conversion formula:

°C = (°F − 32) × 5/9
°F = (°C × 9/5) + 32

Energy:

1 joule = 0.2388 calories (cal)

Abbreviations:

mg	milligram
g	gram
kg	kilogram
oz	ounce (= 28.35 g)
lb	pound (= 0.454 kg)
st	stone (= 6.356 kg)
ml	millilitre
cl	centilitre
l	litre
tsp	teaspoon
tbl	tablespoon
A	amp(ere)
V	volt
W	watt
AC	alternating current
DC	direct current
F	farad
kWh	kilowatt hour
R	resistance
RCD	residual current device
dB	decibel
FM	frequency modulation
UHF	ultra-high frequency
Hz	hertz
MHz	megahertz
GHz	gigahertz
LAN	local area network
WLAN	wireless local area network
LED	light-emitting diode
rpm	revolutions per minute

Common irregular verbs

infinitive, simple past, perfect participle

be	was/were – been	sein
become	became – become	werden
begin	began – begun	anfangen
bring	brought – brought	bringen
build	built – built	bauen
buy	bought – bought	kaufen
catch	caught – caught	fangen
choose	chose – chosen	auswählen
come	came – come	kommen
cost	cost – cost	kosten
cut	cut – cut	schneiden
do	did – done	tun, machen, erledigen
draw	drew – drawn	zeichnen
drink	drank – drunk	trinken, saufen
drive	drove – driven	fahren
eat	ate – eaten	essen, fressen
fall	fell – fallen	hinfallen
feed	fed – fed	füttern
feel	felt – felt	sich fühlen
fight	fought – fought	(be)kämpfen
find	found – found	finden
fly	flew – flown	fliegen
forget	forgot – forgotten	vergessen
give	gave – given	geben
get	got – got	bekommen, erhalten
go	went – gone	gehen
grow	grew – grown	wachsen
hang	hung – hung	(auf)hängen
have	had – had	haben
hear	heard – heard	hören
hide	hid – hidden	verstecken
hit	hit – hit	schlagen, aufprallen auf
hold	held – held	halten
hurt	hurt – hurt	verletzen
keep	kept – kept	behalten
know	knew – known	kennen, wissen
lead	led – led	führen, leiten
leave	left – left	verlassen
lend	lent – lent	(ver)leihen
let	let – let	lassen
light	lit – lit	anzünden
lose	lost – lost	verlieren
make	made – made	machen
mean	meant – meant	bedeuten
meet	met – met	sich treffen
pay	paid – paid	(be-)zahlen
put	put – put	setzen, stellen, legen
read	read – read	lesen
ride	rode – ridden	reiten
ring	rang – rung	klingeln
rise	rose – risen	steigen
run	ran – run	laufen
say	said – said	sagen
see	saw – seen	sehen
sell	sold – sold	verkaufen
send	sent – sent	senden, schicken
shake	shook – shaken	schütteln
sing	sang – sung	singen
sit	sat – sat	sitzen
speak	spoke – spoken	sprechen
spend	spent – spent	ausgeben, verbringen
stand	stood – stood	stehen
steal	stole – stolen	stehlen
swim	swam – swum	schwimmen
take	took – taken	nehmen
teach	taught – taught	unterrichten, lehren
tear	tore – torn	(zer)reißen
tell	told – told	erzählen, mitteilen, sagen
think	thought – thought	denken, meinen
throw	threw – thrown	werfen
understand	understood – understood	verstehen
wear	wore – worn	tragen, anhaben
win	won – won	gewinnen
write	wrote – written	schreiben

Be careful with:

burn	burnt – burnt	(ver)brennen
	burned – burned	
dream	dreamt – dreamt	träumen
	dreamed – dreamed	
learn	learnt – learnt	lernen, erfahren
	learned – learned	
smell	smellt – smellt	riechen
	smelled – smelled	
spell	spellt – spellt	buchstabieren
	spelled – spelled	
spoil	spoilt – spoilt	verderben
	spoiled – spoiled	

Acknowledgements

Fotos
Alamy: S. 37/1/David R. Frazier Photolibrary, Inc., S. 37/3/mediacolor's, S. 38/1/Simon Belcher, S. 88/1/Finnbarr Webster, S. 88/2/ilian food & drink, S. 88/3/razorpix, S. 88/4/Bon Appetit, S. 88/5/Red Fred, S. 88/6/Lenscap, S. 88/8/9/11/drink Alan King, S. 88/unten/INTERFOTO, S. 119/1/Janine Wiedel Photolibrary, S. 128/3/Chad Ehlers, S. 132/1/Arnold Bell, S. 132/5/Jim Parkin, S. 132/7/Peter Bowater, S. 152/1/Simon Price;

Appleton Estate: S. 88/12;

CV Archiv: S. 6/1, S. 15/1;

Fotofinder: S. 9/1/Cultura Images RM/F1 ONLINE, S. 17/2/Bernhard Classen, S. 17/3/vario images, S. 23/1/Petra Steuer/JOKER, S. 35/2/3/vario images, S. 38/2/3/vario images, S. 47/1/die bildstelle/Witschel, Mike, S. 50/2/Kevin Schafer/Peter Arnold, S. 88/10/www.stillsonline.de, S. 92/1/Bildagentur-online/SC-Photos;

Georg Aigner, Landshut: S. 7/1/2/3/4/5/6/7, S. 11/1/2/3/4/5/6/7/8/9/10/11/12/13/14/15/16/17, S. 12/1, S. 13/1/2/3, S. 16/1, S. 17/4/5, S. 20/1/2/3/4/5/6/7, S. 21/1/2, S. 24/unten, S. 30/1, S. 31/1, S. 32/1, S. 33/1, S. 34/1, S. 35/5/6, S. 40/1/2/3/4/5/6/7/8/9/10/11, S. 50/oben, S. 51/1, S. 68/1, S. 69/1/2/3, S. 75/1, S. 78/1, S. 95/1, S. 98/2, S. 99/2, S. 106/1/2/3/4/5/6/7, S. 109/oben, S. 114/1/2/3/4/5/6/7/8, S. 121/1, S. 122/1, S. 128/1/3, S. 141/1, S. 145/1/2, S. 146/1/2/3/4/5/6/7/8, S. 149/1;

GILDEMEISTER: S. 77/1/2/3/4/5/6/7/8/9, S. 79/1, S. 80/1/2;

Hummer: S. 64/1;

International Equipments: S. 116/1;

iStockphoto: S. 50/4, S. 55/4, S. 58/1, S. 60/1, S. 68/2, S. 90/3, S. 125/1, S. 132/3, S.137/1/5;

John Deere: S. 147/6;

Krones AG: S. 89/1/2, S. 90/1/2/3/4;

Kunzmann: S. 25/1, S. 28/1;

Shutterstock: S. 17/1, S. 24/2, S. 35/1/4, S. 37/2, S. 50/3, S. 50/1/6, S. 55/1/2/3/5, S. 58/2, S. 60/2/3/4, S. 68/2/4/5, S. 92/2, S. 98/1, S. 109/1/2/3/4/5/6/7/8, S. 113/1, S. 119/2, S. 132/4/6/8, S. 137/3/4/7/8/9/10;

Siemens AG: S. 128/2, S. 130/1, S. 131/1/2/3/4/5, S. 132/oben, S. 134/1;

Sommer: S. 137/2;

Sütaş: S. 88/7;

TopTier: S. 97/1/2;

United States Stove Company: S. 50/5;

Vogel Germany GmbH: S. 24/6

Illustrationen
Oxford Designers & Illustrators

Nicht alle Copyright-Inhaber konnten ermittelt werden; deren Urheberrechte werden hiermit vorsorglich und ausdrücklich anerkannt. Wir danken allen Instituten, Firmen und Personen, die bei der Erstellung dieses Lehrwerks mit Materialen und Informationen behilflich waren.